Legalines®

Editorial Advisors:
Gloria A. Aluise
   Attorney at Law
Jonathan Neville
   Attorney at Law
Robert A. Wyler
   Attorney at Law

Authors:
Gloria A. Aluise
   Attorney at Law
Daniel O. Bernstine
   Attorney at Law
Roy L. Brooks
   Professor of Law
Scott M. Burbank
   C.P.A.
Charles N. Carnes
   Professor of Law
Paul S. Dempsey
   Professor of Law
Jerome A. Hoffman
   Professor of Law
Mark R. Lee
   Professor of Law
Jonathan Neville
   Attorney at Law
Laurence C. Nolan
   Professor of Law
Arpiar Saunders
   Attorney at Law
Robert A. Wyler
   Attorney at Law

CRIMINAL PROCEDURE

Adaptable to Twelfth Edition* of Kamisar Casebook

By Jonathan Neville
Attorney at Law

*If your casebook is a newer edition, go to www.gilbertlaw.com
to see if a supplement is available for this title.

THOMSON
™
WEST

EDITORIAL OFFICE: 1 N. Dearborn Street, Suite 650, Chicago, IL 60602
REGIONAL OFFICES: Chicago, Dallas, Los Angeles, New York, Washington, D.C.

SERIES EDITOR
Linda C. Schneider, J.D.
Attorney at Law

PRODUCTION MANAGER
Elizabeth G. Duke

FIRST PRINTING—2009

Legalines®

Features Detailed Briefs of Every Major Case,
Plus Summaries of the Black Letter Law

Titles Available

Administrative Law	Keyed to Breyer
Administrative Law	Keyed to Schwartz
Administrative Law	Keyed to Strauss
Antitrust	Keyed to Areeda
Antitrust	Keyed to Pitofsky
Business Associations	Keyed to Klein
Civil Procedure	Keyed to Friedenthal
Civil Procedure	Keyed to Hazard
Civil Procedure	Keyed to Yeazell
Conflict of Laws	Keyed to Currie
Constitutional Law	Keyed to Brest
Constitutional Law	Keyed to Choper
Constitutional Law	Keyed to Cohen
Constitutional Law	Keyed to Rotunda
Constitutional Law	Keyed to Stone
Constitutional Law	Keyed to Sullivan
Contracts	Keyed to Calamari
Contracts	Keyed to Dawson
Contracts	Keyed to Farnsworth
Contracts	Keyed to Fuller
Contracts	Keyed to Kessler
Contracts	Keyed to Knapp
Contracts	Keyed to Murphy
Corporations	Keyed to Choper
Corporations	Keyed to Eisenberg
Corporations	Keyed to Hamilton
Criminal Law	Keyed to Dressler
Criminal Law	Keyed to Johnson
Criminal Law	Keyed to Kadish
Criminal Law	Keyed to Kaplan
Criminal Law	Keyed to LaFave
Criminal Procedure	Keyed to Kamisar
Domestic Relations	Keyed to Wadlington
Estates and Trusts	Keyed to Dobris
Evidence	Keyed to Mueller
Evidence	Keyed to Waltz
Family Law	Keyed to Areen
Income Tax	Keyed to Freeland
Income Tax	Keyed to Klein
Labor Law	Keyed to Cox
Property	Keyed to Cribbet
Property	Keyed to Dukeminier
Property	Keyed to Nelson
Property	Keyed to Rabin
Remedies	Keyed to Rendelman
Securities Regulation	Keyed to Coffee
Torts	Keyed to Dobbs
Torts	Keyed to Epstein
Torts	Keyed to Franklin
Torts	Keyed to Henderson
Torts	Keyed to Prosser
Wills, Trusts & Estates	Keyed to Dukeminier

All Titles Available at Your Law School Bookstore

THOMSON

WEST

SHORT SUMMARY OF CONTENTS

Page

I.   **INTRODUCTION** 1

    A.   Criminal Justice Process 1
    B.   Sources of Criminal Procedure Law 5
    C.   The Right to Counsel; Equality and the Adversary System ... 22
    D.   The Role of Counsel 34

II. **POLICE PRACTICES** 53

    A.   The Role of the Courts in the Administration of Justice ... 53
    B.   Arrest, Search, and Seizure 54
    C.   Undercover Investigations 101
    D.   Network Surveillance 109
    E.   Police Interrogation and Confessions 121
    F.   Pretrial Identification Procedures 155
    G.   Grand Jury Investigations 161
    H.   The Scope of the Exclusionary Rules 177

III. **THE COMMENCEMENT OF FORMAL PROCEEDINGS** ... 191

    A.   Pretrial Release 191
    B.   The Decision Whether to Prosecute 196
    C.   The Preliminary Hearing 204
    D.   Grand Jury Review 207
    E.   The Charging Instrument 213
    F.   The Location of the Prosecution 219
    G.   Joinder and Severance 221
    H.   Speedy Trial and Other Speedy Disposition 232

IV. **THE ADVERSARY SYSTEM AND THE DETERMINATION
     OF GUILT OR INNOCENCE** 236

    A.   Pretrial Discovery and Related Rights 236
    B.   Guilty Pleas 246
    C.   Trial by Jury 260
    D.   Media Rights vs. Fair Trial Rights 270
    E.   The Criminal Trial 279
    F.   Double Jeoparty 287
    G.   Sentencing 295

V.   **APPEALS, POST-CONVICTION REVIEW** 301

    A.   Post-Trial Motions and Appeals 301

    B.   Post Conviction Review: Federal Habeas Corpus 308

TABLE OF CASES 317

TABLE OF CONTENTS AND SHORT REVIEW OUTLINE

Page

I. **INTRODUCTION** 1

  A. **CRIMINAL JUSTICE PROCESS** 1

    1. Introduction 1
    2. State Criminal Procedure 1

      a. Arrest 1
      b. The charge 1
      c. Proceedings before a magistrate 1
      d. Preliminary hearing 1

        1) Sufficient evidence 1
        2) Writ of prohibition 2
        3) Indictment 2
        4) Decision at preliminary hearing 2

      e. Accusatory pleading 2
      f. Arraignment 2
      g. Motions and pleas 2

        1) Motions 2
        2) Pleas 2

      h. Evidence gathering and discovery 2
      i. Extraordinary writs 3
      j. Trial 3
      k. Sentencing 3
      l. Post-trial motions 4

        1) Motion to vacate 4
        2) Motion for a new trial 4

      m. Appeal 4
      n. Habeas corpus 4

    3. Federal Criminal Procedure 4

      a. Gathering of evidence 4
      b. Arrest 4
      c. Appearance before a commissioner 4
      d. Preliminary examination 4
      e. Grand jury indictment 4

   f. Accusatory pleading 4
   g. Arraignment 5
   h. Motions and pleas 5
   i. Evidence gathering and discovery 5
   j. Extraordinary writs 5
   k. Trial 5
   l. Sentencing 5
   m. Post-trial motions 5
   n. Appeal 5
   o. Habeas corpus 5

B. SOURCES OF CRIMINAL PROCEDURE LAW **5**

  1. Basic Principles of the Federal System 5

   a. A federal system 5

     1) National supremacy 5
     2) Separation of powers 5

   b. Limited government 5

  2. Federal Powers 6

   a. Judicial power 6

     1) Scope of federal judicial power 6
     2) Judicial review by the Supreme Court 6

   b. Power of Congress 6

     1) Scope of the granted powers 6
     2) Limitations on the exercise of congressional power 6

  3. Power of the States 7

   a. Tenth Amendment 7
   b. Police power 7
   c. Limitations on the exercise of state power 7
   d. Power of local government 7

  4. Sources of Criminal Procedure Law 7

   a. Provisions of the Constitution 7
   b. State constitutions 7
   c. State and federal statutes 8

    d.   Court regulations 8

5.   Fourteenth Amendment Due Process 8

    a.   Meaning of due process 8
    b.   Incorporation doctrine 8

        1)   Adoption of the selective incorporation approach 8
        2)   Rights incorporated 9
        3)   Scope of incorporation 9

    c.   Bodily extractions and the incorporation doctrine 9

        1)   Introduction 9
        2)   Forced stomach pumping 9
        3)   Blood samples 10

    d.   Criminal procedure and retroactivity 11

        1)   Introduction 11
        2)   Applications 11
        3)   Extent of retroactivity 12
        4)   Retroactivity of Supreme Court decisions in state courts 14

    e.   The federal courts' supervisory power 15

        1)   Purpose of supervisory power 15
        2)   Scope of supervisory power 15

    f.   Trend for greater protection under state law than required by
        the Constitution 15

        1)   State constitution interpretation 15
        2)   Rules of evidence 16
        3)   The new federalism in criminal procedure 16
        4)   Public responses to the new federalism 16
        5)   Supreme Court's responses to the new federalism 16

    g.   Executive detention of enemy combatants 16

        1)   Joint resolution authorizing the use of military force 17
        2)   Detention of United States citizens 17
        3)   Detention of enemy combatants at Guantanamo Bay 19
        4)   Habeas corpus review for foreign detainees after new
            acts of Congress 19

C.   **THE RIGHT TO COUNSEL; EQUALITY AND THE ADVERSARY SYSTEM** **22**

   1.   Attorney General's Committee on Poverty and the Administration of Criminal Justice (1963) 22

       a.   Concept of poverty 22

           1)   Right to counsel 22
           2)   Other problems 22
           3)   Conclusion 22

       b.   Obligation of equal justice 22
       c.   "Indigency" standards and administration 22
       d.   Obligation to repay 23
       e.   Appointed counsel's right to compensation 24

   2.   The Right to Appointed Counsel 24

       a.   Criminal prosecutions 24

           1)   Introduction 24
           2)   Special circumstances approach to due process 24
           3)   Developments after *Betts* 25
           4)   Expansion of special circumstances approach to all felony cases 25
           5)   Right to counsel whenever imprisonment is imposed 26
           6)   Limit on right to counsel 27

       b.   Attachment of right to counsel 27

           1)   Basic rule 27
           2)   Detention alone not a prosecution 28
           3)   Determination of when right to counsel attaches ... 28

   3.   The Griffin-Douglas Equality Principle 29

       a.   Origin of the equality principle 30
       b.   Transcript for any appeal 30
       c.   The right to counsel on appeal 30
       d.   Limitation on the right to appointed counsel on appeal 30
       e.   Right to expert services other than counsel 32

           1)   Psychiatric exam 32
           2)   Criminal Justice Act of 1964 32

   4.   Withdrawal of Appointed Counsel on Appeal 32

		a.	Requirement of brief	32
		b.	Discussion of lack of merit	32
		c.	Alternatives to *Anders*	32
	5.		Proceedings Other than Criminal Prosecutions	33
		a.	Probation revocation hearings	33
		b.	Summary court martial	34
		c.	Proceedings to terminate parental rights	34
		d.	Collateral attack proceedings	34
D.			**THE ROLE OF COUNSEL**	**34**
	1.		The Right to Waive Counsel	34
		a.	Introduction	34
		b.	Right of self-representation	34
		c.	Standby counsel	35
		d.	No specific warning for waiver of counsel	36
		e.	Appointing counsel when pro se representation is denied	37
	2.		Division of Authority over Defense Decisions	38
		a.	Issues to be raised on appeal	38
		b.	Tactical trial decisions	38
	3.		Effective Assistance of Counsel	39
		a.	Reluctance to find denial of effective counsel	39
		b.	Early approach	39
		c.	Effective assistance of appellate counsel	39
		d.	Current two-part test	39
		e.	Proof of prejudice	39
		f.	Failure to file suppression motion	41
		g.	Counsel's refusal to let the client commit perjury	42
		h.	Closing arguments	42
		i.	Scope of duty to review mitigation evidence	43
		j.	Actual proof of prejudice required	45
	4.		Conflicts of Interests	46
		a.	Potential conflicts	46
		b.	Postconviction review	47
		c.	Disqualification of counsel	48
	5.		The Right to Counsel of Choice	49

a. Appointed counsel 49
b. Deprivation of chosen counsel as reversible error 49
c. Defendants not allowed to use forfeitable assets to pay attorney fees 51

II. POLICE PRACTICES 53

A. THE ROLE OF THE COURTS IN THE ADMINISTRATION OF JUSTICE 53

1. Federalism and State Criminal Procedure 53
2. Competing Values 53

    a. Crime control 53
    b. Due process model 53
    c. Supreme Court intervention 53

B. ARREST, SEARCH, AND SEIZURE 54

1. The Exclusionary Rule 54

    a. Violation of the Fourth Amendment 54
    b. Disadvantages of the suppression rule 54
    c. Advantages of the rule 54

        1) Civil remedy 54
        2) Criminal sanctions 54
        3) Intra-police department penalties 54

    d. Effectiveness 55
    e. Exclusionary rule applied to states 55

        1) Early case 55
        2) *Wolf* overruled 55

    f. Good faith exception to the exclusionary rule 56
    g. Violation of "knock-and-announce" rule 58
    h. Other dimensions of the exclusionary rule 60

        1) Questions to grand jury witness 60
        2) Quasi-criminal proceedings 60
        3) Other proceedings 60
        4) Evidence obtained by private persons 60

    i. Other remedies 60

2. Protected Areas and Interests 60

a. Introduction 60
b. People protected, not things 60
c. Consequences of *Katz* 61
d. Limitation on *Katz*'s expectation of privacy 62
e. Application of *Katz* to thermal imaging of residence 63
f. Use of technology 65

    1) Enhancing senses 65
    2) Electronic tracking 65
    3) Aerial photography 65

g. What items can be searched for and seized 65

    1) "Property interest" rule (early view) 65
    2) "Mere evidence" rule (later view) 66
    3) Modern rule—nexus requirement 66
    4) Business records 66
    5) Newspapers 67

3. Probable Cause 69

a. Introduction 69
b. Sufficiency of affidavit supporting request for a warrant 69
c. *Aguilar/Spinelli* two-prong test 69
d. Abandonment of tests in *Aguilar/Spinelli*: totality of circumstances
    standard adopted 70
e. Ramifications of *Gates* 71
f. Challenge to affidavit 72
g. Identity of the informer 72
h. Other sources of probable cause 73
i. Probable cause based on probable joint enterprise 73

4. Search Warrants 74

a. Conditions for receiving a search warrant 74

    1) Location 74
    2) Affidavit 74
    3) Basis 74
    4) Time 74
    5) Receipt 74
    6) Who may issue a warrant 75
    7) Description of place to be searched 75

b. Execution of the warrant 75

1)   Time to execute 75
2)   Announcement of intent to search 75
3)   Items that can be seized 76

c.   Detention and search of persons on the premises 76
d.   Detention while a warrant is sought 76
e.   Seizure of unnamed items 77

5.   Warrantless Arrests and Searches of the Person 77

a.   Warrantless arrests 77
b.   Arrest in public places 77
c.   Seizure when deadly force used 78
d.   Post-arrest probable cause requirement 78
e.   Other warrantless searches of the person 79

1)   Full search of person incidental to arrest 79
2)   Station house search 81
3)   Delayed post-arrest search of clothing 81
4)   Blood test 81
5)   Searches of the body 81
6)   Probable cause but no arrest 82

6.   Warrantless Entries and Searches of Premises 82

a.   Search incident to arrest 82

1)   Reasons for the exception 82
2)   Scope of permissible search 82
3)   Pretext arrests 83
4)   Warrantless searches under exigent circumstances 84
5)   Warrantless entry into residence to arrest 84

7.   Warrantless Seizures and Searches of Vehicles and Containers 85

a.   Vehicle searches 85

1)   Motor homes 85
2)   Searching a container inside a car 87
3)   Exigent circumstances 88
4)   Privacy interests 89

b.   Delayed search of contents of vehicle 89
c.   "Controlled deliveries" 89
d.   Vehicle search when driver outside car 90
e.   Inventory searches 91

8. Stop and Frisk 92

    a. Limited right to stop and frisk 92
    b. Police action short of a seizure 93
    c. No seizure without control 94
    d. Grounds for temporary seizure to investigate 94
    e. Police bulletin or flyer 94
    f. Least intrusive 94
    g. Seizure incident to a "stop" 94
    h. Stop and frisk on informer's tip 95
    i. "Protective" search 95
    j. Other brief detention for investigation—fingerprinting 95

9. Administrative Inspections and Regulatory Searches 95

    a. Inspection of premises 95
    b. Border searches and vehicle checkpoints 96

        1) Routine searches 96
        2) Traffic checkpoints 96
        3) Boats 96
        4) Fixed checkpoints 96

    c. Search of students 97
    d. Search of parolees 97

10. Consent Searches 99

    a. Nature of consent 99
    b. Who can consent? 100
    c. Consent of third party—common authority or sufficient relationship 100
    d. Reasonable belief 100

C.   **UNDERCOVER INVESTIGATIONS** **101**

1. Secret Agents 101

    a. Legal status 102
    b. Incriminating statements in the presence of a confidential informant 102
    c. Electronic Eavesdropping 103

2. The Entrapment Defense 104

    a. Police and informer "encouragement" 104

        1) First case 104

    2) Use in certain class of crimes 104

  b. Tests for Entrapment 104

    1) Overcoming initial refusal to commit a crime 104
    2) Meaning of "inducement" 106
    3) Supplying an essential ingredient for commission of a crime 107

 3. Prolonged Government Involvement 108

D. NETWORK SURVEILLANCE **109**

 1. The Fourth Amendment 109

  a. Fourth Amendment rights when connected to a computer network 110
  b. Rights in content information 111

    1) Sealed container held by common carrier 111
    2) Postal mail privacy 112
    3) Telephone privacy 112

  c. Rights in non-content information 114

 2. Statutory Privacy Laws 115

  a. Federal Communications Act 115
  b. Wiretapping and federal-state relations 116
  c. Nontelephonic electronic eavesdropping 116

    1) Possible eavesdropping devices 116
    2) Protection afforded 116

  d. Federal Wiretap Act 117

    1) Lawful interceptions 117

  e. Meaning of "interception" 119
  f. Exceptions not applicable 120

E. POLICE INTERROGATION AND CONFESSIONS **121**

 1. Some Different Perspectives 121

  a. Inbau—police interrogation a practical necessity 121
  b. Kamisar—equal justice in the gatehouses and the mansions 122

2. Historical Background 122

    a. Statements to police during illegal detention—*McNabb-Mallory* speedy arraignment rule 122

        1) Federal courts 122
        2) State prosecutions 123

    b. The right to counsel and voluntary confessions—early cases 123
    c. The right to counsel—further developments 124

        1) Prelude to *Escobedo* 124
        2) The *Escobedo* approach 125

    d. The privilege against self-incrimination 126

3. The *Miranda* Revolution 126

    a. The case 126
    b. The meaning of *Miranda* 127

        1) A code of criminal procedure 128
        2) Has *Miranda* gone too far? 128
        3) Congressional response 128
        4) Effect on nonconfessions 128
        5) Effect of confession or admission illegally obtained 128

    c. Application of *Miranda* 130

        1) Exploiting a criminal's ignorance 130
        2) Advisement regarding subject matter of questioning 130
        3) Noncustodial interrogation 131
        4) Noncustodial questioning—"threshold" confessions 131
        5) Roadside questioning of motorist 131
        6) Questioning of minor brought to police station by parents 132

    d. Determining what constitutes an interrogation 133

        1) Measure of compulsion 133
        2) The "jail plant" situation 134
        3) Routine booking question exception 134

    e. Public safety exception to *Miranda* 135
    f. Waiver 136
    g. Resumption of questioning 136

		1)	Multiple interrogations	136
		2)	Importance of which party initiates interrogation	137
	h.		Independent subsequent questioning	137
	i.		Presumption against waiver of rights	137
	j.		Interrogation after a third party retains defense counsel	139
	k.		Use of psychiatric exams at sentencing	141
	l.		Comparing *Miranda* and the Fourth Amendment exclusionary rule	141
	m.		Congress cannot overrule *Miranda*	142
4.	Questioning and the Fourteenth Amendment			143
5.	Evidence Obtained After Pre-Warning Statements			145
	a.		Introduction	145
	b.		*Miranda*: subsequent admissions	145
	c.		Physical evidence obtained from pre-warning statement	145
	d.		Use of "second confession"	147
6.	Developments in the Voluntariness Test			148
	a.		Deception	148
	b.		Effect of mental impairment	149
7.	*Massiah* and *Miranda* Compared			150
	a.		Post-arrest interrogations without counsel	150
	b.		Waiver after requesting counsel	150
	c.		Activity considered to be interrogation	151
	d.		Waiver of Sixth Amendment—*Massiah* rights	151
	e.		Use of co-defendant as informer to circumvent the right to counsel	151
	f.		Use of paid informant	152
	g.		Use of passive informant	153
	h.		Right to counsel regarding other crimes	153
F.	**PRETRIAL IDENTIFICATION PROCEDURES**			**155**
1.	Constitutional Concerns over Eyewitness Identifications			155
	a.		Introduction	155
	b.		Right to counsel at post-indictment lineups	155
		1)	Later courtroom identification must have independent source	155
		2)	Application to the states	156
		3)	Crime Control Act	157
2.	Retreat from *Wade*			157

| | | a. | Pre-indictment showups | 157 |
| | | b. | Post-indictment identification | 157 |

| | 3. | Due Process and Other Limitations | 158 |

| | | a. | Introduction | 158 |
| | | b. | Factors considered | 159 |

| | | | 1) | Emergency situation | 159 |

| | | c. | No per se rule | 159 |

G. | **GRAND JURY INVESTIGATIONS** | **161**

| | 1. | The Structure of the Investigative Grand Jury | 161 |

| | | a. | Grand jury composition | 161 |

			1)	Size	161
			2)	Selection	161
			3)	Challenges to selection	161
			4)	Challenges to legal qualification	161
			5)	Challenges based on alleged bias	161

		b.	Role of the prosecutor	161
		c.	Role of the court	162
		d.	Grand jury secrecy	162
		e.	Dual nature	163
		f.	Subpoena power	163

| | 2. | Challenges to the Investigation | 163 |

| | | a. | Fourth Amendment objections | 164 |

			1)	Early approach	164
			2)	Overbreadth doctrine	164
			3)	Overbreadth doctrine inapplicable to subpoena ad testificandum	165
			4)	The exclusionary rule	165

		b.	Chilling effect objections	166
		c.	Subject matter challenges	166
		d.	Relevancy objections	166
		e.	Misuse objections	167
		f.	Limitation of objections allowed	167

| | 3. | The Privilege Against Self-Incrimination | 169 |

   a. Grand jury testimony 169

     1) *Miranda* warnings 169
     2) Witness's comprehension of Fifth Amendment 169
     3) Warning not required 170

   b. Immunity grants 170

     1) Transactional immunity 170
     2) Testimonial immunity 170
     3) Protecting against "taint" 170

   c. Production of documents—the subpoena duces tecum 170

     1) Introduction 171
     2) Papers held by attorney 171
     3) Sole proprietorship 172
     4) Small partnership records 172
     5) Corporate records 173
     6) Act of production immunity 174
     7) Bank records 176

H. THE SCOPE OF THE EXCLUSIONARY RULES **177**

 1. Standing to Object to the Admission of Evidence 177

   a. Federal courts 177
   b. State courts 177
   c. Fourth Amendment rights are "personal" 177

     1) No standing to assert Fourth Amendment by private party 177

   d. "Automatic standing"—interest in the property seized 177

     1) History of the rule 177
     2) "Automatic standing" rule reversed 178

   e. Expectation of privacy 178
   f. Current approach 178

     1) "Legitimately on the premises" test insufficient 178
     2) Mere ownership insufficient 179
     3) Passenger in car sufficient 180
     4) Brief invited stay insufficient 180

 2. "Fruit of the Poisonous Tree" Doctrine 181

a.   Consequences of illegal arrest or search followed by incriminating statements 181

      1)   Introduction 182
      2)   Witnesses 182

b.   Confession as the fruit of an illegal arrest or search 182

      1)   Circumstances considered 182
      2)   *Miranda* warnings insufficient 182

c.   In-court identification by victim 182
d.   Confession after *Payton* violation 183
e.   "Independent source" upon which the warrant was secured 183
f.   Tainted witness 184
g.   "Inevitable discovery" doctrine 185

3.   Use of Illegally Obtained Evidence for Impeachment Purposes 185

a.   Voluntary confession obtained in violation of *Miranda* 186
b.   Exceptions 186
c.   Statements made during cross-examination 187
d.   No impeachment of defense witnesses 187
e.   Use of pre-arrest silence 188
f.   Use of post-*Miranda* warning silence to rebut insanity defense 188

4.   Allocation of the Burden of Proof 189

a.   Burden of proof 189

      1)   Search pursuant to warrant 189
      2)   Search without a warrant 189

b.   Approach in New York 189
c.   Standard of proof on confessions 189
d.   Waiver 190
e.   Other issues relating to the hearing 190

      1)   Testimony by the defendant 190
      2)   Holding the hearing in the presence of the jury 190
      3)   Specific findings 190
      4)   The jury's presence 190

III.   **THE COMMENCEMENT OF FORMAL PROCEEDINGS** **191**

      A.   **PRETRIAL RELEASE** **191**

1. Bail 191

    a.   Setting bail 191
    b.   Purposes of bail 191

        1)   To insure appearance 191
        2)   Crime control 192

    c.   Problems with the bail system 193
    d.   Possible solutions 194

        1)   Release on own recognizance 194
        2)   Speedy trial 194
        3)   Retention of portion of bail bond 194
        4)   Bail Reform Act of 1984 194

    e.   Bail for capital offenses 194

2. Preventive Detention 194

    a.   Bail Reform Act of 1984 194
    b.   District of Columbia statute 195
    c.   Constitutionality of preventive detention 195

B.   THE DECISION WHETHER TO PROSECUTE 196

1. Prosecuting Attorney 196

    a.   Office and duties 196
    b.   Prosecutor's discretion 196
    c.   Factors in exercising discretion 196

2. Challenging the Prosecutor's Discretion 197

    a.   The decision not to prosecute 197

        1)   Constitutional limitations 197
        2)   The district attorney and the grand jury 198
        3)   Checks on the prosecutor's refusal to prosecute 198

    b.   The decision to prosecute 198

        1)   Selective enforcement 198
        2)   Selective prosecution 199
        3)   Vindictive prosecution 200
        4)   Retaliatory prosecution 200

        5)   Desuetude (nonuse) 201

    c.   Selection of the charge 201

        1)   Overlapping provisions of a single federal statute 201
        2)   Overlapping federal and state statutes 202
        3)   Plea bargaining 202
        4)   Due process and substitution of a more serious charge 203
        5)   Prosecutorial vindictiveness 203

C.   THE PRELIMINARY HEARING 204

    1.   Introduction 204

        a.   Requirement 204
        b.   Procedure 204

    2.   Functions 205

        a.   Screening 205
        b.   Discovery 205
        c.   Perpetuation of testimony 205
        d.   Other purposes 205

    3.   Waiver of the Preliminary Hearing 205

    4.   Defendant's Right to a Preliminary Hearing 205

        a.   Federal courts 206
        b.   State courts 206
        c.   Misdemeanors 206

    5.   The Bindover Determination 206
    6.   Preliminary Hearing Procedures 207

        a.   Rules of evidence 207
        b.   Scope of hearing. 207
        c.   Right to counsel 207

D.   GRAND JURY REVIEW 207

    1.   Introduction 207
    2.   Challenges to Grand Jury Composition 208

        a.   Juror selection 208
        b.   Discrimination in foreman appointment 208

3. Challenges to Evidence Before the Grand Jury 208
4. Challenges to Grand Jury Procedures 209

    a. Disclosure of exculpatory evidence not required 209
    b. Nonprejudicial misconduct by the prosecution 210

5. Improper Grand Jury Procedure Not Disclosed Until Trial 212

E. THE CHARGING INSTRUMENT **213**

1. Modern Pleading Requirements 213

    a. "Bill of indictment" 213
    b. Pleading 213
    c. Information 213
    d. Contents of the information 213

2. Providing Notice Through the Pleadings 213

    a. Indictment 214
    b. Information 214
    c. Arraignment 214

        1) Presence of the accused 214
        2) Proceedings 214

    d. Specificity of the offense charged 214
    e. Sufficiency of the term "attempt" in indictment 215
    f. Omission of enhancement fact from indictment 217
    g. Unnecessary portions of an indictment may be disregarded 218

F. THE LOCATION OF THE PROSECUTION **219**

1. Jurisdiction 219

    a. Jurisdiction over the person 219

        1) Extradition 219
        2) Self-help 219

    b. Subject matter jurisdiction 219

        1) Territorial principle 219
        2) Court limitations 219

2. Venue 220

		a.	Venue determined by definition of crime	220
		b.	Constitutional limitations	221
		c.	Venue within the state	221
		d.	Change of venue	221

G. JOINDER AND SEVERANCE **221**

	1.	Joinder and Severance of Offenses	221

| | | a. | Proper joinder | 222 |
| | | b. | Improper joinder | 222 |

			1)	Forced testimony	222
			2)	Cumulative guilt	222
			3)	Factors showing lack of prejudice	223

| | | c. | Proper severance of offenses | 223 |
| | | d. | Improper severance | 224 |

	2.	Failure to Join Related Offenses—Collateral Estoppel	224

		a.	*Blockburger* test	224
		b.	Double jeopardy—continuing criminal enterprise	227
		c.	Defendant asks for separate trials	227
		d.	Collateral estoppel	228

	3.	Joinder and Severance of Defendants	228

		a.	Confrontation and the Sixth Amendment	228
		b.	ABA standards	229
		c.	Continuing joinder when joining charge fails	229
		d.	Improper joinder of defendants	230

| | | | 1) | Inadequate redaction | 230 |
| | | | 2) | Other cases and comments | 231 |

H. SPEEDY TRIAL AND OTHER SPEEDY DISPOSITION **232**

	1.	Constitutional and Statutory Provisions	232

		a.	Sixth Amendment	232
		b.	Purpose	232
		c.	Other protections	232
		d.	Speedy Trial Act of 1974	232
		e.	Balancing test	232

2. When Right to a Speedy Trial Attaches 233

    a. Pre-prosecution delay 233

        1) Statute of limitations 233

    b. Sentencing 233
    c. Fifth Amendment rights 233

3. Waiver 233
4. Determining the Unreasonableness of the Delay 234

    a. Defendant imprisoned in another state 234
    b. Prejudice 235

5. Right to Other Speedy Disposition 235
6. Remedy 235

IV. THE ADVERSARY SYSTEM AND THE DETERMINATION OF GUILT OR INNOCENCE 236

   A. PRETRIAL DISCOVERY AND RELATED RIGHTS 236

    1. Pretrial Discovery by the Defense 236

        a. Introduction 236
        b. Background 236

            1) Preliminary hearing 236
            2) Grand jury minutes 237
            3) Bill of particulars 237
            4) Federal Rules of Criminal Procedure 237

        c. State practice 237
        d. Federal practice 237

            1) Scope 237
            2) Required showing 238
            3) Capital cases 239
            4) Habeas corpus proceedings 239

    2. Discovery by the Prosecution 239

        a. Notice of alibi 239
        b. Choosing when to testify 240
        c. Discovery during trial 240

d.   In general 240

e.   Sanctions for defense violations 240

3.   Access to Evidence by Defendant 242

      a.   Introduction 242

      b.   The *Brady* rule 242

      c.   Impeachment and exculpatory evidence 242

      d.   Standards of materiality 242

            1)   False prosecution evidence 242

            2)   Favorable defense evidence not requested 242

            3)   Specifically requested evidence 243

      e.   Reasonable probability standard 243

      f.   Duty to assist in discovery of exculpatory evidence 244

      g.   Balancing state's interest in confidentiality with defendant's
          right of access to evidence 244

      h.   Access to witnesses 245

      i.   Unavailable evidence 246

      j.   Compulsory process 246

B.   GUILTY PLEAS **246**

1.   Background 246

      a.   Basis of plea 246

      b.   Sentencing 246

2.   Justifications for Guilty Pleas as a Factor in the Judge's Consideration
      of Final Disposition 247

3.   The Plea in the Prosecutor's Office 247

      a.   Alternatives 248

4.   Should a Court Accept a Plea? 248

5.   Some Problems with Guilty Pleas 248

      a.   Coercion by the judge 248

      b.   Claims of innocence 249

      c.   Representation by counsel in the bargaining process 249

6.   Rejected, Kept, and Broken Bargains; Unrealized Expectations 250

      a.   Vindictiveness 250

      b.   Fear of the death penalty 250

		c.	Retraction of promise by judge	251
		d.	Requirement that promise be fully performed	251
		e.	Violation of guilty plea agreements	252
	7.		Professional Responsibility: The Role of the Prosecutor and Defense Counsel	253
		a.	Right to counsel	253
		b.	Discretion of the prosecutor	254
		c.	Prosecutor's refusal to disclose impeachment material prior to entering plea agreement	254
		d.	Prosecutor's discretion to charge and prosecute offenses	255
	8.		Receiving the Defendant's Plea; Plea Withdrawal	256
		a.	Entering the plea	256
		b.	Voluntariness	256
		c.	Understanding	257
		d.	Determining factual basis of guilty plea	257
		e.	Plea withdrawal	257
			1) Timing	257
			2) Procedure	258
			3) Effect of withdrawn plea	258
			4) Federal Rules of Criminal Procedure	258
		f.	Compliance with federal rules	258
		g.	Significance of compliance with requirements for receiving guilty plea	259
		h.	Effect of a guilty plea on right to counsel	259
		i.	Constitutional violations before the guilty plea	260
C.			**TRIAL BY JURY**	**260**
	1.		Right to Jury Trial; Waiver	260
		a.	Right to trial by jury incorporated	260
		b.	Length of sentence	261
		c.	Contempt cases	261
			1) Civil or criminal contempt	261
			2) Criminal contempt	261
		d.	What constitutes "trial by jury"?	262
			1) Number of jurors	262
			2) Unanimous verdict	262

e.	Waiver	262
f.	Instructing the jury on disregarding the law	263
g.	Prosecution's right to jury trial	263

2. Jury Selection 263

    a. Constitutional requirements 263

        1) Federal courts 264
        2) State courts 264
        3) Racial discrimination 264
        4) Sex discrimination 265
        5) Other discrimination 265

    b. Procedure for selecting trial jurors 266

        1) Source of names 266
        2) Examination of jurors (voir dire) 266
        3) Procedures not required 266
        4) Challenges 267
        5) Limitation in capital cases 269

D. MEDIA RIGHTS VS. FAIR TRIAL RIGHTS **270**

1. Introduction 270
2. Control over What Is Published 270

    a. Restraint by newspapers 270
    b. English rule 270

        1) Freedom of the press 270
        2) Positive contributions by newspapers and news media 270
        3) The political process 270

3. Pretrial Publicity and Jury Selection 271

    a. Publication of inadmissible evidence 271
    b. Confession and criminal record 271
    c. Presumption of partiality 272

4. Change of Venue 272
5. Preventing Prejudicial Publicity 273

    a. Reporter and official conduct 273
    b. Restricting public statements 273
    c. Restricting the media 274

   d. Closed proceedings 274
   e. Public right to attend trials 275
   f. Closure standards 275
   g. First Amendment right of access to preliminary hearings 276

  6. Televising Courtroom Proceedings 277

   a. State proceedings 277
   b. Trial by television—inherently prejudicial 277
   c. Televised coverage allowed 278

E. THE CRIMINAL TRIAL **279**

  1. Public Trial 279
  2. Presence and Confrontation 279

   a. Confrontation and the Sixth Amendment 279
   b. Defendant's misconduct 279
   c. Waiver of right to confrontation 280
   d. No right of access to witness competency hearing 280
   e. Holding the defendant in shackles at sentencing 280
   f. Confrontation of out-of-court witness 281

  3. The Defendant's Right to Remain Silent 282
  4. Counsel's Arguments 283

   a. Introduction 283
   b. Improper arguments must deny due process 284

  5. Process of Proof, Argument, and Instruction of the Jury 284

   a. Order of the proceedings 285
   b. Instructing the jury 285

    1) Instructing sua sponte 285
    2) Requested instructions 285
    3) Ruling on requested instructions 286
    4) Hung jury charge 286

   c. Judge-jury relationship—motion for judgment of acquittal 286

  6. Deliberations and Verdict 286

   a. Deadlocked juries 286
   b. Inconsistent verdicts 287
   c. Impeaching verdicts 287

| | 7. | Jury's Role in Sentencing | 287 |

F. | **DOUBLE JEOPARDY** | **287** |

| | 1. | Introduction | 287 |

| | | a. | Origins | 287 |
| | | b. | History in the United States | 287 |

| | 2. | Reprosecution After a Mistrial | 287 |

		a.	Mistrial based on unintentional procedural error	288
		b.	Mistrial caused by defendant or counsel	288
		c.	Standard for allowing reprosecution after a mistrial	289

| | 3. | Reprosecution Following an Acquittal | 290 |

| | | a. | Dismissal pursuant to defendant's motion | 290 |
| | | b. | Post-trial ruling appealed | 291 |

| | 4. | Reprosecution Following a Conviction | 292 |

		a.	The *Ball* rule	292
		b.	Reprosecution following a conviction	292
		c.	Implied acquittals	293

| | 5. | Reprosecution by a Different Sovereign | 293 |

| | | a. | Reprosecution in a sister state | 293 |
| | | b. | Reprosecution by a state after a federal trial | 294 |

G. | **SENTENCING** | **295** |

| | 1. | Introduction | 295 |

| | | a. | Purposes | 295 |
| | | b. | Sentencing guidelines | 295 |

| | 2. | Control of Discretion | 295 |
| | 3. | Constitutional Limitation on Sentencing Procedure | 296 |

		a.	Information used by sentencing judge	296
		b.	Burden of proof	297
		c.	Use of prior conviction	297
		d.	Aggravating facts other than prior convictions must go to the jury	298
		e.	Constitutionality of Federal Sentencing Guidelines	299

V. APPEALS, POST-CONVICTION REVIEW 301

    A. POST-TRIAL MOTIONS AND APPEALS 301

        1. Motions 301

            a. Motion for acquittal or directed verdict 301
            b. Motion to arrest judgment 301
            c. Motion to correct or reduce the sentence 301
            d. Motion for a new trial 301

        2. The Right to Appeal 301

            a. Appeals by the defense 301

                1) No constitutional right 301
                2) Bail 302
                3) Due process and imposition of harsher punishment 302
                4) Greater sentence upon retrial permitted 303

            b. Appeals by the state 304

        3. Scope of Appellate Review 305

            a. Introduction 305
            b. The harmless error concept 305

                1) Contribution to verdict 305
                2) Harmless error situations 306

            c. Automatic reversal required 306
            d. Harmless error and omission of element of offense 306
            e. Issues not properly raised 308

    B. POST-CONVICTION REVIEW: FEDERAL HABEAS CORPUS 308

        1. Translations 308
        2. Constitutional Provisions 308
        3. Remedy 308
        4. Historical Development of Habeas Corpus 308

            a. At common law 308
            b. Federal courts 308
            c. Current statute 309

        5. Procedure 309

     a.   Issuance of the writ of order to show cause 309

     b.   Hearing 309

     c.   Appeal 309

6.   Issues Cognizable 309

     a.   Generally 309

     b.   Exclusionary rule 310

     c.   *Miranda* violations 311

7.   Waivers, Defaults, and Other Bars to Relief 311

     a.   Contemporaneous objection rule 311

     b.   Successive applications for a writ 312

8.   Retroactive Application of New Rules 312

9.   Impact of AEDPA Provisions 313

TABLE OF CASES 317

I. INTRODUCTION

Criminal procedure is the process by which governments may convict and punish persons for crimes. The term encompasses the means of detecting crimes and gathering evidence against a suspect, the process of arrest and detention, and the manner in which the determination of guilt and punishment is made.

A. CRIMINAL JUSTICE PROCESS

1. **Introduction.** Criminal procedure of the states and federal government may differ in substantial respects. For example, California's procedure (which is described below as an example of state procedure) is different from federal procedure.

2. **State Criminal Procedure.**

   a. **Arrest.** The criminal process typically begins with the gathering of evidence concerning a suspect (sufficient to make an arrest). Or perhaps the police, investigating the commission or possible commission of a crime, gather evidence for the purpose of determining suspects and then ultimately making an arrest. Upon arrest, the defendant is brought to the police station.

   b. **The charge.** The police then ask the district attorney to make out a formal charge and an affidavit (*i.e.,* a written complaint charging the accused with a specified crime or crimes). Of course, if the accused had been arrested pursuant to a warrant, the complaint would have been prepared before the arrest and used to secure the warrant.

   c. **Proceedings before a magistrate.** Then the defendant is taken before the committing magistrate (in California, a municipal court judge) who advises the defendant of her rights and sends the defendant back to jail or allows her to post bond. If the charge is a misdemeanor, the defendant is then and there arraigned and required to plead to the pending criminal charge. If the charge is a felony, however, the defendant is normally not required to plead, but a date is set for a preliminary hearing.

   d. **Preliminary hearing.** When a felony has been charged, the defendant is entitled to a preliminary hearing for the purpose of determining whether there are sufficient grounds to bind her over for a trial.

      1) **Sufficient evidence.** The committing magistrate rules on the evidence. If the evidence is suppressed for some reason at this point, then the prosecutor's case collapses and the defendant is set free.

2) **Writ of prohibition.** If the defendant loses here, she can bring a writ of prohibition to appeal the magistrate's findings.

3) **Indictment.** Note that no preliminary hearing is normally required when a grand jury has returned an indictment against the defendant. An indictment is simply a finding by an investigatory body (on a written accusation made by the prosecuting attorney) that there is sufficient evidence to warrant a conviction of the crime. A grand jury indictment may either precede or follow arrest.

4) **Decision at preliminary hearing.** The committing magistrate decides the case at the preliminary hearing. If he decides that the case should go on, the defendant is committed. *Note*: As mentioned above, the prosecution could go to the grand jury for an indictment without a preliminary hearing when it wants to keep its information to itself. The preliminary hearing gives the defendant a chance at cross-examining the prosecution's witness (a good discovery technique).

e. **Accusatory pleading.** The prosecution commences once the government files either an indictment or an information. An indictment has been explained above. An information is simply a written charge on which the defendant will be tried.

f. **Arraignment.** Once the information has been filed, the defendant is brought before a court of competent jurisdiction (a court must have both personal and subject matter jurisdiction), and is informed of the charges against her. The accused is then asked to plead.

g. **Motions and pleas.** The accused is normally permitted to make certain motions or one of several different pleas.

1) **Motions.** The defendant may file a demurrer (a challenge to the legal sufficiency of the accusatory pleading, one basis of which could be the court's lack of jurisdiction), a motion to quash or set aside the indictment or information (on various grounds), a motion to dismiss, a motion for change of venue to another court, discovery motions, or a motion to suppress (for example, to suppress unconstitutionally seized evidence).

2) **Pleas.** After denial of her motions, the defendant may plead guilty, not guilty, or nolo contendere (the same as pleading guilty except that the conviction cannot be used in subsequent civil proceedings; typically this plea can be made only with the consent of the prosecution).

h. **Evidence gathering and discovery.** Typically the next part of the criminal process involves further fact-finding in preparation for trial. This usually involves use of the discovery process in order to find out as much as possible about the opposition's case.

i.   **Extraordinary writs.** The defendant may file certain extraordinary writs before trial begins. The writ of prohibition (mentioned above) is an appeal to a higher (appellate) court to terminate the judicial process, normally on the basis of a lack of proper jurisdiction in the lower court. The other writ in common use is that of habeas corpus ("bring forth the body"), which lies to test any restraint that is contrary to "fundamental law" (*i.e.,* in the case of federal habeas corpus, any restraint that is contrary to the federal Constitution).

j.   **Trial.** A host of criminal procedure problems and issues are raised during the process of trial, including, but not limited to, the following:

1) The competency of the defendant to stand trial, as well as her sanity at the time of the offense.

2) The defendant's right to counsel.

3) The right to a trial by jury and the selection of jurors.

4) The right to a fair trial.

5) The defendant's and witnesses' privilege against self-incrimination, including the right of the defendant not to testify as a witness at all.

6) The right to compulsory process in order to obtain witnesses to testify.

7) The right to cross-examine witnesses.

8) Issues relating to trial of two or more defendants in the same trial; to more than one trial of the same defendant for the same criminal act; and to the trial of the same defendant for more than one crime growing out of the same act.

9) Evidence questions relating to the introduction or order of evidence, the burden of proof, motions—such as a motion to dismiss, a motion for mistrial (for misconduct at the trial)—instructions to the jury, etc.

10) The verdict, the sentence, and the entry of judgment by the court.

k.   **Sentencing.** Ordinarily the judge has substantial discretion in determining the appropriate sentence. However, modern statutes sometimes set a minimum sentence as well as a maximum sentence for a particular offense.

l. **Post-trial motions.** Typically the defendant who has been convicted has at her disposal several possible post-trial motions. The most frequently used are:

1) **Motion to vacate.** The defendant may ask that the judgment be reconsidered because it was based on erroneous facts or was obtained by fraud, deceit, etc. Many states permit this motion only if the defendant did not take an appeal from the trial court judgment.

2) **Motion for a new trial.** States will permit a motion, within certain time limits, for a new trial, but only on specified grounds (such as the fact that new evidence has been discovered). Often the motion must be made before sentencing.

m. **Appeal.** Most states grant a first appeal from a criminal conviction as a matter of right.

n. **Habeas corpus.** The writ of habeas corpus is available at any stage of the criminal process.

3. **Federal Criminal Procedure.**

a. **Gathering of evidence.**

b. **Arrest.** A warrant may be issued on presentation of a complaint by the United States attorney, showing the crime and the accused, and her responsibility therefor (there must be "probable cause" for the issuance of the warrant). [Fed. R. Crim. P. 4(a)] A valid arrest may also be made without a warrant if there is probable cause. Note that only federal crimes are involved in the federal criminal process.

c. **Appearance before a commissioner.** If the accused was arrested without a warrant, then a complaint is prepared. If a warrant was used, the complaint was previously prepared. The accused is next brought before a United States commissioner; this must occur "without unnecessary delay." [Fed. R. Crim. P. 5(a)]

d. **Preliminary examination.** Preliminary examinations are held before United States commissioners. [Fed. R. Crim. P. 5(c)]

e. **Grand jury indictment.** If a grand jury has returned an indictment against the accused, she is not entitled to a preliminary examination, except that Federal Rule of Criminal Procedure 5(c) provides that if a person is taken into custody before the indictment is given, she is entitled to a preliminary examination (this avoids the problem of the lengthy holding of a defendant waiting for a grand jury).

f. **Accusatory pleading.**

g. Arraignment. The defendant is arraigned in federal district court.

h. Motions and pleas. Under Federal Rule of Criminal Procedure 12, the motion to dismiss is used in place of all other motions discussed above under state procedure. This motion attacks all possible defects.

i. Evidence gathering and discovery.

j. Extraordinary writs.

k. Trial.

l. Sentencing.

m. Post-trial motions.

n. Appeal.

o. Habeas corpus.

B. SOURCES OF CRIMINAL PROCEDURE LAW

1. Basic Principles of the Federal System.

a. A federal system. Rather than establish a unitary form of government, where power is concentrated in a single, central government, the framers of the Constitution formed a federal state. Governmental power, and thus the power to pass and enforce laws (including laws of criminal procedure), is divided between the federal government and the states.

    1) National supremacy. This division of power between the states and the federal government creates the possibility of a conflict for supremacy between them. The framers realized that such conflict was bound to arise and provided for its resolution with the Supremacy Clause (Article VI, Section 2), which states that the federal Constitution and laws are the "supreme Law of the Land."

    2) Separation of powers. Governmental power is divided between the federal and state governments. There is a further division of the federal power—among the three branches of the federal government (executive, legislative, and judicial). While not constitutionally required to do so, many state governments follow this principle as well.

b. Limited government. The framers feared the tendency of governments to grow in power and to suppress the liberties of the people. They provided, therefore, for a limited government (i) by specifically enumerating the powers of the federal government and leaving all residual powers to the states or to the people, and (ii) by specifically forbidding the federal and state governments from performing certain acts and by providing that certain individual liberties or rights should be protected from invasion by governmental authority (*i.e.,* the Bill of Rights, etc.). The law of criminal procedure deals principally with these limitations.

2. **Federal Powers.**

a. **Judicial power.** Article III, Section 1 of the Constitution states that "the Judicial Power of the United States, shall be vested in one supreme Court, and in such inferior Courts as the Congress may from time to time ordain and establish."

   1) **Scope of federal judicial power.** Article III, Section 2 outlines the scope of federal judicial power, the most important provision of which provides: "The judicial Power shall extend to all Cases, in Law and Equity, arising under this Constitution, the Laws of the United States, and Treaties made . . . under their Authority. . . . "

   2) **Judicial review by the Supreme Court.** The Supreme Court may review congressional acts, federal court judgments, state court judgments, and state legislative acts for their constitutionality.

b. **Power of Congress.** The Constitution lodges the power to make federal laws in Congress.

   1) **Scope of the granted powers.**

      a) **Delegated powers.** The powers of Congress are specifically enumerated in the Constitution. Among these powers are many that relate specifically to criminal law and criminal procedure.

      b) **Necessary and Proper Clause.** The specific powers of Congress are enlarged by the Necessary and Proper Clause (Article I, Section 8), which states that Congress shall have the power to make all laws that are necessary and proper for executing its powers.

   2) **Limitations on the exercise of congressional power.** There are both implied and express constitutional limitations on the exercise by Congress of its delegated powers. For example, the Fourth Amendment guarantees the individual that she will be free from unreasonable searches and seizures by government officials. Many of these constitutional limitations restrict the power of the federal government in its use of the criminal law.

3. **Power of the States.**

   a. **Tenth Amendment.** The powers of the federal government are specifically mentioned in the Constitution; hence, they are termed delegated powers. The powers of the states, however, are not delegated but are residual; that is, the states have all the power that has not been specifically given to the federal government.

   b. **Police power.** The principal state power is the police power, which is simply another name for the power to enact legislation, including criminal legislation, that will promote the health, peace, morals, education, or good order of the people. Such power, derived from the Tenth Amendment, can be exercised in innumerable ways.

   c. **Limitations on the exercise of state power.** The question concerning state and local legislation or the acts of state and local government officials undertaken pursuant to the police power is usually whether or not they violate any of the limitations that the federal Constitution places on the exercise of state power.

      1) State power may be limited by the United States Constitution. For example, the Fourteenth Amendment prohibits a state from passing a law that denies any person the equal protection of the laws.

      2) The state may have the constitutional power to pass laws in an area, but if the federal government does also and the law passed by the state conflicts with federal law, then the federal law governs.

      3) A state law may not violate the state's own constitution.

   d. **Power of local government.** Legally a state possesses all the power exercised by both the state and local government units. This result is dictated by the Tenth Amendment. However, in practice a state delegates (usually through its constitution and other implementing legislation) both powers and functions to its many local political subdivisions. These local government units are limited in the exercise of their power not only by the provisions of the federal Constitution but also by the provisions of the state's constitution and laws.

4. **Sources of Criminal Procedure Law.** The following are the basic sources of the law of criminal procedure:

   a. **Provisions of the Constitution.** All laws pertaining to criminal procedure must be in accord with the provisions of the United States Constitution.

   b. **State constitutions.** State constitutions are increasingly becoming an important source for laws governing criminal procedure. While such constitutions may add to the rights and privileges of the accused beyond what the federal Constitution provides, they cannot detract or take away from the protections and rights given the accused in the federal Constitution. (In other words, state law may not violate the federal Constitution.)

c.   **State and federal statutes.** State and federal statutes may also apply to and govern criminal procedure, each in its respective sphere of authority (state laws are applicable to state proceedings, federal laws to federal proceedings). Of course, neither may violate the provisions of the federal Constitution, and state laws may not violate the state's constitution.

d.   **Court regulations.** Judges also make laws for the administration of criminal justice. The power to do so is derived from their supervisory powers over the administration of criminal justice within their respective jurisdictions—*i.e.,* the United States Supreme Court makes rules that are applicable in all federal courts, and state courts make rules that are applicable in state proceedings.

5.   **Fourteenth Amendment Due Process.**

a.   **Meaning of due process.** The Fourteenth Amendment Due Process Clause prevents any state from depriving any person of life, liberty, or property without "due process" of law. In the past, the clause was applied primarily to economic regulations. Today, however, the clause is probably most meaningful as a protection of individual rights. The scope of the clause in this area has expanded greatly over the years.

b.   **Incorporation doctrine.** Whether the Due Process Clause incorporated the rights guaranteed at the federal level by the Bill of Rights is an important question. Some commentators and judges argued for total incorporation; *i.e.,* that the Bill of Rights should apply fully to state action. Others argued that "due process" included only "fundamental" principles of liberty.

1)   **Adoption of the selective incorporation approach.** The Supreme Court has consistently held that the Fourteenth Amendment only incorporates the Bill of Rights on a selective basis. Early cases incorporated procedural safeguards that were "implicit in the concept of ordered liberty" [Palko v. Connecticut, 302 U.S. 319 (1937)], so that without them, a fair and enlightened system of justice would be impossible. Later cases, including *Duncan v. Louisiana*, 391 U.S. 145 (1968), have focused on the attributes of the actual criminal justice system involved; *i.e.,* whether, given this kind of system (the Anglo-American system), a particular procedure is fundamental. For example, the exclusionary rule is not necessarily fundamental to fairness in every imaginable criminal

justice system, but it has been considered fundamental in the context of the system used by the various states, and is therefore part of due process. In *Duncan*, the Court applied this approach in holding that the Sixth Amendment right to a jury trial was applicable to the states through the Fourteenth Amendment, even though other criminal justice systems are imaginable that would be orderly, fair, and equitable even without juries.

2) **Rights incorporated.** In a series of cases, the Court has held that the Due Process Clause incorporates: (i) the Fourth Amendment rights to be free from unreasonable searches and seizures and to have excluded from criminal trials any evidence illegally seized; (ii) the Fifth Amendment rights against compelled self-incrimination and double jeopardy (but not the right to a grand jury indictment); and (iii) the Sixth Amendment rights to counsel, to a speedy and public trial, to confrontation of opposing witnesses, and to compulsory process to obtain witnesses.

3) **Scope of incorporation.** Over the objection of several of the Justices, the Court at first apparently incorporated each right to the same extent as applied at the federal level. Then in *Williams v. Florida, infra*, the Court held that the right to a jury trial does not prevent the states from using fewer than the 12 jurors required in federal courts. In *Apodaca v. Oregon, infra*, the Court held that, although the Sixth Amendment requires a unanimous verdict in federal criminal jury trials, the Due Process Clause does not prevent the states from using less-than-unanimous jury verdicts. Accordingly, the application of a federal right to the states through the Fourteenth Amendment does not necessarily mean that the right will include all the features protected at the federal level.

c. **Bodily extractions and the incorporation doctrine.**

1) **Introduction.** The relationship between the Due Process Clause and the specific protections of the Bill of Rights is illustrated best when an issue can be resolved through application of either provision. The Bill of Rights protects a person against "unreasonable searches and seizures" and against being forced to be "a witness against himself." These provisions are more specific than the Due Process Clause, but may not be enough by themselves to resolve issues arising, for example, from forced bodily extractions by police to obtain evidence.

2) **Forced stomach pumping--**

Rochin v. California, 342 U.S. 165 (1952).

Facts. Police illegally entered Rochin's (D's) bedroom and saw two capsules on his nightstand. D took the capsules and swallowed them. The officers tried to retrieve the capsules. When they could not do so, they took D to the hospital and forcibly pumped D's stomach to obtain the capsules, which subsequent testing showed to contain narcotics. This evidence was used in a state court to convict D. The Supreme Court granted certiorari.

Issue. May the police use forcible tactics to extract evidence by pumping the stomach of a suspect?

Held. No. Conviction reversed.

♦ If the methods of obtaining evidence "shock hardened sensibilities," as they did here, the evidence must be excluded under the Due Process Clause. Due process cannot be defined precisely, but it does mean that convictions cannot be brought about by methods that offend a sense of justice.

♦ Coerced confessions cannot be used as evidence, even if the statements are proven true by other evidence, because such coercion offends the community's sense of fair play and decency. To permit the brutal police conduct here would give brutality the cloak of law, thereby discrediting the law.

Concurrence (Black, J.). The Due Process Clause incorporates the Fifth Amendment's protection against compelled self-incrimination, and forced extraction of evidence such as occurred here is therefore unconstitutional. It is better to adhere to such specific guarantees in the Bill of Rights than to nebulous Fourteenth Amendment due process concepts.

Concurrence (Douglas, J.). The Fifth Amendment should apply to the states as well as the federal government. To rely on due process instead of the Fifth Amendment makes the law turn not on the Constitution but on the idiosyncrasies of the Justices on the Supreme Court.

───────────────

3) **Blood samples.** The Court permitted state police to take a blood sample from an unconscious person at an automobile accident scene. The person was convicted based on the blood test, which showed intoxication. [Breithaupt v. Abram, 352 U.S. 432 (1957)] The majority deemed this a slight intrusion outweighed by the interests in scientific determination of intoxication, while the dissenters could not distinguish the case from *Rochin*. Later the Court upheld the taking of a blood sample from an injured person over his objection, again to prove intoxication. [Schmerber v. California, 384 U.S. 757 (1966)] By this time, the Court had held that the Fifth Amendment applied to the states, yet the situation in *Schmerber* satisfied the Fifth Amendment requirements.

d. Criminal procedure and retroactivity.

1) **Introduction.** The Court's decisions on matters of criminal procedure often drastically affect criminal prosecutions. Thus it can be a determinative factor if a particular decision is applied retroactively, especially for those persons previously convicted. As stated in *Desist v. United States*, 394 U.S. 244 (1969), the Court bases its retroactivity decisions on the following factors:

   a) **Purpose of new standard and its effect on truth-finding.** If the new constitutional procedural requirement is intended to promote the truth-finding function of criminal procedure and raises questions about the accuracy of previous guilty verdicts, it will be given retroactive effect. Otherwise, *e.g.,* if the standard has only a prophylactic purpose, the Court will consider two other factors.

   b) **Reliance.** The degree to which police have relied on the existing procedural standards is one factor. When police reliance on the old standard was justified because the standard was clear and widely accepted, the Court is less likely to apply the new standard retroactively.

   c) **Effect.** The practical effect a retroactive application would have upon the administration of justice is the other factor. For example, it may be impossible to retrieve evidence.

2) **Applications.**

   a) **Right to counsel.** In *Gideon v. Wainwright*, *infra*, the Court held that all defendants in felony prosecutions were entitled to counsel, and if they could not afford one themselves, the state must provide one. This holding was given complete retroactive effect because, when a defendant had not been represented by counsel, it was impossible to tell whether his case was adequately presented and thus whether he was innocent.

   b) **Exclusionary rule applied to the states.** In *Mapp v. Ohio*, *infra*, the Court held that the Fourth Amendment's protection against unreasonable searches and seizures was incorporated by the Fourteenth Amendment so as to require state courts to exclude evidence obtained by unlawful searches and seizures. The ruling was not applied retroactively to final state convictions because the purpose of the exclusionary rule—deterrence of lawless police action—would not be promoted by a retroactive application, since any police violations would already have occurred. Also, the rule has no bearing on guilt. [Linkletter v. Walker, 381 U.S. 681 (1965)]

c) **Comment on defendant's failure to testify.** The Court held in *Griffin v. California, infra,* that the Fifth Amendment's privilege against self-incrimination forbids adverse comment by a judge or prosecutor on a defendant's failure to testify, and that this applies to the states. However, the rule was not applied retroactively because the privilege against self-incrimination is not intended to protect the innocent from conviction, but to protect the individual's right to be let alone. The states had also relied on the existing rule in good faith for over 50 years. [Tehan v. United States *ex rel.* Shott, 382 U.S. 406 (1966)]

d) *Miranda* **warning.** The *Miranda* rights case—*Miranda v. Arizona, infra,* was applied only to those cases in which the trial began after the date of the *Miranda* decision. The Court reasoned that the voluntariness of confessions was already a circumstance of the interrogation. *Miranda* provided new safeguards, but existing challenges could be resolved through an involuntariness claim. [Johnson v. New Jersey, 384 U.S. 719 (1966)]

e) **Right to pretrial counsel.** In *United States v. Wade,* 388 U.S. 218 (1967), and *Gilbert v. California,* 388 U.S. 263 (1967), the Court granted the right to counsel at certain pretrial events such as lineups. These holdings applied only to confrontations for identification purposes conducted after the date of the decisions, thus indicating the importance of police reliance on existing procedures.

3) **Extent of retroactivity.**

a) **Prospective application.** Even when the Court determines that a new standard will have only prospective application, it necessarily applies to the case at hand and to that extent is applied retroactively. Justice Harlan objected to this approach in his dissent in *Desist v. United States, supra.* He felt it unprincipled that two similarly situated defendants could be treated differently merely because one's case came before the Court instead of the other's.

b) **Cases on direct appeal.** In *Desist,* the Court did not distinguish between final convictions and those still pending on review so far as retroactivity was concerned. In *United States v. Johnson,* 457 U.S. 537 (1982), however, the Court relied on Justice Harlan's approach and decided that the rule (set forth in *Payton v. New York,* 445 U.S. 573 (1980)) requiring an arrest warrant to enter a suspect's house to make an arrest should be applied to cases still pending on direct appeal when *Payton* was decided. The rule was not applied retroactively to state-court convictions finally affirmed by a state supreme court before *Edwards v. Arizona, infra,* was decided, however. [Solem v. Stumes, 465 U.S. 638 (1984)]

c) **Retroactivity of Fifth Amendment decisions--**

Shea v. Louisiana, 470 U.S. 51 (1985).

Facts. Shea (D) requested a lawyer when he was read his *Miranda* rights. The interview was stopped, but the next day, before D had seen a lawyer, the police reread D his rights and D made a confession. D was convicted on the basis of the confession, and D appealed. Subsequently, the Court held in *Edwards v. Arizona, infra,* that the police cannot initiate a second interrogation once the suspect has requested a lawyer. The Louisiana Supreme Court refused to apply *Edwards* to D's case. The United States Supreme Court granted certiorari.

Issue. Does a new Fifth Amendment standard apply to all cases on direct review at the time the standard is announced?

Held. Yes. Judgment reversed.

♦ The difference between the *Johnson* and *Solem* cases, *supra,* is the difference between a pending and undecided direct view of a conviction and a federal collateral attack upon a state conviction that has become final. There is no reason why the *Johnson* rule should not apply to Fifth Amendment cases. Principled decisionmaking and fairness to similarly situated petitioners requires application of a new rule to all cases pending on direct review.

♦ The distinction between cases on direct review and those presented on collateral review is based on considerations of finality in the judicial process. Finality must attach at some point.

♦ The only fair alternative to applying a new rule to all cases pending on direct appeal would be to make the rule prospective even as to the appellant himself. Such would be an unacceptable result.

Dissent (White, J., Burger, C.J., Rehnquist, O'Connor, JJ.). The Court says that any new constitutional decision, except one that constitutes a "clear break with the past," must be applied to all cases pending on direct appeal when it is handed down. There is no principled reason for distinguishing between direct review and habeas corpus petitions.

Comment. In *Teague v. Lane*, 489 U.S. 288 (1989), the Court held that as a general rule, new rulings should not apply retroactively to cases on collateral review, but did not agree as to what exceptions to the general rule would be recognized.

---

4)   Retroactivity of Supreme Court decisions in state courts--

Danforth v. Minnesota, 128 S. Ct. 1029 (2008).

Facts. After Danforth (D) was convicted of first-degree sexual assault, he filed a motion for postconviction relief, alleging that the admission of the victim's taped interview at trial violated the rule announced in *Crawford v. Washington, infra*, and that *Crawford* should be applied retroactively. The Minnesota Supreme Court held that under *Teague v. Lane*, *supra*, *Crawford* did not apply retroactively and that state courts are not free to give a Supreme Court decision announcing a new constitutional rule of criminal procedure a broader retroactive application than that given by the Supreme Court. The Supreme Court granted certiorari.

Issue. May state courts provide greater retroactivity for new Supreme Court rules of criminal procedure than federal courts provide?

Held. Yes. Judgment reversed and case remanded.

♦   State courts may, but are not required to, apply *Crawford* to cases that were final when *Crawford* was decided. And because *Teague* focused on federal habeas relief, it does not prohibit states from applying *Crawford* retroactively. Nothing in *Teague* prevents state courts from exercising their authority to give broader effect to new rules of criminal procedure than required by *Teague*.

♦   The rule established in *Teague* was meant to be applied in the context of federal habeas and had no bearing on whether states could provide broader relief in their postconviction proceedings. Federalism allows states to define crimes, punishments, rules of evidence, and rules of criminal and civil procedure in different ways, as long as they do not violate the Constitution.

♦   The *Teague* rule of nonretroactivity was tailored to achieve the goals of federal habeas while minimizing federal intrusion into state criminal proceedings. It limits the authority of federal courts to overturn state convictions; it does not limit a state court's authority to grant relief for violations of new rules of constitutional law when reviewing its own state's convictions.

♦   The retroactivity of new rules of constitutional law is primarily concerned with the availability of remedies, not with whether a constitutional violation occurred. The availability of remedies is a mixed question of state and federal law, whereas the question of whether a constitutional violation occurred is a pure question of federal law, and this Court's resolution should be applied uniformly throughout the nation.

Dissent (Roberts, C.J., Kennedy, J.). The question of retroactivity is distinct from the question of remedies and is a question of federal law. State courts are bound by this Court's rulings on the retroactivity of its decisions. The Supremacy Clause requires uniform application of the Court's decisions.

---

e.   **The federal courts' supervisory power.**

1)   **Purpose of supervisory power.** The Supreme Court has supervisory authority over the administration of criminal justice in the federal courts, beyond mere enforcement of minimum constitutional safeguards. There are three purposes for this supervisory power: (i) to implement a remedy for violation of recognized rights; (ii) to preserve judicial integrity by ensuring that a conviction rests on appropriate considerations validly before the jury; and (iii) to design remedies to deter illegal conduct. Pursuant to this power, the Court may hold certain evidence inadmissible apart from constitutional considerations. [McNabb v. United States, 318 U.S. 332 (1943)]

2)   **Scope of supervisory power.** The Court has restricted the scope of the supervisory power. In *United States v. Payner*, 447 U.S. 727 (1980), the Court held that the supervisory power does not allow a federal court to exclude evidence not obtained in violation of the Fourth Amendment. The dissenting Justices suggested that this approach makes supervisory power cases constitutional cases in disguise. In *United States v. Hasting*, 461 U.S. 499 (1983), the Court noted that reversals of convictions under the court's supervisory power must be approached with some caution; *i.e.,* if there is some less drastic means of exercising the supervisory power, it should be used instead.

f.   **Trend for greater protection under state law than required by the Constitution.** In the years since the Warren Court, the Supreme Court has become more conservative in granting rights to the accused. However, a number of the highest state courts have opted to try to keep alive the Warren Court's philosophical commitment to protect the criminal suspect, by granting to the accused greater protection than required by decisions under the United States Constitution.

1)   **State constitution interpretation.** Often the rationale for doing so is the interpretation of state constitutional provisions.

2) **Rules of evidence.** Alternatively, state courts may place their decisions on the basis that they have constitutional power to establish rules of evidence for their own courts.

3) **The new federalism in criminal procedure.** More and more state supreme courts are rejecting or ignoring Supreme Court decisions that have narrowly interpreted the Bill of Rights in criminal cases, relying instead upon state law as a basis for protecting the rights of criminal defendants. In *Commonwealth v. Upton*, 476 N.E.2d 548 (Mass. 1985), the court ruled that the Massachusetts law provided more substantive protection to criminal defendants than the Fourth Amendment in the determination of probable cause and further rejected the totality of circumstances test adopted by the Supreme Court in *Illinois v. Gates*, 462 U.S. 213 (1983). And in *People v. Oates*, 698 P.2d 811 (Colo. 1985), the Colorado Supreme Court ruled that under the Colorado Constitution a legitimate expectation of privacy encompasses the expectation that purchased commercial goods will be free of government surveillance devices such as beepers, notwithstanding Supreme Court decisions interpreting identical language to the contrary.

4) **Public responses to the new federalism.** The general public has not entirely accepted the actions of the state courts in expanding constitutional protections. For example, California voters approved an amendment to the state's Bill of Rights that restricted application of the exclusionary rule to those circumstances mandated by the federal Constitution.

5) **Supreme Court's responses to the new federalism.** Supreme Court decisions have taken an expansive view of its jurisdiction in areas where a state court decision purportedly rests on independent state grounds. In *Michigan v. Long*, 463 U.S. 1032 (1983), the Supreme Court found that it had jurisdiction "in the absence of a plain statement that the decision below rested on an adequate and independent state ground." And in *Florida v. Meyers*, 466 U.S. 380 (1984), the Court summarily reversed the Florida District Court of Appeals, rejecting the contention that the judgment was unreviewable because it rested on an adequate and independent state ground.

g. **Executive detention of enemy combatants**. The Constitution does not contain any general "state of emergency" exception to its provisions that would suspend constitutional rights in the event of a national emergency. The Fifth Amendment does relax the requirement for a grand jury indictment for military cases in actual service in time of war or public danger. The Court has held that the constitutional protections apply even in time of war, such as in *Youngstown Sheet & Tube Co. v.*

Sawyer (the Steel Seizure Case), 343 U.S. 579 (1952). In *Ex Parte Mulligan*, 71 U.S. 2 (1866), the Court held that President Lincoln could not suspend the writ of habeas corpus during the Civil War and could not try civilians in military tribunals. In 1948, Congress enacted the Non-Detention Act, 18 U.S.C. section 4001(a), which provides that no citizen shall be imprisoned or otherwise detained by the United States except pursuant to an Act of Congress.

1) **Joint resolution authorizing the use of military force.** In response to the attack on September 11, 2001, Congress passed a Joint Resolution entitled Authorization for Use of Military Force ("AUMF") that gave the President broad authority to use force against nations, organizations, or persons that the President determines aided the terrorist attacks. No particular enemy was defined. President Bush committed the United States military to combat in Afghanistan and Iraq and detained alleged enemy combatants inside the United States and at Guantanamo Bay, Cuba.

2) **Detention of United States citizens--**

Hamdi v. Rumsfeld, 542 U.S. 507 (2004).

Facts. Hamdi (P), an American citizen, was captured in an active combat zone abroad, detained by the United States military as an "enemy combatant," and held in naval brigs in Virginia and South Carolina. P sought habeas corpus relief against Rumsfeld (D), Secretary of Defense, in federal court in Virginia, claiming that the Non-Detention Act of 1948 barred indefinite detention. The Fourth Circuit held that P was not entitled to habeas relief, despite being a United States citizen, because of military needs. The court held that the AUMF satisfied the requirement in the Non-Detention Act for an Act of Congress authorizing detention. P appeals.

Issue. Does the President have the authority to detain citizens who qualify as "enemy combatants" for an indefinite period of time with no opportunity for an impartial hearing?

Held. No. Judgment reversed.

♦   D claims that the Executive Branch has plenary authority to detain pursuant to Article II, but that question need not be addressed because Congress authorized detention through the AUMF. The detention of individuals falling into the limited category of combatants, for the duration of the particular conflict in which they were captured, is a fundamental incident to war and falls within the AUMF.

♦   There is no reason that the government cannot hold one of its own citizens as an enemy combatant. *Ex Parte Quirin*, 317 U.S. 1 (1942), held that citizenship does not preclude detention for the duration of hostilities.

- While indefinite detention is not authorized by Congress, there are active combat operations in Afghanistan against Taliban combatants, and the United States may lawfully detain Taliban combatants during these hostilities.

- Although the AUMF did authorize the detention of combatants such as P in the narrow circumstances of this case, the writ of habeas corpus remains available to every person detained within the United States. The writ has not been suspended. P may properly seek a habeas determination on the issue of whether P falls within the category of hostile forces subject to detention. Due process demands that a citizen held in the United States as an enemy combatant be given a meaningful opportunity to contest the factual basis for that detention before a neutral decisionmaker.

- To satisfy the minimum requirements for such a hearing, the citizen-detainee must receive notice of the factual basis for his classification and a fair opportunity to rebut the government's factual assertions before a neutral decisionmaker. Evidentiary standards may be relaxed so that the government may use hearsay to support the classification. There may be a rebuttable presumption in favor of the government's evidence.

Concurrence and dissent (Souter, Ginsburg, JJ.). To the extent that the plurality rejects the government's proposed limit on the exercise of habeas jurisdiction, it is correct. However, the plurality goes too far when it agrees that P can be detained if his designation as an enemy combatant is correct. The AUMF does not refer to detention, so it cannot provide a basis for P's detention. The government has failed to justify holding P in the absence of an Act of Congress, criminal charges, a showing that P's detention conforms to the law of war, or a showing that section 4001(a) is unconstitutional. Without a showing of something more, P should be released. In a moment of genuine emergency, the President can detain a citizen if there is a reason to fear he is an imminent threat to the safety of the nation and its people, but such emergency power must be limited by the emergency, and P has been held for over two years, so that exception does not apply here.

Dissent (Scalia, Stevens, JJ.). A citizen who wages war against the United States may be prosecuted for treason, but unless Congress suspends the usual protections under the Suspension Clause, a citizen cannot be detained without charge. The lower court decision should be reversed. The traditional treatment of enemy aliens that includes detention until the cessation of hostilities does not apply to American citizens. The criminal law process is the only means for punishing and incapacitating traitors. Unless the writ of habeas corpus is suspended, a citizen is entitled either to a criminal trial or a judicial decree requiring his release. The AUMF is not a suspension of the writ. The Court's opinion establishes a procedure that makes P's detention legal, but that is an incorrect application of the writ.

Dissent (Thomas, J.). The detention of P falls within the government's war powers, and the courts have no expertise or capacity to second-guess the decision to detain P. The President has constitutional authority to protect the national security and has broad discretion to exercise that authority. The courts should not interfere in these matters. Due process requires only a good-faith executive determination.

Comment. In *Padilla v. Rumsfeld*, 542 U.S. 426 (2004), Padilla, a United States citizen, was arrested in Chicago for participating in a plot to detonate a dirty bomb. He was declared an "enemy combatant" by the President and was turned over to the Department of Defense for detention. Padilla challenged his detention. The Second Circuit held that the President did not have authority to detain Padilla under section 4001(a). The Court reversed on jurisdictional grounds because Padilla should have filed his habeas petition against the commander of the brig he was incarcerated in. The four justices in the minority opinion would have found Padilla's detention to be unauthorized under section 4001(a).

---

3) **Detention of enemy combatants at Guantanamo Bay.** The United States military captured several hundred foreign fighters in Afghanistan and held them as "enemy combatants" at Guantanamo Bay, a territory leased by the United States from Cuba since 1903. Under the lease, the territory remains under the "ultimate sovereignty" of Cuba. Some of the prisoners sought writs of habeas corpus in the federal district court for the district of D.C. In *Rasul v. Bush*, 542 U.S. 466 (2004), the Court held that federal judges do have jurisdiction to consider such habeas petitions from Guantanamo detainees. The Court reasoned that although technically Cuba has sovereignty over the territory, under the lease, the United States exercises "complete jurisdiction and control" over the base and may continue to exercise such control permanently if it chooses. As such, Guantanamo Bay is in every practical respect a territory of the United States. Another consideration is the indefinite status of the detention and the lack of any legal procedure to determine the detainees' status. The dissenters argued that the decision extends the habeas statute to aliens beyond the sovereign territory of the United States to anywhere in the world, and that Congress could have changed the habeas jurisdiction of federal judges if it wanted to.

4) **Habeas corpus review for foreign detainees after new acts of Congress--**

Boumediene v. Bush, 128 S. Ct. 2229 (2008).

Facts. Boumediene and other aliens (Ps) were detained as enemy combatants at the United States naval station at Guantanamo Bay, Cuba. Ps petitioned for a writ of habeas corpus. In *Rasul v. Bush*, *supra*, the Court held that such detainees were entitled to habeas corpus review by the United States district court in Washington, D.C. Congress then passed the Military Commissions Act of 2006 ("MCA"), which stripped United States courts of habeas corpus jurisdiction over detained aliens who were determined to be enemy combatants. Congress had set up an alternative form of review under the Detainee Treatment Act of 2005 ("DTA"), which allowed the D.C. Circuit to review Ps' cases only after the Combatant Status Review Tribunals ("CSRTs") had found Ps to be enemy combatants. Ps claimed that the withdrawal of habeas corpus jurisdiction violated the Suspension Clause, Article I, section 9. The government (D) claimed that the Suspension Clause did not apply to noncitizens held outside the United States and that, even if it did apply, the DTA was an adequate substitute for habeas corpus. The court of appeals held that Ps were not entitled to habeas corpus or the protections of the Suspension Clause. The Supreme Court granted certiorari.

Issue. Are Ps entitled to a habeas corpus hearing without first exhausting the DTA review procedures?

Held. Yes. Judgment reversed and case remanded.

♦ The Constitution cannot be contracted away. The United States has complete control of Guantanamo. The surrendering of formal sovereignty to Cuba, while entering into a lease that granted total control over the territory back to the United States, did not mean that the political branches would govern without legal constraint. If Congress denies Ps the privilege of habeas corpus, Congress must comply with the Suspension Clause.

♦ This Court has never held that noncitizens detained by the federal government in territory over which another country maintains de jure sovereignty have constitutional rights. However, Ps are detained for the duration of a conflict that is already among the longest wars in American history. For this reason, and because Ps are held in a territory over which our government has complete control, the lack of precedent is not a barrier to our holding.

♦ The CSRTs are deficient because Ps have limited means to find and present evidence against the charges they face. The government has essentially no limits on the use of hearsay evidence. There is a high risk of error, with possible consequences of detention for the duration of the hostilities. Therefore, the court that conducts the habeas proceeding must have the means to correct errors that occurred during the CSRT proceedings, including the authority to assess the sufficiency of the government's evidence and the authority to admit and consider relevant exculpatory evidence.

♦ To require DTA review before proceeding with the habeas corpus actions would mean months, if not years, of delay. Ps are entitled to a prompt habeas corpus hearing. The DTA review procedures are an inadequate substitute for habeas corpus in these cases.

♦   The only law we find to be unconstitutional is section 7 of the MCA. The DTA and the CSRT process remain intact. Except in cases of undue delay, federal courts should allow the CSRT process to proceed before entertaining an enemy combatant's habeas corpus petition.

Concurrence (Souter, Ginsburg, Breyer, JJ.). Some Ps have been detained for six years without any real habeas scrutiny. Today's decision is an act of perseverance in trying to make habeas review mean something of value to prisoners and to the nation.

Dissent (Roberts, C.J., Scalia, Thomas, Alito, JJ.).

♦   The majority overreaches when it strikes down the DTA as an inadequate substitute for habeas review without showing what rights Ps have that cannot be vindicated by the DTA system. The majority holds that to be an adequate substitute, any tribunal reviewing Ps' cases must have the power to order the conditional release of a prisoner unlawfully detained. The DTA system meets this requirement. Furthermore, the majority does not explain how the remedy it prescribes will differ from the procedural protections of the DTA. The majority proposes no alternatives of its own, does not address what will become of the CSRT process, or resolve problems of witness availability.

♦   No one has benefitted by the Court's holding. Ps are left with only the prospect of further litigation to determine their new habeas right, followed by further litigation. And the American people have lost a bit more control over the conduct of this nation's foreign policy to unelected, politically unaccountable judges.

Dissent (Scalia, J., Roberts, C.J., Thomas, Alito, JJ.).

♦   The writ of habeas corpus does not extend to aliens abroad. The Suspension Clause does not apply, and the Court's intervention in this military matter is entirely ultra vires.

♦   The majority's opinion will almost certainly cause more American deaths. Former detainees, whom the military concluded were not enemy combatants, have returned to the battlefield. This shows the difficulty of determining who is and who is not an enemy combatant in a foreign land. The Court has no competence to second-guess the judgment of Congress and the President in this area. Requiring military officials to appear in civilian court and release sensitive evidence to defense lawyers will give our enemies access to information they should not have. In the past, trial testimony revealed the military's surveillance of the enemy's cellular network, with the predictable result that the enemy stopped using the network. The nation will regret what the Court has done today.

C. THE RIGHT TO COUNSEL; EQUALITY AND THE ADVERSARY SYSTEM

1. **Attorney General's Committee on Poverty and the Administration of Criminal Justice (1963).**

    a. **Concept of poverty.** Poverty is a relative concept and must be measured by reference to the particular need or service under consideration.

      1) **Right to counsel.** The criterion here is the lack of financial ability to hire a lawyer.

      2) **Other problems.** Problems may arise with respect to any number of other services—finances for an adequate pretrial investigation, to hire expert witnesses, etc.

      3) **Conclusion.** A problem of poverty exists in the system of criminal justice when, at any stage of the proceedings, the accused's lack of means substantially inhibits the proper assertion of a right.

    b. **Obligation of equal justice.**

      1) Criminal justice is a process initiated by the government for the achievement of governmental purposes, and it often results in severe injury to the prosecuted. The government's duty is to avoid reasonably avoidable injuries, and this means the elimination of factors that are irrelevant to just administration of the law—*i.e.,* the influence of poverty.

      2) "Equal justice" is not based alone on humanitarian sentiment but insures a purification of the "system of justice."

        a) The government should eliminate factors inhibiting the effective assertion of grounds relevant to the defendant's liability.

        b) The adversary system is devised to reconcile public and private interests in a crucial area—it contributes to a free society. Since the essence of this system is challenge and the questioning of official decisions, the defense function is vital to the forging of a free society; poverty that impedes proper challenge threatens the adversary system.

    c. **"Indigency" standards and administration.**

      1) A study in the District of Columbia found that 40% of all those arrested were unemployed, 28% lost their jobs prior to arraignment, and most of the remaining defendants had very low-paying

jobs. In short, on any reasonable standard, nearly every defendant would be considered sufficiently impoverished to require free legal services.

2) Many argue that the legal system takes excellent care of the rich and the poor and totally destroys the middle-class defendant, who must borrow against everything to finance a defense. The rich can afford a lawyer and all the necessary aids—investigators, etc.; the poor often have an equally good lawyer, the public defender (who also has the aids available). The person in the middle can afford a lawyer, but maybe only a poor one, and often cannot get the funds for all the necessary aids.

3) Possible standards include:

   a) Using the involved forms and investigations common (and hated) in the welfare system;

   b) Giving the defendant a choice—stay in jail and get a free lawyer or make bail and hire a lawyer; and

   c) Providing free counsel in any case where cost would be a "substantial hardship."

4) Wherever the line is drawn, those just above it will be at a disadvantage when compared to those getting free lawyers, because the indigent will usually get more and better aid than the person just above the line can afford.

d. **Obligation to repay.** Many states now have recoupment laws applicable to counsel fees and other costs.

1) There have been no decisions whether it is a denial of due process to compel an acquitted defendant to repay her defense costs.

2) There have been decisions holding recoupment to violate equal protection. In *James v. Strange*, 407 U.S. 128 (1972), the Court held a recoupment law invalid because the defendant could not avail himself of restrictions on wage garnishment as civil creditors could.

3) Some states require a promise to pay counsel costs as a condition of probation. For example, in *Fuller v. Oregon*, 417 U.S. 40 (1974), the Supreme Court upheld an Oregon statute that required those with the likelihood of being able to repay in the future to accept a contingent obligation to repay counsel fees as a condition of probation. The obligation would not actually be imposed until indigency conditions have ended. *James v. Strange* was distinguished in that

there were no favorable distinctions made in Oregon law relative to civil judgment creditors.

e. **Appointed counsel's right to compensation.** There has never been a constitutional case holding that the attorney must be reimbursed by the government for representing an indigent. Most states and the federal government recognize that, without pay, representation would be inadequate.

2. **The Right to Appointed Counsel.**

a. **Criminal prosecutions.**

1) **Introduction.** The Court held in *Johnson v. Zerbst*, 304 U.S. 458 (1938), that the Sixth Amendment required appointment of counsel in all federal criminal cases if the accused cannot afford an attorney, so long as the accused does not intentionally and competently waive that right. At first, the Court did not extend this right to state cases, except on a case-by-case basis when required by special circumstances.

2) **Special circumstances approach to due process--**

Betts v. Brady, 316 U.S. 455 (1942).

Facts. Betts (D), tried for robbery in a state court, was unable to employ counsel and requested that one be appointed. The state refused. D waived a jury trial, pleaded not guilty, conducted his own defense, and was convicted. He then brought a habeas corpus proceeding in federal court.

Issue. In a felony prosecution by the state for a robbery, must the state provide a lawyer for an indigent defendant?

Held. No. Judgment affirmed.

♦ The Sixth Amendment prevents federal courts from depriving an accused of his life or liberty unless he has counsel or waives the assistance of counsel. However, this rule is not so fundamental and essential to a fair trial that it is obligatory on the states through the Fourteenth Amendment. Most states do not consider this a fundamental right.

♦ In certain cases, such as a capital case where the accused cannot obtain counsel and is unable to effectively defend himself, due process may require appointment of counsel, even in state courts. This can only be evaluated on a case-by-case basis.

♦ D in this case relied on an alibi defense. He called and examined witnesses to support his defense. The trial was before a judge alone, who was able to control the course of the trial and ensure that impartial justice was done. Thus there was no denial of due process.

Dissent (Black, Douglas, Murphy, JJ.). Under the circumstances of this case, D was denied due process. D was an unemployed farmhand who had little education. More importantly, the Fourteenth Amendment made the Sixth Amendment applicable to the states.

---

3)   **Developments after *Betts*.**

a)   *Bute v. Illinois*, 333 U.S. 640 (1948), stated in dictum that there was a flat requirement of counsel in all capital cases. In *Hamilton v. Alabama*, 368 U.S. 52 (1961), the Court held that due process was offended when a defendant at an arraignment in a capital case was not represented by counsel.

b)   Even during the reign of *Betts v. Brady, supra,* the Supreme Court made it clear that denying a defendant the assistance of her own lawyer in any case, at any stage, on any issue, constituted a per se violation of due process. [*See* Chandler v. Fretag, 348 U.S. 3 (1954)]

c)   In many cases before *Gideon v. Wainwright, infra,* the Supreme Court found that the defendant's lack of counsel did prejudice her case. With each case, less and less was required to show such prejudice. This indicated the Supreme Court's search for flat standards.

(1)   For example, in *Chewning v. Cunningham*, 368 U.S. 443 (1962), the Court reversed a conviction in a state court of a 10-year sentence under a recidivist statute—conviction on the basis of being a habitual criminal is so serious, the issues so complex, the potential prejudice of not having counsel so great, that trial without counsel violates due process.

(2)   After this, there was nothing left of *Betts*. *Gideon v. Wainwright* was a foregone conclusion.

4)   **Expansion of special circumstances approach to all felony cases--**

Gideon v. Wainwright, 372 U.S. 335 (1963).

Facts. Gideon (D) was charged in a Florida court with having committed a felony. D was indigent, but his request for counsel was denied. D defended himself and declined to testify. He was convicted and sentenced to five years in prison. D then unsuccessfully brought a habeas corpus proceeding. The Supreme Court granted certiorari.

Issue. When an indigent defendant is prosecuted for a noncapital felony, does the Constitution require that counsel be supplied?

Held. Yes. Judgment reversed.

♦ Even before *Betts*, this Court had declared that the right to the aid of counsel is fundamental. In *Betts*, the Court made an abrupt break with precedent by deciding that appointment of counsel was not a fundamental right.

♦ The necessity of counsel is shown by the fact that the government hires trained lawyers to prosecute and that defendants who can afford to will always hire the best available lawyers. The right to counsel being fundamental and essential to a fair trial, *Betts* is overruled.

Concurrence (Clark, J.). The Constitution does not distinguish between capital and noncapital cases, so there should be no difference in the due process requirements of both types of proceedings.

Concurrence (Harlan, J.). *Betts* was not an abrupt break with the past. It recognized that special circumstances might exist in noncapital cases such that appointed counsel would be necessary. The Court did not find those special circumstances in *Betts* itself, however. Today the Court recognizes that the mere existence of a serious criminal charge is a special circumstance requiring the assistance of counsel at trial. In effect, the special circumstance rule is now abandoned in all capital cases and in all cases where a substantial prison sentence is possible.

---

5) Right to counsel whenever imprisonment is imposed--

Argersinger v. Hamlin, 407 U.S. 25 (1972).

Facts. An indigent petitioner was tried for an offense punishable by imprisonment of six months, fine of $1,000, or both. He received a 90-day sentence. The Florida courts did not provide counsel except for "nonpetty offenses punishable by more than six months."

Issue. Does due process require counsel to be provided to indigents in all criminal cases where imprisonment is possible on conviction?

Held. Yes.

♦ The right to trial by jury may be limited to serious criminal cases, but the right to assistance of counsel may not be denied even in a petty offense prosecution. The issues involved in any case that leads to imprisonment, even for a brief period, require assistance of counsel.

♦ Misdemeanor cases frequently involve guilty pleas, and the volume of cases can create an obsession for speedy disposition regardless of the fairness of the result. These problems require the presence of counsel to insure a fair trial.

♦ Pursuant to this standard, no imprisonment may be imposed, even if permitted by local law, unless the accused is represented by counsel.

Concurrence (Powell, Rehnquist, JJ.). Counsel is often, but not always, essential to a fair trial. Petty offense cases are not prosecuted by lawyers but by arresting police officers. The Court has now extended the right of appointed counsel to indigent defendants in cases where nonindigents would rarely hire counsel. In doing so, it distinguishes between deprivations of liberty and deprivations of property as well. The better approach would permit judges to exercise discretion in providing counsel, by considering: (i) the complexity of the issues; (ii) the probable sentence if a conviction results; and (iii) the peculiar circumstances of each case, such as the accused's ability to present a defense.

---

6) **Limit on right to counsel.** In *Scott v. Illinois*, 440 U.S. 367 (1979), the Court held that an indigent accused was not entitled to appointed counsel, even when he could have been sentenced to one year in jail, because he was actually fined only $50. Actual imprisonment, not fines or the mere threat of imprisonment, is the line that defines the constitutional right to appointment of counsel. If an indigent is not provided counsel, any conviction that results from the proceeding may not be used at a later time to increase the indigent's imprisonment upon a subsequent conviction under a recidivist statute. [Baldasar v. Illinois, 446 U.S. 222 (1980)]

b. **Attachment of right to counsel.**

1) **Basic rule.** A person has a right to counsel at a critical stage of the prosecution. The meaning of these terms has been developed over time. The "prosecution" requirement refers to adversary judicial proceedings against the person. This includes the formal charge, preliminary hearing, indictment, information, and arraignment. Before this time, the right to counsel only comes into play as an aspect of the right against compelled self-incrimination, *e.g.,* the custodial interrogation.

2) **Detention alone not a prosecution.** The Court held in *United States v. Gouveia*, 467 U.S. 180 (1984), that administrative detention alone does not constitute the initiation of adversary proceedings. Gouveia, an inmate, was held in administrative detention for several months after prison officials determined that he had participated in the murders of other inmates. He did not receive appointed counsel during this time. The Court stated that the core purpose for the right to counsel is to assure aid at trial. The right has been extended to critical pretrial proceedings that might settle the accused's fate, but the right does not go so far as to provide a pre-indictment private investigator.

3) **Determination of when right to counsel attaches--**

Rothgery v. Gillespie County, 128 S. Ct. 2578 (2008).

Facts. Police officers relied on erroneous information that Rothgery (D) had a prior felony conviction when they arrested him for unlawful possession of a firearm. The officers brought D before a magistrate judge for an "article 15.17" hearing at which probable cause is determined, bail is set, and the defendant is formally apprised of the accusation against him. The magistrate judge found probable cause for the arrest, set bail at $5,000, and committed D to jail. D was released from jail after posting a surety bond. D had no money for a lawyer and made several requests for a lawyer to be appointed to him, but his requests went unheeded. About six months later, he was indicted for the offense and rearrested. Bail was increased to $15,000. When D could not post it, he was put in jail and stayed there for three weeks. Subsequently, counsel was appointed. D's lawyer got the indictment dismissed. D then sued Gillespie County under 42 U.S.C. section 1983 for violation of his Sixth Amendment right to counsel. D claimed that if the county had provided him with counsel within a reasonable time after the hearing, he would not have been indicted, rearrested, or jailed. The district court granted the county's motion for summary judgment. The court of appeals affirmed, holding that D's right to counsel did not attach at the article 15.17 hearing because the relevant prosecutors were not aware of or involved in D's arrest or appearance at the hearing. The Supreme Court granted certiorari.

Issue. Does the right to counsel attach at a criminal defendant's initial appearance before a judicial officer where the accused learns the charge against him and his liberty is subject to restriction?

Held. Yes. Judgment vacated and case remanded.

♦ The Sixth Amendment gives an accused a right to assistance of counsel in all criminal prosecutions. This means the initiation of adversary judicial criminal proceedings, whether by a formal charge, preliminary hearing, indictment, information, or arraignment. It is the hearing at which a judicial officer informs the defendant of the charge and determines the conditions for pretrial release.

- Therefore, the first formal proceeding is the point at which the right to counsel attaches. This signifies a commitment to prosecute. Counsel must be appointed within a reasonable time after attachment to allow for adequate representation before trial.

Concurrence (Roberts, C.J., Scalia, J.). While Justice Thomas's dissent is compelling, the result here is controlled by precedent.

Concurrence (Alito, J., Roberts, C.J., Scalia, J.). The Court does not hold that a defendant is entitled to the assistance of appointed counsel as soon as his Sixth Amendment right attaches. Attachment means only the beginning of the prosecution, not the beginning of a substantive entitlement to the assistance of counsel. Appointment of counsel is required only as far in advance of trial or any pretrial critical stage as necessary to guarantee effective assistance at trial. D only asked the Court to decide the limited question of whether the hearing marked the beginning of his criminal prosecution under the Sixth Amendment, a question of when the right may be asserted.

Dissent (Thomas, J.).

- The term "criminal prosecution" in the Sixth Amendment refers to the commencement of a criminal suit by filing formal charges in a court with jurisdiction to try and punish the defendant. D's initial appearance before the magistrate in this case did not, therefore, constitute the commencement of a criminal prosecution. No formal charges had been filed, and the only document submitted to the magistrate was the arresting officer's affidavit of probable cause. D's initial appearance was not an arraignment. An arraignment is a postindictment proceeding at which the defendant enters a plea.

- Neither D nor the Court shows how D's ability to receive a fair trial was undermined by the absence of counsel during the time between his initial appearance and his indictment. D's complaint is that if counsel had been appointed earlier, he would have been able to avoid indictment by convincing the prosecutor that he was not guilty of the crime alleged. However, the Sixth Amendment protects against the risk of erroneous conviction, not the risk of unwarranted prosecution. D argues that he had a right to counsel because his liberty was restricted when he was required to post bail. But the accused's right to the assistance of counsel for his defense does not entail a right to use counsel to contest pretrial detention. A defendant's liberty interests are protected by other constitutional guarantees.

- The Court's holding is not supported by the original meaning of the Sixth Amendment right to counsel or any reasonable interpretation of our precedents.

---

3. **The *Griffin-Douglas* Equality Principle.** A disturbing reality of the criminal justice system is that a wealthy defendant can hire the best lawyers,

investigators, experts, and so forth, thus obtaining the best possible defense, while an indigent may receive only a minimal defense. There is no completely satisfactory solution to this problem of inequality, but the Supreme Court has set forth some standards promoting equality.

a.   **Origin of the equality principle.** In *Griffin v. Illinois*, 351 U.S. 12 (1956), the Court relied on the Due Process and Equal Protection Clauses of the Fourteenth Amendment to hold that in a state prosecution where no appeal was possible without a transcript from the trial court, the state must provide indigent defendants a free transcript in all felony criminal cases. The Court reasoned that poverty bears no rational relationship to a defendant's guilt or innocence and is an improper basis for discrimination. States do not have to provide appellate review of criminal cases, but if they do so they cannot be provided in such a way as to discriminate against some defendants because of their poverty. There can be no equal justice where the kind of trial a person gets depends on the amount of money he has.

b.   **Transcript for any appeal.** In *Mayer v. Chicago*, 404 U.S. 189 (1971), the rule in *Griffin*, *supra*, as to transcripts on appeal was held to apply to nonfelonies as well as felonies—even if only a fine was involved. The Court explained that *Griffin* is not a balancing test, but a flat prohibition against pricing indigent defendants out of as effective an appeal as would be available to those able to pay their own way.

c.   **The right to counsel on appeal.** *Douglas v. California*, 372 U.S. 353 (1963), concerned a California rule that required that, when an indigent criminal defendant requested counsel for his appeal, the state appellate court was to make an independent investigation of the record and appoint counsel only if it would likely be helpful to the defendant or to the court. The Court held the rule to be unconstitutional, stating that denial of counsel in this situation is the same kind of invidious discrimination against indigents as was involved in *Griffin*, *supra*. The Court explained that there is no equal justice if the kind of appeal available depends on the amount of money the appellant has. Justice Harlan, joined by Justice Stewart, dissented. Justice Harlan argued that equal protection does not impose on the states an affirmative duty to lift the handicaps flowing from differences in economic circumstances.

d.   **Limitation on the right to appointed counsel on appeal--**

Ross v. Moffitt, 417 U.S. 600 (1974).

Facts. North Carolina provided appointed counsel only for an initial appeal to the state court of appeals. Moffitt (D), who had been convicted in two separate trials, sought appointment of counsel for discretionary review in both the state supreme court and the United States Supreme Court. The state courts denied D's request, but the federal court of appeals, acting on D's federal habeas corpus petition, held that under *Douglas*, counsel should have been appointed. The Supreme Court granted certiorari.

Issue. Is an indigent entitled to appointed counsel to assist in discretionary appellate review?

Held. No. Judgment reversed.

♦ The rationale behind the *Griffin-Douglas* approach is based on both the Equal Protection and Due Process Clauses. Due process requires appointment of counsel at a criminal trial because the prosecutor is a lawyer. Due process does not even require that the state provide for an appeal, or that, having provided one, the state also provide counsel. The requirement for appointed appellate counsel rests primarily on equal protection grounds.

♦ Unfairness results when indigents are singled out by the state and denied access to the appellate system because of their poverty. The Equal Protection Clause does not demand complete equality of economic conditions, but it does require that indigents have an adequate opportunity to present their appellate claims. The state has satisfied this requirement by providing counsel for the initial appeal.

♦ Discretionary review depends on factors other than the perceived correctness of the challenged judgment, including the public interest in the subject matter and any potential contributions such review might have on jurisprudence. Although counsel might assist in procuring discretionary review, the fact that a particular service might benefit an indigent does not make provision of the service a constitutional requirement.

Dissent (Douglas, Brennan, Marshall, JJ.). The most meaningful review of constitutional questions is found in the highest court of the jurisdiction involved. Certiorari proceedings are specialized and require expert attention. The right to discretionary review is substantial.

Comment. In *Halbert v. Michigan*, 545 U.S. 605 (2005), the Court held that *Douglas*, *supra*, rather than *Ross*, applies in cases of first-tier discretionary appellate review of convictions on guilty or nolo contendere pleas. One reason was that the state appeals process required the appellate court's examination of the merits of the claims made in the application for review. Another reason was that indigent defendants were ill-equipped to represent themselves when pursuing first-tier review. The dissent contended that such a right was not found anywhere in the Constitution and that *Douglas* did not support extending the right to counsel to any form of discretionary review.

———————————

e. **Right to expert services other than counsel.** The Court has held that fundamental fairness entitles indigent defendants to an adequate opportunity to present their claims fairly within the adversary system. This means that the government must provide the basic tools of an adequate defense or appeal, such as a trial transcript for appeal or a blood grouping test in a paternity action.

1) **Psychiatric exam.** In *Ake v. Oklahoma*, 470 U.S. 68 (1985), the Court applied this analysis to an indigent's request for a psychiatric evaluation at state expense. Such a request need not be automatically granted. The defendant must first demonstrate that his sanity at the time of the offense is likely to be a significant factor at trial. If he does so, the state must provide access to a competent psychiatrist. Additionally, the state must provide access to psychiatric assistance if, at a capital sentencing proceeding, the prosecution presents psychiatric evidence of the defendant's future dangerousness.

2) **Criminal Justice Act of 1964.** In federal courts, indigent defendants are assured the right to counsel *and* "investigative, expert, and other services necessary for adequate representation." [18 U.S.C. §3006A]

4. **Withdrawal of Appointed Counsel on Appeal.**

a. **Requirement of brief.** *Anders v. California*, 386 U.S. 738 (1967), involved a California appellate court's summary dismissal of an indigent defendant's appeal after the court permitted withdrawal of the defendant's appointed counsel, who had informed the court that he thought there was no merit to the appeal. The Supreme Court held that if appointed counsel finds a case to be wholly frivolous, he may advise the court and request to withdraw, but he must accompany the request with a brief referring to anything in the record that arguably supports the appeal. Then the court must examine the proceedings to see if the claim is frivolous—if it is, permission to withdraw may be given and the case dismissed. If it is not frivolous, counsel must be afforded to the defendant to prosecute the appeal.

b. **Discussion of lack of merit.** In *McCoy v. Court of Appeals of Wisconsin*, 486 U.S. 429 (1988), the Court upheld the constitutionality of a Wisconsin Supreme Court rule requiring court-appointed counsel to explain in an *Anders* brief why a client's appeal lacks merit.

c. **Alternatives to *Anders*.** In *Smith v. Robbins*, 528 U.S. 259 (2000), the Court held that states may adopt alternatives to the *Anders* requirement as long as the procedures afford adequate and effective appellate review to indigent defendants. In *Robbins*, a California lawyer complied with the state's procedure under which the lawyer was to file a brief summarizing the case, explain his evaluation of the case to his client, provide the client with a copy of the brief, inform the client of his rights, and request that the appellate court independently examine the record for arguable issues. The Court found that this was sufficient to resolve the appeal in a way that was related to the merit of the appeal.

5. **Proceedings Other than Criminal Prosecutions.** Outside of the actual criminal prosecution and appeals process, the Court continues to apply an approach similar to *Betts*; *i.e.,* the particular circumstances of the case dictate whether counsel must be appointed.

a. **Probation revocation hearings--**

Gagnon v. Scarpelli, 411 U.S. 778 (1973).

Facts. Scarpelli (D) was sentenced to 15 years' imprisonment for armed robbery. His sentence was suspended and he was placed on probation for seven years. Later, D was caught burglarizing a house. His probation was revoked without a hearing after he admitted his role in the burglary. He successfully sought a writ of habeas corpus and the Supreme Court granted certiorari.

Issue. Is an indigent probationer or parolee always entitled to appointed counsel at a revocation hearing?

Held. No. Judgment affirmed in part, reversed in part, and case remanded.

♦ Even though parole and probation revocation are not part of the criminal prosecution process, due process requires that the state provide a preliminary and a final revocation hearing because of the serious liberty interest involved.

♦ Providing counsel at revocation hearings would greatly add to the complexity and expense of such hearings. The need for counsel at a criminal prosecution arises from the formal and invariable attributes of such trials. At a revocation hearing, however, the need for counsel, if any, derives from the peculiarities of the particular case.

♦ The decision to appoint counsel at a revocation hearing must be made on a case-by-case basis. Counsel should be provided upon request when the probationer or parolee makes a timely and colorable claim that (i) he did not violate his probation or parole; or (ii) even if he did violate the conditions, a case of justification or mitigation can be made that is complex or difficult enough that assistance of counsel is necessary.

---

b. **Summary court martial.** In *Middendorf v. Henry*, 425 U.S. 25 (1976), the Court determined that members of the armed forces are not entitled to counsel at a summary court martial. The Court reasoned that the summary court martial is not an adversary proceeding, it is not available except for offenses that would not be criminal in a civilian setting, the punishment that can be given is severely limited, and the setting is military rather than civilian. These factors indicate that the proceeding is not a criminal proceeding for purposes of the Sixth Amendment. *In re Gault*, 387 U.S. 1 (1967) and *Gagnon, supra,* held that juvenile court proceedings and parole hearings are not criminal prosecutions within the scope of the Sixth Amendment, and a summary court martial proceeding is of a similar nature. The Court noted that defendants can request a general court martial if they desire and can have counsel for that hearing.

c. **Proceedings to terminate parental rights.** In *Lassiter v. Department of Social Services*, 452 U.S. 18 (1981), the Court determined that due process does not require that the state appoint counsel in every proceeding to terminate parental rights. The right to counsel exists only when the defendant risks losing physical liberty if the trial is lost. The right to appointed counsel diminishes as the risk to personal liberty diminishes. The facts of each case must be considered to determine whether counsel should be appointed. In this case, the Court reasoned, no reversible error resulted from the refusal to appoint counsel.

d. **Collateral attack proceedings.** The ABA Standards provide that counsel should be available to applicants for post-conviction relief, such as habeas corpus proceedings. There is great variation in state and federal practice in this area.

D. THE ROLE OF COUNSEL

1. The Right to Waive Counsel.

a. **Introduction.** The courts recognize a presumption against waiver of fundamental rights, including the right to counsel. An accused must intelligently and understandingly reject an offer of counsel in order to waive the right. [Carnley v. Cochran, 369 U.S. 506 (1962)]

b. **Right of self-representation--**

Faretta v. California, 422 U.S. 806 (1975).

Facts. Faretta (D) asked to defend himself at his trial for grand theft. He had represented himself in a prior criminal prosecution. Prior to trial, the judge held a hearing on D's request. After questioning D about the hearsay rule and voir dire, the judge denied

D's request and appointed the public defender to represent D. D was convicted. D appeals.

Issue. Does a criminal defendant have a constitutional right to defend himself without the assistance of counsel?

Held. Yes. Judgment reversed.

♦ The right of self-representation is supported in the structure of the Sixth Amendment itself, as well as in the common law. The accused, not counsel, must be informed of the charges, must be confronted with the witnesses against him, and must be given compulsory process to obtain witnesses. Counsel is merely an assistant to the accused.

♦ Counsel is intended to be a defense tool to aid a willing defendant, not an organ of the state interposed between an unwilling defendant and his right to defend himself personally. Representation not desired by the defendant cannot present the defendant's true defense.

♦ Even if it is unwise for a defendant to conduct his own defense, his choice must be honored. So long as the decision is made knowingly and intelligently, the court may not override it by providing unwanted counsel.

Dissent (Burger, C.J., Blackmun, Rehnquist, JJ.). The spirit and logic of the Sixth Amendment go towards providing every person accused of a crime with the fullest possible defense. The trial judge can best determine whether counsel is necessary.

Dissent (Blackmun, J., Burger, C.J., Rehnquist, J.). No amount of pro se pleading can cure the injury to society of an unjust result. Today's decision will create many procedural problems for trial courts in the future.

Comment. The competency standard for waiving the right to counsel is not higher than the competency standard for standing trial. There is no reason to believe that the decision to waive the right to counsel requires an appreciably higher level of mental functioning than the decision to waive other constitutional rights. [Godinez v. Moran, 509 U.S. 389 (1993)]

---

c. **Standby counsel.** A trial judge can appoint standby counsel even over the defendant's objection. [McKaskle v. Wiggins, 465 U.S. 168 (1984)] Such counsel may assist the defendant to overcome routine obstacles that prevent him from achieving his own clearly indicated goals, and may relieve the judge from having to explain and enforce rules of courtroom protocol. There are some limits on how much such counsel may participate over the defendant's objections, especially when he makes the objections clearly known.

d.   No specific warning for waiver of counsel--

Iowa v. Tovar, 541 U.S. 77 (2004).

Facts. In November 1996, 21-year-old Tovar (D) was arrested for operating a vehicle while under the influence of alcohol ("OWI"). At his arraignment, D waived his right to a court-appointed attorney and pleaded guilty after the court discussed with D the maximum penalty for OWI. At his sentencing hearing the next month, D also waived his right to an attorney. In 1998, D was convicted of OWI a second time. He was represented by counsel. In 2000, D was charged a third time with OWI. Under the law of Iowa, a third offense of OWI was a felony. D was represented by counsel and pleaded not guilty. D's counsel moved for a ruling that D's first OWI conviction could not be used to enhance his 2000 offense into a felony. D claimed that his 1996 waiver of counsel was invalid because he was not made aware by the court of the dangers and disadvantages of self-representation. The trial court denied D's motion, but the Iowa Supreme Court held that under the Sixth Amendment, a defendant cannot choose to plead guilty without the assistance of an attorney unless the court advises him that he will risk overlooking viable defenses and lose the chance to have an independent opinion on the advisability of pleading guilty. The Supreme Court granted certiorari.

Issue. Does the Sixth Amendment require that a court give a defendant who waives his right to counsel a warning that he may be overlooking a valid defense and losing the chance to have independent advice regarding the advisability of pleading guilty?

Held. No. Judgment reversed.

♦   While the Sixth Amendment gives a defendant facing a prison term a right to have counsel present at both the plea stage and at the trial, the court cannot force a lawyer upon him. To be valid, the waiver of the right to counsel must be knowing, voluntary, and intelligent.

♦   There are no specific notices that a court must give a defendant who waives the right to counsel, so long as he is warned specifically of the hazards ahead. At the trial stage, the warning must be rigorous, but at earlier stages of criminal proceedings, the warning need not be as searching.

♦   The law normally considers a waiver to be knowing, voluntary, and intelligent if D fully understands the nature of the right and how it would likely apply in general to the circumstances. Even if D lacked a full and complete appreciation of all the consequences flowing from his waiver, so long as he competently and intelligently waived his right to counsel, the Sixth Amendment is satisfied.

♦   The information that a defendant must be given in order to intelligently waive the right to counsel depends on the facts of each case.

Comment. In this case, D's challenge to his waiver of counsel was a collateral attack. This put the burden of proof on D to show that he lacked the minimum constitutional understanding.

---

e. Appointing counsel when pro se representation is denied--

Indiana v. Edwards, 128 S. Ct. 2379 (2008).

Facts. Edwards (D) tried to steal a pair of shoes from a store. When he was discovered, he shot a gun at a security officer and hit a bystander. He was charged with attempted murder, battery with a deadly weapon, criminal recklessness, and theft. The court found D incompetent to stand trial and committed him to a state hospital. After seven months, doctors determined that his condition had improved to the point where he could stand trial. The court found that he was competent to assist his attorneys and stand trial. Seven months later, a subsequent evaluation led the court to decide that D was not competent to stand trial. After another eight months in the hospital, doctors said he could stand trial. A year later, just before the trial was to start, D asked to represent himself. D asked for a continuance, which the court denied, and D was represented by counsel. D was convicted of criminal recklessness and theft, but the jury was unable to reach a verdict on the charges of attempted murder and battery. Before retrial, D asked to represent himself again. The court found that D was competent to stand trial but not to represent himself. He was represented by counsel at his retrial and was convicted of both attempted murder and battery. D appealed. The appellate courts held that D had the right to represent himself and reversed. The Supreme Court granted certiorari.

Issue. May a state require a defendant to proceed to trial with counsel, denying the defendant the right to represent himself?

Held. Yes.

♦   The Court's "mental competency" cases focus on a defendant's understanding of the proceedings against him and his present ability to consult with his lawyer, assuming representation by counsel. These cases do not address the relation of the mental competence standard to the right of self-representation. Yet they provide a standard that focuses on a defendant's ability to consult with his lawyer, and they emphasize the importance of counsel. Thus, these cases suggest that the circumstances are very different when a defendant chooses to forgo counsel at trial; this calls for a different standard.

♦   The foundational self-representation case, *Faretta, supra*, did not address the problem of mental competency, but its conclusion was based in part on cases that are consistent with a competency limitation on a defendant's right to represent himself.

- There should not be a single mental competency standard for deciding both whether a defendant who is represented by counsel can proceed to trial and whether a defendant must be permitted to represent himself at trial. Mental illness varies in degrees and can vary over time. D's own history illustrates the complexity of the problem. The American Psychiatric Association points out that a defendant may be able to play the lesser role of represented defendant even if he is incapable of playing the significantly expanded role of self-representation.

- A right of self-representation will not affirm the dignity of a defendant who lacks the mental capacity to conduct his own defense, and it could result in his humiliation. It could even result in an improper conviction or sentence. This would undercut the most basic of the Constitution's criminal law objectives—providing a fair trial. The trial judge is often best able to make mental capacity decisions, tailored to the circumstances of a particular defendant.

- Therefore, the Constitution permits judges to make a realistic assessment of a defendant's mental capacity if the defendant seeks to represent himself. States may require that defendants who are competent to stand trial, but are not competent to represent themselves, be represented by counsel.

Dissent (Scalia, Thomas, JJ.). D filed some incoherent written pleadings, but he also filed several intelligible pleadings. He complained that the lawyer in his first trial did not prepare well and did not share legal materials for use in his defense. The judge concluded that D knowingly and voluntarily waived his right to counsel, but the judge denied his request to represent himself because the judge did not want to grant D a continuance. In the second trial, D told the judge that he and his lawyer disagreed about which defense to present to the attempted murder charge. D was in favor of self-defense, but his lawyer pursued a lack of intent to kill. As long as D appreciated the risk of forgoing counsel and chose to do so voluntarily, the Constitution protects his ability to present his own defense, even if that harms his case.

---

2. **Division of Authority over Defense Decisions.**

   a. **Issues to be raised on appeal.** Although appointed counsel may not withdraw from a nonfrivolous appeal, counsel has no obligation to raise every nonfrivolous issue requested by the client. Strategic decisions rest within counsel's professional judgment and include the methods to utilize for a vigorous and effective advocacy. [Jones v. Barnes, 463 U.S. 745 (1983)]

   b. **Tactical trial decisions.** In *Gonzalez v. United States*, 128 S. Ct. 1765 (2008), the Court held that express consent by counsel suffices to allow a federal magistrate judge to preside over jury selection in a felony trial, even without the client's own express consent. The Court explained that a presiding judge has significant discretion over jury selection and that acceptance of a judge at the jury selection phase is a tactical decision. The lawyer must have full authority to manage the conduct of the trial and should make tactical decisions, which may be difficult to explain to a layperson.

3. **Effective Assistance of Counsel.** As a matter of constitutional law, a defendant may challenge a conviction on the basis that his lawyer was so incompetent as to deprive him of the effective assistance of counsel. [Powell v. Alabama, 287 U.S. 45 (1932)] This claim, although raised more frequently in recent years, is rarely upheld.

    a. **Reluctance to find denial of effective counsel.** Courts are generally reluctant to find a denial of "effective assistance." They fear that: (i) honoring the claim is an implicit censure of the trial court; (ii) it forces the trial judge to intervene whenever possible error is being committed; (iii) it makes most lawyers even more reluctant to accept court assignments; and (iv) it permits a lawyer with a desperate case to insure that the client gets a new trial through the lawyer's deliberate errors.

    b. **Early approach.** The standard test for effectiveness was whether the challenged representation was so inadequate that it was a "mockery of justice." This test gave great latitude to defense counsel. Many commentators argued that the test was inadequate, and several alternative tests were proposed.

    c. **Effective assistance of appellate counsel.** In *Wainwright v. Torna*, 455 U.S. 586 (1982), the Court held that because there is no constitutional right to counsel to pursue discretionary review, there was no deprivation of effective assistance of counsel when counsel failed to file the application for review in a timely manner. But in *Evitts v. Lucey*, 469 U.S. 387 (1985), the Court held that counsel's failure to comply with appellate procedural rules for an appeal as of right was a deprivation of the right to effective assistance of counsel. It does not matter whether counsel is retained or appointed.

    d. **Current two-part test.** Under the Court's current approach, a convicted defendant can prevail on a claim of ineffective assistance of counsel only by showing (i) that counsel's performance was so deficient as not to qualify as counsel under the Sixth Amendment and (ii) that the deficient performance prejudiced the defense.

    e. **Proof of prejudice--**

Strickland v. Washington, 466 U.S. 668 (1984).

Facts. Washington (D) committed, during a 10-day period, three groups of crimes, including murders, torture, kidnapping, and attempted murders. Against his counsel's advice, D pleaded guilty to all charges and further chose to be sentenced by the trial judge. For the sentencing hearing, counsel did not seek out character witnesses other than D's wife and mother; did not request a psychiatric examination; and did not request a presentence report. D was sentenced to death. D sought federal habeas corpus relief, claiming ineffective assistance of counsel. The district court held that no errors of trial counsel had affected the outcome of the sentencing proceeding. On rehearing, the former Fifth Circuit reversed and remanded. The Supreme Court granted certiorari.

Issue. To successfully claim ineffective assistance of counsel, must the defendant show that, but for counsel's unprofessional errors, the result of the sentencing proceeding would have been different?

Held. Yes. Judgment reversed.

♦   The basis for an ineffectiveness claim is that counsel's conduct rendered the trial unreliable. Thus, the claimant must show that counsel's performance was short of professional standards and that it prejudiced the defense.

♦   In substantiating an ineffectiveness of counsel claim, a defendant must show that there is a reasonable probability that, but for counsel's unprofessional errors, the result of the proceeding would have been different. A reasonable probability is one sufficient to undermine confidence in the outcome. In assessing the defendant's proof of prejudice, the court must consider the totality of the evidence before the judge or jury.

♦   Here, the conduct of D's counsel cannot be found unreasonable, and even assuming it was unreasonable, D has suffered insufficient prejudice to warrant setting aside his death sentence. Counsel chose to rely as fully as possible on respondent's acceptance of responsibility for his crimes. The aggravating circumstances were overwhelming. Restricting testimony on D's character ensured that contrary evidence of character would not be admitted. The omitted psychiatric evidence would not have changed the conclusion, given the overwhelming aggravating factors. Admission of the presentence report might even have been harmful to D's case. Counsel's actions were not outside the range of professionally competent assistance.

♦   Failure to show either deficient performance or sufficient prejudice defeats D's ineffectiveness of counsel claim.

Concurrence and dissent (Brennan, J.). The Court's opinion setting forth the "reasonable probability test" provides useful standards. These standards should take into consideration the special circumstances of a capital sentencing proceeding, however.

Dissent (Marshall, J.). The standard set forth by the Court is too malleable. Had evidence been admitted on D's character, D would have had a significant chance that the outcome would have been different.

––––––

f.   Failure to file suppression motion--

Kimmelman v. Morrison, 477 U.S. 365 (1986).

Facts. Morrison (D) was prosecuted for rape. Until the day before trial, D's attorney did not know that D's bedsheet had been seized. Consequently, D's attorney failed to make a timely suppression motion, and the trial judge permitted the prosecution to use the sheet as evidence. D was convicted. D appealed, claiming ineffective assistance of counsel. The state courts upheld the conviction. D sought federal habeas corpus relief. The district court granted relief, the court of appeals remanded for consideration under *Strickland*, and the Supreme Court granted certiorari.

Issue. Does a Sixth Amendment ineffective assistance of counsel claim arise in a habeas corpus action from counsel's failure to file a timely motion to suppress evidence allegedly obtained in violation of the Fourth Amendment?

Held. Yes. Judgment vacated and case remanded.

♦   D's attorney was unaware of the search and of the state's intention to introduce the bedsheet into evidence because he had conducted no pretrial discovery. His failure to request discovery was based on his mistaken beliefs that the state was required to turn over all of its inculpatory evidence to the defense and that the case would not go to trial because the victim was reluctant to testify. The attorney's decision to forgo discovery was unreasonable and contrary to prevailing professional norms. His failure to conduct pretrial discovery fell below the level of reasonable professional assistance.

♦   D's Fourth and Sixth Amendment claims are distinct. The Fourth Amendment protects all citizens and is not a trial right, but the Sixth Amendment right to counsel applies specifically to criminal defendants.

♦   The state argues that D's habeas petition is an attempt to litigate his defaulted Fourth Amendment claim. Under *Stone, infra,* a federal habeas corpus proceeding may not relitigate a Fourth Amendment claim already litigated in state court because the exclusionary rule is not a personal constitutional right, but merely a deterrent. But D seeks to vindicate his Sixth Amendment right to counsel. If D was deprived of effective assistance of counsel, the state unconstitutionally deprived him of his liberty.

♦   D claims that he has proven prejudice, but the state has never conceded that the search was illegal. It should be permitted to try to show that the search was lawful. D may be unable to show that the absence of the bedsheet would have raised a reasonable doubt.

Concurrence (Powell, J., Burger, C.J., Rehnquist, J.). The issue has not been raised, but it is questionable whether the admission of illegally seized but reliable evidence can ever constitute prejudice under *Strickland*, *supra*. The harm suffered by D was merely the absence of a windfall, not the denial of a fair and reliable trial. The Court merely holds that the right to effective assistance of counsel is equally enforceable on direct appeal and on federal collateral review.

---

g. Counsel's refusal to let the client commit perjury--

Nix v. Whiteside, 475 U.S. 157 (1986).

Facts. During preparations for his murder trial, Whiteside (D) told Robinson, his attorney, that he intended to lie during his testimony. Robinson warned D that he would withdraw from the case if D committed perjury and would advise the court about his reasons. D did not perjure himself. D was convicted. After state appeals failed, D sought federal habeas corpus relief for lack of effective assistance of counsel. The district court denied relief, the court of appeals reversed, and the Supreme Court granted certiorari.

Issue. Does a defense attorney's successful effort to prevent his client from committing perjury provide a basis for a claim of ineffective assistance of counsel?

Held. No. Judgment reversed.

♦   Mere breach of an ethical standard does not necessarily constitute a denial of the Sixth Amendment guarantee of assistance of counsel. Standards of professional conduct are established by the states, not the Constitution. However, virtually all such standards include a specific exception from the attorney-client privilege for disclosure of a client's perjury. The attorney is required, not just permitted, to disclose such perjury. Thus, Robinson's conduct did not constitute serious attorney error under *Strickland*.

Concurrence (Blackmun, Brennan, Marshall, Stevens, JJ.). D has failed to show any prejudice. We need not decide whether Robinson acted correctly.

---

h. **Closing arguments.** In *Yarborough v. Gentry*, 540 U.S. 1 (2003), the Court held that the state appellate court's rejection of a defendant's claim of ineffective assistance of counsel was not objectively unreasonable. Gentry had been convicted of assault with a deadly weapon for stabbing his girlfriend. Gentry claimed that the stabbing was accidental. The federal district court denied Gentry's petition for federal habeas relief, but the Ninth Circuit reversed. The Supreme Court reversed the decision of the Ninth Circuit. The Court stated that although Gentry's defense attorney had omitted some potential issues in his closing argument, some of them were ambiguous and others may have backfired. The Court explained that counsel has wide latitude in deciding how best to represent a client and that deference to counsel's tactical decisions in his closing argument is important because of the broad range of legitimate strategy at that stage. "When counsel focuses on some issues to the exclusion of others, there is a strong presumption that he did so for tactical reasons rather than through sheer neglect. . . . [E]ven if an omission is inadvertent, relief is not automatic. The Sixth Amendment guarantees reasonable competence, not perfect advocacy judged with the benefit of hindsight."

    i.   **Scope of duty to review mitigation evidence--**

Rompilla v. Beard, 545 U.S. 374 (2005).

Facts. When Rompilla (D) was indicted for murder, the Commonwealth gave notice of its intent to ask for the death penalty. D was convicted. At the penalty phase, the prosecution established three aggravating factors: (i) the murder was committed in the course of another felony; (ii) the murder was committed by torture; and (iii) D had a significant history of felony convictions that indicated the use or threat of violence. The mitigation evidence that D's lawyers presented was not very helpful—D was not interested in helping his lawyers; the reports of three mental health experts revealed nothing useful; D's son testified that he loved his father and would visit him in prison; and five of D's family members asked for mercy. D's lawyers argued for residual doubt. The jury sentenced D to death. The state courts upheld the conviction and sentence. D obtained new lawyers and sued under the state's postconviction relief act. D's claim alleged that his trial lawyers were ineffective because they did not offer mitigating evidence about D's childhood, his mental capacity and health, and his alcoholism. The state courts denied relief. D sought a writ of habeas corpus in federal district court. The district court granted relief for ineffective assistance of counsel. The Third Circuit reversed. The Supreme Court granted certiorari.

Issue. Was D entitled to federal habeas relief?

Held. Yes. Judgment reversed.

♦   D is entitled to federal habeas relief if he shows that the state court's decision was not only incorrect or erroneous, but was also objectively unreasonable. Defense counsel's investigation is judged by looking to norms of adequate investigation in preparing for the sentencing phase of a capital trial. The standard of review of the reasonableness of a defense counsel's judgments considers the facts from counsel's own position at the time investigative decisions were made. Deference is given to counsel's judgments.

♦ Here, counsel did pursue mitigation evidence, but none of it explained why D might have done what he did. Counsel did not examine D's school records, records of his juvenile and adult incarcerations, or evidence of D's history of alcohol dependence.

♦ Counsel does not have a duty to "scour the globe" in search of evidence, but D's counsel seriously compromised D's case by failing to thoroughly examine the court file on D's prior conviction. Counsel did not even look at the file until the prosecution warned counsel a second time that it was going to use the information within the file. The file was a public document that was readily available. D's counsel had a duty to make all reasonable efforts to learn what they could about D's prior violent offense and to determine whether there were extenuating circumstances. Otherwise, there was no hope of presenting a convincing argument for residual doubt.

♦ ABA standards require defense counsel to secure information in the possession of the prosecution and law enforcement authorities. No reasonable lawyer would forgo examination of D's file.

♦ The failure to look at the file was without doubt prejudicial. It would have provided leads to other relevant mitigation evidence, including test results that indicated mental disorders, test scores showing that D had a third grade level of cognition, D's family history of alcoholism, and abuse and neglect of D as a child.

♦ Postconviction counsel's investigation indicated a need for further tests of D. These tests revealed that D suffered from organic brain damage and probable fetal alcohol syndrome and that D's capacity to appreciate the criminality of his conduct or to conform his conduct to the law was substantially impaired at the time of the crime. This mitigating evidence may well have influenced the jury's appraisal of D's culpability.

Dissent (Kennedy, J., Rehnquist, C.J., Scalia, Thomas, JJ.).

♦ The majority creates a new requirement that defense counsel review all documents in a case file of any prior conviction that the prosecution might rely on at trial. Such a per se rule is a radical departure from the *Strickland*, *supra*, line of cases. A detailed set of rules for counsel's conduct would interfere with the constitutionally protected independence of counsel and would restrict the wide latitude counsel must have in making tactical decisions. ABA standards are only guides and do not establish the constitutional baseline for effective assistance of counsel.

♦   Regardless of the adequacy of D's counsel, D is not entitled to habeas relief. D has the burden of demonstrating prejudice. The mitigation leads that the Court says D's counsel should have discovered consist of a handful of notations within a single 10-page document, an "Initial Transfer Petition," prepared by the department of corrections to determine D's initial prison assignment. Nothing in the record indicates that D's trial lawyers would have discovered the transfer petition if they had reviewed the old file. They would have looked at the transcript of the trial testimony and perhaps at probative exhibits or forensic evidence. It is unlikely that they would have read such an obscure document as the transfer petition. To require defense counsel to look at every document will consume limited defense resources.

---

j.   Actual proof of prejudice required--

United States v. Cronic, 466 U.S. 648 (1984).

Facts. Cronic (D) and two associates were indicted for federal mail fraud, involving a check kiting scheme. Shortly prior to trial, D's attorney withdrew. The district court appointed a young lawyer whose principal practice was real estate to represent D; he had never before participated in a jury trial. D's appointed attorney was allowed only 25 days for pretrial preparation, even though it had taken the government (P) over four and one-half years to investigate the case, and even though the case involved thousands of documents. D was convicted of 11 of 13 counts in the indictment. The court of appeals reversed, inferring that, based on the circumstances, D's Sixth Amendment right to effective assistance of counsel had been violated. The Supreme Court granted certiorari.

Issue. May defense counsel's inexperience and lack of preparation time raise a presumption that a conviction was insufficiently reliable to satisfy his client's Sixth Amendment right to effective counsel?

Held. No. Judgment reversed and case remanded.

♦   Because we presume that counsel is competent to represent a defendant, the burden rests on the defendant to establish a constitutional violation.

♦   The court of appeals in this case based its inference that the defendant's right to the effective assistance of counsel had been violated on five factors: (i) the time afforded for investigation and preparation; (ii) the experience of counsel; (iii) the gravity of the charge; (iv) the complexity of possible defenses; and (v) the accessibility of witnesses to counsel. These factors are relevant to an evaluation of a lawyer's effectiveness in a particular case, but they do not provide a basis for concluding that counsel was unable to provide the defendant with the competent representation that the Constitution guarantees.

---

4.   Conflicts of Interests.

    a.   Potential conflicts--

Cuyler v. Sullivan, 446 U.S. 335 (1980).

Facts. Sullivan (D) was one of three defendants jointly indicted for murder, but D was tried separately. All three were represented by the same two co-counsel. D was tried first and convicted. The other two defendants were subsequently acquitted. D appealed, claiming he was denied effective assistance of counsel because of a conflict of interest. The state courts denied relief. D sought a federal writ of habeas corpus, which he obtained. The United States Supreme Court granted certiorari.

Issue. May a state prisoner obtain a federal writ of habeas corpus merely by showing that his retained counsel represented potentially conflicting interests?

Held. No. Judgment vacated and case remanded.

◆   Although state trial courts must investigate timely objections to multiple representation, the Sixth Amendment does not require state courts themselves to initiate inquiries into the propriety of multiple representation in each case. Defense counsel has an ethical obligation to avoid conflicting representations and to advise the court if a conflict of interest arises. Unless the trial court knows or reasonably should know that a conflict exists, the court need not initiate an inquiry.

◆   Nothing in this case indicates that the trial court had a duty to inquire into whether there was a conflict of interest. There were separate trials for D and his codefendants; there was no objection to the multiple representation during the trial; D's lawyer's opening argument outlined a defense compatible with the view that none of the defendants was involved in the murders; the opening argument suggested that counsel was willing to call witnesses whose testimony might be needed at the trials of D's codefendants; D's counsel's decision not to call those witnesses, but to rest D's defense instead, was a reasonable tactical response to the weakness of the prosecution's evidence.

Concurrence (Brennan, J.). The trial court, to ensure that defendants do not give up their right to effective counsel, must make appropriate inquiries whenever multiple representation exists.

Concurrence and dissent (Marshall, J.). D should be required only to show that an actual conflict of interest existed.

----

b. **Postconviction review--**

Mickens v. Taylor, 535 U.S. 162 (2002).

Facts. Saunders, a lawyer, had been appointed to represent Hall as his defense attorney. Mickens (D) sexually assaulted and murdered Hall. Without inquiring into the potential conflict, the same judge who appointed Saunders to represent Hall appointed him to represent D. Saunders never told the trial judge or D about the potential conflict. D was convicted and sentenced to death. D brought a habeas corpus petition in federal court. The lower courts denied relief on the ground that D failed to show both an actual conflict of interest and an adverse effect from the conflict. The Supreme Court granted certiorari.

Issue. Where a trial court fails to inquire into a potential conflict of interest about which it knew, must a defendant show a reasonable probability that, but for counsel's unprofessional errors, the result of the proceeding would have been different?

Held. Yes. Judgment affirmed.

◆ Generally, under *Strickland*, a defendant alleging a violation of the Sixth Amendment must show a reasonable probability that, but for counsel's unprofessional errors, the result of the proceeding would have been different. Such a probable effect may be presumed when assistance of counsel has been denied entirely or during a critical stage of the proceedings, but the presumption arises only in circumstances of that magnitude.

◆ If D's attorney actively represented conflicting interests, the case may have involved a circumstance of the magnitude sufficient to raise the presumption. In *Holloway v. Arkansas*, 435 U.S. 475 (1978), the Court established a duty to inquire where defense counsel was forced to represent codefendants over his timely objection; failure to so inquire leads to automatic reversal.

◆ In *Cuyler v. Sullivan, supra*, the Court required a court to inquire when it knows or reasonably should know that a particular conflict exists. This duty to inquire arises only where there is an actual conflict that affects counsel's performance. There is no requirement for a trial court to inquire, even if it is aware of a potential conflict, if the conflict does not affect counsel's performance.

◆ In this case, D did not establish that the conflict of interest adversely affected his counsel's performance, and the lower courts properly denied relief.

Concurrence (Kennedy, O'Connor, JJ.). The district court held an evidentiary hearing on D's claim and found that D's counsel's brief representation of the victim had no effect on the course of D's trial. The prior representation did not influence the choices he made during D's trial. At trial, D testified that he had never met the victim, so his claim that he would have asserted consensual sex with the victim but for his counsel's alleged conflict is inconsistent.

Dissent (Stevens, J.). D had a right to know that his counsel had represented the victim and a right to reject the appointment of that counsel. The trial court had a duty to inquire into the conflict. At this point, all we know is that D did not receive the kind of representation the Constitution guarantees. The Court should not uphold a rule that allows the state to foist a murder victim's lawyer onto his accused.

Dissent (Souter, J.). The Court essentially denies relief to D because his counsel did not formally object to the conflict. The trial court judge was on notice of a prospective potential conflict and had a duty to inquire, whether D's counsel formally objected or not.

Dissent (Breyer, Ginsburg, JJ.). This case is not governed by *Holloway* and *Sullivan* because the representational incompatibility is egregious, involved a capital murder case, and was created by the same judge who had dismissed the prior case against the victim.

Comment. The Court noted that *Sullivan* has not been extended to cases of successive representation.

---

c.   **Disqualification of counsel--**

Wheat v. United States, 486 U.S. 153 (1988).

Facts. Wheat (D), Gomez-Barajas, Bravo, and others were charged in a drug conspiracy. Initially, Gomez-Barajas and Bravo were represented by Iredale; D had another attorney. Iredale negotiated guilty pleas on certain charges for his two clients. D moved to substitute Iredale to represent him as well. The government objected on grounds that a conflict of interest would arise (i) if the court rejected Gomez-Barajas's guilty plea (which had not yet been accepted) and (ii) if Bravo were called as a witness at D's trial (Bravo would likely have testified only that he did not know D). D argued that the potential for conflict was remote under the circumstances, and stated that he was willing to waive any right to conflict-free counsel. The district court denied D's motion. D was convicted after trial with his original counsel, and the Ninth Circuit affirmed.

Issue. Does a defendant have a right to the attorney of his own choosing when that attorney has represented other defendants in the same conspiracy?

Held. No. Judgment affirmed.

♦ The Sixth Amendment right to counsel is not absolute but is circumscribed in several respects; *e.g.,* the chosen counsel must be a member of the bar and must not be representing an opposing party.

♦ Federal courts have an interest in ensuring that criminal trials are conducted fairly and within ethical standards. Federal Rule of Criminal Procedure 44(c) specifically directs trial judges to investigate cases involving multiple representation.

♦ D's offer to waive any possible conflicts does not resolve the issue, since the courts of appeals have shown a willingness to entertain ineffective assistance claims by defendants who specifically made such waivers.

♦ While there is a presumption in favor of D's right to counsel of choice, the district court must be given substantial latitude in refusing waivers of conflicts of interest. The district court's analysis of the situation takes place before trial when the exact relationships among the defendants are not yet clear, and not with the benefit of hindsight. Based on the situation as it appeared before trial, the district court here acted within its discretion.

Dissent (Marshall, Brennan, JJ.). The trial court's decision as to whether a potential conflict justifies rejection of a defendant's chosen counsel should not be entitled to any special deference on appeal; the trial court does not have broad latitude to vitiate D's Sixth Amendment right to counsel of choice. However, even under the Court's deferential standard, the facts of this case require reversal.

Dissent (Stevens, Blackmun, JJ.). Here, the Court exaggerates the significance of the potential conflict and gives inadequate weight to the informed and voluntary character of the waiver.

---

5. **The Right to Counsel of Choice.**

   a. **Appointed counsel.** An indigent defendant does not have the right to designate which attorney he wants appointed to represent him. Selection of the attorney is within the discretion of the court. In *Morris v. Slappy*, 461 U.S. 1 (1983), where the defendant's appointed counsel was hospitalized shortly before trial and the defendant wanted to wait for him rather than be appointed a new attorney, the Court held that there is no Sixth Amendment right to a "meaningful attorney-client relationship."

   b. **Deprivation of chosen counsel as reversible error--**

United States v. Gonzalez-Lopez, 548 U.S. 140 (2006).

Facts. Gonzalez-Lopez (D) was charged in Missouri with conspiracy to distribute marijuana. D's family hired Fahle to represent D, but D also hired Low, a California lawyer. A magistrate judge granted Low a provisional entry of appearance. On the ground that Low had violated a court rule restricting the cross-examination of a witness to one lawyer, the magistrate revoked the provisional acceptance after Low passed notes to Fahle during an evidentiary hearing. D later told Fahle that he wanted Low to be his only attorney, and Low filed an application for admission pro hac vice. The district court denied his application without comment. Fahle moved to withdraw as counsel and sought sanctions against Low for contacting D while Fahle was representing him. The court granted Fahle's motion to withdraw. D hired Dickhaus, a local attorney, who requested to have Low at counsel table with him. The court refused to allow Low to participate. D was convicted. D appealed and the Eighth Circuit vacated the conviction, holding that the district court's denial of Low's admission was erroneous and violated D's Sixth Amendment right to choose his own counsel. The Supreme Court granted certiorari.

Issue. Does a trial court's erroneous deprivation of a criminal defendant's choice of counsel entitle the defendant to reversal of his conviction?

Held. Yes. Judgment affirmed and case remanded.

◆   The government does not dispute that an element of the Sixth Amendment right to assistance of counsel is the right of a defendant who does not require appointed counsel to choose who will represent him. However, the government contends that the defendant must show that substitute counsel was ineffective or that, even if substitute counsel's performance was not deficient, there is a reasonable probability that the results of the proceedings would have been different if he had been represented by his counsel of choice. The government argues that the Sixth Amendment is not violated unless a defendant has been prejudiced.

◆   The purpose of the Sixth Amendment is to ensure a fair trial, but that does not mean that rights can be disregarded as long as the trial is fair. The right to counsel of choice guarantees the fairness of allowing a defendant to be represented by the counsel he believes to be the best. The right at stake here is the right to counsel of choice, not the right to a fair trial. There need not be an additional showing of prejudice.

◆   There is a difference between the right to counsel of choice and the right to effective counsel. The violation of the right to the effective assistance of counsel generally requires a defendant to establish prejudice. An inquiry into prejudice is not necessary when the right to select counsel of one's choice has been wrongly denied. Here, the trial court violated D's right to counsel of choice. The next question is whether this error is subject to review for harmlessness.

♦ There are two classes of constitutional errors. The first, trial error, arises during presentation of the case to the jury. Whether these errors are harmless beyond a reasonable doubt can be determined by quantitative assessment. The second, structural error, includes problems such as deprivation of the right to counsel of choice, denial of counsel, and denial of the right of self-representation. It is impossible to know in such cases what different choices different counsel would have made, which means that harmless-error analysis would be a speculative inquiry into what might have occurred.

♦ A choice-of-counsel error occurs whenever a defendant's choice is wrongly denied. This is different from the issue of effective representation, where the inquiry determines whether a violation even occurred.

♦ There are limits on the right to choose counsel, such as when a court appoints counsel or when a defendant desires representation by a person who is not a member of the bar or who has a conflict of interest. But none of these limitations is relevant here. The district court erred when it denied D his choice of counsel. That error violated D's Sixth Amendment right to counsel of choice; this violation is not subject to harmless-error analysis.

Dissent (Alito, J., Roberts, C.J., Kennedy, Thomas, JJ.).

♦ The Sixth Amendment protects the right to have the assistance that the defendant's counsel of choice is able to provide. The focus of the right is the quality of the representation, not the identity of the lawyer who provides the representation. The erroneous disqualification of counsel does not violate the Sixth Amendment unless it diminishes the quality of assistance that the defendant would have otherwise received. Thus, a defendant would be entitled to a new trial if he could show an identifiable difference in the quality of representation between the disqualified attorney and the attorney who represented him at trial.

♦ We have never held that the erroneous disqualification of counsel violates the Sixth Amendment when there is no prejudice. Even if the erroneous disqualification of counsel of choice always violated the Sixth Amendment, reversal would not be required in all cases. The touchstone of structural error is fundamental unfairness and unreliability. Automatic reversal should be reserved for constitutional errors that always or necessarily produce unfairness. There should be at least some showing of prejudice or harmless-error review. Otherwise, a defendant whose first choice of counsel is erroneously disqualified would automatically be entitled to a new trial even if his attorney performed brilliantly.

---

    c.   **Defendants not allowed to use forfeitable assets to pay attorney fees.** In *Caplin & Drysdale, Chartered v. United States*, 491 U.S. 617

(1989), the Supreme Court held that the federal statute authorizing forfeiture to the government of property acquired as a result of drug-law violations did not impermissibly burden a defendant's Sixth Amendment right to retain counsel of his choice. A narcotics defendant's attorney had challenged the forfeiture statute because it did not provide an exception for property used to pay attorney fees. The Court noted that a defendant has no Sixth Amendment right to spend another person's money to pay his lawyer, even if he will not otherwise be able to retain the attorney of his choice. The Court stated three governmental interests in the forfeiture: (i) forfeitable assets are deposited in a fund that supports law-enforcement efforts in a variety of important ways; (ii) rightful owners of forfeited assets may make claims for forfeited assets before they are retained by the government; and (iii) a major purpose of the racketeer-influenced and corrupt organizations ("RICO") and the continuing criminal enterprise ("CCE") forfeiture provisions is the desire to decrease the economic power of organized crime and drug enterprises. The Court found that the governmental interests override any Sixth Amendment interest in allowing criminals to use forfeitable assets to pay for their defense.

II. POLICE PRACTICES

A. THE ROLE OF THE COURTS IN THE ADMINISTRATION OF JUSTICE

1. **Federalism and State Criminal Procedure.** Many of the safeguards in criminal procedure have come relatively late. For example, the right to counsel in federal courts meant nothing until 1938. Of course, Supreme Court power to review state criminal convictions has always existed when federal constitutional rights have been involved. But the real beginning of federal activity came with the Fourteenth Amendment (and the legislation passed to guarantee rights thereunder). For example, Congress created civil and criminal actions to enforce constitutional rights and in 1867 extended habeas corpus to prisoners in state custody in violation of the Constitution. The uncertainty of the law in the area of criminal procedure therefore results from the newness of the issues; also, the problems demand difficult choices between conflicting social policies. As a result, it is presently unclear in many areas exactly what is demanded of the states.

   As far as supervision of the states is concerned, there has been little congressional action. Federal supervision is through the judicial process; this is sometimes difficult, because unlike other areas of constitutional law, in criminal procedure strong interests compete against an abstract ideal; *i.e.,* the state interest in a particular case versus a general idea of "fair procedure." Another problem is that the content of due process is even more general than the standards that govern other areas of federalism. It is not thought to merely crystallize the English common law or simply incorporate the Bill of Rights, and it cannot be confined to a particular set of existing procedures because due process at any given time includes those procedures that are fair and feasible in light of then existing values and capabilities. There can be little doubt that the Supreme Court is the arbiter of what these procedures shall be.

2. **Competing Values.** There are inherently competing values involved in the criminal process:

   a. **Crime control.** The efficient, expeditious screening and disposition of people suspected of crimes is largely an administrative function.

   b. **Due process model.** Crime control is subordinate to maintenance of the dignity and autonomy of the individual under this model. Providing due process is a judicial function. The criminal process is moving more and more in this direction.

   c. **Supreme Court intervention.** Typically, the Supreme Court has started out with highly particular decisions, dealing on a narrow basis with the facts of the case before it; it then has moved toward an increasing generality of statement. For example, "this confession was coerced (for such and such reasons)" to "all confessions are bad when obtained from an arrestee who has not been promptly brought before a magistrate."

B. ARREST, SEARCH, AND SEIZURE

1. The Exclusionary Rule.

a. Violation of the Fourth Amendment. If it is determined that the police have violated the Fourth Amendment rules on search and seizure to obtain evidence, what remedy is available for the defendant because of the illegal search? In *Weeks v. United States*, 232 U.S. 383 (1914), the Supreme Court first enunciated the exclusionary rule. It stated that when the Fourth Amendment requirements on search and seizure have been violated, evidence illegally obtained thereby may be suppressed or excluded in a prosecution for a federal crime.

b. Disadvantages of the suppression rule.

1) The rule is so strong and so drastic that it inhibits the development of other, perhaps more sophisticated methods of deterring objectionable police actions.

2) It carries a penalty that frequently exceeds the character of the police mistake. Regardless of the error, the evidence is excluded. This may mean that as a result of a trivial mistake, a dangerous criminal goes free.

3) It prevents experiment in the means used to discipline police methods.

c. Advantages of the rule. Viewing the Fourth Amendment requirements strictly, there may be no other way of protecting these rights. Alternatives include:

1) **Civil remedy.** Because of sovereign immunity, a cause of action can be brought only against the officer committing the violation, who usually will not have much money. Furthermore, the officer will have the backing of the municipality; it would be very expensive for defendants to win such suits.

2) **Criminal sanctions.** This would mean that the district attorney would be suing fellow police officers.

3) **Intra-police department penalties.** These do not work. Police hierarchies do not care if searches are illegal, as they feel that the defendants are the "bad guys" anyway.

d.   **Effectiveness.** Although there may be no viable alternative to the exclusionary rule, this does not exclude the necessity of having to show that the rule is effective in preventing violations of illegal search and seizure. Although there is no data on this, probably the rule does some good and in the long run will cut down police abuses. Possibly by so doing it will cut down crime itself and cure other social ills. Protecting people's constitutional rights may prevent citizen alienation.

e.   **Exclusionary rule applied to states.**

   1)   **Early case--**

Wolf v. Colorado, 338 U.S. 25 (1949).

Facts. Police seized a doctor's records without a search warrant, but no physical violence was used.

Issue. Does the Fourteenth Amendment incorporation of the Fourth Amendment include the federal exclusionary rule (which prohibits introduction in evidence of material seized in violation of the Fourth Amendment)?

Held. No.

♦   In this instance, the Fourteenth Amendment incorporated the Fourth Amendment, making the police action a violation of the Fourth Amendment's search and seizure provision.

♦   Even though the Fourth Amendment applies to the states, it does not follow that the federal remedy (exclusion of all illegally seized evidence) applies to the states. Therefore, the illegally seized evidence may be admitted.

Concurrence (Black, J.). The federal exclusionary rule is not a command of the Fourth Amendment but is a judicially created rule of evidence that Congress might negate.

Dissent (Murphy, Rutledge, JJ.). The only alternative to the exclusionary rule is no sanction at all.

---

   2)   *Wolf* overruled--

Mapp v. Ohio, 367 U.S. 643 (1961).

Facts. The police forcibly entered the home of Mapp (D) without a warrant. They found obscene books, pictures, and photographs. D was convicted for the unlawful possession of these items, even though the police did not enter the house to find these particular things. The Supreme Court of Ohio upheld her conviction while recognizing that the evidence introduced against her was obtained by an unlawful search and seizure. D appeals.

Issue. Does the Fourth Amendment (as incorporated by the Fourteenth Amendment) require state courts to exclude evidence obtained by unlawful searches and seizures?

Held. Yes. Judgment reversed and case remanded.

♦ Since 1914 (when *Weeks* was decided), the use of illegally seized evidence has been prohibited in federal prosecutions. The states have not adequately protected the individual's right to privacy. To allow state courts to convict individuals on the basis of illegally seized evidence would be granting the right of privacy, but withholding its enjoyment and privilege.

♦ Since *Wolf, supra,* many states have adopted the *Weeks* approach. California adopted the rule after concluding that other remedies failed to secure compliance with the constitutional provisions. *Wolf* is now expressly overruled.

♦ While some criminals may go free because of this holding, there is a greater consideration here—the imperative of judicial integrity. Nothing can destroy a government more quickly than its failure to observe its own laws. If the government becomes a lawbreaker, it breeds contempt for the law.

♦ Today's holding requires state governments to observe the individual's right to privacy. The Fourth Amendment right to privacy is no longer revocable at the whim of any police officer who, in the name of law enforcement itself, chooses to suspend its enjoyment.

Dissent (Harlan, Frankfurter, Whittaker, JJ.). I would not impose the federal exclusionary remedy on the states. One-half of the states still follow the common law rule. The question remains one of state power. This is not the same as admission in evidence of an involuntary confession.

---

f.   **Good faith exception to the exclusionary rule--**

United States v. Leon, 468 U.S. 897 (1984).

Facts. Pursuant to a facially valid search warrant, searches were conducted, which uncovered a large quantity of drugs. The evidence was suppressed in the district court on the ground that the warrant was not issued on probable cause, in that the affidavit, upon which the warrant was based, contained allegations of an untested informer and limited corroboration by the police. The court of appeals affirmed, rejecting the government's invitation to adopt a good faith exception to the exclusionary rule. The Supreme Court granted certiorari.

Issue. Should the Fourth Amendment exclusionary rule be modified so as not to bar the use of evidence obtained by officers acting in reasonable reliance on a search warrant issued by a neutral magistrate but ultimately found to be unsupported by probable cause?

Held. Yes. Judgment reversed.

♦   Evaluation of the costs and benefits of the exclusionary rule lead to the conclusion that the evidence should be admissible in the government's case-in-chief. First, the rule is designed to deter police misconduct, not to punish the errors of judges and magistrates. Second, no evidence exists suggesting that judges subvert the Fourth Amendment, which would require the extreme sanction of exclusion. Third, there is no basis for believing that exclusion of evidence seized pursuant to a warrant will have a deterrent effect on the issuing judge.

♦   The rule should not be applied to deter objectively reasonable law enforcement activity, particularly when the officer acting with objective good faith has obtained a warrant and acted within its scope. Suppression is appropriate only if the officers were dishonest or reckless in preparing their affidavit or could not have harbored an objectively reasonable belief in the existence of probable cause.

♦   Here, the affidavit reflected the results of extensive investigation. The officer's reliance on the magistrate's determination of probable cause was objectively reasonable. Exclusion of the evidence is therefore inappropriate.

Concurrence (Blackmun, J.). The Court's decision is based on an empirical judgment, which shall have to be reconsidered if it should emerge that the good faith exception materially changes police compliance with the Fourth Amendment.

Dissent (Brennan, Marshall, JJ.). Admission of illegally obtained evidence implicates the same constitutional concerns as does the initial seizure of that evidence. The chief deterrent function of the exclusionary rule is to promote institutional compliance with the Fourth Amendment on the part of law enforcement agencies generally.

Dissent (Stevens, J.). There is no need to announce a new rule of law in light of the Court's decision in *Gates, infra.* Were it given the opportunity, the court of appeals would probably conclude that the warrant here satisfied the Fourth Amendment.

Comment. In a companion case, the Court ruled that, under *Leon*, evidence obtained by police acting in reasonable reliance (*i.e.,* good faith) on an improper type of search warrant, which was ultimately found to be unsupported by probable cause because it did not name the items to be seized with particularity, may be admitted and used at trial. [Massachusetts v. Sheppard, 468 U.S. 981 (1984)]

g. Violation of "knock-and-announce" rule--

Hudson v. Michigan, 547 U.S. 586 (2006).

Facts. Police officers executed a warrant to search the home of Hudson (D) for drugs and firearms. The officers announced their presence and waited just three to five seconds before entering D's house. The officers found drugs and a firearm. D moved to suppress the evidence, claiming that the premature entry violated the "knock-and-announce" requirement under the Fourth Amendment. The trial court granted the motion. The court of appeals reversed. D was convicted at trial and appealed. The court of appeals upheld the conviction. The Supreme Court granted certiorari.

Issue. Does violation of the "knock-and-announce" rule require the suppression of all evidence found in the search?

Held. No. Judgment affirmed.

◆ The exclusionary rule generates substantial social costs, and it should only be applied where its remedial objectives are most effectively served; *i.e.*, where its deterrence benefits outweigh the social costs. In this case, the costs are considerable. In addition to the risk of releasing dangerous criminals into society that arises in all exclusion cases, excluding evidence for a knock-and-announce violation would generate substantial litigation over whether the police waited a "reasonable" time or whether there was "reasonable suspicion" that the officers' knocking and announcing their presence would be dangerous or futile. This is not like the straightforward question of whether the police had a warrant or gave the *Miranda* warning.

◆ Another social cost would be police officers' refraining from timely entry after knocking and announcing. The appropriate amount of time they must wait is uncertain, and application of the exclusionary rule would lead officers to wait longer than the law requires, resulting in preventable violence against them and the destruction of evidence.

◆ At the same time, the exclusionary rule would provide few deterrence benefits in these cases. The value of deterrence depends on the strength of the incentive to commit the forbidden act. If police ignore the knock-and-announce rule, they do not achieve anything except the prevention of destruction of evidence and the avoidance of dangerous resistance. If there is reasonable suspicion of either situation, the knock-and-announce requirement is suspended anyway.

◆ The exclusionary rule was adopted when it was more difficult to deter with civil liability. But now 42 U.S.C. section 1983 provides meaningful relief, and the federal civil rights laws provide for legal fees and damages against municipalities and the federal government. Civil liability is an effective deterrent.

♦ Finally, police forces have become increasingly professional, with a new emphasis on internal police discipline. There have been reforms in the education, training, and supervision of officers. Internal discipline can limit successful careers and has a deterrent effect.

Concurrence (Kennedy, J.). Today's decision does not minimize the seriousness of knock-and-announce violations. Also, it does not call into doubt the continued operation of the exclusionary rule. The Court's decision determines only that a violation of the knock-and-announce requirement is not sufficiently related to the later discovery of evidence to justify suppression.

Dissent (Breyer, Stevens, Souter, Ginsburg, JJ.).

♦ Absent the exclusionary rule, police know they can ignore the Constitution without risking suppression of evidence. The cases show a widespread pattern of violations of the knock-and-announce requirement. The deterrent effect of civil litigation is not significant. Civil suits have produced nothing more than nominal damages, and actions for damages are expensive, time-consuming, not readily available, and rarely successful. The majority's argument that new remedies, such as section 1983 actions and better trained police, make suppression unnecessary is an argument that *Wolf*, *supra*, not *Mapp*, *supra*, is now the law.

♦ No precedent supports the majority's holding. The Court has declined to apply the exclusionary rule only where, unlike this case, admissibility in proceedings other than criminal trials was at issue, and where there is a specific reason to believe that application of the rule would not result in appreciable deterrence, such as where an officer executes a defective search warrant in good faith. This does not apply here because officers who violate the rule are not acting as a reasonable officer would act in similar circumstances. The deterrence rationale would not be served if the rule applied to police officers acting in good faith because the deterrent purpose of the exclusionary rule assumes that the police have engaged in willful, or at least negligent, conduct. There is no reason to think that in the case of knock-and-announce violations the exclusion of evidence at trial would not sufficiently deter future errors.

♦ The only substantial social costs that the Court mentions are those that are typical when the exclusionary principle is applied. The majority's substantial social costs argument is an argument against the exclusionary rule itself. The Court has always rejected that argument in the past. The knock-and-announce rule is important, and violations can only be effectively deterred through the exclusionary rule.

h. **Other dimensions of the exclusionary rule.**

   1) **Questions to grand jury witness.** In *United States v. Calandra, infra*, the Court held that a grand jury witness may not refuse to answer questions on the ground that they are based on evidence obtained from him in an earlier unlawful search.

   2) **Quasi-criminal proceedings.** Evidence obtained by government agents according to methods that violate the Fourth Amendment and used in "quasi-criminal" cases is excludable according to the *Mapp* standard. [*See* One 1958 Plymouth Sedan v. Pennsylvania, 380 U.S. 693 (1965)—forfeiture proceedings]

   3) **Other proceedings.** The exclusionary rule does not apply in civil deportation hearings [INS v. Lopez-Mendoza, 468 U.S. 1032 (1984)], or in civil cases brought by a sovereign different from the one that obtained the evidence [United States v. Janis, 428 U.S. 433 (1976)].

   4) **Evidence obtained by private persons.** Generally, evidence obtained by private persons is not excluded, except when the private person acted on behalf of the police. Also, no privacy interest in the contents of a package exists after private employees find the unsealed package, examine it, and invite federal agents to the premises for the purpose of viewing its contents. The viewing by federal agents of what the private party had made freely available to inspect did not violate the Fourth Amendment. [United States v. Jacobsen, 466 U.S. 109 (1984)]

i. **Other remedies.** Title 42 U.S.C. section 1983 imposes tort liability on any person who, under color of state law, deprives a United States citizen of his constitutional rights. The Court has also recognized a federal constitutional cause of action for such violations by federal officers. [*See* Bivens v. Six Unknown Named Agents, 403 U.S. 388 (1971)]

2. **Protected Areas and Interests.**

   a. **Introduction.** Before the Supreme Court decided *Katz* (below), property concepts had dominated search and seizure cases. That is, a search violated the Fourth Amendment only if it involved a physical trespass on the subject's tangible property. This notion was repudiated in *Katz*.

   b. **People protected, not things--**

Katz v. United States, 389 U.S. 347 (1967).

Facts. The FBI monitored telephone conversations by attaching a listening device to the outside of a public telephone booth. Information gathered about wagering was used as evidence to convict Katz (D), who appealed his conviction. The court of appeals held that the search was not illegal because there was no physical entrance into the area occupied by D. The Supreme Court granted certiorari.

Issue. Must the police obtain a search warrant before wiretapping a public telephone booth?

Held. Yes. Conviction reversed.

◆ Areas or places are not protected, but people are. What a person could reasonably expect to preserve as private (a conversation), even in an area accessible to the public, is protected from unlawful invasion without a warrant. Wherever a person is, he is entitled to know that he will remain free from unreasonable searches and seizures.

◆ Physical intrusion and the theory of seizure only of material items as unlawful is discredited. The government, however, could have made the search had it first obtained a search warrant.

Concurrence (Harlan, J.). The critical factor here is that the booth becomes a temporarily private place when someone enters it and shuts the door.

Dissent (Black, J.). The Fourth Amendment does not forbid eavesdropping. Wiretapping is the modern equivalent of eavesdropping.

Comment. The *Katz* court added that no electronic surveillance may be undertaken without a search warrant. Such searches without warrants are per se unreasonable. The decision goes on to set forth the standards under which such warrants will be issued.

––––––––––––––

    c.   **Consequences of *Katz*.** A number of questions remain after the *Katz* decision. Does protection depend on whether the police use artificial means of surveillance? What if the police are in a "public place" and simply observe what the defendant wants to keep private?

        1)   Formerly searches were illegal only when they constituted an unauthorized intrusion by the police into an area where "privacy would normally be expected by the owner or occupant of the property." Therefore, observing that which was open to the public view did not constitute an illegal search. This is probably still the law.

        2)   For example, the Supreme Court held in *Harris v. United States*, 331 U.S. 145 (1947), that objects falling into the "plain view" of

an officer are subject to seizure without a warrant; or what a person knowingly exposes to the public, even in her own home, is not protected by the Fourth Amendment. Of course, if the police use some artificial means to observe the defendant's conduct, then the "search" may fall within the proscription of *Katz*.

d.   Limitation on *Katz's* expectation of privacy--

California v. Greenwood, 486 U.S. 35 (1988).

Facts. Greenwood (D) was suspected of narcotics trafficking. A police investigator asked a neighborhood trash collector to pick up D's trash bags and turn them over to the police without mixing them with trash from other houses. The collector did so, and the investigator found evidence of narcotics use, which she then used to obtain a search warrant. In executing the warrant, the police found cocaine and hashish in D's house. D was arrested and released on bail. Subsequent searches of D's trash produced additional evidence of drug use, which in turn led to another search of D's house and another arrest of D. The trial court dismissed the charges on the ground that the search of D's trash was unconstitutional under the Fourth Amendment and the California Constitution. The court of appeals affirmed, and the state supreme court denied certiorari. The Supreme Court granted certiorari.

Issue. Does a person have an objectively reasonable expectation of privacy in the contents of trash put out on the street for pickup?

Held. No. Judgment reversed.

♦   A warrant is required to search property in which the owner manifests a subjective expectation of privacy that society accepts as objectively reasonable.

♦   D in this case claims to have had such an expectation of privacy in his trash. D intended that the trash be on the street temporarily, pending pickup, and did not expect that the contents of the bags would become known to the public generally or the police specifically. Such a subjective expectation of privacy does not, by itself, give rise to Fourth Amendment protection, however.

♦   It is common knowledge that plastic garbage bags left on the street are accessible to the public, including animals, children, scavengers, and snoops. D intended to convey the trash to the trash collector, a third party, who might sort through it or permit others, including the police, to do so. A person has no legitimate expectation of privacy in information he voluntarily gives to third parties. Accordingly, society would not view D's subjective expectation of privacy in trash left in a public place for collection as a reasonable expectation.

♦   We cannot reasonably expect police to avert their eyes from evidence of criminal activity that anyone could observe. What a person knowingly exposes to the public is not protected by the Fourth Amendment, even if it is in his own home.

Dissent (Brennan, Marshall, JJ.). A sealed trash bag contains evidence of the intimate details of a person's life, including financial, political, personal, and romantic interests, the privacy of which the Fourth Amendment is intended to protect. It is not enough to say that D placed his trash at the curb to convey it to a third party who might have sorted through it or allowed others, such as the police, to go through it. Under a county ordinance, D was not to dispose of his trash in any other way. Moreover, even the voluntary relinquishment of property does not necessarily amount to a relinquishment of a privacy expectation in it.

Comment. Open fields do not fall within the Fourth Amendment because an open field does not provide the setting for the intimate activities that the Fourth Amendment is intended to protect from government interference. [Oliver v. United States, 466 U.S. 170 (1984)] The Court has also upheld helicopter surveillance of a partially covered greenhouse in a residential backyard from a height of 400 feet, on the ground that there was no reasonable expectation of privacy when any member of the public could legally fly at that altitude. [Florida v. Riley, 488 U.S. 445 (1989)]

---

  e. **Application of *Katz* to thermal imaging of residence--**

Kyllo v. United States, 533 U.S. 27 (2001).

Facts. A federal agent suspected that Kyllo (D) was growing marijuana in his home in Florence, Oregon. Because indoor marijuana growing requires high-intensity lamps, the agent used a thermal imager to scan D's residence to see if D's walls were relatively hot. The agent scanned D's home in a few minutes from the seat of the agent's car, parked in the streets in the front and back of D's home. The scan showed that D's garage roof and a side wall of D's home were hotter than the rest of the home and neighboring homes. The agent used this information together with utility bills and informants' tips to obtain a search warrant. Inside, the agents found over 100 marijuana plants growing. D was indicted for manufacturing marijuana. The courts denied his motion to suppress and he entered a conditional guilty plea. The court of appeals affirmed. The Supreme Court granted certiorari.

Issue. Does it constitute a search for the police to use sense-enhancing technology to obtain information about the interior of a home that could not otherwise have been obtained without physical intrusion?

Held. Yes. Judgment reversed.

◆   The courts have recognized that new technology has affected the degree of privacy protected by the Fourth Amendment. Airplanes have made possible observation of homes and curtilage that were previously considered private. But there are legal limits upon the power of technology to shrink the realm of guaranteed privacy.

◆   The *Katz* test, which courts use to determine whether an individual has an expectation of privacy that society recognizes as reasonable, is difficult to apply in close cases. But there is a minimal expectation of privacy, acknowledged to be reasonable, in the interior of homes.

◆   The use of sense-enhancing technology to obtain information about the interior of a home that could not have been obtained without physical intrusion must be considered a search under the Fourth Amendment. This rule preserves the degree of privacy against government that existed when the Fourth Amendment was adopted.

◆   The government claims that the agents were merely detecting heat radiating from the external surface of the house, an "off-the-wall" observation distinct from "through-the-wall surveillance." But this analogy fails because a powerful microphone would pick up only sound emanating from a house, even though the sounds were generated inside the house. The government's approach would leave citizens defenseless against advanced imaging technology that could penetrate the walls.

◆   The government also claims the thermal imaging was constitutional because it did not detect private activities occurring in private areas. That type of distinction would lead to a jurisprudence that would distinguish between home activities that are intimate and those that are not.

◆   The Fourth Amendment draws a firm line at the entrance to the house, and the bright line rule announced in this case will protect the minimal expectation of privacy in one's home.

Dissent (Stevens, J., Rehnquist, C.J., O'Connor, Kennedy, JJ.). The agents in this case collected off-the-wall information that was exposed to the general public from the outside of D's home. The infrared scanners did not penetrate the interior of D's home. Using ordinary senses, any citizen could have detected heat emanating from D's house if snow was melting faster there. Using sense-enhancing technology to measure this public information is reasonable. The Court has previously allowed the use of sense-enhancing technology in the form of drug dogs, which sniff the exterior of luggage. The majority has improperly anticipated future technology that actually may some day penetrate the walls of the home.

f. **Use of technology.** The rapid development of technology has provided new tools for law enforcement to detect and solve crimes, but it has also enabled greater intrusion of privacy. The courts continue to balance the competing interests, but generally permit the use of technology when it is readily available in public places.

1) **Enhancing senses.** When an officer lawfully present at a certain place detects something by one of his natural senses, it is not a search. Use of a flashlight or binoculars to enhance vision does not make the detection a search. Likewise, use of a trained canine to detect drugs in luggage located in a public place does not constitute a "search" within the meaning of the Fourth Amendment. [United States v. Place, 462 U.S. 696 (1983)] In the same way, police can use an on-the-spot chemical test to determine whether an exposed powder is cocaine. [United States v. Jacobsen, *supra*]

2) **Electronic tracking.** The police may use electronic "beepers" placed inside a container that is sold as part of a "sting" operation to assist police in tracking the item. [United States v. Knotts, 460 U.S. 276 (1983)] The Court has held that such use of a beeper, when installed with the consent of the original owner, is not by itself a search or seizure because the transfer of a container with unmonitored beepers does not infringe any privacy interest. However, monitoring the beeper does constitute an unreasonable search when it reveals information that could not have been obtained through visual surveillance, such as information about the container's location within a house and the duration of its time in the house. [United States v. Karo, 468 U.S. 705 (1984)]

3) **Aerial photography.** The use of aerial photography of a large industrial plant is not a search under the Fourth Amendment, because such a plant is more like an open field that is open to the view of persons in aircraft lawfully in the public airspace above or near the area for the reach of cameras. [Dow Chemical Co. v. United States, 476 U.S. 227 (1986)] A device that could penetrate walls or windows might be a search, however.

g. **What items can be searched for and seized.**

1) **"Property interest" rule (early view).** Historically, the right to search for and seize property depended upon assertion by the government of a valid claim to a superior interest in the property seized.

a) **Contraband.** Under this approach, contraband (narcotics, counterfeit money and plates, etc.) clearly could be seized— it was illegal for any person to possess it, and the government's interest was therefore superior.

b)   **Fruits of crime.** Likewise, a person wrongfully in possession of stolen goods had no valid claim thereto, and the government's interest was deemed superior.

c)   **Instrumentalities of crime.** The same result applied in the case of objects used to perpetrate a crime (weapons, burglary tools, etc.). *Rationale:* Use of an object for illegal purposes "renders it forfeit," and hence subject to government seizure.

2)   **"Mere evidence" rule (later view).** However, the Court subsequently held that objects that were "merely evidence" of a crime could not be seized. The rationale was that the government had no superior right to such property. Indeed, the property owner could maintain an action in trespass and replevin to recover property from governmental officers who took it, even though such evidence might be essential to the government's case against the accused. [*See* Gouled v. United States, 255 U.S. 298 (1921)—Fourth Amendment barred seizure of incriminating correspondence from defendant's files even with a search warrant]

3)   **Modern rule—nexus requirement.** In *Warden v. Hayden*, 387 U.S. 294 (1967), the Supreme Court overruled and discarded the "mere evidence" rule. The Court held that the primary purpose of the Fourth Amendment, in its modern setting, was to protect privacy, not property. Hence, any kind of property—be it contraband, "fruits" or "instrumentalities," or even "mere evidence" of a crime—is subject to lawful search and seizure. The Court found no reason to protect a person's privacy more as to one kind of evidence than as to another. (The "mere evidence" seized in *Hayden* was items of clothing useful in identifying the accused as the perpetrator of the crime.)

a)   **"Nexus."** The Court made it clear, however, that police could seize only those items of property that appear reasonably necessary to aid in a particular apprehension or conviction. This is deemed automatically to be the case for "fruits," instrumentalities, or contraband. As to other evidence ("mere evidence"), there must be probable cause for believing that the item is related to criminal behavior.

4)   **Business records--**

Andresen v. Maryland, 427 U.S. 463 (1976).

Facts. Law enforcement personnel executed a search warrant at Andresen's (D's) offices. They found the papers sought for regarding a fraudulent sale of land. Over D's objection, the papers were used to convict D. The Supreme Court granted certiorari on the search issue.

Issue. May personal business papers seized during a search of business premises be used as evidence against the owner of the papers?

Held. Yes. Judgment affirmed.

♦ A person may not be required to produce incriminating evidence pursuant to a subpoena because that would constitute compulsory self-incrimination. Here, however, D was not asked to say or do anything. A party is privileged from producing the evidence but not from its production.

♦ The Fifth Amendment does not provide protection against voluntary statements such as these made before D was charged with a crime. There was nothing unreasonable about the search itself because all the warrant requirements were satisfied.

Dissent (Brennan, J.). There should be no difference between protecting private documents from being the subject of a subpoena and protecting them from seizure during a search. The inner sanctum of individual feeling and thought is the interest sought to be protected by the Fifth Amendment, and these business records fall into the protected area.

―――――――――

5)   Newspapers--

Zurcher v. Stanford Daily, 436 U.S. 547 (1978).

Facts. Nine policemen were injured by demonstrators. A warrant was obtained to search the offices of the *Stanford Daily* newspaper (P) for film or negatives relevant to identification of the assailants. P later brought a civil action in federal district court where declaratory relief was granted. The trial court held that: (i) the Fourth Amendment forbade the issuance of a warrant to search for materials in the possession of one not suspected of a crime except upon showing of probable cause that a subpoena duces tecum would be impractical; and (ii) the First Amendment bars searching of a newspaper office except upon a clear showing that evidence would be lost. The court of appeals affirmed, and the Supreme Court granted certiorari.

Issue. May a search warrant be issued to search property belonging to an innocent third party?

Held. Yes. Judgment reversed.

- A valid warrant under the Fourth Amendment may be issued to search any property, whether or not occupied by a third party, for which there is probable cause to believe that fruits, evidence, or instrumentalities of a crime will be found. The Fourth Amendment itself strikes the balance between privacy and public need, and a new emphasis on the subpoena duces tecum (as indicated by the trial court) is unwarranted.

- Whether the third party occupant is suspect or not, the state's interest remains the same. Furthermore, if the third party is aware of the presence of the evidence, he is sufficiently culpable to justify the warrant. If he is unaware, the warrant will so inform him of such presence.

- Denying search warrants against third parties and insisting on subpoenas could seriously undermine law enforcement efforts. Search warrants are often used early in an investigation before all of the perpetrators are known. A seemingly blameless third party in possession of evidence may not actually be innocent or may be sympathetic with the culpable party. There is the possibility that he cannot be relied upon to preserve the evidence or that he might notify those who would be damaged by it to let them know that the police are aware of its location.

- The privacy of the third party is not more protected by a subpoena duces tecum, because a warrant is more difficult to obtain and has inherent judicial safeguards that a subpoena duces tecum does not have.

- The framers of the First Amendment did not preclude warrants where the press is involved. Properly administered, the requirements for a warrant—probable cause, specificity, and overall reasonableness—afford adequate protection. If the evidence is sufficient to obtain a warrant, it is sufficient to obtain a subpoena.

Dissent (Stewart, Marshall, JJ.). The First Amendment is violated by such a use of the warrant. The operation of the newspaper is disrupted. There is great possibility of disclosure of confidential information, which inhibits the social purpose of the press. Under such a warrant the police can ransack and look for anything, while under a subpoena there is orderly delivery of particular items.

Dissent (Stevens, J.). The only justification for an unannounced search of an innocent citizen is the fear that he would conceal or destroy the object of the search if he were given notice. If there is probable cause to believe that he is actually a criminal or that he holds a criminal's weapons, contraband, etc., that fear is justified. But if nothing in the warrant application shows the need for an unannounced search by force, the probable-cause requirement is not satisfied and the search violates the Fourth Amendment.

3. Probable Cause.

a.   **Introduction.** The Fourth Amendment provides: "The right of the people to be secure in their persons, houses, papers, and effects, against unreasonable searches and seizures, shall not be violated, and no Warrants shall issue, but upon probable cause, supported by Oath or affirmation, and particularly describing the place to be searched, and the persons or things to be seized." The amendment indicates that arrests are seizures of the person and are, therefore, also covered. Furthermore, a finding of probable cause is required as a condition for getting a search or an arrest warrant.

b.   **Sufficiency of affidavit supporting request for a warrant.** The rationale for the warrant system is that there should be a separation between the police and the determination of whether probable cause exists. Therefore, the judge must determine, from the evidence the police present, whether there is in fact probable cause.

   1)   In order to show probable cause, the police must state sufficient facts of which they have actual knowledge or information from a reliable source.

   2)   Probable cause to arrest may require a somewhat different kind of showing and conclusion than probable cause to search.

      a)   Probable cause to arrest is reasonable grounds to believe that a crime has been committed by the person to be arrested.

      b)   Probable cause to search requires reasonable grounds to believe: (i) that items sought are seizable because they are connected with criminal activity; and (ii) that the items will be found in the place to be searched.

c.   *Aguilar/Spinelli* **two-prong test--**

Spinelli v. United States, 393 U.S. 410 (1969).

Facts. Spinelli (D) appeals from a conviction of violating gambling statutes. The search warrant that enabled the state to secure damaging evidence against D was based on simple hearsay conclusions by an informer of unknown reliability.

Issue. May hearsay conclusions alone be used to establish probable cause necessary to issue a search warrant?

Held. No. Judgment reversed.

♦   An application for a warrant must set forth the underlying circumstances necessary to enable the magistrate independently to judge the validity of the informer's conclusions about where evidence is. It must also support the credibility of the informer or the reliability of his information.

♦ Here, the magistrate was given no information to show the informer was reliable. Worse, the statement of the underlying circumstances was not specific with respect to the criminal activity.

♦ The informer's tip was insufficient to support a finding of probable cause, so the warrant was illegally issued.

Concurrence (White, J.). Since the informant's specific information about D using two phones with particular numbers had been verified, his allegation about gambling became more believable. It was not neutral, irrelevant information but was material to proving the allegation. Two phones in an apartment indicates a business use in operation where multiple phones are needed.

Comment. The Court stated that both prongs of the test enunciated in *Aguilar v. Texas*, 378 U.S. 108 (1964), are needed to base a search warrant on an informer's tip; *i.e.,* to establish the reliability of the inferences made by the informer from his facts and to establish the reliability of the informer. Corroboration of minor aspects of the tip that do not directly involve the alleged criminal conduct does not suffice.

---

d. **Abandonment of tests in *Aguilar/Spinelli:* totality of circumstances standard adopted--**

Illinois v. Gates, 462 U.S. 213 (1983).

Facts. An anonymous handwritten letter was sent to the Bloomingdale police alleging that Lance and Susan Gates (Ds) were selling drugs out of their condominium. The letter stated that on May 3, Susan would drive to Florida and a few days later Lance would fly down and drive back. The police investigated, finding that Lance had made a plane reservation to Florida, had flown there, and went to a room registered to Susan, and the next morning drove northbound with an unidentified woman on an interstate leading to Chicago. Based on these facts, a circuit court issued a search warrant for Ds' residence and automobile. On May 7, the police searched Ds' house and car, which revealed marijuana, weapons, and contraband. The circuit court ordered suppression of all these items on the ground that the affidavit failed to support a determination of probable cause. The appellate and Illinois Supreme Courts affirmed. The Supreme Court granted certiorari.

Issue. Given all the circumstances set forth in the affidavit, including the veracity and basis of knowledge of persons upon which the affidavit is based, was there probable cause to believe that contraband would be found in Ds' house and car?

Held. Yes. Judgment reversed.

♦ The two-pronged test established in *Aguilar* and *Spinelli* is abandoned. Instead, the totality of circumstances should be considered to determine whether there is fair probability that contraband will be found in a particular place. The informer's veracity, reliability, and basis of knowledge are all highly relevant, but not exclusive or mandatory, factors in evaluating the totality of the circumstances.

♦ Florida is well-known as a source of narcotics. Lance's flight to Florida and his immediate return north to Chicago is suggestive of a prearranged drug trip. The magistrate could rely on the anonymous letter as well, which contained facts detailing the time of the trip and future actions of third parties. Corroboration of major portions of the letter indicates a fair probability that the writer of the letter obtained his information from either Ds or someone they trusted. There was probable cause to believe that drugs would be found in Ds' home and car.

♦ The issuing magistrate must simply make a practical, common sense decision whether, given all the circumstances set forth in the affidavit, including the informer's veracity and basis of knowledge, there is a fair probability that contraband or evidence of a crime will be found in a particular place.

♦ A magistrate's determination of probable cause is entitled to great deference by reviewing courts. Appellate courts should not engage in de novo review. The evidence presented to the magistrate in this case supported his finding of probable cause.

Concurrence (White, J.). I agree that the warrant should be upheld but reach this conclusion based on the tests in *Aguilar* and *Spinelli*.

Dissent (Brennan, Marshall, JJ.). The warrant is invalid even under the totality of circumstances test. It is inadvisable to depart from the *Aguilar-Spinelli* test, which insures greater accuracy in probable cause determinations.

Dissent (Stevens, Brennan, JJ.). There was no probable cause before Ds arrived in Bloomingdale to justify a search of a private home. Unlike the informer's claim, Ds left no one home to protect the contraband supposedly left in the house.

———————

e. **Ramifications of *Gates*.** The extent of the deference to be accorded a magistrate's decision after *Gates* was illustrated in *Massachusetts v. Upton*, 466 U.S. 727 (1984). The state courts had held that probable cause was lacking because the basis for the informer's knowledge was not forcefully apparent, her credibility and reliability were not established, and the corroborating evidence related to innocent or public activities. The Supreme Court reversed, noting that while no single piece of evidence was conclusive, "the pieces fit neatly together and, so viewed, support the magistrate's determination that there was a fair probability that contraband or evidence of crime would be found."

f. **Challenge to affidavit.** Despite the deference to a determination of probable cause, a defendant may challenge an affidavit by making a substantial preliminary showing that a false statement knowingly and intentionally, or with reckless disregard for the truth, was included by the affiant in the warrant affidavit. If the allegedly false statement is necessary to the finding of probable cause, the Fourth Amendment requires that a hearing be held at the defendant's request. If the defendant's allegation is established by a preponderance of the evidence, the search warrant must be voided and the fruits of the search excluded to the same extent as if probable cause was lacking on the face of the affidavit. [Franks v. Delaware, 438 U.S. 154 (1978)]

g. **Identity of the informer--**

McCray v. Illinois, 386 U.S. 300 (1967).

Facts. McCray (D) was arrested without a warrant, searched incident to the arrest, and convicted on the basis of the heroin that was found on his person. At trial, one of the officers testified that the informer was reliable because information he had previously given had led to many past arrests. The officers refused, however, to disclose the identity of the informer. D was convicted of possession of narcotics. He appeals.

Issue. May a warrantless arrest and subsequent search be valid if the police do not reveal the identity of the informer?

Held. Yes. Judgment affirmed.

♦ The issue presented is probable cause for a search, not guilt or innocence. Evidence presented at trial proved that the officers did rely in good faith upon credible information supplied by a reliable informer. The Constitution does not require a judge to assume the arresting officers are committing perjury.

♦ The informer's privilege against disclosure of his identity is valid so long as he is not a witness against the accused on the merits.

Dissent (Douglas, J., Warren, C.J., Brennan, Fortas, JJ.). Today we are encouraging arrests and searches without warrants. A judicial mind should be interposed between the police and the citizen.

---

h.   **Other sources of probable cause.** Prior reliability need not be established when the information is provided by an alleged victim of, or a witness to, a crime. Unlike informers, who have other motivations for giving information, ordinary citizens act out of concern for society in general or their own personal safety. Police officers may also act on their own direct observations.

i.   **Probable cause based on probable joint enterprise--**

Maryland v. Pringle, 540 U.S. 366 (2003).

Facts. Pringle (D) was the front-seat passenger in a vehicle that was stopped by a police officer for speeding. The officer observed a wad of cash in the open glove compartment. After denying that he had any weapons or narcotics in the vehicle, the driver consented to a search. The officer found $763 in the glove compartment and five plastic baggies containing cocaine behind the back-seat armrest. Neither D, the driver, nor the back-seat passenger admitted owning the drugs or the money. They were all arrested. D later confessed that he owned the cocaine. At trial, D sought to have his confession suppressed as the fruit of an illegal arrest. The court denied D's motion. D was convicted and sentenced to 10 years in prison. The court of appeals reversed, holding that the presence of drugs in the back armrest was insufficient to establish probable cause for the arrest of a front-seat passenger under the Fourth and Fourteenth Amendments. The Supreme Court granted certiorari.

Issue. Does the presence of narcotics in a back-seat armrest constitute probable cause to believe that a front-seat passenger may have committed the crime of possession?

Held. Yes. Judgment reversed.

♦   The probable-cause standard cannot be precisely defined or quantified into percentages because it is based on probabilities and depends on the totality of the circumstances. It requires a reasonable ground for belief of guilt, particularized with respect to the person to be searched or seized.

♦   The facts in this case give rise to a reasonable inference that any or all three of the occupants of the car had knowledge of, and exercised dominion and control over, the cocaine. The officer could reasonably conclude that there was probable cause to believe P possessed the cocaine, either solely or jointly.

♦   This is not a case of guilt by association, which the Court has disapproved in *Ybarra v. Illinois*, 444 U.S. 85 (1979). In that case, a patron in a tavern was searched when officers had a warrant to search the tavern and the bartender. Mere proximity to others independently suspected of criminal activity does not constitute probable cause.

♦ In this case, unlike in *Ybarra*, P's presence in the car with two others and a quantity of cocaine was sufficient to infer a common enterprise among the three men.

---

4. **Search Warrants.**

   a. **Conditions for receiving a search warrant.** Federal Rule of Criminal Procedure 41 sets forth the conditions on which a federal search warrant will be issued. State procedure is substantially the same.

      1) **Location.** Any United States judge or commissioner within the district where the property is sought may issue a search warrant. But *Coolidge v. New Hampshire*, 403 U.S. 443 (1971), held that the Fourth and Fourteenth Amendments require that warrants be issued by "neutral and detached magistrates." Thus a search warrant issued in a case by the state's chief investigator and prosecutor (who was also a justice of the peace) was invalid even though based on probable cause.

      2) **Affidavit.** A warrant can be issued only on a sworn affidavit to the judge or commissioner, establishing the grounds for a warrant. The judge or commissioner issues the warrant if she is satisfied that there is probable cause to believe that the grounds for the application for a warrant exist. Probable or reasonable cause to believe that the items to be seized are in fact seizable by reason of their being connected with criminal activity and that the items will be found in the place named to be searched is necessary.

      3) **Basis.** The warrant is directed to a civil officer of the United States and must state the grounds for its issuance and the names of those who gave affidavits in support of it.

      4) **Time.** The warrant must designate the judge or commissioner to whom the warrant must be returned and must be executed and delivered (*i.e.,* the search conducted) within 10 days of its issuance.

      5) **Receipt.** The officer executing the warrant must give a copy of it and a receipt to the person from whom the property is seized or else leave a copy and a receipt on the premises. A written inventory must be taken. The return must be made promptly, accompanied by a written inventory.

6) **Who may issue a warrant.** Under the Fourth and Fourteenth Amendments, a municipal court clerk may issue an arrest warrant for violations of municipal ordinances. In *Shadwick v. City of Tampa*, 407 U.S. 345 (1972), the Court held that the clerk was "neutral and detached" because he was "independent of police and prosecution" and "capable of determining whether probable cause exists," since it was not shown to be a difficult task. Note that clerks are neither judges nor attorneys.

7) **Description of place to be searched.** The Fourth Amendment requirement of particularity in describing the place to be searched is satisfied by a description that allows the officer using reasonable effort to ascertain and identify the place intended. In *Maryland v. Garrison*, 480 U.S. 79 (1987), the warrant allowed the search of McWebb and a third-floor apartment, but after finding contraband during the search, they discovered they were in Garrison's separate apartment, also on the third floor. Because the warrant was valid when issued and the officers' failure to realize the overbreadth of the warrant was objectively understandable and reasonable, the search was valid.

b. **Execution of the warrant.**

1) **Time to execute.** Warrants must be executed promptly, or within a period of time specified by statutes and court rules, usually 10 days or less. In many jurisdictions, warrants cannot be served in the nighttime without express permission. There is no constitutional requirement for a daytime execution, however. [Gooding v. United States, 416 U.S. 430 (1974)]

2) **Announcement of intent to search.** The federal government and many states have statutes requiring that an officer announce his purpose and his authority prior to breaking into a dwelling to conduct a search (or to make an arrest). These statutes' purpose is to permit voluntary compliance with the police request and thus avoid violence.

a) **Failure to comply.** Failure to make the required announcement normally results in making the entry and the search unlawful (and the evidence obtained thereby is excluded by the exclusionary rule).

b) **Exceptions.** Most courts have held that there are exceptions to the statutory rule requiring announcement. Such exceptions occur where the officer would be put in danger by the prior announcement, or the intended arrestee might escape or destroy evidence. The exception must be based on the facts of the particular situation and cannot be based on a "general assumption" that in all such cases the exception applies. [*See* People v. Gastelo, 432 P.2d 706 (Cal. 1967)—no general assumption in narcotics cases that suspected person will attempt to destroy the evidence]

    c)   **Constitutional requirement.** The Supreme Court has held that the announcement rule is a constitutional requirement. However, the Court also indicated the general rule is subject to broad exceptions. In some states statutes also authorize magistrates to allow "no knock" searches.

3)   **Items that can be seized.**

    a)   **Described in warrant.** The general rule is that the searching officer can seize only those items that are particularly described in the search warrant. If he sees other offending items, he must get another warrant before seizing them.

    b)   **Pursuant to arrest.** However, items may be lawfully seized under the rule that a search may be made pursuant to a lawful arrest. Therefore, if the original warrant does not describe some item but during the search a lawful arrest is made, it may be possible to justify the seizure of items not described in the warrant as part of a "search incident to a lawful arrest."

c.   **Detention and search of persons on the premises.** In *Ybarra v. Illinois, supra,* the Court refused to uphold a state law as applied to a search of customers, not identified in the warrant, conducted during a search of the premises. The state law would have permitted admission of the evidence so obtained, but the Court found that there was no danger justifying a frisk for weapons under *Terry v. Ohio, infra,* and that a person's constitutional protection against unreasonable searches outweighs the state's interest in controlling drug traffic.

d.   **Detention while a warrant is sought--**

Michigan v. Summers, 452 U.S. 692 (1981).

Facts. Police officers obtained a warrant to search a house owned by Summers (D) for narcotics. As they went to execute the warrant, they found D leaving the house. They detained D while they searched the house. When they found narcotics in the house, they arrested D, searched him, and found drugs on his person. The state courts suppressed the evidence of drugs found on D, and the Supreme Court granted certiorari.

Issue. May police detain the owner of premises for which they have a search warrant during the time they are executing the warrant?

Held. Yes. Judgment reversed.

♦ Here the police had a valid search warrant, which authorized them to intrude on D's privacy. The detention was justifiable as a means of reducing the risk of harm to D's property, because it facilitated an orderly search. The detention was only an incremental intrusion of D's personal liberty when the search was already authorized.

♦ The police, being authorized to require D to remain at his house, could properly arrest him and perform a search of his person when the search under the warrant produced evidence creating probable cause.

Dissent (Stewart, Brennan, Marshall, JJ.). Detention without probable cause requires a governmental interest independent of the ordinary interest of investigating crime and detaining suspects, which was absent here. Also, a detention during a search could last for hours, constituting more than an incremental intrusion.

---

e. **Seizure of unnamed items.** Items found in "plain view" may be seized if it is immediately apparent to the police that they have evidence before them, even if not named in the warrant. There is no requirement that the discovery of such unnamed items be inadvertent, but if the scope of the search exceeds that permitted by the terms of the warrant or the character of the relevant exception from the warrant requirement, the seizure is unconstitutional. [Horton v. California, 496 U.S. 128 (1990)]

5. **Warrantless Arrests and Searches of the Person.**

   a. **Warrantless arrests.** A lawful arrest may be made without a warrant, but the arresting officer must act on facts sufficient to constitute "probable cause."

   b. **Arrest in public places--**

United States v. Watson, 423 U.S. 411 (1976).

Facts. Watson (D), identified by a reliable informer as a possessor of stolen credit cards, was arrested without a warrant during a prearranged meeting between D and the informer. D was searched, but no cards were found. D consented to a search of his car after receiving *Miranda* warnings, and two stolen cards were found. D was convicted, despite his motion to suppress. D appealed, and the court of appeals reversed. The government appeals.

Issue. May an authorized law enforcement officer make a warrantless arrest in a public place despite an opportunity to procure a warrant after developing probable cause for arrest and when authorized by statute?

Held. Yes. Judgment reversed.

- The common law rule permitted a police officer to arrest without a warrant for a misdemeanor or felony committed in his presence as well as for a felony not committed in his presence if there were reasonable grounds for making the arrest. This rule survived the Fourth Amendment and is permitted by most states.

- The arrest was based on probable cause, occurred in a public place, in the daytime, and the officers acted in strict compliance with the governing statute and regulations conferring arrest authority.

- The judicial preference for an arrest warrant should not be transformed into a constitutional rule. Therefore, neither the lack of exigent circumstances nor the possibility of obtaining a warrant are sufficient to invalidate the arrest and subsequent consensual search.

Concurrence (Powell, J.). This result merely recognizes historical experience and practical considerations. Warrantless arrests were permitted at the adoption of the Fourth Amendment. Changing the rule now would severely hamper law enforcement.

Dissent (Marshall, Brennan, JJ.). The arrest and search both are intrusions on protected rights and should be conducted only with a warrant. Common law allowed arresting officers to make an arrest when a felony was committed in their presence, but the class of crimes that today constitute felonies is larger and comprises many crimes that never were felonies at common law. The police would not be hampered by the warrant requirement since once probable cause for an arrest exists, it usually continues into the indefinite future, and therefore a delay in obtaining a warrant for the purpose of gathering more evidence would not hamper law enforcement. The effect of the majority opinion is to weaken the probability that warrants will ever be obtained for felony arrests.

---

c. **Seizure when deadly force used.** In *Tennessee v. Garner*, 471 U.S. 1 (1985), the Supreme Court held that a "seizure" occurs when police use deadly force to apprehend a suspect, and it is unreasonable to use such force unless there is probable cause to believe that the suspect poses a significant threat of death or serious injury to the officers or others.

d. **Post-arrest probable cause requirement--**

Gerstein v. Pugh, 420 U.S. 103 (1975).

Facts. Florida state law permitted the prosecutor to bring noncapital criminal actions based on information without holding a preliminary hearing. Thus, Pugh and Henderson (Ds) were charged with noncapital crimes and detained without a hearing as to the probable cause for their arrests.

Issue. Is a defendant entitled to judicial determination of probable cause as a prerequisite to pretrial detention?

Held. Yes.

♦ A police officer may arrest a person based on his immediate assessment of probable cause. Once the suspect is in custody, however, there is no further justification for dispensing with a magistrate's neutral judgment.

♦ The Fourth Amendment requires a fair and reliable determination of probable cause as a prerequisite to extended restraint on liberty following arrest, which determination must be made by a judicial officer either before or promptly after arrest.

Comments.

♦ "Prompt" under *Gerstein* means within 48 hours of arrest. [County of Riverside v. McLaughlin, 500 U.S. 44 (1991)] Prior to that, an arrested individual may still prove that the delay was unreasonable. After 48 hours, the government has the burden to show that the delay was due to a bona fide emergency or other extraordinary circumstance.

♦ In *Michigan v. Doran*, 439 U.S. 282 (1978), the Court held that in extradition proceedings, courts in the asylum state may not pursue questions of probable cause once the demanding state has made a judicial determination that probable cause exists.

e.   **Other warrantless searches of the person.** As a general rule in "emergency" situations (where evidence might be destroyed or life endangered), a search may be made without a warrant. Normally there must be a showing that police had "probable cause."

1)   **Full search of person incidental to arrest--**

United States v. Robinson, 414 U.S. 218 (1973).

Facts. Robinson (D) was lawfully arrested for driving while his license was revoked. The officer knew from previous investigation that D's operator's permit had been re-voked, and driving after revocation was an offense with a mandatory minimum jail term. Pursuant to his arrest, a full body search uncovered heroin in a cigarette package on his person. D was then convicted of possession and concealment of heroin. The court of appeals reversed and the Supreme Court granted certiorari.

Issue. Is a full body search incident to a lawful arrest permissible even if the officer does not suspect that the arrestee is carrying weapons or has evidence on his person?

Held. Yes. Judgment reversed.

♦ It is "reasonable" under the Fourth Amendment for the police to make a full body search incident to a lawful arrest, at least when the person arrested is taken into custody. This is true regardless of the nature of the crime for which the arrest was made.

♦ A full body search ensures that the person taken into custody does not bring weapons or other contraband into the police vehicle or police station.

♦ The fact of custodial arrest gave rise to the authority to search. Once the police found the cigarette package, they were entitled to inspect it. They were then entitled to seize whatever contraband they found.

Dissent (Marshall, Douglas, Brennan, JJ.). The reasonableness of a search must be determined on a case-by-case basis, not by applying a formula. The patdown of D's coat pocket was clearly lawful. The removal of the unknown object was not justifiable, however, because it did not feel like a weapon. But even if it was reasonable to remove the object, there was clearly no justification for opening the package and looking in-side.

Comments.

♦ In *Gustafson v. Florida*, 414 U.S. 260 (1973), the defendant also committed a driving infraction, but one that was not punishable by a minimum jail sentence. The Court upheld the search on the basis of *Robinson*, finding no distinction between the two cases.

♦ In *Virginia v. Moore*, 128 S. Ct. 1598 (2008), the Court held that the Fourth Amendment did not require the exclusion of evidence that police obtained dur-ing a search incident to an arrest even though, as a matter of state law, they should have issued a summons instead of arresting the defendant for the misde-meanor of driving with a suspended license.

2) **Station house search.** When an arrested person is taken to the police station, the police may make a full inventory search of his person and all property in his possession before he is jailed. This is "reasonable" to protect the suspect's property, to protect the police against false claims of theft of the property, to discover dangerous objects, and to assist in identifying the suspect. [Illinois v. Lafayette, 462 U.S. 640 (1983)] Although a less intrusive means to protect the property might have been used, such as placing the entire bag in a locker or box, the Constitution does not require such steps. Treatment of such property is a matter of administrative procedure to deter theft by and false claims against police employees.

3) **Delayed post-arrest search of clothing.** In *United States v. Edwards*, 415 U.S. 800 (1974), a warrantless search of the defendant's clothes that revealed incriminating paint chips was upheld, although it occurred 10 hours after his arrest. There was a legitimate reason for the delay—no substitute clothing was available—so the search was "incidental" to the arrest.

4) **Blood test--**

Schmerber v. California, 384 U.S. 757 (1966).

Facts. Schmerber (D) was being treated at a hospital following a car accident. The police directed a blood sample of D to be taken. This evidence was used to convict D for drunk driving.

Issue. Does warrantless taking of the defendant's blood constitute an unreasonable seizure in contravention of the Fourth Amendment?

Held. No. Judgment affirmed.

♦ The search was conducted in a reasonable manner, and there was imminent fear of "destruction of evidence" as the percentage of alcohol in the blood naturally decreases with time.

♦ Under these special circumstances, taking blood for the blood alcohol test was appropriate incident to the arrest.

---

5) **Searches of the body.** The reasonableness of searches into the human body depends on weighing society's need for the evidence against the magnitude of the intrusion on the individual, including

the threat to health, safety, and dignity of the individual. In *Winston v. Lee*, 470 U.S. 753 (1985), the Court held that a surgical procedure under general anesthesia—to remove a bullet—involved significant risks to health and a severe intrusion on privacy; such a procedure was thus unreasonable, at least when there existed substantial other evidence.

6) **Probable cause but no arrest.** If the police have probable cause to arrest but do not do so, they may nonetheless make a limited search of the person without a warrant if the evidence is readily destructible. [Cupp v. Murphy, 412 U.S. 291 (1973)—scraping fingernails]

6. **Warrantless Entries and Searches of Premises.**

a. **Search incident to arrest.** There are specific situations that permit a search to be conducted without a warrant. A search made incident to a lawful arrest is one such situation.

1) **Reasons for the exception.**

a) The arrestee may have a concealed weapon.

b) He may have concealed a means to escape.

c) He may destroy evidence.

2) **Scope of permissible search--**

Chimel v. California, 395 U.S. 752 (1969).

Facts. Police lawfully arrested Chimel (D) when he returned home from work and thereafter conducted a warrantless search of the entire house. The search led to evidence used to convict D of burglary. D unsuccessfully appealed his conviction. The Supreme Court granted certiorari.

Issue. May a search of a defendant's entire house be constitutionally justified as incident to the defendant's arrest?

Held. No. Judgment reversed.

♦ Under the Fourth and Fourteenth Amendments, a search made without a warrant but incidental to a valid arrest may extend only to a search of the person and the area within his immediate control; *i.e.,* the area from within which he might grab a weapon or destructible evidence. Anything beyond this must be justified, and the government has the burden of justification.

♦ The more expansive approach adopted in *United States v. Rabinowitz*, 339 U.S. 56 (1950), which would permit a search of the entire area in the "possession" of the arrested person, is disapproved. That rule gave law enforcement officials the opportunity to engage in searches not justified by probable cause merely by choosing the place of arrest.

♦ The search of D's house in this case went far beyond the area from within which he could have obtained a weapon or an item of evidence. Therefore, the scope of the search was unreasonable.

Concurrence (Harlan, J.). The only thing that has given me pause is that as a result of *Mapp v. Ohio, supra*, every change in Fourth Amendment law must now be obeyed by state officials facing widely different problems of local law enforcement. We do not know to what extent cities are prepared to administer the greatly expanded warrant system.

Dissent (White, Black, JJ.). It is unreasonable to require the police to leave the scene of the arrest to obtain a search warrant, especially when, as in this case, they have probable cause to support a warrant. While the police are gone, D's wife could easily destroy the evidence. If circumstances justify a warrantless arrest, it is strange that they do not also justify a warrantless search.

Comments.

♦ Many of the cases since *Chimel* seem to suggest that the area within "immediate control" may be very large. For example, search of a box six feet away for stolen money orders was upheld. Also, police may enter premises "looking" for the defendant and in effect conduct a search *before* arrest. [*See* Washington v. Chrisman, 455 U.S. 1 (1982)]

♦ In *Arizona v. Hicks*, 480 U.S. 321 (1987), the Court held that a police officer conducted an unreasonable search when, after lawfully entering an apartment from which a shot had been fired, the officer moved some stereo components to read their serial numbers. When he called in the numbers, he was told the components were stolen. The Court held that such a search would require probable cause, not merely reasonable suspicion.

------

3) **Pretext arrests.** If the police can arrest a person close enough to the place they want to search, can they search without a warrant? Can police deliberately arrest a man at his home in order to search it? Or enter a home looking for a person whom they have probable cause to arrest and make a search? Yes, if they are not too unsubtle about it. For example, if the police are shown to have had many opportunities to arrest a person but waited until he entered his home,

then evidence seized from the home incident to the arrest may be thrown out as the fruit of an illegal search. However, the police need only show some small reason for having arrested the defendant at his home to sustain the search. The police always testify that there were such reasons. In some cases, when the police have merely used the arrest (usually on some small technicality) as a pretext to search, the search has not been upheld (search incident to a technically lawful arrest for a traffic offense). Unfortunately, the cases are not consistent.

4) **Warrantless searches under exigent circumstances.** A search is incident to an arrest only if it is substantially contemporaneous with the arrest and is confined to the immediate vicinity of the arrest. In *Vale v. Louisiana*, 399 U.S. 30 (1970), the Court found that the warrantless search of a house when the arrest took place on the front steps was not justified. The dissent argued that the police were justified to search the house because there could have been other people in the house who would have been alerted by the arrest to destroy the contraband that the police believed was inside. In *Segura v. United States*, 468 U.S. 796 (1984), the Court upheld a warrantless entry into an apartment when the person who answered the door was arrested. The police remained in the apartment for 19 hours while waiting to get the search warrant, which was justified to secure the premises.

5) **Warrantless entry into residence to arrest--**

Payton v. New York, 445 U.S. 573 (1980).

Facts. Police officers, having probable cause to believe that Payton (D) had committed a murder, forcibly entered D's apartment to arrest him. They had not obtained a warrant. No one was home, but the officers seized a shell casing that was in plain view. The casing was admitted into evidence at D's trial and D was convicted. D appeals.

Issue. May police officers forcibly enter a private residence, without a warrant, to make a routine felony arrest?

Held. No. Judgment reversed.

♦   The officers had ample time to obtain a warrant. No exigent circumstances were involved. On the other hand, under the Fourth Amendment, searches and seizures inside a home without a warrant are presumptively unreasonable.

♦   An entry to arrest implicates the same interests as an entry to search and seize. In both situations, a warrant must be obtained before entry, absent exigent circumstances. This is an unequivocal constitutional command.

Dissent (White, J., Burger, C.J., Rehnquist, J.). This rule is cumbersome and presents officers with the difficult task of deciding whether the circumstances are sufficiently exigent to justify entry to arrest without a warrant. The common law rule would be much clearer and fairer. Once police knock and announce their presence, they may enter a home to make a daytime arrest without a warrant if they have probable cause to believe that the person committed a felony and is present in the house.

Comment. The Court relied on *Dorman v. United States,* 435 F.2d 385 (D.C. Cir. 1970), which listed six factors for finding exceptional circumstances: (i) a grave offense, especially one of violence; (ii) a reasonable belief that the suspect is armed; (iii) a clear showing of probable cause to believe the suspect committed the crime; (iv) a strong reason to believe the suspect is in the premises being entered; (v) a likelihood that the suspect will escape if not swiftly apprehended; and (vi) the circumstance that the entry is made peaceably. In *Welsh v. Wisconsin,* 466 U.S. 740 (1984), the Court held that an arrest of a person in his own bedroom for a noncriminal traffic offense was unjustified when the only potential emergency was the need to ascertain the suspect's blood alcohol level. In *Minnesota v. Olson,* 495 U.S. 91 (1990), the suspect had allegedly driven the getaway car in a robbery/homicide. The Court upheld a state court determination that the warrantless entry was not justified because, despite the gravity of the offense, there were no exigent circumstances because the police knew where the suspect was and he posed no danger to those with him.

———————

7.   **Warrantless Seizures and Searches of Vehicles and Containers.**

    a.   **Vehicle searches.** Warrantless searches of automobiles may be permitted in circumstances that would not support searches of a home or office. The inherent mobility of autos creates an "exigent circumstance" (given the possibility of movement or destruction of evidence while a search warrant is obtained). Moreover, there is substantially less expectation of privacy in the case of autos than with a home or office—since they are subject to licensing, inspection, and other frequent contacts with authority. Accordingly, an auto may often be subject to search without a warrant solely on the basis of probable cause to believe that the vehicle contains something subject to seizure.

    1)   **Motor homes--**

———————

California v. Carney, 471 U.S. 386 (1985).

———————

Facts. Having received information that a particular motor home had been used as a place to exchange marijuana for sex, drug enforcement agents kept it under surveillance. An agent watched Carney (D) meet a youth, accompany him to the motor home, and close the window shades. Over an hour later, the youth left the motor home. Upon being stopped and questioned, the youth said that he had received marijuana for sex. The agents accompanied the youth back to the motor home. The youth knocked, D stepped out, and an agent entered the motor home, where he found marijuana on a table. D was ultimately convicted of possession of marijuana for sale, but the state supreme court reversed on grounds that the search was unreasonable because the agents did not get a warrant. The Supreme Court granted certiorari.

Issue. Does the automobile exception to the search warrant requirement apply to motor homes?

Held. Yes. Judgment reversed.

♦   In *Carroll v. United States*, 267 U.S. 132 (1925), the Court recognized that the privacy interests in an automobile, while constitutionally protected, deserve a diminished protection because of the vehicle's mobility. It is not practicable to obtain a warrant when the vehicle to be searched can be quickly moved.

♦   Another reason for the vehicle exception is the reduced expectation of privacy resulting from pervasive government regulation of vehicles, including inspection and licensing requirements, as recognized in *South Dakota v. Opperman, infra.* Vehicles are always subject to being stopped and searched if probable cause exists to believe that the vehicle contains contraband.

♦   D's vehicle possessed many attributes of a home. Yet it was readily mobile, and, being licensed to operate on public streets, it was subject to regulation and inspection. Its potential for use as a home does not override these pertinent characteristics.

♦   Because the agents had probable cause to believe that D's vehicle contained contraband, and because the exigencies attendant to ready mobility were present, the warrantless search was not unreasonable.

Dissent (Stevens, Brennan, Marshall, JJ.). The automobile exception has never before been applied to a parked vehicle that could easily be detained while a warrant is issued. There were no actual exigencies here that prevented the officers from seeking a warrant. D's vehicle was obviously used as a home, containing furniture and sleeping and eating space. It thus differed from a mere passenger vehicle.

Comment. In *Chambers v. Maroney*, 399 U.S. 42 (1970), police investigating a service station robbery were given a description of the getaway car and the robbers. They saw a car fitting the description; the passengers fit the description of the robbers. The police stopped the car, made the arrests, and searched the car after first driving it to the police station. The search turned up the stolen property and guns used in the holdup. The Court held that officers may search a vehicle without a warrant if they have probable cause to believe that it contains contraband or other items subject to seizure (since a car can rapidly leave the jurisdiction before a warrant can be obtained). If such probable cause exists, the police can also take the car to the police station and there search it without a warrant. Note that the rationale for this exception is that cars can leave the jurisdiction before a warrant can be obtained; seizure would prevent this problem.

---

2) Searching a container inside a car--

California v. Acevedo, 500 U.S. 565 (1991).

Facts. Two hours after Daza took a package of marijuana to his apartment, Acevedo (D) entered the apartment. D left with a paper bag large enough to contain a marijuana package, put the bag in the trunk of his car, and drove off. The police who were monitoring the entire situation stopped him and found the marijuana in the bag. D was convicted, but the state appellate court reversed. The Supreme Court granted certiorari.

Issue. Does the Fourth Amendment require police to obtain a warrant to open a sack in a movable vehicle when they lack probable cause to search the entire car?

Held. No. Judgment reversed.

♦ *United States v. Ross*, 456 U.S. 798 (1982), held that a warrantless search of an automobile under the *Carroll* doctrine could include a search of a container or package found inside the car when the search was supported by probable cause. However, *United States v. Chadwick*, 433 U.S. 1 (1977), and *Arkansas v. Sanders*, 442 U.S. 753 (1979), held that a person expects more privacy in his luggage and personal effects than he does in his automobile, so the police may not search personal luggage merely because it is located in an automobile. These cases provided that if the police have probable cause to search personal luggage, they must obtain a warrant.

♦ A container found after a general search of an automobile and a container found in a car after a limited search for the container are equally easy for the police to store and for the suspect to hide or destroy. The distinction between probable cause to search a vehicle and probable cause to search a package in that vehicle is not always clear, and provides the police with an incentive to search the entire car instead of focusing on searching for a particular container. It does not make sense to have a rule that requires police to conduct a more intrusive search in order to justify a less intrusive one. The *Chadwick-Sanders* rule has come to mean that the more likely the police are to discover drugs in a container, the less authority they have to search it.

♦ For these reasons, the *Chadwick-Sanders* rule must be discarded in favor of a rule that the Fourth Amendment does not compel separate treatment for an automobile search that extends only to a container within the vehicle. Accordingly, the police may search a vehicle and all of its containers without a warrant if their search is supported by probable cause. If probable cause extends only to the specific container, however, the search may not extend to the entire vehicle.

Concurrence (Scalia, J.). While it is anomalous for a briefcase to be protected by the general requirement of a prior warrant until it is placed into an automobile, the Court's rule is more consistent with the Fourth Amendment and does eliminate the anomaly that previously existed whereby a locked compartment inside an automobile was less protected than an unlocked briefcase carried in the vehicle. There are many other anomalies in Fourth Amendment jurisprudence. The better approach to this case would not make the closed container subject to the "automobile" exception to the general warrant requirement, but would simply allow the search of a closed container, outside a privately owned building, based on probable cause to believe it contains contraband.

Dissent (Stevens, Marshall, JJ.). The Fourth Amendment is an important protection against police practices that prevail in totalitarian regimes, and it reflects the public policy that the decision to invade the privacy of an individual's personal effects should be made by a neutral magistrate instead of a police agent. The burden thereby imposed on the police is outweighed by the individual interest in privacy. The *Chadwick-Sanders* rule was adopted by the Court to balance the competing interests, and it should not be overruled.

---

3) **Exigent circumstances.**

    a) **Moving vehicles.** The police may stop and search a moving vehicle without a warrant if they have probable cause to believe that it contains contraband. Such a search is justified by sheer necessity, the vehicle being a "fleeting target." [*See* Carroll v. United States, *supra*]

        (1) It is immaterial whether the police had time to obtain a search warrant—the mobility of the vehicle (the fact that it may get away) justifies the immediate search.

        (2) The right to stop and search a vehicle in such cases does *not* depend on the arrest of its occupants. The police need only have probable cause to believe that the *vehicle* contains contraband, not that the occupants are guilty of criminal acts.

    b) **Vehicle taken to police station.** The right to search without a warrant continues when the police have "immobilized" the vehicle—as when they have stopped the car on the highway, arrested the occupants, and instead of searching the vehicle there, have taken it into custody. Since the search would have been lawful when the vehicle was stopped on the highway, it is lawful at the police station (regardless of whether removal of the car to the station was reasonable). [*See* Texas v. White, 423 U.S. 67 (1975)]

    c) **Parked vehicles.** Here, again, "exigent circumstances" must be shown to justify the failure to obtain a search warrant. For example, a police search of a defendant's auto (parked in his driveway) was held unlawful—although the car was believed to have been used in a crime—when it was no longer being used for any illegal purpose, there was no probable cause to believe it contained contraband or other evidence subject to seizure, and the police had ample opportunity to obtain a warrant but failed to do so. [*See* Coolidge v. New Hampshire, *supra*—the defendant had been arrested, so his car was not likely to be moved]

        (1) However, recovery of the ***getaway car*** shortly after commission of a robbery involves exigent circumstances justifying a search for clues as to the identity or location of suspects.

        (2) A few courts have suggested that probable cause (without exigent circumstances) may be sufficient to justify a search of parked vehicles, but this is a minority view.

  4) **Privacy interests.** Further elucidation of the *Chambers* and *Coolidge* cases was given by the Supreme Court in *Cardwell v. Lewis*, 417 U.S. 583 (1974), where the Court held that since no consideration of the owner's privacy interest was involved, police having probable cause could impound a vehicle and search its exterior (here taking a paint scratching and a print of the rear tires) without a warrant.

b. **Delayed search of contents of vehicle.** In *United States v. Johns*, 469 U.S. 478 (1985), the Court ruled that if the police have probable cause to search containers found in an automobile, they need not do so immediately unless the delay adversely affects legitimate privacy interests.

c. **"Controlled deliveries."** The "border search" rule permits the authorities to open containers shipped into the country. If the container has contraband, the police may close it and deliver it to the owner—and may then reopen it ***without a warrant*** if there is no "substantial likelihood" that its contents have been changed by the owner during some gap in the police control of the container. In such circumstances, the owner has no legitimate expectation of privacy in the previously law-fully searched container. [*Illinois v. Andreas*, 463 U.S. 765 (1983)]

    d.   Vehicle search when driver outside car--

Thornton v. United States, 541 U.S. 615 (2004).

Facts. A police officer, suspicious of Thornton (D), checked D's license plates and discovered they were issued for a different vehicle. Just then, D drove into a parking lot, parked, and left the vehicle. The officer stopped D and asked whether D had illegal drugs with him. D pulled out marijuana and cocaine. The officer handcuffed D and put him in the patrol car. The officer then searched D's vehicle and found a handgun under the driver's seat. The search was upheld as constitutional. The Fourth Circuit affirmed. The Supreme Court granted certiorari.

Issue. Where an officer arrests a defendant who has already exited his vehicle, may the officer then search the passenger compartment of the vehicle?

Held. Yes. Judgment affirmed.

♦   Under *New York v. Belton*, 453 U.S. 454 (1981), a police officer who makes a lawful custodial arrest of an automobile's occupant may also search the passenger compartment as a contemporaneous incident of the arrest. The rationale was based on *Chimel, supra*, which recognized the need to remove weapons an arrestee might use to resist arrest or escape, and the need to prevent the concealment or destruction of evidence.

♦   The area within an arrestee's immediate control does not depend on whether the officer initiates contact while the person is in the car. A suspect who is next to a vehicle presents the same concerns about officer safety and destruction of evidence as a suspect who is inside the car. It may make more sense for an officer to hide until the suspect exits his vehicle, and the scope of an incidental search should not depend on this decision.

♦   Officers need a clear rule to follow, not dependent on different estimates of what might be within the reach of an arrestee at any particular moment. Thus, once an officer determines that there is probable cause to make an arrest, the officer may search the entire passenger compartment to ensure safety and preserve evidence.

Concurrence (O'Connor, J.). Justice Scalia's approach would be an improvement to existing law, but it was not addressed by the parties to this case.

Concurrence (Scalia, Ginsburg, JJ.). When the officer searched D's car, D was handcuffed in the back of the patrol car. There was only an extremely remote risk that D would grab a weapon or evidentiary item from his car. There has never been a case of a handcuffed suspect retrieving arms or evidence from his car. The only justification for *Belton* searches is to gather evidence relevant to the crime for which the suspect is arrested. *Belton* searches should therefore be limited to cases where it is reasonable to believe evidence relevant to the crime of arrest might be found in the vehicle. This is such a case.

Dissent (Stevens, Souter, JJ.). The extension of *Belton* to cases where the suspect has already left the car at the time of arrest is justified only to uncover evidence, but this goal should yield to the citizen's privacy interest. This broadening of the automobile exception is not justified.

---

e.   **Inventory searches--**

Colorado v. Bertine, 479 U.S. 367 (1987).

Facts. Bertine (D) was arrested for DUI and was taken into custody. The police conducted an inventory search of D's vehicle before the tow truck arrived to take the vehicle to an impoundment lot. The search included an examination of the contents of a closed backpack, including drugs, paraphernalia, and cash. D was charged with drug offenses in addition to the DUI. D's suppression motion was granted under Colorado law, and specifically not under the Fourth Amendment. The Colorado Supreme Court affirmed on interlocutory appeal, but relied on the Fourth Amendment. The Supreme Court granted certiorari.

Issue. May items discovered during a proper inventory search, even of the contents of a closed bag, be used in evidence in a criminal prosecution?

Held. Yes. Judgment reversed.

♦   Inventory searches are a clear exception to the Fourth Amendment warrant requirement. Such a search is a routine, noncriminal procedure, so long as it is not a subterfuge for criminal investigation.

♦   The Court upheld an inventory search of an automobile in *South Dakota v. Opperman*, 428 U.S. 364 (1976), and an inventory search of the personal effects of an arrestee at a police station in *Illinois v. Lafayette*, *supra*. The cases cited by the Colorado Supreme Court involved criminal investigations, not inventory searches.

♦   In this case, there was no indication that the police acted in bad faith or for the sole purpose of investigation. As in other inventory search situations, the police were potentially responsible for the property they took into custody, and had to guard against any danger that could have been posed to themselves or the public by the property. It does not matter that the vehicle was subsequently towed to a secure, lighted facility. The Fourth Amendment does not require any resort to alternatives to an inventory search or less intrusive means such as applying a balancing test.

Concurrence (Blackmun, Powell, O'Connor, JJ.). The police are justified in inventorying closed containers only if their standard procedures mandate the opening of such containers in every impounded vehicle.

Dissent (Marshall, Brennan, JJ.). The officer who conducted the inventory in this case exercised his own individual discretion in deciding to inventory the vehicle instead of parking and locking it. His discretion was not limited by any standardized criteria. He could have allowed a third party to take custody, or he could have parked and locked the car; in either case, he could not conduct an inventory of closed containers unless there was an indication that they contained valuables or a weapon. The search was not a caretaking function, but a discretionary act that presents an unreasonable danger of abuse of discretion. In fact, the officer's "inventory" failed to include numerous items of value.

Comment. On remand in *Opperman*, the South Dakota Supreme Court held that the inventory search violated the state constitution.

---

8. **Stop and Frisk.** An "arrest" implies restraint of a person. However, not all restraints have been held to be arrests. A police officer who reasonably concludes that preventive action to protect himself or others is called for is privileged to stop a person for investigation. If facts would reasonably lead the officer to believe that the suspect may be armed, he may also conduct a carefully limited search of the outer clothing for weapons and may seize any weapons so uncovered. Such a "stop and frisk" is permissible even if the officer does not have probable cause to make an arrest.

    a. **Limited right to stop and frisk--**

Terry v. Ohio, 392 U.S. 1 (1968).

Facts. An experienced police officer saw Terry (D) and another person walking back and forth in front of a store window very early in the morning. The officer stopped D and "patted him down," feeling a gun in the process. D was convicted of carrying a concealed weapon and appealed. Admittedly the police did not have "probable cause" to arrest D. The state supreme court affirmed the conviction and D appeals to the Supreme Court.

Issue. Is a stop and frisk by a police officer constitutionally permissible when the officer has neither probable cause nor a warrant?

Held. Yes. Judgment affirmed.

♦ Police must be granted a limited license to stop and frisk; the Fourth Amendment countenances a "frisk" or "patdown" but only when a police officer observes unusual conduct that leads him reasonably to conclude (*i.e.,* the reasonable person test), in light of his experience as a police officer, that criminal activity may be afoot and that the persons with whom he is dealing may be armed and presently dangerous; and where in the course of investigating this behavior he identifies himself as a police officer and makes reasonable inquiries; and where nothing in the initial stages of the encounter serves to dispel his reasonable fear of his own or others' safety.

♦ Moreover, in these limited circumstances the police are entitled only to conduct a carefully limited search of the outer clothing of such persons in an attempt to discover weapons that might be used to assault the police. Anything beyond this limited stopping and searching is unreasonable and prohibited by the Fourth Amendment.

Concurrence (Harlan, J.). A "frisk" can occur only after a permissible stopping, which could occur on less than probable cause if the circumstances would reasonably lead an experienced police officer to suspect that a person was about to commit a crime.

Concurrence (White, J.). The Constitution does not prevent a police officer from asking questions of anyone on the streets. The person addressed may refuse to cooperate and walk by without being detained or frisked. But in circumstances such as those in this case, the person may be briefly detained against his will to be asked questions, but the person still need not cooperate.

Dissent (Douglas, J.). The police could not have obtained a warrant in this case because they lacked probable cause. Now the Court says the police have greater authority to make a "seizure" and conduct a "search" than a judge has to authorize such action.

---

    b.   **Police action short of a seizure.** The Court has reaffirmed the constitutionality of a police officer approaching an individual and asking questions. In *Florida v. Bostick*, 501 U.S. 429 (1991), two police officers approached Bostick, a bus passenger, and asked to see his ticket and identification. Bostick provided them, and they were in order. The police then told Bostick they were narcotics agents looking for illegal drugs, and asked for Bostick's consent to search his luggage. Bostick gave his consent, and the police found drugs in the luggage. The Court held that this encounter did not trigger Fourth Amendment scrutiny because it was entirely consensual. The fact that Bostick did not feel free to leave the bus did not make the encounter a seizure. His freedom of movement was restricted by his being a passenger on the bus, not by any action of the police. The dissenting Justices considered the intimidating show of authority to suffice to make the encounter a seizure. Bostick had a choice of remaining seated while refusing to respond to the officers, or of trying to escape the officers by leaving the bus. The whole purpose of the encounter on the bus was to pressure passengers to consent.

c. **No seizure without control.** In *California v. Hodari D.*, 499 U.S. 621 (1991), the Court held that a person who flees from an encounter with the police has not been arrested. Hodari D. had fled when he saw a police car approach. He was pursued on foot and threw away a small object, which turned out to be crack cocaine. The state court deemed the cocaine to be the fruit of an illegal seizure. The Court reversed, noting that a seizure cannot occur if the subject does not yield, whether the police merely show authority or actually apply physical force.

d. **Grounds for temporary seizure to investigate.** In *Sibron v. New York*, 392 U.S. 40 (1968), the Court held that a frisk that recovered heroin was unlawful because there were no facts supporting a reasonable belief that the defendant was armed and dangerous. In *Alabama v. White*, 496 U.S. 325 (1990), the Court upheld a stop based on information provided by an anonymous tipster to the effect that the individual would drive a particular vehicle to a specific location and would be in possession of cocaine in a specific attaché case. The individual's actions were consistent with the tip. The Court held that the tip satisfied the reasonable suspicion standard, even if it would not have satisfied the probable cause standard.

e. **Police bulletin or flyer.** In *United States v. Hensley*, 469 U.S. 221 (1985), the Supreme Court held that a police officer need not have personal knowledge of the evidence creating a reasonable suspicion when making a stop and frisk in reliance on a flyer or bulletin issued by other police. The Court held that such a stop and frisk is valid as long as the bulletin has been issued on the basis of proper evidence.

f. **Least intrusive.** An investigatory stop must be temporary and no longer than necessary to effectuate its purpose. The investigative methods must be the least intrusive reasonably available to verify or dispel the officer's suspicion. [Florida v. Royer, 460 U.S. 491 (1983)—removal of detainee without his consent from public area in airport to police room in airport converted "stop" to "seizure"] However, it is not a seizure for police in a car to drive alongside a pedestrian a short distance. [Michigan v. Chesternut, 486 U.S. 567 (1988)]

g. **Seizure incident to a "stop."** If the police have a reasonable suspicion (the standard for making a "stop") that a person's luggage contains narcotics, they may detain the unopened luggage *temporarily* to investigate the circumstances. Although this is a "seizure" within the meaning of the Fourth Amendment, the strong government interest outweighs the minimal intrusion. [United States v. Place, 462 U.S. 696 (1983)—90-minute detention of luggage unreasonable under the circumstances]

h. **Stop and frisk on informer's tip.** In *Adams v. Williams,* 407 U.S. 143 (1972), a police officer received a tip from an informer (known to him), given near the scene of the arrest, that Williams was armed and sitting in a car. The police officer went to the car and asked Williams to roll down the window; then the officer reached into the car and took the concealed weapon, not visible from outside the car, from under Williams's coat. Williams was then arrested for unlawful possession of a gun. A search incident to the subsequent arrest disclosed heroin and other contraband on Williams and in the vehicle. The Court held that this was a reasonable investigatory stop and protective search. The informer's information had sufficient reliability to justify a forcible detention and protective search. The "reasonable belief" required by *Terry* for stop and frisk need not be based on personal observation by the police but can be based on an unnamed informer's tip that has some reliability, although such is not sufficient to constitute probable cause for a valid arrest or search warrant. It is noteworthy that the informer could be arrested for "false complaint" if the information was not correct and the informer was known to the police officer personally. This is not the same thing as a tip by an anonymous phone caller.

i. **"Protective" search.** If the police have lawfully detained an automobile and have an "articulable suspicion" that an occupant may gain immediate control of weapons, then the police may—before the suspect reenters the auto—search those parts of the passenger area that may contain weapons. [Michigan v. Long, 463 U.S. 1032 (1983)]

j. **Other brief detention for investigation—fingerprinting.** *Davis v. Mississippi,* 394 U.S. 721 (1969), suggested that perhaps detention for fingerprinting may be made, consistent with the Fourth Amendment, under "narrowly circumscribed procedures," when there is less than probable cause to arrest. The Court noted that such detention may constitute a much less serious intrusion upon personal security and be subject to fewer abuses than other types of police searches and detentions.

9. **Administrative Inspections and Regulatory Searches.**

a. **Inspection of premises.** In *Camara v. Municipal Court*, 387 U.S. 523 (1967), the Court held that the Fourth Amendment requires that a warrant procedure be employed, in the absence of an emergency situation (such as involved in the seizure of unwholesome food), for administrative inspections of commercial and residential premises pursuant to fire, health, and housing regulations, unless the consent of the occupant has been obtained. Such a warrant need not be based on a finding that there is "probable cause" to believe that conditions in a particular dwelling violate the regulations; rather warrants may issue (usually only after the occupant refuses entry, unless there has been a citizen complaint or other satisfactory reason for securing immediate entry) on reasonable need to conduct periodic, area-wide inspections. What is "reasonable need" for such area inspections "will vary with the municipal program being enforced, [and] may be based on the passage of time, the nature of the building, or the condition of the entire area."

b. Border searches and vehicle checkpoints.

1) Routine searches. In *Almeida-Sanchez v. United States*, 413 U.S. 266 (1973), the Court held that the search of a car by a "roving patrol," without either consent, a warrant, or probable cause, on a road more than 20 miles from the border, violated the Fourth Amendment. However, the Court stated that "routine" searches of persons and their effects at an international border or its functional equivalent (*i.e.,* at an established station near the border or at a place where an airplane first lands in the United States) may be made without a warrant or probable cause.

2) Traffic checkpoints. At established traffic checkpoints removed from the border and its functional equivalents, private vehicles may not be searched without consent or probable cause. The Court left as an open question whether a vehicle may be stopped for questioning at an established checkpoint without reason to believe (*i.e.,* with less than probable cause) that it is carrying illegal aliens. [United States v. Ortiz, 422 U.S. 891 (1975)]

3) Boats. Congress may authorize customs officials—without any suspicion of wrongdoing—to make the "limited intrusion" of boarding a boat, in waters with ready access to the open sea, to inspect its documents. *Rationale:* The nature of sea vessels, in contrast to automobiles, does not lend itself (i) to establishing fixed checkpoints or roadblocks, or (ii) to prescribed external markings (*e.g.,* license plates) disclosing compliance with legal requirements. [United States v. Villamonte-Marquez, 462 U.S. 579 (1983)]

4) Fixed checkpoints. In *United States v. Martinez-Fuerte*, 428 U.S. 543 (1976), the Court held that a vehicle may be stopped at a fixed checkpoint away from the international border, for the purpose of briefly questioning its occupants, without reason to believe the vehicle contains illegal aliens. In contrast to the concerns expressed in *Almeida-Sanchez* regarding inspections by roving patrol units, routine checkpoint stops do not intrude similarly on the motoring public. In some situations, as discussed in *Camara*, the governmental interests involved in the inspection simply outweigh those of the private citizen, even in the absence of individualized suspicion. Although selective-referral inspection may be somewhat annoying, because of its public and routine nature, it should not prove frightening or offensive.

c.   **Search of students.** The Fourth Amendment applies to searches conducted by public school officials of students, including the purses or bags they carry. In *New Jersey v. T.L.O.*, 469 U.S. 325 (1985), the Court ruled that it was reasonable for officials to search a student's purse after a teacher had accused the student of smoking in school in violation of school rules. The standard, the Court ruled, for a school official's search of a student is "reasonableness under all of the circumstances." Such a search will ordinarily be justified if there are "reasonable grounds for suspecting" that it will turn up evidence of violation of the law or school rules. The scope of the search will be permissible if it is reasonably related to its objectives and "not excessively intrusive in light of the age and sex of the student and the nature of the infraction."

d.   **Search of parolees--**

Samson v. California, 547 U.S. 843 (2006).

Facts. Samson (D) was on parole after being convicted for possessing a firearm as a felon. Conditions of his parole included an agreement, consistent with California law, to be subject to search or seizure by a parole officer or other peace officer at any time of the day or night, with or without a search warrant and with or without cause. An officer who recognized D stopped him on the street and asked if D had any parole warrants outstanding. D said no. The officer verified this over his radio but searched D anyway. He found methamphetamine on D. D was tried for possession. D sought to suppress the results of the search, but the trial court denied his motion. D was convicted. He appealed, but the state appellate court upheld the conviction. The Supreme Court granted certiorari.

Issue. May a condition of release eliminate a parolee's reasonable expectation of privacy such that a suspicionless search by a police officer is not a violation of the Fourth Amendment?

Held. Yes. Judgment affirmed.

♦   The Fourth Amendment requires examination of the totality of the circumstances to determine whether a search is reasonable. This requires a balancing of the degree of intrusion on an individual's privacy against the degree to which the search is needed to promote legitimate governmental interests.

♦ In *United States v. Knights*, 534 U.S. 112 (2001), this Court held that a probationer's home could be searched without a warrant, based on police suspicion that he had been involved in vandalism and arson. We said that probation is one point on the continuum of possible punishments ranging from solitary confinement to community service. Probationers do not enjoy the absolute liberty that law-abiding citizens enjoy. Knights's probation order clearly set out the probation search condition, and Knights was clearly informed of the condition. Thus, Knights had a diminished expectation of privacy. Probation searches are necessary to the promotion of legitimate governmental interests. The government has a dual interest in integrating probationers back into the community and in combating recidivism. Probationers have more incentive to conceal their criminal activities and to quickly dispose of evidence than the ordinary criminal because probationers are subject to supervision and face revocation of probation. Thus, the police could search without a warrant, based on reasonable suspicion.

♦ This case is similar to *Knights* except that here the officer acted without reasonable suspicion and D was a parolee instead of a probationer. On the punishment continuum, parolees have fewer expectations of privacy than probationers because parole is more like imprisonment. A parolee is in the legal custody of the state and must comply with strict conditions that severely diminish his expectations of privacy by virtue of his status alone. And D signed an order submitting to the condition of being subject to suspicionless searches by any police officer at any time. D did not have a legitimate expectation of privacy.

♦ The state has a strong interest in close supervision of parolees. California's parolee population has a 68% to 70% recidivism rate. California's ability to conduct suspicionless searches of parolees serves its interest in reducing recidivism in a manner that aids, rather than hinders, the reintegration of parolees into society. If individualized suspicion were required, the state's ability to effectively supervise parolees and protect the public from criminal acts by recidivists would be undermined. Parolees would have greater opportunity to anticipate searches and conceal criminality. The incentive to conceal is even greater for parolees than for probationers.

♦ D points out that the majority of states and the federal government have systems that require that parolee searches are based on some level of suspicion. D argues that California's system is constitutionally defective. However, the requirement of some states and the federal government that there be a level of individualized suspicion is of little relevance to whether California's supervisory system meets its needs and is reasonable.

♦ Finally, officers do not have unbridled discretion to search parolees, because California prohibits arbitrary, capricious, or harassing searches.

Dissent (Stevens, Souter, Breyer, JJ.).

♦ The Fourth Amendment has always provided some degree of protection for probationers and parolees, even if it is less than that provided to ordinary citizens. No precedent supports a regime of suspicionless searches. This is the very evil the Fourth Amendment was intended to eliminate.

♦ Individualized suspicion has been dispensed with only when programmatic searches were required to meet a "special need," divorced from the state's general interest in law enforcement. The majority does not contend that there are special needs in this case. Even if the supervisory relationship between a probation officer and the probationer may properly be characterized as one giving rise to needs divorced from the state's general interest in law enforcement, the relationship between an ordinary law enforcement officer and a probationer unknown to him does not. In special needs cases, there must be programmatic safeguards to ensure evenhandedness—measures to protect against the state actor's unfettered discretion. Here, there are no standards, guidelines, or procedures to protect against the arbitrary exercise of discretion.

♦ The logic that prisoners have no legitimate expectation of privacy, that parolees are like prisoners, and that, therefore, parolees have no legitimate expectation of privacy rests on false premises. A parolee's status is not tantamount to that of a prisoner or even materially distinct from that of a probationer. It is untrue that a parolee legitimately expects only so much privacy as a prisoner. The traditional Fourth Amendment right of privacy is denied those who are incarcerated because of the institutional needs and objectives of prison facilities. These institutional needs do not apply to parolees.

---

10. **Consent Searches.**

   a. **Nature of consent--**

Schneckloth v. Bustamonte, 412 U.S. 218 (1973).

Facts. Bustamonte (D) and five others were in a car with a burned-out headlight. Police stopped the car; the driver had no license. A passenger, Alcala, had a license and told the police the car was his brother's. The police asked if they could search the car; Alcala said yes and opened the trunk, where the police found stolen checks. D was convicted of theft and appeals.

Issue. In order for a defendant's consent to be voluntary, must he be warned that he is under no obligation to give his consent?

Held. No. Conviction sustained.

♦ The consent was voluntary (*i.e.,* not the result of duress or coercion). Voluntariness is determined from all the surrounding circumstances. While a defendant's knowledge of his right to refuse consent is one factor to be taken into account, it is not an absolute prerequisite to voluntariness—at least when the defendant is not in custody.

Dissent (Marshall, J.). I would hold that the prosecutor may not rely on purported consent if the subject of the search did not know that he could refuse to give consent.

---

    b.   **Who can consent?** The easiest cases are those where the defendant is alleged to have given his consent for himself. The more difficult cases involve third parties giving consent for the defendant.

        1)   In *Stoner v. California*, 376 U.S. 483 (1964), the Supreme Court held that search of a defendant's hotel room without his consent, with neither search nor arrest warrants, violated his constitutional rights, despite police having received consent from the hotel clerk.

        2)   But the court has permitted consent to apply when one occupant of an apartment has given his consent while the other occupant was absent.

    c.   **Consent of third party—common authority or sufficient relationship.** In *United States v. Matlock*, 415 U.S. 164 (1974), the Court stated that effective consent to a warrantless search may be given either by the accused or by any third party who possesses common authority or other sufficient relationship to the premises or effects sought to be inspected. "Common authority" rests on mutual use of the property by persons generally having joint access or control, so that each may be deemed to have assumed the risk that the other would permit the common area to be searched. For example, family members or other persons who share a house or apartment may have sufficient joint access and control over the premises so that the consent of either occupant is effective against the absent, nonconsenting person with whom the premises are shared.

    d.   **Reasonable belief--**

Illinois v. Rodriguez, 497 U.S. 177 (1990).

Facts. Fischer told police she had been assaulted by Rodriguez (D) in what she referred to as "our" apartment. She showed signs of a severe beating. She told the police D was asleep in the apartment and that she had a key with which she could let them into the apartment. Fischer said she had clothes and furniture in the apartment. She accompanied the police to the apartment, unlocked the door, and gave the officers permission to enter. Upon entering, the officers saw drug paraphernalia and white powder in plain view. They arrested D and seized the drugs. D was charged with possession with intent to deliver. He moved to suppress the evidence on the ground that Fischer had moved out of the apartment several weeks earlier and had no authority to consent to the entry. The trial court granted the motion. The Illinois Court of Appeals affirmed. The Supreme Court granted certiorari.

Issue. If the police enter a dwelling based on the reasonable but mistaken belief that a third party who consented to the entry had authority to consent, may evidence found inside be used against the resident of the dwelling?

Held. Yes. Judgment reversed and case remanded.

♦   The Fourth Amendment does not prohibit the warrantless entry of a dwelling when voluntary consent has been obtained, either from the individual whose property is searched, or from a third party who possesses common authority over the premises.

♦   Common authority rests on mutual use of the property by persons generally having joint access or control for most purposes. In this case, Fischer had lived in the apartment, but had moved out before the search. She had a key, but she had taken it without D's knowledge. Thus, Fischer did not have common authority over D's apartment.

♦   The Fourth Amendment protects only against "unreasonable" searches. A search is reasonable if it is done with the consent of the person. A factual determination made by agents of the government need not be correct, so long as it is reasonable. The issue is not whether the right to be free of searches has been waived by D, but whether the right to be free of unreasonable searches has been violated. If the officers' determination of consent to enter would "warrant a man of reasonable caution in the belief" that the consenting party had authority over the premises, then the search was valid.

♦   On remand, the court must determine whether the officers reasonably believed that Fischer had the authority to consent.

Dissent (Marshall, Brennan, Stevens, JJ.). Third-party consent searches are not based on an exigency and serve no compelling social goal. If faced with the choice of relying on third-party consent or securing a warrant, they should secure a warrant or accept the risk of error should the third party giving consent turn out not to have authority to do so.

C. UNDERCOVER INVESTIGATIONS

    1.   **Secret Agents.** Law enforcement relies on undercover investigations to uncover conspiracies, trafficking in illegal drugs, and other crimes such as prostitution. The people who work undercover are either disguised police or confidential informants who are private citizens who have a motive for working with the police.

a. **Legal status.** Because they work for the police, confidential informants are state actors whose activities, like those of undercover police, are subject to the Fourth Amendment. Questions of admissibility arise when the police plant a transmitter or recording device on the informer to listen to incriminating statements. In such cases, the informer's own testimony is admissible. Alternatively, the police who overhear the conversations can testify about them, and recordings are admissible to corroborate the testimony of both the informer and the police who listen in.

b. **Incriminating statements in the presence of a confidential informant--**

Hoffa v. United States, 385 U.S. 293 (1966).

Facts. Hoffa (D), the president of the International Brotherhood of Teamsters, was tried for violating a provision of the Taft-Hartley Act. The trial, known as the Test Fleet trial, ended with a hung jury. D and three others were later tried and convicted for trying to bribe the jury, based in part on testimony from Partin, a Teamsters Union official, who accompanied D during the Test Fleet trial at D's hotel suite, in the courthouse, and elsewhere. Partin made frequent reports to a federal agent concerning D's conversations about bribing the jury. Before the Test Fleet trial, Partin was in jail on a state criminal charge and was under a federal indictment for embezzling union funds. He was released on bail on the state criminal charge, and proceedings under the federal indictment were postponed before Partin's initial meeting with D. After the Test Fleet trial, Partin's wife received payments from government funds, and the charges against Partin were either dropped or were not actively pursued. D claimed that Partin's testimony should have been excluded. The Supreme Court granted certiorari.

Issue. Does the Fourth Amendment protect a wrongdoer against testimony by a confidential informant in whom the wrongdoer confided?

Held. No. Judgment affirmed.

♦   D claims that Partin's failure to disclose that he was a government informer vitiated D's consent to Partin's entries into D's hotel suite. D contends that by listening to D's statements under these circumstances, Partin conducted an illegal "search" for verbal evidence.

♦   It is true that a hotel room is a constitutionally protected area and that the Fourth Amendment can apply to oral statements as well as tangibles. However, the Fourth Amendment protects against unwarranted governmental intrusion, but in this case, D was not relying on the security of his hotel suite when he made incriminating statements to Partin. Partin was not a surreptitious eavesdropper; he was an invitee. D was not relying on the security of the hotel room, but on his misplaced confidence that Partin would not reveal his wrongdoing. The Fourth Amendment does not protect a wrongdoer's misplaced belief that a person to whom he voluntarily confides his wrongdoing will not reveal it.

♦ D also makes a due process claim that the government's conduct in this case offends canons of decency and fairness under *Rochin v. California, supra*. However, courts have always allowed the use of informers, and in cases of conspiracy or when the crime consists of preparing for another crime, it is usually necessary to rely on informers or accomplices. Although Partin may have had motives to lie, this does not mean that his testimony was untrue or was constitutionally inadmissible. A witness's testimony is subject to cross-examination and his credibility is determined by a properly instructed jury.

Dissent (Warren, C.J.).

♦ It cannot be said that every use of an informer is proper or that it is never proper. But to ensure that the protections of the Constitution are respected and to maintain the integrity of federal law enforcement, this Court should give careful scrutiny to practices of government agents when they are challenged in cases before us.

♦ Partin contacted federal authorities while he was in jail and offered to become an informer against D. His motive was to get out of jail and out of his legal entanglements with the state and federal governments, which were more serious than the indictment against D. After becoming part of D's entourage, Partin was in a position to overhear conversations not directed to him, including those between attorneys and defense witnesses. The government paid him well, through secret payments to his wife and, presumably, by promises not to pursue his prior indictments. Using such an informer raises a serious potential for undermining the integrity of the truth-finding process, and his testimony should not be allowed to become the primary basis for a conviction. This Court need not reach D's constitutional arguments because the affront to the quality and fairness of federal law enforcement presented here requires the Court to exercise its supervisory powers.

———————

c. **Electronic Eavesdropping.** In *United States v. White*, 401 U.S. 745 (1971), the Court stated that, for constitutional purposes, there is no difference between a government agent writing down his conversations with a defendant and testifying concerning them or carrying radio equipment that records the conversations or transmits them to other agents. The Court noted that an electronic recording is often more reliable than the unaided memory of an agent. In his dissent, Justice Harlan asserted that warrants should be necessary for the more extensive intrusions, such as electronic eavesdropping, which significantly jeopardize the sense of security that is the paramount concern of Fourth Amendment liberties.

2. The Entrapment Defense.

a. **Police and informer "encouragement."** The police or their agent "encourage" the commission of a crime by: (i) acting as a willing participant in the commission of a crime; (ii) communicating this feigned willingness to the suspect; and (iii) thereby having some influence on the suspect's commission of the crime.

1) **First case.** The entrapment defense was first recognized in *Sorrells v. United States*, 287 U.S. 435 (1932), in which the Court held that the defense focuses on the intent or predisposition of the defendant to commit the crime. Entrapment occurs when law enforcement officers instigate a criminal act by persons otherwise innocent in order to lure them to its commission and to punish them. A concurring opinion in that case would have closed the courts to any trial of a crime instigated by government agents.

2) **Use in certain class of crimes.** "Encouragement" is used in the detection of a certain class of crimes—prostitution, liquor sales, narcotics, gambling, etc.—because they are committed privately with a willing person who will not complain, thus making normal detection impossible.

a) **Necessity of use.** The practice is commonly used only after the police have a reasonable suspicion that a person or institution is currently engaged in the commission of a crime. Police may use these unconventional methods to get the proof required for arrest even if they have enough for "reasonable suspicion" because: (i) the quality of evidence to show probable cause might not otherwise be obtainable; or (ii) police might be able to get evidence to show probable cause but not enough to show guilt beyond a reasonable doubt (enough to convict).

b) **Problem.** Questions arise about distinguishing encouragement from entrapment; *i.e.,* what types of inducements are proper?

b. **Tests for entrapment.**

1) **Overcoming initial refusal to commit a crime--**

Sherman v. United States, 356 U.S. 369 (1958).

Facts. Sherman (D) met Kalchinian at a doctor's office where the two were being treated for addiction to narcotics. They ran into each other several more times and began discussing their efforts to overcome addiction. Finally, Kalchinian started asking D if he knew of a source of drugs. D tried to avoid the issue, but Kalchinian persisted, claiming that he was suffering. D obtained the drugs and shared them with Kalchinian. Kalchinian eventually informed government agents, who observed three sales of drugs by D to Kalchinian. D was tried and claimed entrapment as a defense. The jury convicted D. The Second Circuit affirmed. The Supreme Court granted certiorari.

Issue. Where a government agent overcomes a person's initial refusal to commit a crime by resorting to repeated persuasion and an appeal to sympathy, does the agent's conduct constitute entrapment?

Held. Yes. Judgment reversed.

♦ As recognized in *Sorrells*, *supra*, the defense of entrapment is available in federal court and applies when government officials implant in the mind of an innocent person the disposition to commit an offense and induce its commission so they may prosecute.

♦ Entrapment does not arise solely because government agents merely afford opportunities for the commission of the crime. The criminal conduct must be "the product of the creative activity" of law enforcement officials. The difference is between a trap for the unwary innocent and a trap for the unwary criminal.

♦ The facts in this case established entrapment as a matter of law. Kalchinian resorted to sympathy and persistence to overcome D's initial refusal, then his evasiveness and his hesitancy to get drugs. Kalchinian also induced D to return to his own habit of use. Kalchinian had instigated at least two previous prosecutions. Although the government did not pay Kalchinian, he was likely motivated to cooperate with the government because he was under criminal charges for illegally selling drugs and had not yet been sentenced.

♦ The government contends that D was ready and willing to sell drugs. However, there is no evidence to support this contention. When D's apartment was searched, no drugs were found. And although D had two prior narcotics convictions, one was a nine-year-old sales conviction and the other was a five-year-old possession conviction. This is insufficient to prove that D was ready to sell drugs when Kalchinian approached him, especially since D was trying to overcome his habit at that time.

♦ The government played on D's weakness and beguiled him into committing crimes he otherwise would not have attempted.

Concurrence (Frankfurter, Douglas, Harlan, Brennan, JJ.).

♦ The courts do not allow entrapped defendants to be convicted because such governmental methods cannot be countenanced, even if the defendant's conduct falls within the criminal statute. The obligation to apply proper standards for the enforcement of the federal criminal law in federal courts goes beyond the conviction of a particular defendant before the court. Public confidence in the fair and honorable administration of justice is the transcending value at stake.

♦ Criminal statutes define and prohibit the substantive offense. A statute prohibiting the sale of narcotics is silent on the issue of entrapment. We cannot look to a statute for guidance in the application of a policy that was not within the contemplation of Congress when it enacted the statute.

♦ The crucial question is whether the police conduct in a particular case fell below standards for the proper use of governmental power. It is irrelevant whether the "intention" to commit the crime originated with the defendant or with government officers. In every case of this kind, the intention that the crime be committed originates with the police, and without their inducement, the crime would not have been committed. There is no entrapment if the police simply provide the opportunity for the commission of the crime.

♦ The test for entrapment should focus on whether the police conduct would induce to the commission of crime those who would normally avoid crime, not any particular defendant's character disposition, for that involves prejudicial evidence of prior crimes. Determinations of entrapment are appropriate for the court, rather than a jury, to make. It is the province of the court to protect itself and the government from the debasement of the criminal law and the violation of the principles of justice.

---

2) **Meaning of "inducement."** In *United States v. Gendron*, 18 F.3d 955 (1st Cir. 1994), the court stated that an inducement consists of an opportunity plus something else, which is typically excessive pressure on a defendant by the government or the government's taking advantage of an alternative, non-criminal type of motive. The court explained that a "sting" that combines an ordinary opportunity with these extra elements may catch, not only those who might have committed the crime in the absence of the sting, but also those who would not have done so in its absence. Also, the court gave examples of improper inducements, such as where a government official: used intimidation and threats against a defendant's family; called and threatened the defendant; and told the defendant that she was suicidal and in desperate need of money.

3) Supplying an essential ingredient for commission of a crime--

United States v. Russell, 411 U.S. 423 (1973).

Facts. An undercover agent agreed with Russell (D) to supply propanone, an essential ingredient of methamphetamine, which was difficult for D to obtain, in return for one-half of the methamphetamine D produced. The agent provided the chemical; D produced the methamphetamine and gave the agent one-half; and D was convicted of unlawfully manufacturing and selling methamphetamine. D claimed that the extent of the agent's involvement denied D due process, even if D had been predisposed to commit the offense. The Ninth Circuit reversed. The Supreme Court granted certiorari.

Issue. May a conviction for a criminal offense be upheld even when a government agent supplied a necessary ingredient for the commission of the crime?

Held. Yes. Judgment reversed.

♦ The agent's contribution of propanone to the criminal enterprise already in progress does not violate fundamental fairness and is not objectionable. Agents' infiltration of drug rings and limited participation in the unlawful enterprise is a common and practicable means of gathering evidence. But an agent will not be taken into the confidence of the criminals unless he offers them something of value.

♦ Entrapment is a relatively limited defense. It is based on the notion that Congress did not intend criminal punishment for a defendant who committed all of the elements of a crime but was induced to do so by the government. The judiciary does not have the authority to dismiss a prosecution just because it feels that the law enforcement officers were overzealous.

♦ D was an active participant in manufacturing the drug before and after the agent's appearance on the scene. His predisposition to commit the charged offenses is supported by the evidence. In the words of *Sherman, supra*, D was not an "unwary innocent," but an "unwary criminal."

Dissent (Stewart, Brennan, Marshall, JJ.). The approach that focuses on the actions of the governmental agents is an objective one, and is more consistent with the rationale of the defense, which is to prevent unlawful governmental activity in instigating crime. Any person who commits an offense is not "innocent," and no one would commit a crime without being to some extent predisposed to do so. Thus, it should make no difference that the successful temptor is a government agent instead of a private individual. Government activity that provides an opportunity to a person ready and willing to commit a crime is permissible; if the activity induces or instigates the commission of the crime by one who is not ready and willing to commit it, entrapment has occurred. Here the agent supplied an essential ingredient for the manufacture of the drug, which D could not have obtained otherwise.

---

3. Prolonged Government Involvement--

Jacobson v. United States, 503 U.S. 540 (1992).

Facts. Jacobson (D), a 56-year-old Nebraska resident, ordered two *Bare Boys* magazines from a California adult bookstore. The magazines contained photos of nude boys aged younger than 18, not engaged in sexual activity. The material was legal under both federal and Nebraska law, but D had expected photos of young men 18 years or older. Three months later, the Child Protection Act of 1984 was adopted, which made illegal the receipt through the mails of sexually explicit depictions of children. Postal inspectors found D's name on the bookstore's mailing list. Over the next two-and-one-half years, two government agencies used five fictitious organizations and a bogus pen pal (a government "prohibited mail specialist") to explore D's willingness to order material in violation of the Act. Many of these mailings referred to a fight against censorship and a need to protect individual rights. D responded to the various surveys and correspondence he received from the government, but he never provided evidence that he had ever intentionally possessed or been exposed to child pornography. Twenty-six months after the government started sending material to D, a bogus company used by the Postal Service invited D to send for more information about its pornography. D responded, and the company sent him a catalogue. D ordered a magazine titled *Boys Who Love Boys,* which depicted young boys engaged in various sexual activities. D was arrested after a controlled delivery of a photocopy of the magazine. A search of his home revealed material the government had sent him, but no other evidence that D collected child pornography. D was convicted. The Eighth Circuit affirmed, holding that D was not entrapped as a matter of law. The Supreme Court granted certiorari.

Issue. May the government overcome an entrapment defense when it has spent 26 months repeatedly attempting to induce a person to commit a crime when there is no evidence prior to these attempts that the individual was predisposed to commit the crime?

Held. No. Judgment reversed.

♦   The government may not originate a criminal design, give an innocent person the disposition to commit a criminal act, and then induce commission of the crime in order to prosecute. To prevail over a defense of entrapment, the prosecution must prove beyond a reasonable doubt that the defendant was disposed to commit the criminal act prior to first being approached by government agents.

♦ In this case, the government does not dispute that it induced D to commit the crime; it merely had to prove that D was predisposed to violate the law before the government intervened. If the government had merely offered D the opportunity to order child pornography through the mails and D had promptly done so, D would probably not have even been entitled to a jury instruction on entrapment.

♦ In this case, D was the target of repeated mailings for 26 months. By the time he finally ordered, he had become predisposed to break the law, but the government did not prove that D's predisposition was independent and not the product of the government's efforts over 26 months.

♦ The only evidence of predisposition prior to the investigation was D's order and receipt of the *Bare Boys* magazines, but this activity was legal at the time and is not, by itself, sufficient to show predisposition to commit illegal acts. D's responses to the government's repeated mailings do not support an inference that he would commit the crime of receiving child pornography through the mails. In this situation, rational jurors could not find beyond a reasonable doubt that D possessed the requisite predisposition prior to the government's investigation and that it existed independent of the government's repeated approaches to D.

Dissent (O'Connor, J., Rehnquist, C.J., Kennedy, Scalia, JJ.). D ordered child pornography on the only two opportunities the government gave him. The government started by sending him questionnaires to make sure he was generally interested in the subject matter, and his responses gave the government reason to think D would be interested in the illegal materials. This evidence was sufficient to allow a reasonable jury to find that D was predisposed to commit the crime. A defendant's predisposition should be evaluated as of the time the government first suggests the crime, not as of the time the government first gets involved. The government never actually suggested the crime until the point that D responded by ordering the illegal material. The majority opinion would require the government to prove a defendant's predisposition before it ever contacts him, which is a new approach to entrapment.

D. NETWORK SURVEILLANCE

The evolution of technology has created new legal concerns over the expectation of privacy in communications networks. Litigation now involves privacy in communication through such means as email, text messages, and the Internet, in addition to phone calls and postal mail. The Fourth Amendment and statutes regulate the government's collection and use of evidence obtained through these channels.

1. The Fourth Amendment.

a. Fourth Amendment rights when connected to a computer network--

United States v. Heckenkamp, 482 F.3d 1142 (9th Cir. 2007).

Facts. A computer system administrator for Qualcomm Corporation in San Diego discovered that someone had hacked into Qualcomm's computer network. He traced the intrusion to a computer on the network of the University of Wisconsin. He contacted FBI agent Rankhorn and the university's computer help desk. Savoy, the university's network investigator, discovered that someone using a computer on the university network was hacking into Qualcomm's system and had also gained unauthorized access to the university's system. Savoy was concerned that the user had gained access to a server on the university's system that housed accounts for 60,000 individuals on campus and processed approximately 250,000 emails each day. He traced the unauthorized access to a computer with an Internet Protocol ("IP") address ending in 117. Savoy determined that the computer at that IP address had been used regularly to check the email account of Heckenkamp (D), a computer science graduate student, who had been fired from his job at the university help desk for unauthorized network activity. Later that night, Savoy discovered that the computer was changed to an IP address ending in 120. He decided that he had to get the computer off line immediately as a security measure. Rankhorn asked Savoy to wait for a warrant, but Savoy decided to act promptly and went to the dorm room assigned to D, where the computer was located. Savoy and a university police detective entered through an open door and disconnected the computer from the network. The detective questioned D and got his password. Savoy used the password to access the computer and verify that it was the one used to gain the unauthorized access. D was charged with various offenses, including recklessly causing damage by intentionally accessing a protected computer without authorization. His motions to suppress the evidence gathered from the search of his computer were denied, and D was convicted. D appeals.

Issue. Does a computer user have a reasonable expectation of privacy in his personal computer if he connects it to a university network, where the university network does not have an announced network monitoring policy?

Held. Yes. Judgment affirmed on other grounds.

♦ D must show that he had a reasonable expectation of privacy in the computer, which requires both a subjective expectation and an expectation recognized by society as reasonable. Both of these elements were satisfied with respect to D's personal computer, standing alone.

♦ A person's reasonable expectation of privacy may be diminished in transmissions over the Internet or through email that have already arrived at the recipient. But accessing a network does not by itself extinguish privacy expectations. Privacy expectations may be reduced if the user is advised that information transmitted through the network is not confidential and that administrators may monitor such communications.

◆ The university in this case did not have such a monitoring policy, however. Therefore, D had a reasonable expectation of privacy in his personal computer, which he protected with the password.

Comment. Although D had a reasonable expectation of privacy, the court upheld the denial of the suppression motion under the "special needs" exception to the search warrant requirement. Savoy had a need to secure the server that was separate from and not motivated by the needs of law enforcement. Savoy acted within the scope of his role as a system administrator.

---

   b. Rights in content information. The Fourth Amendment protects legitimate expectations of privacy in the contents of closed containers, including envelopes, boxes, and other packages.

    1) Sealed container held by common carrier--

United States v. Villarreal, 963 F.2d 770 (5th Cir. 1992).

Facts. Villarreal and Gonzalez (Ds) arranged to receive two 55-gallon drums containing over 100 kilograms of marijuana. The drums were labeled phosphoric acid and shipped under a fictitious name. Employees at the transport terminal suspected that something was wrong because the drums were too light to contain acid and the contents did not slosh when moved. They contacted customs agents, who arrived and opened the drums when their sniffing dog reacted to the drums. After they found marijuana in one of drums, they resealed it and made a controlled delivery to Ds. Ds were charged with possessing and conspiring to possess more than 100 kilograms of marijuana with intent to distribute it. Ds sought to exclude the evidence from the warrantless search. The trial court granted the motion. The government appeals.

Issue. May government agents search a sealed container held by a common carrier without a warrant or consent if they have probable cause to believe it contains contraband?

Held. No. Judgment affirmed.

◆ The Fourth Amendment protects legitimate expectations of privacy in closed containers that conceal their contents from plain view. Shipping by mail or common carrier does not constitute a surrender of expectations of privacy.

◆ If a common carrier or private party searches a package, the Fourth Amendment is not implicated, because it protects only against unreasonable government action. The police may be called in to confirm the presence of contraband and to determine what to do with it without converting the private search into a government search subject to the Fourth Amendment. However, if government agents themselves open containers that are sent by mail or private carrier, the requirements of the Fourth Amendment must be satisfied, even if the agents have probable cause to believe that they contain contraband. In this case, the customs agents themselves opened the container.

♦ Even though the consignee of the drums was a fictitious person, individuals may assert a reasonable expectation of privacy in packages addressed to them under fictitious names. Also, it does not matter what kind of container it is, with the exception of containers that by their very nature cannot support any reasonable expectation of privacy because their contents can be inferred from their outward appearance, such as a gun case or burglar kit.

♦ The government contends that Ds had no expectation of privacy because the drums' labels indicated that the drums contained phosphoric acid; thus, there was no reasonable expectation of privacy in the contents. However, a label is not an invitation to search the contents.

♦ There was no justification for a warrantless search of the drums. Although the government had probable cause, no amount of probable cause can justify a warrantless search or seizure absent exigent circumstances. There were no exigent circumstances here. The agents should have obtained a warrant, and failure to do so requires that the evidence be excluded.

---

2) **Postal mail privacy.** In *ex parte Jackson*, 96 U.S. 727 (1877), the Court drew a distinction between what is intended to be kept free from inspection, such as letters and sealed packages subject to letter postage, and what is open to inspection, such as newspapers and magazines that are purposely left in a condition to be examined. The Court stated that while letters and sealed packages are in the mail, they are under the constitutional protection against unreasonable searches and seizures and can only be opened and examined if there is a warrant.

3) **Telephone privacy.**

   a) **Constitutional permission.** In *Olmstead v. United States*, 277 U.S. 438 (1928), the FBI listened to bootleggers over a tapped telephone line, and the information was then used to convict them. The Court found that there was no violation of the Fourth Amendment in securing the wiretap because the evidence was secured without entering the defendants' house and because the privacy of a sealed letter in the mail did not apply to telephone communications. At the time, the Court stated that the amendment protects only against search and seizure of tangible, material things—*i.e.*, persons, papers, houses, and effects. This has since been rejected.

b) **The *Berger* rule.** The Supreme Court imposed a high standard for statutes that would allow wiretapping or electronic eavesdropping. In *Berger v. New York*, 388 U.S. 41 (1967), a recording device was placed in Berger's office under a New York statute that permitted such eavesdropping by judicial order if there is reasonable ground to believe evidence may thus be obtained. Berger was convicted with the evidence obtained through wiretapping. The Court held that a state may not authorize wiretapping without specifying precise and discriminate procedures. The state eavesdropping statute in this case, permitting trespassory intrusions by court order, was invalid because: (i) it laid down no requirement for particularity in the warrant (*i.e.*, it was like a "general warrant") as to what specific crime had been or was being committed, nor the place to be searched, nor the persons or things (conversations) to be seized, as is specifically required by the Fourth Amendment; (ii) its authorization of eavesdropping for up to two months was equivalent to a series of intrusions, searches, and/or seizures pursuant to a single showing of probable cause; (iii) it placed no termination date on the eavesdrop; and (iv) it gave no notice (to the person eavesdropped on), as conventional warrants do.

c) **Modern rule.** In *Katz v. United States, supra,* the Supreme Court held that Fourth Amendment restrictions applied to evidence obtained even by a nontrespassory wiretap. (Recall that in *Katz*, federal agents bugged the defendant's telephone conversations by placing a device on the outside of a public telephone booth where he regularly conveyed gambling information.)

(1) **Rationale.** "The Fourth Amendment protects people, not places." The presence or absence of physical intrusion is irrelevant if a person justifiably expected that the communication would be private.

(2) **Binding on states.** The *Katz* decision is binding also on the states. [*See* Kaiser v. New York, 394 U.S. 280 (1969)]

(3) **Effect.** Without prior judicial authorization, wiretapping or electronic eavesdropping without the consent of one party to the conversation is now an unreasonable search or seizure per se, and evidence obtained thereby is inadmissible in either federal or state criminal prosecutions.

c.   Rights in non-content information--

Smith v. Maryland, 442 U.S. 735 (1979).

Facts. McDonough was robbed. She described the robber to the police and said that a 1975 Monte Carlo was near the scene. She began receiving threatening and obscene phone calls from a man who claimed he was the robber. The police spotted a man matching the description driving a 1975 Monte Carlo in the victim's neighborhood. They traced the license plate to Smith (D). At police request, the phone company installed a pen register that recorded phone numbers dialed from D's home. The register recorded that a call was placed from D's home to the victim's phone. Using this and other evidence, the police obtained a warrant to search D's home, where they found a page in D's phone book that was turned down to the name and number of the victim. After the victim identified D in a lineup, D was indicted. He sought to suppress the evidence derived from the pen register. The trial court denied his motion. D was convicted. The Supreme Court granted certiorari.

Issue. Does the use of a pen register to record phone numbers constitute a search within the meaning of the Fourth Amendment?

Held. No. Judgment affirmed.

♦   As this Court stated in *Katz, supra*, a search can occur even when there has not been a physical intrusion into a constitutionally protected area, because the Fourth Amendment protects people, not places. Thus, an electronic listening device attached to a public phone booth violates the privacy of the person using the booth and is a search.

♦   The pen register in this case was installed on telephone company property at the company's offices. Thus, D cannot claim that his property was invaded or that the police intruded into a constitutionally protected area. And a pen register does not acquire the contents of communications as did the listening device used in *Katz*. Thus, the only way the installation and use of the register could constitute a search would be if D had a legitimate expectation of privacy regarding the numbers he dialed on his phone.

♦   Phone numbers must be conveyed to the telephone company to be switched and connected. Phone users know that the phone company records all the numbers they dial because long distance numbers are listed on monthly bills. Therefore, telephone subscribers could not have an expectation that the numbers they dial will remain secret.

♦   D claims an expectation of privacy because he called from the phone in his house, but the site of the call is immaterial to the number called. He may have expected to keep the contents of his call private by calling from his home, but regardless of his location, he had to convey the number that he dialed to the phone company if he wanted to complete his call.

♦ Even if D had a subjective expectation that the number he dialed would remain private, this expectation is not reasonable. A person has no legitimate expectation of privacy in information that he voluntarily turns over to third parties.

♦ D concedes that if he had placed his calls through an operator, he would have no legitimate expectation of privacy. He contends that an operator may be able to remember every number that callers convey to him but that automatic switching equipment, such as was used to process the numbers D placed, usually does not record local calls, such as his call to McDonough. However, regardless of whether the phone company chose to make a record of the number that D dialed, he voluntarily conveyed the number, and the phone company had the facilities to record it. D did not have a legitimate expectation of privacy in the numbers he dialed.

Dissent (Marshall, Brennan, JJ.). The Court asserts that those who convey information to third parties assume the risk of disclosure to the government. The concept of assumption of risk implies that there is choice. However, unless a person is willing to forgo the use of telephonic communication, he cannot help but accept the risk. It is pointless to speak of assuming risks when there is no realistic alternative. The use of pen registers is an extensive intrusion. There are legitimate reasons why people may wish to avoid disclosure of their personal contacts. A person should be entitled to assume that the numbers he dials in the privacy of his home will be recorded, if at all, solely for the phone company's business purposes. Law enforcement officials should be required to obtain a warrant before getting such information from phone companies.

Comment. In *United States v. Forrester*, 512 F.3d 500 (9th Cir. 2008), the court held that the government's monitoring of a person's "to" and "from" addresses of email messages, the addresses of websites he visited, and the total amount of data transmitted to or from his Internet account did not amount to a search in violation of the Fourth Amendment. The court stated that the computer surveillance techniques used were indistinguishable from the use of the pen register in *Smith*.

---

2.   **Statutory Privacy Laws.**

    a.   **Federal Communications Act.** The first federal statute outlawing wiretapping was the 1934 Federal Communications Act. "[N]o person not being authorized by the sender shall intercept any communication and divulge or publish the existence, contents, substance, purport, effect, or meaning of such intercepted communication to any person." [47 U.S.C. §605]

1) The statute was held to bar use of wiretap evidence in both federal and state criminal prosecutions. [*See* Lee v. Florida, 392 U.S. 378 (1968)]

2) *Nardone v. United States*, 308 U.S. 338 (1939), held that this statute covered wiretapping by state or federal officers as well as by private persons.

3) *Weiss v. United States*, 308 U.S. 321 (1939), held the statute applicable to intrastate as well as interstate communications.

4) However, the Act was subject to a major limitation—it was construed as applying only to interceptions accomplished by some physical intrusion ("tap") on the wire, and therefore did not prevent purely electronic ("nontrespassory") eavesdropping. [*See* Goldman v. United States, 316 U.S. 129 (1942)]

b. **Wiretapping and federal-state relations.**

1) In *Lee v. Florida, supra,* the Court held that the exclusionary rule would protect intercepted communications from divulgence in any court or any other place.

2) In *Benanti v. United States*, 355 U.S. 96 (1957), the Court barred state-gathered wiretap evidence from a federal prosecution, even though there was no collusion between the two sovereignties.

c. **Nontelephonic electronic eavesdropping.** In addition to the exceptions mentioned above, section 605 did ***not*** cover electronic eavesdropping since it was not "wiretapping."

1) **Possible eavesdropping devices.** Modern developments have made it possible to transform a telephone into a microphone that will transmit every sound in the room when the receiver is on the hook; directive microphones make it possible to eavesdrop on a conversation over 100 feet away, etc.

2) **Protection afforded.**

a) **Federal Communications Act.** The Act applies only when telephone, telegraph, or radiotelegraph conversations are overheard.

b) **United States Constitution.** Over time, protection against unreasonable search and seizure has applied only when electronic snooping was accomplished by a "physical invasion" or a "trespass."

(1) For example, the Court held in *Goldman v. United States, supra,* that there was no violation where federal officers placed a detectaphone against the wall of a private office, since there was no trespass.

(2) In *Silverman v. United States*, 365 U.S. 505 (1961), the Court held that inserting an electronic device into a party wall and making contact with a heating duct servicing the house occupied by the defendants, thus converting the entire heating system into a conductor of sound, violated the defendants' protection against unreasonable search and seizures. Here there was a trespass.

d. **Federal Wiretap Act.** The Federal Wiretap Act [18 U.S.C. §§2510-22] was enacted in response to *Katz.* It is considerably broader than the Federal Communications Act and bars the unauthorized interception by any kind of device of any communication by wire or any oral conversation uttered in expectation of privacy.

1) **Lawful interceptions.** Eavesdropping or wiretapping is permitted wherever authorized by a federal or state court order or warrant based on a showing of probable cause as to commission of specified crimes or (in state orders) crimes "dangerous to life, limb or property and punishable by imprisonment for more than one year." [18 U.S.C. §2516]

a) **Who may apply.** In the case of federal intercepts, application for the wiretap must be made by the Attorney General or an Assistant Attorney General expressly designated for this purpose. No other official will do. [*See* United States v. Giordano, 416 U.S. 505 (1974)] Similar limitations are imposed on state officials. However, incorrect identification of the authorizing official will not invalidate the application if the correct officer in fact authorized the application. [*See* United States v. Chavez, 416 U.S. 562 (1974)]

b) **Information required.** Each application and order must include the following information:

(1) Identity of the law enforcement officer making the application and officer authorizing application.

(2) A statement of probable cause, which includes:

(a) Details of the offense;

(b) Location of the place where the communication is to be intercepted;

(c) A particular description of the type of communication to be intercepted; and

(d) Identity of all persons (if known) committing the offense whose communications are expected to be intercepted.

(3) A full and complete statement as to whether other investigative procedures have been tried and have failed or, if not tried, why they are not satisfactory.

(4) The period of time for which the interception must be maintained, including whether or not the interception will automatically terminate when the communication sought is first obtained. [18 U.S.C. §2518(1), (4)]

c) **Notice requirement.** In addition to the requirements of an application and order, notice must be sent within 90 days after the interception ends to the party named in the order and (at the court's discretion) to persons whose conversations were intercepted. [18 U.S.C. §2518(8)(d)]

(1) In order that the court may properly decide whether "intercepted" parties should be notified, the government must supply the court with the names of all such parties or a description of the categories into which such persons fall.

d) **Admissibility of evidence.** Provided a proper court order was secured, any evidence obtained from the wiretap is admissible. This includes unanticipated conversations that are unrelated to the crime originally specified as the basis for the tap, as long as the tap procedure minimizes eavesdropping on conversations not subject to interception. [*See* Scott v. United States, 436 U.S. 128 (1978)] And the court may authorize surreptitious entry of a defendant's premises to place the wiretap.

(1) If any provisions of the Act are violated, evidence obtained from the wiretap is *not* automatically inadmissible. The evidence will be suppressed only if:

(a) It was obtained in violation of the Fourth Amendment; or

(b) The provision violated is one that directly and substantially implements the congressional policy of limiting the use of intercept procedures. [*See* United States v. Giordano, *supra*]

e) **Grand jury witnesses.** In *Gelbard v. United States*, 408 U.S. 41 (1972), the Court held that grand jury witnesses may refuse to testify when their testimony is sought on the basis of illegal wiretaps, since section 2511 of Title III prohibits use of evidence derived from violations of Title III.

f) **ECPA.** The Electronic Communications Privacy Act of 1986 ("ECPA") extended Title III to electronic media including e-mail. It covers prospective surveillance (wiretaps), retrospective surveillance (data stored in computer systems), and pen registers (numbers dialed from phones), so that these cannot be used without a court order. It also provides for roving wiretaps (electronic surveillance of an individual rather than a location or specific telephone).

g) **USA Patriot Act of 2001**. Six weeks after the September 11, 2001, attacks on the World Trade Center and Pentagon, Congress adopted the Patriot Act, which included hundreds of amendments to federal law. It extended the pen register provisions to the Internet and provided for roving wiretaps under the Foreign Intelligence Surveillance Act ("FISA"), as well as subjected United States citizens to surveillance under FISA under specified conditions. It also encouraged use of the FBI's Internet-surveillance program named DCS-1000.

e. **Meaning of "interception"--**

United States v. Turk, 526 F.2d 654 (5th Cir. 1976).

Facts. Acting on a tip, officers stopped a car, discovered cocaine and firearms inside, and arrested the occupants, including Kabbaby. They also removed two cassette tapes, but Kabbaby told them that nothing was on the tapes. Later, the officers listened to the tapes without Kabbaby's permission and without a warrant. One of the tapes was a recording of a private telephone conversation between Kabbaby and another man, Turk (D). D was subpoenaed to appear before a federal grand jury. Once granted immunity, D testified and denied trafficking in marijuana or other drugs. D was subsequently charged with making irreconcilably contradictory statements, obstruction of justice, and perjury based on the contents of the tape. D was found guilty of perjury for denying his involvement in marijuana trafficking. D appeals.

Issue. When police listen to a tape recording of a telephone conversation, does that constitute an interception of the communication?

Held. No. Judgment affirmed.

- Title III of the 1968 Omnibus Crime Control and Safe Streets Act, 18 U.S.C. sections 2510-2520, concerns the interception or disclosure of wire or oral communications. D claims that the action of the officers in listening to the tape was an impermissible "interception" of D's oral communication, as defined in section 2510(4). Under the statute, "intercept" means the aural acquisition of the contents of any wire or oral communication through the use of any electronic, mechanical, or other device.

- Kabbaby intercepted his conversion with D, but the statute exempts situations in which one party to the conversation is himself the interceptor, so this interception did not violate the act. Whether the officers' seizure and replaying of the tape was also an interception depends on the definition of "aural acquisition."

- The language of section 2510 and the policies reflected in the legislative history suggest that the central concern of the statute is with the activity at the time of the oral communication, which causes the communication to be overheard by uninvited listeners. Secretly recording a conversation between two others may be considered an aural acquisition. On the other hand, it could be asserted that an aural acquisition means a combination of the initial acquisition by the device and the hearing of the communication by the person responsible for the recording. Either definition would require participation by the one charged with an interception in the contemporaneous acquisition through the use of the device.

- To argue that an "aural acquisition" occurs each time a recording is replayed is not logical. Under that approach, a single recording could lead to innumerable "interceptions" and thus violations of the Act. It is the act of surveillance, not the hearing, that is the target of congressional concern.

---

f.   Exceptions not applicable--

Deal v. Spears, 980 F.2d 1153 (8th Cir. 1992).

Facts. The Spears (Ds) owned and operated a store. They lived in a mobile home adjacent to the store and had one phone line with an extension in each location. Deal (P) was an employee of Ds'. Ds' store was burglarized, and Ds suspected that P was involved. Ds bought a recording device and installed it on the phone extension in their home. The machine recorded all conversations on the phone in their home and the phone in their store. Ds told P that they might monitor calls because she used the phone too much during work. Ds started taping and listening to the recordings of P's calls. P conducted long conversations with a man with whom she was having an affair. While listening to the recordings, Ds discovered that P had sold her lover a keg of beer at cost, in violation of store policy. Ds fired P and told P's husband and the wife of P's paramour about the tapes. P sued for the intentional interception and disclosure of her phone conversations, a violation of the Omnibus Crime Control and Safe Streets Act of 1968. The district court found for P. Ds appeal.

Issue. May an employer monitor the phone calls of an employee suspected of stealing if the employer does not use equipment provided by the phone company and listens to conversations unrelated to the interests of the business?

Held. No. Judgment affirmed.

♦ Under the relevant provisions of the Omnibus Crime Control and Safe Streets Act, criminal liability attaches and a federal civil cause of action arises when a person intentionally intercepts a wire or electronic communication or intentionally discloses the contents of the interception.

♦ Ds claim that they are exempt from civil liability because P consented to the interception of her calls made from and received at the store. However, there was no evidence of express consent. Ds merely told P that they might monitor calls, not that they were actually doing so. They hoped to catch her discussing the burglary, which she would not do if she knew her calls were being monitored. These facts do not show implied consent.

♦ Ds also claim a business use exemption. But this exemption applies when telephone-related equipment is furnished by the phone company and is used in the ordinary course of its business. Ds did have a legitimate business reason to monitor P's calls—they suspected P of being involved in the burglary. In addition, P was abusing her phone privileges as an employee. However, Ds recorded 22 hours of calls and listened to all of them even when they did not pertain to Ds' business interests. Ds cannot avail themselves of the business use exemption.

E. POLICE INTERROGATION AND CONFESSIONS

1. Some Different Perspectives.

a. Inbau—police interrogation a practical necessity.

1) Many cases cannot be solved by investigation of physical evidence—it just is not available; thus, interrogation is essential. The counter-argument is that the police practice is often to use confessions as a short-cut to finding physical evidence or to obviate altogether doing so.

2) If interrogation is to be worthwhile, privacy and a sufficiently long time are essential.

3) In dealing with criminal offenders and suspects, it is necessary to use methods different from those used in ordinary affairs between law-abiding citizens. Thus, deceit, trickery, etc., may be justified.

4) The test of confessional evidence should be: would it be likely to induce a false confession?

b. **Kamisar—equal justice in the gatehouses and the mansions.**

1) The idea of our criminal system is that society carries the burden of proving its charge against the accused. It must establish its case, not by interrogation of the accused (at least not without judicial safeguards), but by evidence independently secured through skillful investigation.

2) In practice, this idea has never been upheld, at least not in the police station, where in the past the police have been allowed to carry on an inquisitorial system.

3) Nothing said in the police station by the suspect is really "voluntary." We carefully protect his rights in the courtroom with the privilege against self-incrimination and the right to counsel; there is at least as much necessity to do so in the police station.

2. **Historical Background.**

a. **Statements to police during illegal detention—*McNabb-Mallory* speedy arraignment rule.**

1) **Federal courts.** In the federal system, the Supreme Court held that any statements made by the arrestee while being detained "unnecessarily" before being taken to a magistrate for arraignment must be excluded at trial—the so-called *McNabb-Mallory* rule. [*See* McNabb v. United States, 318 U.S. 332 (1943); Mallory v. United States, 354 U.S. 449 (1957)]

   a) **Definition.** "Unnecessary delay" is anything more than the time required for booking procedures and perhaps a quick investigation to verify an alibi tendered by the arrestee.

   b) **Not a constitutional requirement.** This "speedy arraignment" rule was not a principle of constitutional law, but a matter of federal judicial policy to implement Federal Rule of Criminal Procedure 5a, which requires prompt arraignment of all persons arrested.

(1) Nevertheless, the rule—particularly before *Miranda, infra*—did assure that an accused would be brought promptly before a magistrate, at which time he would be advised of his constitutional rights, would perhaps be released on bail, and in any event would not be subjected to coercive interrogations.

(2) Some courts extended the rule to exclude evidence of eyewitness identification at police lineups held while the defendant was being "unnecessarily" detained before arraignment.

c) **Statute.** The *McNabb-Mallory* rule was substantially overturned by the Omnibus Crime Control and Safe Streets Act of 1968. [18 U.S.C. §3501] Under the Act, any statement made voluntarily within six hours following arrest or detention is admissible, even though the defendant was not yet arraigned.

(1) If the delay in arraignment is more than six hours, incriminating statements by the accused will be admissible only if the delay is shown to have been reasonable, considering the means of transportation and the distance to be traveled to the magistrate.

(2) Even if the delay is found to be unreasonable, the defendant's confession may still be admissible if the delay is shown not to have had any effect on its voluntariness.

(3) Section 3501 was struck in *Dickerson v. United States, infra*.

2) **State prosecutions.** The *McNabb-Mallory* rule was never binding on the states and has in fact been rejected by most of them. However, many states permit the jury to consider a delay in arraignment in determining the voluntariness and weight of statements given to the police, and permit the court to consider such delay in determining the fairness of the trial.

b. **The right to counsel and voluntary confessions—early cases.**

1) In *Brown v. Mississippi*, 297 U.S. 278 (1936), the Court reversed a state court decision that upheld a jury finding that the defendant's confession was voluntary even though the defendant had been beaten and held 11 days.

2) In *Crooker v. California*, 357 U.S. 433 (1958), the Court held that a defendant's confession was voluntary, even though the defen-

dant had been held for three days, had been questioned a total of three hours, and had been denied permission to speak with his attorney. The fact that the defendant had been a law student and knew of his right to remain silent indicated that his confession was voluntary.

3) In *Cicenia v. La Gay*, 357 U.S. 504, decided the same day as *Crooker*, *supra*, the Court again upheld the admissibility of a confession although the police denied the defendant's request to consult with his lawyer. Not only was Cicenia less educated than Crooker, but his lawyer was at the police station asking to see him while he was being interrogated.

4) In *Spano v. New York*, 360 U.S. 315 (1959), the defendant was also denied permission to see his attorney, and the confession was induced by trickery. The defendant had been questioned only after an indictment had been returned against him. The Court held the confession invalid because of trickery, but ignored the question of when the right to counsel attaches.

c. **The right to counsel—further developments.** Some of the cases above discussed the issue of interrogation and police coercion in the context of the Fifth Amendment privilege against incrimination. Several of the cases looked at the fact of the presence or absence of counsel during interrogation as going to the issue of voluntariness. Finally, the courts focused on the Sixth Amendment issue of when the right to counsel existed in the interrogation context.

1) **Prelude to *Escobedo*--**

Massiah v. United States, 377 U.S. 201 (1964).

Facts. Massiah (D) was arrested and indicted on a narcotics offense, retained counsel, and then was released on bail. One of D's criminal associates cooperated with the police and, with a transmitter planted on his person, engaged D in a conversation in which D made incriminating statements that were overheard by the police. D appeals his conviction.

Issue. Once a defendant has been indicted, may the police extract incriminating statements without the presence of counsel?

Held. No. Judgment reversed.

♦ The right to counsel arises at least at the time of indictment and continues thereafter. The statements cannot be used against D.

Dissent (White, Clark, Harlan, JJ.). I do not see how this case presents an unconstitutional interference with a defendant's right to counsel. D was not being interrogated while in custody, was not surrounded by police officers, and was not forbidden access to others. Moreover, D was not prevented from consulting with counsel, and no meetings with counsel were disturbed or spied upon.

Comment. The case may be better explained, however, as an expansion of the Fifth Amendment privilege against self-incrimination. Investigation can certainly continue after indictment, but here the prosecution was using D's own self-incriminating statements against him.

---

2)   The *Escobedo* approach--

Escobedo v. Illinois, 378 U.S. 478 (1964).

Facts. Escobedo (D), having been picked up and questioned in regard to a shooting, was released on a habeas corpus petition, then arrested a second time. He requested and was denied the opportunity to confer with his counsel, and counsel's repeated requests to see him were likewise denied. Subsequently he confessed, not realizing that he was guilty under Illinois law even though he did not do the actual shooting.

Issue. Does a defendant have a right to counsel when he is being held for the purpose of eliciting a confession?

Held. Yes. Judgment reversed.

♦   The accused has been denied the right to counsel in violation of the Sixth Amendment when: the inquiry has ceased to be generally investigatory and has focused on a particular suspect; the suspect has been taken into custody and interrogated; the suspect has requested and been denied an opportunity to consult with his lawyer; and the police have not informed him of his absolute constitutional right to remain silent.

Dissent (Stewart, J.). *Massiah, supra,* does not govern, because Massiah had already been indicted when he made incriminating statements. The present case does not involve interrogation of a defendant after the initiation of judicial proceedings against him. The institution of formal judicial proceedings, through indictment, information, or arraignment, marks the point at which a criminal investigation has ended and adversary proceedings have begun. This is when the constitutional guarantees attach.

Dissent (White, Stewart, Clark, JJ.). Under the Court's holding, after an accused becomes a suspect and is arrested, any admission made to the police is inadmissible into evidence unless the accused has waived his right to counsel. But the Sixth Amendment provision for counsel was not meant to amend or supersede the Fifth Amendment self-incrimination provision, which resolves the issue of incriminating admissions by proscribing compelled statements.

Comment. The American Civil Liberties Union filed a brief asking for the overruling of *Crooker*, *supra*. Three reasons were listed: the privilege against self-incrimination, the right to counsel, and due process—unfair police practices.

─────────────

      d.   **The privilege against self-incrimination.** The Fifth Amendment privilege against self-incrimination did not extend to pretrial interrogation in the early cases. However, the Court began to find a greater significance in that right when it held that the privilege applied to the states through the Fourteenth Amendment. [*See* Malloy v. Hogan, 378 U.S. 1 (1964)]

3.   **The *Miranda* Revolution.**

    a.   **The case--**

─────────────

Miranda v. Arizona, 384 U.S. 436 (1966).

─────────────

Facts. Miranda (D) was arrested, taken to the police station, and questioned without being advised of any right to remain silent or to have an attorney.

Issue. When a defendant is taken into custody, is it required that his legal right to remain silent and his right to have an attorney present be explained to him?

Held. Yes. Judgment reversed.

♦   To protect one's Fifth Amendment privilege against self-incrimination the following warnings must be given: (i) that the defendant has a right to remain silent; (ii) that anything the defendant says may be used against him in a court of law; (iii) that the defendant has the right to the presence of an attorney; and (iv) that if the defendant cannot afford an attorney, he has the right to have one appointed.

♦   The prosecution cannot use statements, exculpatory or inculpatory, stemming from "custodial interrogation" of the defendant unless it is shown that procedural safeguards have been applied to protect persons against self-incrimination. By custodial interrogation we mean questioning after a person has been taken into custody or otherwise deprived of his freedom of action in a significant way.

- The person must be warned of his Fifth Amendment privileges. It makes no difference whether or not the defendant knows of his rights; the police still must warn him. The object of these procedural safeguards is to insure that the person makes use of his privilege against self-incrimination based on real understanding and knowledge of the consequences of what he chooses to do.

- The presence of counsel at the interrogation is indispensable to protect the defendant's right to remain silent. If the defendant's lawyer is present, police coercion is less likely to occur. Also, if the defendant gives a statement, his lawyer can ensure that his statement is accurately reported at trial.

- At any point that a defendant asks for counsel, the questioning must stop until the defendant's lawyer arrives.

- If the interrogation continues without the presence of counsel, a heavy burden rests on the State to show that the defendant knowingly and intelligently waived his rights to counsel and to remain silent.

- Waiver of the privilege against self-incrimination may not be presumed from silence after a defendant has been warned of his rights; the defendant must expressly articulate a waiver.

- The defendant can withdraw a waiver once given. The defendant's privilege is a continuous one; thus once it has been relinquished, it can be reasserted at any time. It is unconstitutional to persuade a defendant not to withdraw his waiver.

- There can be no admissions by silence when the defendant is in custody.

- The privilege against self-incrimination applies only to interrogation initiated by the police. Statements given freely and voluntarily are not barred.

Dissent (Clark, J.). The majority's arbitrary Fifth Amendment rule is unnecessary and its effect unpredictable.

Dissent (Harlan, Stewart, White, JJ.). The new rule does not protect against police brutality or other overt coercion; it merely discourages any confession at all. It frustrates an instrument of law enforcement long accepted. D confessed in a short time without any force, threats, or promises.

Dissent (White, Harlan, Stewart, JJ.). The new rule is not supported by history or the language of the Fifth Amendment itself. The Court has simply made new law and policy without an adequate empirical basis.

---

b. **The meaning of *Miranda*.**

1) **A code of criminal procedure.** The Supreme Court has in effect laid down a detailed code of criminal procedure.

2) **Has *Miranda* gone too far?** The right against self-incrimination should protect one against being the instrument of one's own conviction. But to what extent? Police should not lie about what a defendant said, or about what they told him (about his rights), or about what they did to him. But protection against police abuses of these things can be afforded without going as far as *Miranda* did (for example, police could employ tape recorders at interrogation sessions). Our system should protect innocent people and the dignity and privacy of all, but should it go as far as to say that we cannot ever convict a person because he provides the information to do so?

3) **Congressional response.** 18 U.S.C. section 3501 was adopted in the Crime Control Act of 1968, supposedly to overrule *Miranda*. However, that provision was invalidated by the United States Supreme Court in *Dickerson v. United States, infra.*

4) **Effect on nonconfessions.** The privilege does not prevent a defendant from being forced to talk for some purposes: identification, giving fingerprints, etc. A defendant's refusal here can be introduced against him as evidence of a consciousness of guilt.

5) **Effect of confession or admission illegally obtained.**

   a) **Prosecution not barred.** The defendant's only remedy for an illegally obtained confession—aside from a civil or criminal action against the police for violation of his civil rights—is to have the confession or admission, and perhaps the evidence derived therefrom (*see* below), excluded from trial as evidence of his guilt. Prosecution for the crime itself will not be barred. [*See* United States v. Blue, 384 U.S. 251 (1966)]

   b) **Used to impeach defendant's testimony.**

      (1) **Involuntary confessions.** An involuntary statement by a defendant cannot be used to impeach. *Rationale:* The fact that it is involuntary means that its trustworthiness is questionable. [Mincey v. Arizona, 437 U.S. 385 (1978)]

      (2) **Statements obtained in violation of *Miranda*.** Such statements are not necessarily untrustworthy. Hence, as long as they otherwise appear to be voluntary and trustworthy, they may be used to impeach any contradictory

testimony given by a defendant at his trial—whether the defendant's pretrial statement relates to a "collateral" matter or directly to the crime charged, *Harris v. New York, infra*, and whether a proper warning was given, *Oregon v. Hass*, 420 U.S. 714 (1975).

    (a)   **Rationale.** Exclusionary rules unrelated to the trustworthiness of the evidence cannot be used as a "shield for perjury."

    (b)   **Compare—silence at time of arrest as impeachment.** However, the *Harris* rule does not permit the prosecutor to impeach the defendant's testimony at trial by showing that he remained silent at the time of arrest (*i.e.,* failed to offer the alibi he now claims).

c)   **"Fruits" of inadmissible confessions and admissions.** An unresolved issue is whether the prosecution can use evidence uncovered through a confession that is otherwise inadmissible. For example, suppose a defendant's confession indicates the whereabouts of stolen property or a murder weapon that the police then recover. The property or gun has the defendant's fingerprints on it. Can this be used in evidence against the defendant, even though his confession could not?

    (1)   Courts generally hold that evidence otherwise admissible is not barred because it was uncovered through an inadmissible confession. [*See, e.g.,* Michigan v. Tucker, 417 U.S. 433 (1974)—witness discovered through confession obtained in violation of *Miranda* may testify]

    (2)   However, some courts apply the same principles to the "fruits" of illegal confessions as to the "fruits" of illegal searches or arrests.

d)   **Public safety exception.** In *New York v. Quarles, infra*, the Court recognized an exception to *Miranda* for statements that are not actually compelled by police conduct but are responsive to questions in a situation posing a threat to the public safety.

e)   **Consecutive confessions.** Suppose the defendant makes an otherwise voluntary confession after he had made a prior confession that was coerced or otherwise inadmissible. Does the inadmissibility of the first confession make the later confession inadmissible?

(1) Test. The Supreme Court has held that the second confession is admissible if free from the coercive influences affecting the first. [*See* Leyra v. Denno, 347 U.S. 556 (1954)]

(2) Proof. The prosecution has the burden to prove that the later confession was not produced because of the existence of the earlier confession.

(3) Subsequent incriminating statements. If a statement made without the benefit of *Miranda* warnings is not the product of coercion or improper police tactics, a subsequent voluntary statement made after the *Miranda* warnings are given is admissible. [Oregon v. Elstad, *infra*] In *Elstad*, the Court reasoned that the failure to give the *Miranda* warnings is a prophylactic and not in itself a violation of the Fifth Amendment. The Court has suggested—but not held—that the "fruits" derived from such statements obtained in violation of *Miranda*—*i.e.,* physical evidence such as weapons or contraband—may be admissible.

c. Application of *Miranda*.

1) Exploiting a criminal's ignorance. In *State v. McKnight*, 243 A.2d 240 (1968), the Court stated that it is consistent with the Constitution and good morals to exploit a criminal's ignorance or stupidity during the detectional process; the government's primary mission is to protect the right of the individual to live free from criminal attack. The Court held that if a suspect was given the *Miranda* warnings, but chose to confess without conferring with a lawyer, it is irrelevant that he did not recognize his need for counsel.

2) Advisement regarding subject matter of questioning. In *Colorado v. Spring*, 479 U.S. 564 (1987), the Court held that a suspect need not be aware of all the possible subjects of questioning in advance of interrogation. The suspect in that case waived his *Miranda* rights after being arrested while purchasing stolen firearms. After questioning him about the firearms offense, the police, who suspected Spring of murder, asked if he had ever shot anyone. Spring's admission led to a murder conviction. It was not relevant to determining whether Spring voluntarily, knowingly, and intelligently waived his privilege against self-incrimination that he did not know the police would ask about the murder when he waived his rights. Spring's decision to talk was unqualified because the rights warning told him that anything he might say could be used against him.

3) Noncustodial interrogation--

Beckwith v. United States, 425 U.S. 341 (1976).

Facts. Beckwith (D) was investigated by the intelligence division of the IRS for possible tax fraud and was informed of that fact by the agents. D cooperated with the agents, answered most of their questions, and provided them with personal tax records. The interview and the records provided the basis for his conviction of tax fraud. D appeals the admission of the evidence obtained before he had been given the warnings required by *Miranda*.

Issue. When the court finds as a fact that the situation is noncustodial in character, are the *Miranda* warnings required?

Held. No. Judgment affirmed.

◆ The concern of *Miranda* was for the inherently coercive nature of the custodial interrogation. D was not in custody in this case, so there could not be the level of coercion noted in *Miranda* as giving rise to the requirements of a warning.

◆ The government is not required to give warnings every time it suspects a person of criminal activity. The warnings are required when a decision has been made to deprive a person of his freedom by taking him into custody.

4) **Noncustodial questioning—"threshold" confessions.** *Miranda* warnings need not be given during general on-the-scene questioning in the fact-finding process of a criminal investigation, nor need the police stop a person who enters the police station and offers a confession or other statement he desires to make. (Similarly, a "threshold" confession, volunteered by the defendant immediately upon arrest and prior to any interrogation, would seem to be admissible even though no *Miranda* warning had yet been given.)

5) **Roadside questioning of motorist.** In *Berkemer v. McCarty*, 468 U.S. 420 (1984), the Court held that an officer who stops a motorist need not give *Miranda* warnings before questioning the motorist to confirm or dispel the officer's suspicions. The Court recognized that *Miranda* does apply to misdemeanor traffic offenses, but only in the context of custodial interrogation. A routine traffic stop does not normally impose upon the detained person pressures that so impair his free exercise of his privilege against self-incrimination as to require the officer to give *Miranda* warnings.

6) Questioning of minor brought to police station by parents--

Yarborough v. Alvarado, 541 U.S. 652 (2004).

Facts. Alvarado (P), who was 17, helped Soto try to steal a truck. During the incident, Soto shot and killed the truck's owner. P was called in for an interview with Comstock, a detective. P's parents brought him to the police station for the interview and waited there for two hours while Comstock interviewed P. P did not receive *Miranda* warnings and initially denied involvement in the shooting. Eventually, P admitted that he had helped Soto. During the interview, Comstock twice asked P if he needed a break. At the conclusion, Comstock returned P to his parents, who drove him home. P was charged with murder and attempted robbery. The trial court denied P's motion to suppress the interview on the ground that he had not been in custody. P brought a habeas petition against Yarborough (D), the warden. The district court denied relief, but the Ninth Circuit reversed in light of P's youth and inexperience. The Supreme Court granted certiorari.

Issue. Is a 17-year-old deemed to be in custody for *Miranda* purposes when his parents take him to a police station and wait for him while he is undergoing a two-hour interview?

Held. No. Judgment reversed.

♦ Prior cases have established that custody, for *Miranda* analysis, must be determined based on how a reasonable person in the suspect's situation would perceive his circumstances. Generally, questioning is not custodial if it takes place in a context where the suspect is free to depart.

♦ In this case, P was not transported to the station by the police and was not required to appear at any particular time. P was not threatened with arrest. His parents waited the whole time, suggesting that the interview would be brief. The interview focused on Soto's crimes, not P's. Comstock did not threaten P, but appealed to P's interest in telling the truth and helping the police. While the interview did take two hours and his parents were not allowed to attend, the trial court's finding is supported by the facts and can be overturned only if it is objectively unreasonable. Here, it is reasonable.

♦ The *Miranda* custody inquiry is an objective test, intended to relieve police from having to guess about particular circumstances. As such, it differs from other tests that depend on the actual mindset of a particular suspect, such as the test for voluntariness.

Concurrence (O'Connor, J.). There may be cases in which a suspect's age will be relevant to the *Miranda* custody determination, but in this case, P was almost 18.

Dissent (Breyer, Stevens, Souter, Ginsburg, JJ.). P was clearly in custody when the police questioned him without *Miranda* warnings. A reasonable person in these circumstances would not feel at liberty to terminate the interrogation and leave, especially a person as young and inexperienced as P.

---

d. Determining what constitutes an interrogation.

1) Measure of compulsion--

Rhode Island v. Innis, 446 U.S. 291 (1980).

Facts. Innis (D) was arrested as a suspect in the robbery and murder of a taxicab driver. The crime was committed with a shotgun that had not yet been found. D was read his *Miranda* rights and asked to see a lawyer. The police took D to the station in a patrol car. On the way, two officers in the car with D discussed the danger of a child finding the still-missing shotgun. D then told the officers he would show them where the shotgun was hidden. He proceeded to do so. D was subsequently convicted, with the prosecution using the evidence of the discovery of the shotgun. The state supreme court reversed, holding that D's admissions were unlawfully elicited. The Supreme Court granted certiorari.

Issue. Does a conversation between police officers in the presence of a suspect who has requested a lawyer constitute an interrogation whenever the suspect makes admissions in response to the conversation?

Held. No. Judgment reversed.

- An interrogation under *Miranda* does not consist solely of police interrogation practices that involve express questioning of a defendant while in custody. An interrogation may consist of other techniques of persuasion that create an interrogation environment such that the individual's will is subjugated to the examiner's and the privilege against compulsory self-incrimination is undermined.

- Not all statements obtained by the police after a person has been taken into custody and asks for a lawyer are to be considered the product of interrogation, however. Interrogation must reflect a measure of compulsion beyond that inherent in custody itself. Thus, the *Miranda* safeguards apply whenever a person in custody is subjected to either express questioning or its functional equivalent.

- In this case, D responded not to a question but to the conversation between the police officers. Even if he was subjected to subtle compulsion, D must also establish that his response was the product of words or actions on the part of the police that they should have known were reasonably likely to elicit an incriminating response. This was not established by D.

Dissent (Marshall, Brennan, JJ.). The Court's definition of "interrogation" is correct under *Miranda*, but this objective standard applied to this case must lead to the conclusion that there was an interrogation. The police used the classic interrogation technique of appealing to D to confess in order to protect others, in this case children.

Dissent (Stevens, J.). The effectiveness of the *Miranda* warnings depends on whether the police scrupulously honor the suspect's rights. Here, the police officers engaged in a conversation that was the functional equivalent of a direct question. There is evidence that the statements were intended to elicit a response from D.

---

2)   **The "jail plant" situation.** In *Illinois v. Perkins*, 496 U.S. 292 (1990), the Court held that *Miranda* warnings were not required before an undercover agent, posing as a prisoner, asked a fellow inmate questions that could elicit an incriminating response regarding a crime unrelated to that for which he was incarcerated. The Court reasoned that coercion is determined from the perspective of the suspect, and when a suspect thinks he is in the company of cellmates, the coercive atmosphere is absent.

3)   **Routine booking question exception.** *Pennsylvania v. Muniz*, 496 U.S. 582 (1990), involved the admissibility of evidence obtained during the booking process. Muniz was arrested for driving under the influence of alcohol. He was taken to a booking center, was told that his actions and voice would be videotaped, and was asked routine questions regarding his name, address, height, weight, eye color, date of birth, age, and the date of his sixth birthday. He was unable to give the date of his sixth birthday and stumbled over two other responses. He also made incriminating statements while he performed physical sobriety tests. After he refused to take a breathalyzer test, he was advised of his *Miranda* rights for the first time. The video and audio portions of the tape were admitted at his trial, and he was convicted. The Supreme Court granted certiorari and held that: the slurred nature of his answers to the questions was a nontestimonial component of his responses; the first seven questions were routine booking questions, related to police administrative concerns, and Muniz's answers were admissible; his incriminating statements during the sobriety tests were admissible because the police instructions as to how the tests were to be performed were not likely to be perceived as calling for any verbal responses; and his remarks regarding his refusal to take the sobriety tests were admissible because they were not prompted by an interrogation within the meaning of *Miranda*. However, the Court held that the answer to the question regarding the date of his sixth

birthday was testimonial and inadmissible. Muniz could have either admitted that he did not then know the date of his sixth birthday and incriminated himself or answered untruthfully and given a date that he did not think was correct, but an incorrect guess would also be incriminating. Thus, the Court concluded that, on remand, his response to the question regarding his sixth birthday had to be suppressed, but not the entire videotape.

e.   **Public safety exception to *Miranda*--**

New York v. Quarles, 467 U.S. 649 (1984).

Facts. Police apprehended Quarles (D) in the rear of a supermarket after a woman had told the police that the man who raped her just entered the supermarket. D matched the description given by the woman. D was frisked and was found to be wearing an empty shoulder holster. An officer, after handcuffing D, asked D where the gun was and D nodded in the direction of some empty cartons and stated "the gun is over there." At the time, D was surrounded by four officers whose guns had just been returned to their holsters. D was formally placed under arrest and advised of his *Miranda* rights. D waived his rights and, in response to questions, stated that he owned the revolver. The New York courts suppressed the statement "the gun is over there," the gun itself, and D's statement that he owned the gun.

Issue. Do overriding considerations of public safety justify the officer's failure to provide *Miranda* warnings to D before D was asked questions regarding locating the weapon?

Held. Yes. Judgment reversed.

♦   The need for answers to questions in a situation posing a threat to public safety outweighs the need for the rule protecting a person's Fifth Amendment privilege against self-incrimination.

♦   The police were confronted with the immediate necessity of locating a gun that they had every reason to believe D had just removed and discarded in the supermarket. So long as the gun was concealed in the store, it posed more than one danger to public safety. The police needed an answer to their question to insure that further danger to the public did not result.

Concurrence and dissent (O'Connor, J.). I would suppress D's statement that "the gun is over there," but not the gun itself because nothing in *Miranda* requires exclusion of nontestimonial evidence.

Dissent (Marshall, Brennan, Stevens, JJ.). The majority opinion is based on a mistaken factual assumption that the public was at risk during D's interrogation. The majority misreads *Miranda*; the rule in *Miranda* was designed to protect defendants against prosecution based on coerced, self-incriminating statements.

---

f. **Waiver.** The government bears a "heavy burden" to demonstrate that a defendant knowingly and intelligently waived his rights after having received *Miranda* warnings. One way to satisfy this burden is to record the warning, any waiver, and any further questioning and statements. However, an officer's testimony about a waiver need not be corroborated. Waiver may be implied from the defendant's actions and words [North Carolina v. Butler, 441 U.S. 369 (1979)], but mere silence is not enough. For example, a defendant may refuse to sign a written waiver, or to permit the officer to take notes, yet agree to talk. In *Connecticut v. Barrett*, 479 U.S. 523 (1987), the suspect refused to make a written statement without counsel, but he did make oral admissions, which were used against him. This use of evidence was permitted, on the rationale that the suspect exercised his right to speak.

g. **Resumption of questioning.** Once the defendant exercises the right to remain silent by requesting counsel or just refusing to answer questions, the police must scrupulously honor that right.

1) **Multiple interrogations--**

Michigan v. Mosley, 423 U.S. 96 (1975).

Facts. Mosley (D) was arrested for participating in two robberies in bars. He was informed of his rights in conformance with *Miranda* and was interrogated by a police detective. The interrogation was terminated when D exercised his right to do so. Two hours later another detective interrogated D about a different robbery in which the victim was killed. D was given the warnings again and then made incriminating statements that were used to obtain a first degree murder conviction. The court of appeals reversed.

Issue. Once a defendant exercises his right to terminate an interrogation, may he later be interrogated on another subject as long as a reasonable time has passed and new warnings are given?

Held. Yes. Judgment reversed.

♦ There was no evidence that the police used interrogations as a pattern of coercion to deprive D of his right against compulsory self-incrimination.

♦ The passage of time, the different subject matter of interrogation, and the giving of the warnings anew tend to indicate that no pressure above that allowed was put on D.

Comment. Note that Mosley asserted only his right to remain silent; he did not ask for an attorney. Compare *Mosley* with *Edwards, Roberson,* and *Bradshaw, infra,* in which attorneys were requested.

---

2) **Importance of which party initiates interrogation--**

Edwards v. Arizona, 451 U.S. 477 (1981).

Facts. Edwards (D) was arrested for felony offenses and initially waived his *Miranda* rights, but then stated that he wanted an attorney "before making a deal." The next day two detectives approached D, gave him his *Miranda* rights, and let him hear recorded statements of another suspect who had implicated D. D then made incriminating statements. D was convicted. The Arizona Supreme Court affirmed on the basis that D voluntarily waived his rights. D appeals.

Issue. Once a defendant invokes his right to have a lawyer, may he subsequently waive his *Miranda* rights when the police initiate an interrogation before providing a lawyer?

Held. No. Judgment reversed.

♦   The state courts erred in considering the voluntariness of D's admission without considering whether D understood his right to counsel and whether he knowingly and intelligently waived it.

♦   When an accused requests counsel, additional safeguards are necessary. After making such a request, the accused may not be interrogated further before counsel is provided, unless he initiates further communication with police on his own. An accused who requests counsel does not waive his rights by responding to a subsequent interrogation.

---

h.   **Independent subsequent questioning.** In *Arizona v. Roberson,* 486 U.S. 675 (1988), the Court held that the *Edwards* rule applied to a defendant in custody when a different police officer questioned him about a different crime than that for which he was in custody and had invoked his right to counsel. The Court found that the presumption that the defendant considered himself unable to deal with custodial interrogation without counsel was not overcome by the second custodial interrogation, even if it did pertain to a separate investigation.

i.   **Presumption against waiver of rights--**

Minnick v. Mississippi, 498 U.S. 146 (1990).

Facts. Minnick (D) escaped from jail in Mississippi with Dykes, a fellow prisoner. The two of them committed a burglary and killed two people in the process. They escaped to Mexico, where they split up. D was later arrested in California. Two FBI agents questioned him, and after a rights advisement, D stated that Dykes had killed one of the victims and forced D to shoot the other. D then asked for a lawyer. An appointed attorney met with D on a few occasions. Denham, a deputy sheriff from Mississippi, visited D in San Diego, advised D of his rights, and questioned him. He made several incriminating statements to Denham. D was tried for murder in Mississippi (P). He moved to suppress the statements given to the FBI and Denham. The court denied the motion with respect to the statements to Denham, but suppressed the other statement. D was convicted, and the state supreme court affirmed. The Supreme Court granted certiorari.

Issue. Does *Edwards's* protection cease once the suspect has consulted with an attorney?

Held. No. Judgment reversed.

- The *Edwards* rule ensures that statements made in interrogation after a prisoner has asserted *Miranda* rights are not the result of coercive pressures. It prevents police from badgering a defendant into waiving his previously asserted *Miranda* rights and is a clear guide to the police.

- Consultation with an attorney does not eliminate the coercive pressures that accompany custody. To create an exception for *Edwards* once a defendant has consulted counsel would undermine the defendant's right to have counsel present at custodial interrogation. It would also raise new issues about what would constitute a consultation; *i.e.,* a telephone call or a brief visit would not suffice, while a longer consultation would. Some official would have to make a determination about the adequacy of the consultation. And it could affect the attorney's relationship with the client, because by consulting with the client, the attorney would subject the client to further interrogation.

- For these reasons, once counsel is requested, interrogation must cease and officials may not reinitiate interrogation without counsel present, whether or not the accused has consulted with his attorney.

Dissent (Scalia, J., Rehnquist, C.J.). There is no justification for applying the *Edwards* irrebuttable presumption that a criminal suspect can never validly waive the *Miranda* rights, once invoked, to situations where a criminal suspect has consulted with his attorney. The Constitution's prohibition against compelled testimony does not remotely authorize suppression of confessions that are not compelled and are given by individuals who are fully aware of their rights and have consulted counsel. A clear and simple rule is desirable, but not if it exceeds constitutional authority. A better approach would be to hold that *Edwards* ceases to apply, permanently, once consultation with counsel has occurred. The Court's new rule reflects not genuine concern about suspects who do not know their right to remain silent, or who have been coerced to abandon it, but instead an effort to protect suspects against their own folly. But the law should not regard an honest confession as a "mistake." It is more virtuous for a wrongdoer to admit his offense and accept punishment than to stand silent, even though everyone is entitled to remain silent.

Comments.

- The type of conversation initiated by a suspect after he asserts his right to counsel determines the permissible scope of police involvement. In *Oregon v. Bradshaw*, 462 U.S. 1039 (1983), the plurality opinion held that it was not a violation of the *Edwards* rule for police to suggest that a suspect take a lie detector test after the suspect reinitiated a conversation after first requesting counsel. The suspect had initiated a conversation about the investigation by asking what would happen to him. This was sufficient to avoid application of the *Edwards* rule, whereas a conversation about the incidents of the custodial relationship such as a request to use the telephone or for a drink would not be. The dissent in that case argued that the suspect did not demonstrate a desire to discuss the investigation.

- In *Davis v. United States*, 512 U.S. 452 (1994), the Court emphasized that a suspect must unambiguously request counsel. In that case, the suspect stated, "Maybe I should talk to a lawyer," but then stated he was not asking for a lawyer. Law enforcement officers are not required to cease questioning immediately whenever a suspect makes an ambiguous or equivocal reference to an attorney.

- The assertion of the *Miranda* right to counsel cannot be inferred from the invocation of the Sixth Amendment right. In *McNeil v. Wisconsin*, 501 U.S. 171 (1991), McNeil was represented by a public defender at his bail hearing after his arrest for armed robbery. He was later visited in jail by a deputy sheriff who asked about an unrelated murder. McNeil waived his *Miranda* rights and made incriminating statements. He was convicted of murder. The Court held that McNeil did not invoke his *Miranda* right to counsel by appearing with counsel at the bail hearing for the armed robbery. The Sixth Amendment right to counsel is offense-specific, and does not attach until a prosecution is commenced.

---

j. **Interrogation after a third party retains defense counsel--**

Moran v. Burbine, 475 U.S. 412 (1986).

Facts. Burbine (D) was arrested with two others in connection with a burglary. Shortly prior to the arrest, police had been informed that a man with D's address and first name had committed an unsolved murder several months earlier. D was questioned but refused to waive his *Miranda* rights in writing. After D's two burglary companions further implicated D in the murder, more detectives were brought in to question D. Unknown to D, D's sister had contacted the public defender on D's behalf. The public defender called the police and was told that D would not be questioned further that night. D was never told about this call. Later that evening, he was again questioned. D waived his *Miranda* rights and provided written confessions to the murder. After unsuccessfully moving to suppress his statements, D was convicted of first degree murder. He appealed, then sought federal habeas corpus relief. The court of appeals granted relief. The Supreme Court granted certiorari.

Issue. Must a pre-arraignment confession, made after a valid waiver of *Miranda* rights, be suppressed because the police lied to defense counsel about their interrogation plans or because they did not tell the suspect that his attorney tried to reach him?

Held. No. Judgment reversed.

♦ D claims that he did not knowingly waive his Fifth Amendment rights because the police deprived him of the information he needed to make that choice—his attorney's attempt to contact him. To be effective, a waiver of *Miranda* rights must be made voluntarily, knowingly, and intelligently. The choice must not be coerced, and the suspect must have a full awareness both of the nature of the right being abandoned and the consequences of the decision to abandon it.

♦ In this case, the totality of the circumstances shows that D validly waived his rights. Events occurring unknown to D, such as his attorney's phone call, had no bearing on his capacity to comprehend and knowingly relinquish his constitutional right. D clearly would have validly waived his rights had the phone call not been made. The possibility that D would have made a different choice had he known of the call is irrelevant. Also irrelevant is the state of mind of the police when they failed to tell D that his attorney had called.

♦ Police misconduct such as that here, despite its offensiveness, is unrelated to any federal right or privilege. Thus there is no basis for a federal exclusionary rule based on how the police treat an attorney.

♦ *Miranda* already strikes a delicate balance between competing interests. Expanding *Miranda* rights to include notification of defense counsel's attempt to contact a suspect would intrude too far into society's legitimate and substantial interest in securing admissions of guilt.

♦ The right to counsel does not attach merely upon retention of an attorney, but upon the person's request for counsel, or upon initiation of adversarial judicial proceedings. D confessed before either event occurred.

Dissent (Stevens, Brennan, Marshall, JJ.). The police conduct in this case violates fundamental fairness. The Court has determined that the state has a compelling interest in lawyer-free, incommunicado custodial interrogation. The failure to inform D of the call from his attorney should make the subsequent waiver of his constitutional rights invalid. Deception of D's attorney is tantamount to deception of D himself, since the attorney was D's agent.

---

k. Use of psychiatric exams at sentencing--

Estelle v. Smith, 451 U.S. 454 (1981).

Facts. Smith (D) was to be tried for murder. The trial judge ordered a psychiatric examination of D to determine his competence to stand trial. The psychiatrist did not obtain permission from D's counsel to examine D, nor did he give D any rights warnings. He reported that D could stand trial. After conviction, the psychiatrist testified in the sentencing proceeding as to D's future dangerousness, over defense objections. D was sentenced to death. D's conviction and death sentence were upheld on appeal. D obtained a writ of habeas corpus in federal court, and his sentence was vacated. The Supreme Court granted certiorari.

Issue. Must *Miranda* warnings be given before eliciting statements to be used at a sentencing proceeding?

Held. Yes. Judgment affirmed.

♦ D cannot be used as a "deluded instrument" of his own execution any more than he could be used to obtain his own conviction. The protection against self-incrimination does not vary between the guilt and penalty phases of a capital murder trial.

♦ A defendant may not be compelled to respond to a psychiatrist if his statements could be used against him at a capital sentencing proceeding unless he himself initiates a psychiatric examination or attempts to introduce psychiatric evidence. However, he could be compelled to respond on the condition that the results would be used only for determining competency.

---

l. **Comparing *Miranda* and the Fourth Amendment exclusionary rule.**
In *Stone v. Powell, infra,* the Court held that where the state had provided an opportunity for full and fair litigation of a Fourth Amendment claim, a state prisoner could not be granted habeas corpus relief on the

ground that evidence obtained through an unconstitutional search and seizure was introduced at his trial. In *Withrow v. Williams*, 507 U.S. 680 (1993), the Court held that the *Stone* restrictions on the exercise of federal habeas jurisdiction in Fourth Amendment cases do not extend to a state prisoner's claim that his conviction rested on statements obtained in violation of *Miranda* safeguards. Comparing the Fourth Amendment exclusionary rule to the *Miranda* rule, the Court explained that the exclusionary rule does not involve a personal constitutional right, and the exclusion of evidence at trial does not improve the reliability of evidence introduced at trial. On the other hand, *Miranda* safeguards a fundamental trial right, and by protecting against the possibility of unreliable statements made during in-custody interrogation, *Miranda* guards against the use of unreliable statements at trial. The Court also pointed out that eliminating habeas review of *Miranda* issues would not significantly benefit the federal courts in their exercise of habeas jurisdiction, because it would not prevent a state prisoner from converting his *Miranda* claim to a due process claim that his conviction rested on an involuntary confession.

m.   **Congress cannot overrule *Miranda*--**

Dickerson v. United States, 530 U.S. 428 (2000).

Facts. Two years after *Miranda* was decided, Congress enacted 18 U.S.C. section 3501, which provided that a confession would be admissible in evidence if it is voluntarily given. Dickerson (D) had been indicted for bank robbery. He moved to suppress a statement he gave to the FBI before he had been given *Miranda* warnings. The district court granted the motion, but the court of appeals reversed, holding that under section 3501, *Miranda* warnings were not required if, in fact, the confession was given voluntarily. The rationale was that *Miranda* was not a constitutional holding, so that Congress could have the final say on the question of admissibility. The Supreme Court granted certiorari.

Issue. May Congress overrule the *Miranda* holding?

Held. No. Judgment reversed.

♦   The courts applied a voluntariness test prior to *Miranda*. *Miranda* reflected increased concern about modern custodial police interrogation, concluding that this type of interrogation blurs the line between voluntary and involuntary statements. *Miranda* set forth "concrete constitutional guidelines for law enforcement agencies and courts to follow."

♦   Section 3501 expressly designates voluntariness as the touchstone of admissibility and omits any warning requirement. It was intended to overrule *Miranda*.

Congress does have the power to specify the rules of procedure and evidence, subject to the requirements of the Constitution. But it cannot overrule constitutional rules.

♦ *Miranda* was intended to be a constitutional decision. This is evident from the fact that it applied to the state courts, over which we have no authority except to enforce the Constitution. The language of the *Miranda* opinion referred to it as a constitutional rule. *Miranda* invited legislative action to protect against coerced self-incrimination that would be "at least as effective" as the *Miranda* warnings.

♦ Subsequent opinions have recognized exceptions to *Miranda*, but other opinions have expanded it. This illustrates that, although *Miranda* is a constitutional rule, it is not immutable and must be adapted to new developments.

♦ Section 3501 does provide protection against coerced confessions, but the protection is less than what *Miranda* provides. *Miranda* held that something more than the totality test was necessary under the Constitution. Because it reinstates the totality test, section 3501 is inadequate.

Dissent (Scalia, Thomas, JJ.). The Court has authority to hold unconstitutional any act of Congress that violates the United States Constitution. Section 3501 does not violate the Constitution. In spite of this, the Court now disregards a statute because it contradicts a decision of the Court. The Court does not say that custodial interrogation not preceded by *Miranda* warnings violates the Constitution, and prior cases have recognized that the police can violate *Miranda* without also violating the Constitution. The Court is assuming authority to expand the Constitution by creating a prophylactic, extraconstitutional constitution that is binding on Congress and the states.

━━━━━━━━━━

4.   **Questioning and the Fourteenth Amendment--**

Chavez v. Martinez, 538 U.S. 760 (2003).

Facts. Martinez (P) was shot five times by a police officer. Chavez (D), a patrol supervisor, arrived at the scene shortly after the shooting and accompanied P to the hospital. D questioned P for about 10 minutes in the emergency room, without giving *Miranda* warnings. P was never charged with a crime and his answers to D were never used against him in any criminal prosecution. P sued D under section 1983, claiming that D violated P's Fifth Amendment right against self-incrimination and P's Fourteenth Amendment due process right to be free from coercive questioning. The district court held that D was not entitled to qualified immunity. The Ninth Circuit affirmed. The Supreme Court granted certiorari.

Issue. Does a police officer violate a suspect's constitutional rights by interviewing him when the testimony is never used against the suspect?

Held. No. Judgment reversed.

♦   D is entitled to qualified immunity if he did not violate P's constitutional rights.

♦   Because P was never prosecuted for a crime, and was never compelled to be a witness against himself in a criminal case, his Fifth Amendment right against self-incrimination could not be violated. The "criminal case" language in the Fifth Amendment does not extend to the entire criminal investigatory process. A constitutional violation can occur only at trial.

♦   D's questioning of P was not so egregious as to shock the conscience, which would be necessary to constitute a deprivation of P's liberty interest. D did not interfere with the medical treatment P was receiving, and D did not worsen P's injuries. D had a justifiable interest in questioning P in case P died without giving his side of the story.

Concurrence (Souter, Breyer, Stevens, Kennedy, Ginsburg, JJ.). [Part II] Whether P can pursue a claim of liability for a substantive due process violation is an issue to be addressed on remand.

Concurrence (Scalia, J.). P's Fifth Amendment claim is invalid, so his section 1983 claim cannot stand. Section 1983 does not provide remedies for violations of judicially created prophylactic rules such as the *Miranda* rule.

Concurrence and dissent (Stevens, J.). D's interrogation of P was the functional equivalent of an attempt to obtain an involuntary confession from a prisoner by torturous methods, and constituted an immediate deprivation of P's constitutionally protected interest in liberty.

Concurrence and dissent (Kennedy, Stevens, JJ.). The failure to give a *Miranda* warning does not establish a completed violation when the unwarned interrogation ensues, but an essential part of the Self-Incrimination Clause is the protection against compelled self-incrimination even if it is not used in a criminal trial. In addition, the government may not prolong or increase a suspect's suffering against the suspect's will. In this case, D caused P to believe his treatment would be delayed if he did not answer questions. This states a cause of action under section 1983. However, to assure a controlling judgment, I join Part II of Justice Souter's opinion.

Concurrence and dissent (Ginsburg, J.). D's conduct violated P's right to be spared from self-incriminating interrogation, and the court of appeals was correct, but to assure a controlling judgment, I join Part II of Justice Souter's opinion.

Comment. The second part of Justice Souter's opinion was the only portion of the Court's opinions with which a majority of the Justices agreed.

---

5.   **Evidence Obtained After Pre-Warning Statements.**

   a.   **Introduction.** Because *Miranda* warnings tend to encourage suspects not to talk, police sometimes try to gather information before giving the warnings. The *McNabb-Mallory* rule, *supra*, excludes from federal trials confessions obtained during a period of "unnecessary delay" in taking a suspect before a magistrate for arraignment. However, such confessions, when followed by an unlawful delay, are not rendered inadmissible because they are not the product of the delay.

   b.   *Miranda*: **subsequent admissions--**

Oregon v. Elstad, 470 U.S. 298 (1985).

Facts. Police officers went to Elstad's (D's) home to question him about a burglary. D said, "Yes, I was there." D was transported to sheriff headquarters and approximately one hour later was read his *Miranda* rights for the first time. D waived his rights and made a statement detailing his involvement in the burglary. The state court found both statements inadmissible. The Supreme Court granted certiorari.

Issue. Does the initial failure of the police to administer *Miranda* warnings taint subsequent admissions made after a suspect has been fully advised of and has waived his *Miranda* rights?

Held. No. Judgment reversed.

♦   While *Miranda* requires that an unwarned admission must be suppressed, the admissibility of any subsequent statement turns on whether it is knowingly and voluntarily made. Absent deliberately coercive or improper tactics in obtaining the initial statement, the fact that a suspect has made an unwarned admission does not warrant a presumption of compulsion.

♦   A suspect who had once responded to unwarned yet uncoercive questioning is not thereby disabled from waiving his rights and confessing after he has been given the requisite *Miranda* warnings.

---

   c.   **Physical evidence obtained from pre-warning statement--**

United States v. Patane, 542 U.S. 630 (2004).

Facts. A federal agent was told that Patane (D), a convicted felon, illegally possessed a pistol. The agent started giving D his *Miranda* warning, but D interrupted and said he knew his rights. The agent asked about the pistol. D told him it was in his bedroom. The agent found the pistol where D said it would be. D was indicted for being a felon in possession of a firearm. D moved to suppress the pistol. The district court granted the motion to suppress on the ground that the officers lacked probable cause to arrest him. The Tenth Circuit reversed as to the probable-cause ruling, but upheld the suppression order on the ground that the gun was the fruit of an unwarned statement. The Supreme Court granted certiorari.

Issue. May evidence obtained by questioning a suspect without giving full *Miranda* warnings be used against the suspect?

Held. Yes. Judgment reversed and case remanded.

♦ The *Miranda* rule is a prophylactic used to protect against violations of the Self-Incrimination Clause. The Clause is not implicated by the admission into evidence of the physical fruit of a voluntary statement, so there is no basis for extending the *Miranda* rule to these facts.

♦ The Self-Incrimination Clause protects against having a criminal defendant testify against himself at trial. The introduction of non-testimonial evidence obtained through voluntary statements cannot violate the Clause.

♦ A mere failure to warn does not violate the Constitution, or even the *Miranda* rules for that matter, so the exclusionary rule does not apply. Potential violations occur, if at all, only upon the admission of unwarned statement into evidence at trial, at which point exclusion is a complete and sufficient remedy for any *Miranda* violations.

♦ In *Dickerson, supra,* the Court held that *Miranda* announced a constitutional rule, but this did not change the *Miranda* cases and did not affect the Court's insistence that the closest possible fit be maintained between the Self-Incrimination Clause and any rule designed to protect it. There is no fit here, since the introduction of the gun in this case is not self-incrimination.

♦ While it is true that physical fruit of actually coerced confessions must be excluded, statements taken without sufficient *Miranda* warnings are presumed coerced only for certain purposes and then only when necessary to protect the privilege. In this case, suppression of the gun is not necessary to protect the privilege.

Concurrence (Kennedy, O'Connor, JJ.). *Dickerson* does not undermine the *Miranda* precedents. However, it is not necessary to decide how the failure to give D full *Miranda* warnings should be characterized, so long as the unwarned statements are not later used at trial.

Dissent (Souter, Stevens, Ginsburg, JJ.). The majority's decision not to apply the fruit of the poisonous tree doctrine where police omit full *Miranda* warnings before custodial interrogation gives an evidentiary advantage to those who ignore *Miranda*. A *Miranda* violation raises a presumption of coercion, and the Self-Incrimination Clause extends to the exclusion of derivative evidence.

Dissent (Breyer, J.). The fruit of the poisonous tree approach should be extended to exclude physical evidence derived from unwarned questioning, unless the failure to provide *Miranda* warnings was in good faith, a determination to be made by the trial court.

---

d. Use of "second confession"--

Missouri v. Seibert, 542 U.S. 600 (2004).

Facts. Officer Hanrahan had another officer arrest Seibert (D) without advising D of her *Miranda* rights. Hanrahan then questioned D for over 30 minutes and D made an incriminating statement. Hanrahan gave D a 20-minute break, then resumed questioning after giving D her *Miranda* warnings. D waived her rights, and Hanrahan confronted D with her previous statements. D repeated her confession. D moved to suppress the statements. The trial court suppressed the prewarning statement but admitted the postwarning statement into evidence. The Missouri Supreme Court reversed on the ground that the postwarning statement was a product of the invalid prewarning statement. The Supreme Court granted certiorari.

Issue. May statements given after *Miranda* warnings be admitted if the questioning officer first obtained similar statements without giving the warnings?

Held. No. Judgment affirmed.

♦ If an officer gives the *Miranda* warning and gets a waiver, any subsequent statements are virtually guaranteed to be admissible. Failure to give the *Miranda* warning and obtain a waiver before custodial questioning generally requires exclusion of any statements obtained. This principle is based on the assumption that *Miranda* warnings are given under circumstances that reasonably suggest a real choice between talking and not talking.

♦ The technique of interrogating in successive, unwarned and warned phases challenges the validity of the *Miranda* assumptions. Essentially, this technique renders the *Miranda* warnings ineffective because they are given only after the suspect has confessed. In most situations, there is no justification for accepting the second stage of interrogation as distinct from the first, which is unwarned and inadmissible.

◆ The state claims that *Elstad* authorizes admission of a confession repeated under the question-first strategy. In *Elstad*, the police were arresting the suspect at his home when he admitted being at the scene of a burglary. The suspect was subsequently given *Miranda* warnings at the station house, after which he gave a confession. There was little if any causal connection between the first and second responses, and the failure to give *Miranda* warnings at the suspect's house was only a good-faith mistake.

◆ In this case, unlike in *Elstad*, the first and second rounds of questioning of D were closely related. The unwarned interrogation was conducted in the station house, the interrogation was systematic, and when the police gave the *Miranda* warning, they did not explain that D's prior statement could not be used. The question-first tactic threatens to thwart *Miranda*. Therefore, D's postwarning statement is inadmissible, just as her prewarning statement was.

Concurrence (Breyer, J.). Courts should simply exclude the fruits of an initial unwarned questioning unless the failure to warn was in good faith.

Concurrence (Kennedy, J.). *Miranda* is an important and accepted element of the criminal justice system. The strategy used in this case distorts *Miranda* and does not further a legitimate countervailing interest. The admissibility of postwarning statements should be governed by *Elstad* unless the officers deliberately fail to provide the warning.

Dissent (O'Connor, J., Rehnquist, C.J., Scalia, Thomas, JJ.). The plurality correctly follows *Elstad* to conclude that D's statement cannot be held inadmissible under a "fruit of the poisonous tree" theory. The factors considered under a fruits analysis would focus on the balance between deterrence value and the social cost of excluding reliable evidence. The plurality instead uses those same factors to focus on the psychological judgment about whether D was informed effectively of her right to remain silent. The officer's subjective intent is irrelevant, as the plurality recognizes. In this sense, Justice Kennedy's approach is ill-advised. However, the plurality incorrectly ignores the second argument of *Elstad*, which disregards the psychological impact of a suspect's sense of having let the "cat out of the bag." If the court finds that D's first statement was involuntary, it needs to determine whether any taint was dissipated through the passing of time or a change in circumstances.

---

6. **Developments in the Voluntariness Test.**

   a. **Deception.** The *Miranda* rule prohibits the use of deception and trickery by the police to obtain a waiver of *Miranda* rights, but it does not necessarily preclude such tactics to obtain a confession once the suspect waives his *Miranda* rights. In *Miller v. Fenton*, 796 F.2d 598 (3d Cir. 1986), the court applied a balancing test to define the limits of permissible interrogation. The two factors are the extent of police pressure and the suspect's power of resistance. In that case, the court permitted the interrogating officer's use of feigned sympathy and understanding, as well as falsehoods, to obtain a confession after the suspect waived his *Miranda* rights.

b. Effect of mental impairment--

Colorado v. Connelly, 479 U.S. 157 (1986).

Facts. On his own initiative, Connelly (D) flew to Denver from Boston and told a police officer that he had killed someone and wanted to talk about it. The officer handcuffed D and read him his *Miranda* rights. D stated that he understood his rights and continued talking. When a homicide detective arrived, he reinformed D of his *Miranda* rights. D explained that he had killed a young girl nine months earlier in Denver and wanted to tell the police about it. He told the detective the girl's name and eventually took the police to the site of the murder. Initially, the trial court found D incompetent to stand trial, but after six months of treatment, he became competent. In D's defense, a psychiatrist testified that D had confessed because of "command auditory hallucinations," also characterized as the "voice of God," that commanded D to confess. The psychiatrist testified that D could not make a free and intelligent decision about whether to confess to the police. The trial court suppressed D's statements, finding that they were involuntary. The state supreme court affirmed. The Supreme Court granted certiorari.

Issue. May a court suppress a confession on the grounds that the accused felt "compelled" to make the confession due to a mental disorder, even if the police exercised no coercion over the accused?

Held. No. Judgment reversed.

♦ The confession cases have involved a substantial element of coercive police conduct. When there is no police conduct that causes the confession, there is no basis to conclude that the state has deprived the accused of due process of law.

♦ In prior cases that involved mental problems, such as *Blackburn v. Alabama*, 361 U.S. 199 (1960), and *Townsend v. Sain*, 372 U.S. 293 (1963), the police took advantage of the individual's weaknesses. Without a link between coercive activity of the state and a resulting confession by a defendant, there is no reason to refuse to admit the confession. The Due Process Clause does not limit the admissibility of confessions to only those that the defendant made when totally rational and properly motivated.

♦ The rules of evidence deal with problems of unreliability, not the Due Process Clause.

---

7. *Massiah* and *Miranda* Compared.

    a. **Post-arrest interrogations without counsel.** Recall that *Massiah, supra,* held that once proceedings have been initiated, a defendant cannot be interrogated by the police unless he has been advised of and consciously waived his right to counsel. The defendant was unaware that the police were listening to his conversation, so he could not have consciously waived his right; the evidence obtained was not admissible, even though the defendant was not in the custody of the police when he divulged the information to his friend. *Miranda,* however, is limited to custodial interrogations.

    b. **Waiver after requesting counsel--**

Brewer v. Williams (Williams I), 430 U.S. 387 (1977).

Facts. Williams (D) was suspected of the abduction and murder of a young girl and contacted an attorney when an arrest warrant was issued for him. His attorney made an agreement with the police that D would turn himself in and the police were not to interrogate D during his transportation to the place of trial. D consulted with another attorney who reiterated the instructions of the first attorney to the police officers who transported D. During the trip, one of the officers engaged in conversation with D and was successful in inducing him to show the location of the body. (The officer mentioned that the girl at least deserved a Christian burial.) D was convicted of first degree murder over motions to suppress the evidence. The conviction was upheld by the state supreme court. The district court in a habeas corpus proceeding granted a new trial, and that ruling was upheld by the Eighth Circuit.

Issue. May the right to counsel be waived after affirmative assertions of the desire to have the assistance of counsel by the defendant, on the basis that the defendant understood his right to counsel?

Held. No. Judgment affirmed.

♦ The issue of the waiver of the right to counsel is resolved by applying the constitutional standard to the facts, not by a factual determination. Here, D evidenced a strong desire for the assistance of counsel, and the police used the trip for the purpose of obtaining a waiver of the right as well as of D's Sixth Amendment rights.

♦ The police officers should have refrained from the interrogation entirely or made the warnings of the effects of the waiver just prior to the interrogation.

Dissent (Burger, C.J.). The majority in effect holds that once a defendant makes an election to retain counsel, that election is not freely revocable. The facts here show an effective waiver of the right to counsel.

Dissent (White, Blackmun, Rehnquist, JJ.). D knew he had a right not to say anything to the officers. There is no evidence in the record that D's decision to talk was anything but an exercise of his own free will. This case is unlike *Massiah* because here the officers did not deliberately isolate D from his lawyers; they merely had to transport D. The officer's purpose was not solely to obtain incriminating evidence, and he was hoping to find out if the girl was dead or alive. Not every attempt to elicit information should be regarded as an interrogation.

---

    c.   **Activity considered to be interrogation.**

        1)   The "Christian burial speech" in *Brewer* appears to have been an interrogation within the meaning of *Miranda*, mainly because of the officer's intent.

        2)   Confronting a suspect with physical evidence or with an accomplice who has already confessed may or may not be a *Miranda* interrogation.

        3)   Conversation between officers in a defendant's presence may be an interrogation under *Miranda*.

        4)   It is uncertain whether the *Massiah* right to counsel applies before commencement of adversary judicial proceedings against a defendant.

    d.   **Waiver of Sixth Amendment—*Massiah* rights.** In *Patterson v. Illinois*, 487 U.S. 285 (1988), the Court held that a waiver of *Miranda* rights includes a waiver of the Sixth Amendment right to counsel as well as the Fifth Amendment right against self-incrimination.

    e.   **Use of co-defendant as informer to circumvent the right to counsel.** *Maine v. Moulton*, 474 U.S. 159 (1985), involved the police investigation of possible uncharged offenses, as well as the crime for which formal charges had already been filed. After formal charges of theft were filed against him, Moulton made incriminating statements to his codefendant, who was operating as an undercover agent for the state. The Court held that Moulton's recorded statements were inadmissible at trial, even though the police had a legitimate reason for recording the statements—to investigate Moulton's alleged plan to kill a state witness and to ensure his codefendant's safety. The Court ruled that incriminating statements pertaining to pending charges are inadmissible at the trial of those charges, even though the police were investigating other crimes, if, in obtaining the statements, they violated the Sixth Amendment by knowingly circumventing the accused's right to the assistance of counsel.

f. Use of paid informant--

United States v. Henry, 447 U.S. 264 (1980).

Facts. Henry (D) was incarcerated pending trial under an indictment for bank robbery. A fellow inmate, Nichols, was a paid FBI informant who was serving a sentence for a local offense. Nichols was instructed to be alert to any statements made by the other prisoners, but he was not to question them or initiate conversations about their crimes. After Nichols was released, he told a government agent what D had told him about the bank robbery. Nichols was paid for the information. D was convicted after Nichols's in-court testimony. D filed a petition to vacate his sentence, which was denied by the district court. The court of appeals reversed, and the Supreme Court granted certiorari.

Issue. May the government use statements obtained through a paid informant who, as a fellow inmate, engages in conversation with the defendant?

Held. No. Judgment affirmed.

♦ Under *Massiah*, the government may not interfere with D's Sixth Amendment right to counsel by deliberately eliciting incriminating statements. Here, D was unaware of Nichols's informant role. Thus, D could not have waived his right to counsel. The government may have instructed Nichols not to take affirmative steps to elicit information, but it must have known that such action would likely occur under the circumstances. The jail setting was also essential to D's confidence in Nichols as one sharing a common plight.

♦ D's Sixth Amendment right to counsel was violated because the government intentionally created a situation likely to induce D to make incriminating statements without the assistance of counsel.

Concurrence (Powell, J.). The mere presence of an informant in a jail setting, with instructions to overhear conversations and even to converse with the other inmates, is not necessarily unconstitutional. The error consists in the informant deliberately eliciting incriminating evidence, as was done here.

Comment. The Court in *Henry* specifically distinguished and reserved decision on the situation where an informant is placed in close proximity with the defendant but makes no effort to stimulate conversations about the crime charged. [*See* Kuhlmann v. Wilson, below]

---

g. Use of passive informant--

Kuhlmann v. Wilson, 477 U.S. 436 (1986).

Facts. Wilson (D) and two others shot a garage employee in the course of a robbery. A few days later, D came forward as a witness and described what happened but denied any involvement. The police had proof of D's involvement but did not know who the other perpetrators were. After he was arraigned, D was put in a cell with Lee, a police informant. D told Lee his original story. Lee told D that his story did not "sound too good." Later, after his brother visited him, D told Lee the truth. Lee told the police. D's motion to suppress was denied on a finding that Lee had only listened to D's unsolicited statements. D was convicted of murder. On his second petition for habeas corpus relief, the court of appeals granted relief based on *Henry*, *supra*. The Supreme Court granted certiorari.

Issue. May police use a passive secret informant to record a suspect's admission in jail?

Held. Yes. Judgment reversed.

♦   So long as the informant takes no action, beyond merely listening, that is designed deliberately to elicit incriminating remarks, the informant may report statements to the police.

♦   The state courts specifically found that Lee merely listened to D's spontaneous and unsolicited statements. The court of appeals made a different finding based on Lee's comment that D's story "didn't sound too good." But the state court findings are entitled to a presumption of correctness.

Dissent (Brennan, Marshall, JJ.). The court of appeals accepted the state court's finding but held that deliberate elicitation includes more subtle conduct beyond overt questioning. Here, Lee stimulated conversation about D's role in the robbery and murder by saying that D's story did not "sound too good."

---

h. Right to counsel regarding other crimes--

Texas v. Cobb, 532 U.S. 162 (2001).

Facts. Cobb (D) was indicted for burglary after confessing to the crime. While in police custody, he waived his *Miranda* rights and confessed that he murdered two occupants of the house during the burglary. D was convicted of murder and sentenced to death. The Texas Court of Appeals reversed on the ground that, although he had not been charged with murder, his right to counsel had attached to that crime because it was closely related factually to the charged offense. The Supreme Court granted certiorari.

Issue. When the Sixth Amendment right to counsel attaches, does it encompass offenses that, even though not formally charged, would be considered closely related?

Held. No. Judgment reversed.

♦ Under *McNeil v. Wisconsin, supra*, the Sixth Amendment right to counsel is offense specific. It does not attach until a prosecution is commenced. Even after the right to counsel attaches for charged offenses, a defendant's statements regarding uncharged offenses may be admissible.

♦ Some courts have held that there is an exception for uncharged crimes that are "factually related" to charged crimes. This type of exception is unwarranted.

♦ In *Blockburger v. United States*, 284 U.S. 299 (1932), the Court articulated a test for double jeopardy that inquired whether each offense contains an element not contained in the other. If not, they are the same offense and double jeopardy applies. The *Blockburger* test applies as well to the right to counsel. The right to counsel attaches to the charged offenses and any other offenses that would be considered the same offense under *Blockburger*.

♦ In Texas, burglary and capital murder are not the same offense under *Blockburger*. Therefore, D's Sixth Amendment right to counsel for the burglary charge did not prohibit the police from interrogating D about the murders, and D's confession was admissible.

Concurrence (Kennedy, Scalia, Thomas, JJ.). The Sixth Amendment right to counsel begins with the initiation of adversary judicial proceedings, not upon a suspect's choice to speak with investigators after a *Miranda* warning. The dissent would find that once a suspect has accepted counsel at the beginning of the prosecution, he may not be forced to confront the police during interrogation without the assistance of counsel. But nothing prevents a suspect from desiring counsel to guide him through a trial while still choosing to give an account of the events that occurred.

Dissent (Breyer, Stevens, Souter, Ginsburg, JJ.). The Court's rule leaves the Fifth Amendment's protections in place but diminishes the additional protection provided by the Sixth Amendment right to counsel. Now law enforcement officials may question those charged with a crime without first approaching counsel so long as they ask questions about any other related crime not actually charged in the indictment. The

Texas court followed the commonly accepted approach of applying the right to counsel to all "closely related" crimes, whether charged or not.

F. PRETRIAL IDENTIFICATION PROCEDURES

1. Constitutional Concerns over Eyewitness Identifications.

   a. Introduction. The police use a variety of procedures to verify that the suspect who has been taken into custody is in fact the perpetrator of the crime. These procedures have the functions of solving crimes and providing evidence for the trial of the suspect. It is the latter function that is of interest to the courts, who review pretrial identification procedures to assure that they do not infringe on the rights of the suspect. The issues involved normally concern both the Fifth Amendment (privilege against self-incrimination) and the Sixth Amendment (right to counsel). The rule enunciated in *Schmerber, supra* (only "testimonial compulsion" violates the Fifth Amendment privilege against incrimination), plays a large role in these cases.

   b. Right to counsel at post-indictment lineups. The Sixth Amendment right to counsel (that counsel be notified and be present), which applies to all "critical stages of criminal proceedings," extends to post-indictment, pretrial lineups as conducted for identification purposes.

   1) Later courtroom identification must have independent source--

---

United States v. Wade, 388 U.S. 218 (1967).

Facts. Wade (D) and an accomplice were indicted for bank robbery. Counsel was appointed. Then, without notification or presence of counsel, the police held a lineup with D and several others; two witnesses to the holdup were present. D and the others were dressed like the described robbers and were asked to speak similar words. The witnesses identified D. At trial, the witnesses again identified D. D was convicted and appeals, alleging that the in-court identification should be thrown out because it was based on the post-indictment lineup, which was improperly conducted.

Issue. Does a post-indictment lineup require the presence of counsel?

Held. Yes. Judgment vacated and case remanded.

♦   Any pretrial confrontation of the accused without counsel must be scrutinized to determine whether the presence of counsel is necessary to protect the defendant's basic right to a fair trial as affected by his right to meaningfully cross-examine the witnesses against him and to have effective assistance of counsel at the trial itself.

♦ The right to counsel extends to the present situation because the "accused's inability effectively to reconstruct at trial any unfairness that occurred at the lineup may deprive him of his only opportunity meaningful to attack the credibility of the witness' courtroom identification."

♦ Even if the lineup identification, made without the presence of counsel, is not mentioned at trial, a courtroom identification is inadmissible unless the state shows that it is the product of an independent source other than the pretrial lineup. Factors to consider in determining whether the courtroom identification is independent include: the prior opportunity to observe the alleged criminal act; the existence of any discrepancy between any pre-lineup description and the defendant's actual description; any identification prior to the lineup of another person; the identification by picture of the defendant prior to the lineup; failure to identify the defendant on a prior occasion; and the lapse of time between the alleged act and the lineup identification.

Concurrence and dissent (Black, J.). I would reverse D's conviction if the prosecution had attempted to make use of the lineup identification, but here the defense brought out the identification. The rule established by the Court is unsound; a witness is not able to draw a sharp line between a courtroom identification based on an earlier lineup and one based on independent memory.

Concurrence and dissent (White, Harlan, Stewart, JJ.). Under this rule, for all intents and purposes courtroom identifications are barred if pretrial identifications have occurred without counsel being present. The rule applies no matter how well the witness knows the suspect. The basis for the rule is to avoid improper police conduct, but there is no evidence this rule is necessary. Absent limits on counsel's role at the lineup, I doubt the rule will contribute to more reliable pretrial identifications.

Comment. The Court left open the question of whether substitute counsel might not suffice if notification and presence of the suspect's own counsel would result in prejudicial delay. The Court also noted that neither the lineup itself nor anything D was asked to do there (*i.e.,* repeat words that the robber had actually used, etc.) violated the accused's Fifth Amendment privilege against self-incrimination (it was not testimonial compulsion).

———————————

2) **Application to the states.** *Gilbert v. California*, 388 U.S. 263 (1967), made the rule in *United States v. Wade, supra,* applicable to the states via the Fourteenth Amendment. It also held that neither the Fifth nor the Sixth Amendment (self-incrimination or right to counsel) bars the taking of a defendant's handwriting sample,

obtained from him in the absence of counsel and without advice that it could be used against him.

> **3) Crime Control Act.** Congress in the 1968 Crime Control Act overturned, in federal prosecutions only, the result in *Wade*, providing for the admissibility of eyewitness identification even if the accused was not represented by counsel at the lineup. The constitutionality of the Act has not yet been determined.

2. Retreat from *Wade*.

> **a. Pre-indictment showups--**

Kirby v. Illinois, 406 U.S. 682 (1972).

Facts. Shard was robbed. Kirby (D) and a companion were stopped for interrogation on another matter. Each of them had articles on them with the name "Shard" on them. The two were arrested for a different crime and taken to the station, where the arresting officers connected D with the Shard robbery. Shard was immediately sent for, and he identified the two as the robbers. D was not advised on his right to counsel. D was indicted for robbery six weeks later. He was convicted at trial where Shard again identified him.

Issue. Does a defendant have a right to counsel at a pretrial showup before being charged with a criminal offense?

Held. No. Judgment affirmed.

♦ Before suspects become formally accused, *i.e.,* indictment, information, preliminary hearing, or arraignment, they have no absolute right to counsel.

Dissent (Brennan, Douglas, Marshall, JJ.). There is no reason for concluding that a post-arrest confrontation is different from a post-charge confrontation.

Comment. *Wade* extends only to identifications made *after* a defendant is indicted or otherwise formally charged with a crime. This case can be seen as a retreat by the Court from the position it took in *Wade*. Thus, all the police need to do in order to avoid *Wade* is not formally charge the defendant after arrest until the identification procedures are completed.

> **b. Post-indictment identification--**

United States v. Ash, 413 U.S. 300 (1973).

Facts. After Ash (D) was indicted, prosecution witnesses identified him using photographs without D's counsel being present. The United States Court of Appeals for the D.C. Circuit found that D's right to counsel had been violated. The Supreme Court granted certiorari.

Issue. Does the defendant have a right to have counsel present at a post-indictment photographic identification?

Held. No. Judgment reversed and case remanded.

♦   Unlike a lineup, a photographic display is not an adversarial confrontation. Unlike a post-indictment lineup, this is not a "critical stage" of the proceedings. The accused is not confronted by the prosecution and does not require the assistance of counsel to deal with the intricacies of the law or the advocacy of the public prosecutor.

Concurrence (Stewart, J.). A photographic identification is different from a lineup because there are fewer possibilities for impermissible suggestion and the display can be reconstructed at trial.

Dissent (Brennan, Douglas, Marshall, JJ.). Retention of the photographs cannot reveal the suggestive manner in which the photographs might have been displayed or reveal any accompanying comments or gestures. The reason a lineup is a critical stage is not because of the physical "presence of the accused" at a "trial-like confrontation." A counsel's function at a lineup is that of a trained observer, who is able to detect suggestive influences and understand the legal implication of the events.

Comment. This again is a retreat by the Court from *Wade, supra.* In effect, the Court is uneasy over the possibility that the right to counsel after indictment might have been extended to every situation where a prosecutor was interviewing possible witnesses. In effect the Court has said that this is not a "critical" stage of the proceeding. Arguably, a distinction could have been made between merely interviewing witnesses and identification by witnesses from photographs.

---

3.   **Due Process and Other Limitations.**

   a.   **Introduction.** In addition to the right to counsel that may attach, a defendant may be able to allege that a pretrial confrontation for purposes of identification resulted in such unfairness that his right to due process of law was violated. For example, in *Moore v. Illinois*, 434 U.S. 220 (1977), the defendant was identified in a preliminary hearing, although there was no lineup. The Court held that the victim's identification of the defendant could be reversible error if it was not shown to be harmless.

b. **Factors considered.** In determining what is "unfair," the courts consider all the circumstances surrounding the identification, including the necessity involved for prompt identification (a possible justification for the police procedures used). Also considered is the reliability of the methods the police used for identification. Finally, the court will consider whether alternative means were available to the police that would have protected the defendant's rights more fully.

1) **Emergency situation--**

Stovall v. Denno, 388 U.S. 293 (1967).

Facts. Stovall (D) was arrested and arraigned. At the arraignment, D said he would obtain his own lawyer. Arraignment proceedings were put over until counsel was obtained. The New York police then took D to the hospital room of his stabbing victim, where she identified him by sight and voice. The victim recovered. At trial the prosecutor mentioned the first identification at the hospital. D, on cross-examination of the victim's in-court identification, brought out all the facts concerning the first identification, charging that the first identification violated due process and prejudiced the second identification.

Issue. Was the first identification of D improper because he did not have counsel present?

Held. No.

◆ A claimed violation of due process in the conduct of a confrontation depends on the totality of the circumstances surrounding it. Here, the immediate hospital confrontation was imperative. The victim was the only person who could have exonerated D by saying that he was not her attacker, and no one knew how long she might live. The usual police station lineup was out of the question.

c. **No per se rule--**

Manson v. Brathwaite, 432 U.S. 98 (1977).

Facts. An undercover police officer made an identification of D from a single photograph that was presented to him two days after the officer encountered the person believed to be D. The photograph was obtained pursuant to the officer's general description of the person. The lower court found this to be too suggestive and granted D's petition for habeas corpus.

Issue. Should a per se rule be adopted to exclude evidence obtained from improperly suggestive photographic identification even though such evidence might otherwise be considered reliable?

Held. No. Grant of habeas corpus reversed.

♦ The per se rule would go too far in satisfying the requirement that the jury not hear eyewitness testimony unless that evidence has aspects of reliability. The desire to deter police misconduct is served by the possibility that police actions will lead to the exclusion of identifications as unreliable. The per se rule would not effectively serve the administration of justice, since it would deny the trier of fact reliable evidence. Because of its rigidity, the per se rule would make error by the trial judge more likely. Reliability is therefore the linchpin in determining the admissibility of identification testimony for both pre- and post-*Stovall* confrontations. The jury can then weigh it in its consideration of the evidence.

Concurrence (Stevens, J.). The rules needed in this area are better left to the legislative process. In evaluating the reliability of particular identification testimony, other evidence of guilt should be put entirely to one side, as the Court does in this decision.

Dissent (Marshall, Brennan, JJ.). The Court ignores the due process distinctions of earlier cases. An unnecessarily suggestive pretrial confrontation itself violates due process per *Stovall*. The Court takes the standard from *Simmons v. United States*, 390 U.S. 377 (1968), for assessing the constitutionality of an in-court identification—"a very substantial likelihood of irreparable misidentification"—and transforms it into an out-of-court standard, deleting the word "irreparable." The Court does not sufficiently weigh the following factors: (i) deterrence favors the per se rule; (ii) the dangers of mistaken identity are simply too great to permit unnecessarily suggestive identifications; (iii) repeated miscarriages of justice have resulted from juries' willingness to credit inaccurate eyewitness testimony; (iv) the per se rule is not flexible since identification evidence, by its very nature, can be readily and effectively reproduced; (v) exclusion here both protects the integrity of the truth-seeking function of the trial and discourages police use of needlessly inaccurate and ineffective investigatory methods: and (vi) if the police and the public erroneously conclude, on the basis of an unnecessarily suggestive confrontation, that the right man has been caught and convicted, the real outlaw must still remain at large. The Court seems to be applying a standard based on whether it thinks D was probably guilty, thus denying equal justice under the law. Strong evidence that a defendant is guilty should be relevant only to the determination of whether an error of constitutional magnitude was nevertheless harmless beyond a reasonable doubt. Assuming the applicability of the Court's totality test, the facts of this case require that the officer's testimony be held inadmissible.

Comment. In *Neil v. Biggers*, 409 U.S. 188 (1972), a rape victim had two occasions to see the face of her rapist in dim light. Seven months after the crime and after numerous viewings of lineups, photos, etc., she identified Neil in a showup at the station house. The identification was found admissible. In determining what is "fair" or "unfair" in identification procedures (the due process question), the courts consider all the circumstances leading up to the identification. Unfairness will be found only when, in the light of all the circumstances, the identification procedure was so impermissibly suggestive as to give rise to a real and substantial likelihood of irreparable misidentification. Note that one-person showups are not favored, as they are highly suggestive. But in-court identifications will not be disallowed (when they may be based on such showups) if, under all the circumstances, the showup seems to have been reliable or not probable to have led to a misidentification. In effect, the Court in *Neil* thought the victim was a reliable witness.

G. GRAND JURY INVESTIGATIONS

1. The Structure of the Investigative Grand Jury.

a. Grand jury composition.

1) **Size.** The grand jury normally has 16 to 23 members, with 12 required for indictment.

2) **Selection.** The members are normally chosen from the same group and in the same manner as petit jurors.

3) **Challenges to selection.** Many jurisdictions permit pre-indictment challenge to grand juror selection, at least in limited circumstances (as where a defendant has already been arrested).

4) **Challenges to legal qualification.** Many jurisdictions permit a pre-indictment challenge to legal qualifications of an individual juror, at least in limited circumstances.

5) **Challenges based on alleged bias.** Most states do not permit challenges for alleged bias, but some do, in a wide variety of circumstances.

b. Role of the prosecutor. The prosecutor has no legal authority to exercise absolute control over the grand jury, but she does have significant authority.

1) The prosecutor is legal advisor to the grand jury, which may also seek additional advice.

2) The prosecutor is present during presentation of evidence.

3) Normally, the prosecutor can present whatever evidence she wants; the jury can consider additional evidence.

4) In most jurisdictions, the prosecutor can negate an indictment by refusing to sign and prosecute it.

5) In most jurisdictions, the prosecutor can resubmit a prosecution if the first grand jury has refused to indict.

6) In many jurisdictions, the grand jury can appoint a special prosecutor to assist it.

c. **Role of the court.** The court normally exercises various controls over the grand jury.

1) Often the initial decision to call a grand jury rests with the court.

2) The court normally states the purpose for which the grand jury has been called.

3) The court may order that specific evidence be presented.

4) The court has discretion in issuing subpoenas.

5) The court has authority to insure proper conduct by the prosecutor.

6) The court has power to discharge the grand jury. Often there is a requirement of "good cause."

7) Most jurisdictions permit the court to dismiss the indictment under certain limited circumstances.

d. **Grand jury secrecy.** Generally, grand jury proceedings are held in secret.

1) Courts generally prevent disclosure of juror voting or deliberations.

2) Many jurisdictions do not permit disclosure of such matters as receipt of inadmissible evidence, presence of unauthorized persons, misconduct of the prosecutor, etc. Others (and the Federal Rules of Criminal Procedure) permit such disclosure in connection with a motion to dismiss an indictment.

3) Most jurisdictions do not impose secrecy on witnesses.

4) A trial witness may be questioned about prior testimony for purposes of impeachment, and most courts recently have held that the witness's grand jury transcript can be introduced as well. Some states prohibit this without a showing of "particularized need."

5) Most courts deny disclosure of grand jury testimony to assist a defendant in trial preparation; some allow it of prosecution witnesses.

6) Disclosure may be made to the prosecuting attorney, but most states limit disclosure to other agencies. Federal Rule of Criminal Procedure 6 allows disclosure in judicial proceedings when need outweighs secrecy.

7) Most jurisdictions are beginning to record all grand jury proceedings so that transcripts are available.

e. **Dual nature.** The grand jury acts both as protector and prosecutor. Indictments are required in all federal felony cases and many state felony cases; grand juries help prevent unjust indictments. Various procedural rules apply to assure adequate protection of the innocent, but in many cases, grand juries are in effect merely stamps of approval for prosecutors. Grand juries are also granted various powers to exercise as prosecutors in reaching an indictment.

f. **Subpoena power--**

Blair v. United States, 250 U.S. 273 (1919).

Facts. Some witnesses were subpoenaed to testify before a grand jury in New York investigating Senate campaign practices in Michigan under the Corrupt Practices Act. The witnesses refused to testify, alleging that the grand jury had no jurisdiction and that the Act was unconstitutional. The court ordered the testimony; the witnesses refused and were held in contempt.

Issue. May witnesses be required to testify before a grand jury?

Held. Yes.

♦ Every person within the jurisdiction of the government is bound to testify in court or before a grand jury after being properly summoned. This public duty is subject to mitigation in exceptional circumstances, such as the constitutional exemption from being compelled in any criminal case to be a witness against oneself. A witness is not entitled to claim objections of incompetency or irrelevancy to challenge the authority of the court or of the grand jury or to set limits to the investigation that the grand jury may conduct.

---

2. **Challenges to the Investigation.**

a. **Fourth Amendment objections.** When an investigatory body seeks physical evidence, it may issue a subpoena duces tecum. Such a subpoena can raise Fourth Amendment issues because it is in the nature of a search.

1) **Early approach--**

Boyd v. United States, 116 U.S. 616 (1886).

Facts. Boyd (D) imported 35 cases of glass without paying the required customs fee. The United States (P) obtained a court order requiring D to produce an invoice covering the glass. The applicable federal law permitted such court orders and specified that a defendant's failure to comply would constitute a confession of the government's allegations. D complied with the order under objection. P prevailed at trial and D's property was forfeited. D appeals.

Issue. May the government force a person to produce personal and incriminating documents?

Held. No. Judgment reversed.

- The statute does not authorize the search and seizure of books and papers, but it accomplishes the same thing by forcing D to produce evidence against himself. Such compulsory production of a person's private papers is within the scope of the Fourth Amendment.

- A search and seizure is not unconstitutional unless it is unreasonable. A search for stolen or illegally untaxed goods is entirely different from a search for incriminating private books and papers. Every invasion of private property is a trespass unless justified or excused. The Fifth Amendment's protection against compulsory self-incrimination suggests the kind of search that is unreasonable. Compelling D to produce incriminating evidence is therefore an unreasonable search and seizure.

Concurrence (Miller, J., Waite, C.J.). The statute is unconstitutional as applied in this case because it requires D to incriminate himself. It is not a search and seizure under the Fourth Amendment, however.

Comment. Much of the *Boyd* analysis has since been rejected. [*See, e.g.,* Andresen v. Maryland, *supra*] The Fourth Amendment does still protect against unreasonable subpoenas, however.

2) **Overbreadth doctrine.** In *Hale v. Henkel*, 201 U.S. 43 (1906), the Court separated Fourth and Fifth Amendment challenges to

subpoenas. It held the subpoena in that case unconstitutionally overbroad under the Fourth Amendment, applying the same specificity requirements to a subpoena that apply to search warrants.

3)   Overbreadth doctrine inapplicable to subpoena ad testificandum--

---

United States v. Dionisio, 410 U.S. 1 (1973).

Facts. During a police investigation of gambling, recorded conversations were taken. Dionisio (D) and about 20 others were subpoenaed before the grand jury to give voice exemplars for comparison with these recorded conversations. D refused. The district judge ordered D to comply with the subpoena. When D again refused, he was held in contempt. The court of appeals reversed. The government appeals.

Issue. Does the requirement by the grand jury that a defendant produce voice exemplars for comparison with conversations recorded by the police violate a defendant's Fourth Amendment rights?

Held. No. Judgment reversed and case remanded.

♦   A subpoena to appear before the grand jury is not the "seizure" of the person. Every citizen has the duty to appear before and give evidence to the grand jury absent a constitutional, common law, or statutory privilege not to do so.

♦   The order to give a voice exemplar was not a "seizure." What a person knowingly exposes to the public is not protected. Physical characteristics are not expected to be private. Thus, the grand jury need not decide reasonableness prior to ordering an exemplar.

Dissent (Marshall, J.). The Court seems to base its decision on the relative unintrusiveness of an appearance before a grand jury. When we move beyond the realm of grand jury investigation limited to testimonial evidence, the danger increases that law enforcement officials will usurp the process in order to gain real evidence.

Comment. The Third Circuit Court of Appeals introduced a relevancy challenge to grand jury requests for handwriting samples, photographs, and fingerprints. [*See In re* Grand Jury Proceedings (Schofield), 486 F.2d 85 (3d Cir. 1973)] Since the government failed to show that the requested items were relevant to its investigation of an offense within its jurisdiction, the defendant could not be found in contempt for failure to produce the items.

---

4)   The exclusionary rule--

United States v. Calandra, 414 U.S. 338 (1974).

Facts. Calandra's (D's) business was illegally searched. At a grand jury investigation, D was asked questions based on the evidence that the police gathered in the search. He refused to answer because the search was unlawful.

Issue. May a witness summoned to testify before a grand jury refuse to answer questions derived from illegally obtained evidence?

Held. No.

♦ The exclusionary rule does not bar the admission of illegally seized evidence in all proceedings and against all persons. The suppression rule interferes with the historical function of the grand jury, which is investigation. Traditionally, the grand jury has been allowed to pursue its purposes without all of the same restrictions that have applied to criminal trials.

♦ The deterrence value gained from not permitting questions to be asked based on illegally seized evidence is far outweighed by the damage done to the grand jury function.

b. **Chilling effect objections.** The grand jury has the power to call witnesses, who may be held in contempt for refusing to testify. Being investigatory bodies, grand juries may ask wide-ranging questions. Some commentators claim that this power was abused during grand jury investigations of anti-Vietnam War activists. In *Branzburg v. Hayes*, 408 U.S. 665 (1972), the Court held that a reporter does not have a First Amendment privilege to refuse to reveal confidential sources. Part of the rationale was that judicial control over the grand jury process can prevent harassment of the press.

c. **Subject matter challenges.** A grand jury witness generally cannot object to the questions posed by claiming that the investigation exceeds the jurisdiction of the grand jury or the court. [Blair v. United States, *supra*] The grand jury is permitted to develop facts to determine whether it has jurisdiction. A grand jury may indict only for offenses committed within the jurisdiction of the court that impaneled it.

d. **Relevancy objections.** Most federal circuits do not uphold relevancy objections unrelated to overbreadth challenges to a subpoena duces tecum. The Third Circuit, however, requires the government to make a preliminary showing of validity when it seeks to enforce a subpoena.

[*In re* Grand Jury Proceedings (Schofield), *supra*] This includes a showing by affidavit that the evidence sought is relevant to the investigation.

  e. **Misuse objections.** The government may not use the powers of the grand jury to gather evidence for civil enforcement. Materials gathered by a grand jury may not be disclosed except under limited circumstances. Before the government may obtain a disclosure order, it must satisfy the court that the grand jury proceeding was not used as a subterfuge for obtaining evidence for a civil investigation or proceeding.

  f. **Limitation of objections allowed--**

United States v. R. Enterprises, Inc., 498 U.S. 292 (1991).

Facts. A federal grand jury in Virginia was investigating interstate transportation of obscene materials and subpoenaed records from three companies (Ps): R. Enterprises, Inc. ("Enterprises"); Model Magazine Distributors, Inc. ("Model"); and MFR Court Street Books, Inc. ("MFR"). All three companies were owned by Rothstein. Ps moved to quash the subpoenas on the ground that they asked for materials irrelevant to the grand jury's investigation and that enforcement of the subpoenas would infringe Ps' First Amendment rights. The district court denied the motions, based on the evidence that the companies were related and at least one of them did ship sexually explicit material into Virginia. Ps refused to comply with the subpoenas and were found in contempt, with the fine stayed pending appeal. The court of appeals upheld the subpoena for Model's records because Model did do business in Virginia, but quashed the subpoenas to Enterprises and MFR. The court applied the trial subpoena standards set forth in *United States v. Nixon*, 418 U.S. 683 (1974). This requires the government to show relevancy, admissibility, and specificity, but in this case there was no evidence that Enterprises or MFR had any link with Virginia. The Supreme Court granted certiorari.

Issue. Do the standards for enforcement applicable to trial subpoenas apply to grand jury subpoenas as well?

Held. No. Judgment reversed.

 ◆ The grand jury has a unique role in the criminal justice system. It can investigate based on suspicion, and has wide discretion in pursuing its investigations. A grand jury can compel the production of evidence or the testimony of witnesses it alone considers appropriate, and its operation need not comply with technical procedural and evidentiary rules that govern criminal trials.

 ◆ The special nature of the grand jury makes its subpoenas much different from criminal trial subpoenas, which focus on specific charges and defendants. Grand juries should be free to act without delays to allow courts to rule on the relevancy and admissibility of evidence sought by a grand jury subpoena. Grand jury proceedings must remain strictly secret, and disclosure of the specific reasons for a subpoena would compromise this important secrecy. For these reasons, the *Nixon* standards do not apply.

♦ Federal Rule of Criminal Procedure 17(c) does provide that courts may quash a subpoena if compliance would be "unreasonable or oppressive." Applying this rule in the grand jury context is difficult because the party challenging the grand jury subpoena typically does not know the purpose for the subpoena, making it difficult to persuade the court that the subpoena is unreasonable or could not serve any legitimate investigative purpose.

♦ The proper approach to enforcement of grand jury subpoenas is to give them a presumption of legitimacy. A challenge on relevancy grounds must be denied unless the court determines that there is no reasonable possibility that the material sought will produce information relevant to the general subject of the grand jury's investigation. To make this determination, the court may require the government to reveal the general subject of the grand jury's investigation. This may involve an in camera disclosure prior to disclosure to the party challenging the subpoena.

♦ In this case, such a disclosure was not necessary because Ps' owner was well aware of the general subject of the grand jury investigation. Ps' denial of any connection to Virginia was insufficient to eliminate the reasonable possibility that Ps' business records could produce information relevant to the grand jury's investigation of interstate transportation of obscene materials.

Concurrence (Stevens, Marshall, Blackmun, JJ.). Federal Rule of Criminal Procedure 17(c) requires courts to balance the burden of compliance against the governmental interest in obtaining the documents. A higher degree of probable relevance would justify a more burdensome subpoena. The moving party has the burden of showing the court that there is a valid objection to compliance, at which point the court inquires into the relevance of the subpoenaed materials. In the grand jury context, the law enforcement interest will almost always prevail, but the court should still apply the balancing test.

Comment. The Court noted that the First Amendment claim had not been decided by the court of appeals and the case was remanded on that issue. When the Fourth Circuit did hear that claim, it rejected it. [*See In re* Grand Jury 87-3 Subpoena Duces Tecum, 955 F.2d 229 (4th Cir. 1992)] Ps had argued for application of the "substantial relationship" test that would require the government, once Ps made a prima facie showing of a First Amendment infringement, to establish that the subpoena serves a compelling governmental interest and that the requested evidence substantially relates to the investigation. Instead, the Fourth Circuit held that a simple balancing of the conflicting interests was appropriate, without any special burden on the government.

---

3. **The Privilege Against Self-Incrimination.**

   a. **Grand jury testimony.**

      1) *Miranda* **warnings--**

United States v. Mandujano, 425 U.S. 564 (1976).

Facts. Mandujano (D) agreed to obtain heroin for a government narcotics agent, made some phone calls to that end, took $650 from the agent to make the purchase, and returned an hour later without having made the purchase. D was later called as a witness before a grand jury, where before testifying he was informed of his duty to answer questions, his right against self-incrimination, his right to counsel, and the possibility of punishment for perjury. D testified, was indicted for perjury and for selling heroin, and moved to suppress his grand jury testimony. The motion was granted by the district court and upheld on appeal.

Issue. Does the Fifth Amendment right against self-incrimination protect a witness from perjury committed during a grand jury hearing where full *Miranda* warnings have not been given?

Held. No. Judgment reversed.

♦   The grand jury proceeding is not equivalent to custodial interrogation by the police, so the warnings are not needed.

♦   The right against self-incrimination must be asserted by the defendant.

♦   The Fifth Amendment does not protect a witness from perjury prosecutions. The law will not tolerate falsehoods propagated from the witness stand under the guise of trying to avoid self-incrimination when the possibility of invoking the Fifth Amendment privilege is available.

Concurrence (Brennan, Marshall, JJ.). D should still be liable for his perjury before a grand jury, but a putative defendant should not be called before a grand jury for the purpose of eliciting incriminating evidence from him.

Comment. The Court also suggested that a witness has no right to be represented by counsel when testifying at a grand jury.

---

   2) **Witness's comprehension of Fifth Amendment.** In *United States v. Wong*, 431 U.S. 174 (1977), the Court held that a witness indicted for perjury committed before a grand jury did not have a constitutional right to suppression of her false testimony, even

though she may have been unable to comprehend the prosecuting attorney's explanation of her Fifth Amendment privilege.

   3) **Warning not required.** In *United States v. Washington*, 431 U.S. 181 (1977), the Court answered one of the issues left open by *Mandujano*: a witness need not be warned that he is a target of the grand jury investigation.

b. **Immunity grants.** The Fifth Amendment was intended to protect the witness against criminal prosecution. Hence, if a witness is granted immunity from prosecution, she may be compelled to testify even about her own crimes.

   1) **Transactional immunity.** Transactional immunity precludes prosecution for any transaction about which the witness testifies. It does not preclude a prosecution for perjury, however, and it applies only to responsive testimony. A witness may not gain immunity for unrelated crimes by volunteering testimony about them without being asked.

   2) **Testimonial immunity.** In 18 U.S.C. section 6002, Congress provided for testimonial immunity, which prohibits only the use, including derivative use (using immunized testimony as an investigatory lead), of the witness's testimony in any subsequent prosecution. It does not, however, prohibit prosecution for the offense about which the witness is compelled to testify. *Kastigar v. United States*, 406 U.S. 441 (1972), upheld testimonial immunity as being all that the Fifth Amendment requires.

   3) **Protecting against "taint."** The most difficult practical effect of granting testimonial immunity is in insuring that any subsequent prosecution is not "tainted" by derivative use of the immunized testimony. In *United States v. North*, 910 F.2d 843 (D.C. Cir. 1990), a grand jury was convened to investigate the Iran-Contra affair. While the grand jury was under way, the defendants gave immunized testimony at congressional hearings. When the defendants were indicted, they sought to avoid prosecution on the ground that their immunized testimony had refreshed the memory of certain witnesses who had heard or read about it, or who had been questioned by the congressional committees about it. The court held that to the extent the testimony of the witnesses was shaped by having their memories refreshed by the congressional activity, the government was "using" the immunized testimony in violation of *Kastigar*.

c. **Production of documents—the subpoena duces tecum.**

1) **Introduction.** A common method of obtaining evidence is the issuance of a subpoena duces tecum, or a subpoena requiring production of specified documents. When the subpoena is directed at an individual who would be incriminated by the contents of the documents requested, a self-incrimination issue arises. Generally, the Supreme Court has held that the act of production may constitute protected testimonial communication because it could entail implicit statements of fact, *i.e.,* a witness who produces documents would thereby admit that the documents existed, were in her possession or control, and were authentic. Accordingly, the privilege against self-incrimination does apply to an act that implies an assertion of fact. The test is whether the communication itself, explicitly or implicitly, relates a factual assertion or discloses information.

2) **Papers held by attorney--**

Fisher v. United States, 425 U.S. 391 (1976).

Facts. Fisher (D) was investigated by an IRS agent for possible civil and criminal violations of the Internal Revenue Code, and thereafter D procured documents used by his accountants in the preparation of his returns and gave them to his attorney. The IRS subpoenaed the documents from the attorney, and D claimed the documents were protected by his Fifth Amendment rights.

Issue. Are business papers prepared by another but relating to the business activities of a defendant protected under the Fifth Amendment from compulsory production?

Held. No.

♦ The papers are protected in the hands of the attorney (not by the Fifth Amendment) by the attorney-client privilege, so that the status of the documents is determined by their character in the hands of the client.

♦ Documents like these are not protected because they are not testimonial in nature, and the Fifth Amendment is a protection against compulsory testimony.

Concurrence (Brennan, J.). The papers were not protected in this case because they are business papers and were not prepared for the purpose of being private memoranda of the sort protected by the Fifth Amendment.

Concurrence (Marshall, J.). The Court should focus on the content of the documents, protecting those of a private nature.

3) Sole proprietorship--

United States v. Doe (Doe I), 465 U.S. 605 (1984).

Facts. A grand jury subpoena was issued directing the respondent (R), a sole proprietor, to produce his business records. The district court sustained R's Fifth Amendment challenge on the basis that the act of producing the documents would require R to admit the records exist and are authentic. The Third Circuit affirmed, adding that an individual's private papers were privileged even if voluntarily created and thus so were the business records of a sole proprietor. The United States Supreme Court granted certiorari.

Issue. Does the Fifth Amendment privilege against compelled self-incrimination apply to the business records of a sole proprietorship?

Held. No. Judgment affirmed in part and reversed in part and case remanded.

♦   No Fifth Amendment privilege exists with regard to papers that are prepared voluntarily. The Fifth Amendment protects the person asserting the privilege from compelled self-incrimination, but these business papers were prepared voluntarily.

♦   Even though the papers themselves are not privileged, the act of producing them would be self-incriminating. Thus, D cannot be compelled to produce the records without a grant of immunity.

Concurrence (O'Connor, J.). The Fifth Amendment provides absolutely no protection for the contents of private papers of any kind.

Concurrence and dissent (Marshall, Brennan, JJ.). Contrary to what Justice O'Connor contends, I do not view this opinion as applying to "private papers of any kind." If the opinion stood for that proposition, I would dissent. The documents at stake here are business records, which implicate a lesser degree of concern for privacy than, for example, private diaries. There are certain documents that no person ought to be compelled to produce.

4)   **Small partnership records.** In *Bellis v. United States*, 417 U.S. 85 (1974), the Court held that the Fifth Amendment protects against compelled production of an individual's personal papers. However, an individual cannot rely upon that privilege to avoid producing the records of a collective entity, which he possesses in a representative capacity, even if those records might incriminate him personally. Therefore, a partner in a small law firm may be

required to produce the firm's business records, even when the records will incriminate that partner.

5) **Corporate records--**

Braswell v. United States, 487 U.S. 99 (1988).

Facts. Braswell (D) was the president of two closely held corporations, and had sole authority over their business affairs. D received a grand jury subpoena directing him to produce the books and records of the corporations. D sought to quash the subpoena on Fifth Amendment self-incrimination grounds. The lower courts denied D's motion, and the Supreme Court granted certiorari.

Issue. May the custodian of corporate books and records assert the Fifth Amendment self-incrimination privilege and refuse to deliver such records pursuant to a subpoena?

Held. No. Judgment affirmed.

◆ Under *United States v. Doe (Doe I) (supra)*, the contents of subpoenaed business records are not privileged, and under *Bellis (supra)*, artificial entities such as corporations and partnerships have no Fifth Amendment privilege. D instead asserts his individual privilege on the ground that his act of producing the documents has independent testimonial significance that would incriminate him personally.

◆ If D had conducted his business as a sole proprietor, under *Doe* he would have had the opportunity to show that his act of production would entail testimonial self-incrimination. But the collective entity rule, which recognizes no Fifth Amendment privilege for organizations that have impersonal characters and embody the common interests of their members instead of their purely private or personal interests, applies to corporations.

◆ A corporate officer cannot invoke his personal privilege as to corporate documents because the documents belong to the corporation. The Fifth Amendment applies only to natural individuals and private papers. D is an agent of the corporations and holds the documents in a representative, not a personal, capacity. Even though *Fisher* and *Doe* moved away from the privacy-based collective entity rule by focusing on the act of production, the agency rationale remains valid.

◆ Even though D cannot refuse to comply with the subpoena on the ground that his act of production will be personally incriminating, he acts in a representative capacity and the government may make no evidentiary use of the "individual act" against the individual. The government may establish that the corporation produced the records subpoenaed, thereby creating an inference that the records were authentic corporate records, but it may not present evidence that D was the person who produced the records. Thus, any nexus between D and the documents arises from the corporation's act of production.

Dissent (Kennedy, Brennan, Marshall, Scalia, JJ.). The majority's holding that a corporate agent must incriminate himself even when he is named in the subpoena and is a target of the investigation, and even when compliance requires compelled, personal, testimonial, incriminating assertions, is not supported by any precedent. The fact that the government designates a specific individual in the subpoena belies the agency rationale behind the court's decision. The Fifth Amendment does not provide for exceptions to make it easier for the government to investigate organizations at the expense of the individual employee's right against self-incrimination.

Comment. The collective entity doctrine was held not to apply to a small family partnership consisting of the accused and his wife. [*In re* Grand Jury Subpoena Duces Tecum Dated November 13, 1984, 605 F. Supp. 174 (E.D.N.Y. 1985)] In that case, the court relied on the suggestion in *Bellis* that the collective entity rule might not apply to a small family partnership or one with a preexisting relationship of confidentiality between the partners. If there could ever be partners who could assert the Fifth Amendment, it would be this husband-wife partnership.

---

6)   Act of production immunity--

United States v. Hubbell, 530 U.S. 27 (2000).

Facts. Hubbell (D) pleaded guilty to mail fraud and tax evasion. His plea bargain required him to provide the Independent Counsel full information about matters related to the Whitewater investigation. While D was in prison, he was served with a subpoena duces tecum for the production of 11 categories of documents. He refused to provide the documents or answer questions about them by invoking his Fifth Amendment privilege against self-incrimination. After receiving immunity under 18 U.S.C. section 6002, D produced over 13,000 pages of documents. The contents of those documents led to a second prosecution of D for tax-related crimes and mail and wire fraud. The district court dismissed the indictment because the prosecution's evidence was based on the testimonial aspects of D's production of the documents. The court of appeals vacated and remanded, holding that the prosecution could continue only if the Independent Counsel could show a prior awareness of the documents. The parties entered a conditional plea agreement whereby the charges would be dismissed if the Supreme Court's opinion on appeal made it reasonably likely that D's "act of production immunity" would not significantly impair the prosecution. The Supreme Court granted certiorari.

Issue. Does a witness have a Fifth Amendment protection against being compelled to disclose the existence of incriminating documents that the government is unable to describe with reasonable particularity?

Held. Yes. Judgment affirmed.

♦   The privilege against self-incrimination protects against compelled communications, but it does not protect a suspect against being compelled to engage in conduct that may be incriminating, such as providing a blood sample.

♦   Thus, a person may be required to produce specific documents, even if they contain incriminating information, because the original creation of those documents was not "compelled." However, the "act of production" itself may implicitly communicate statements of fact, such as an admission that the papers existed, were in the suspect's control, and were authentic.

♦   The privilege protects against compelled statements that lead to the discovery of incriminating evidence.

♦   Section 6002 requires the prosecution to prove the evidence it desires to use is derived from a legitimate source wholly independent of the compelled testimony. In this case, the compelled testimony is D's act of producing the documents.

♦   The Independent Counsel needed D's assistance both to identify potential sources of information and to produce those sources. The subpoena was very broad. D had to use "the contents of his own mind" in order to identify and provide the documents requested by the subpoena. This required more of D than merely a physical non-testimonial act of production.

♦   The privilege against self-incrimination protects a grand jury target from being compelled to answer questions designed to elicit information about the existence of sources of potentially incriminating evidence. D's immunity under section 6002 is co-extensive with the constitutional privilege. Because the prosecution cannot prove that its evidence against D was derived from legitimate sources "wholly independent" of D's immunized conduct in providing the documents, the case must be dismissed.

Dissent (Rehnquist, C.J.). The prosecution relied on the documents only for the information they contained, and so did not use any testimonial elements of D's act of production.

Concurrence (Thomas, Scalia, JJ.). Originally, the Fifth Amendment protected against the compelled production of any incriminating evidence, not just of incriminating testimony. When the Amendment was adopted, the term "witness" applied to anyone who furnished evidence, not just to one who testifies, so it would have applied to someone responding to a subpoena duces tecum.

---

7) Bank records--

Doe v. United States (Doe II), 487 U.S. 201 (1988).

Facts. A federal grand jury was investigating Doe (D) for certain financial offenses of which bank records would constitute critical evidence. D was directed to produce bank records from three named foreign banks. He did so, and claimed he possessed no further records, but when questioned about the existence of further records, D claimed his Fifth Amendment privilege against self-incrimination. The grand jury issued subpoenas to the banks, but the banks refused to comply without their customer's consent, which was required under their home country's law. The prosecution sought a court order that D be required to sign the consent form. The consent form covered "any bank" at which D had an account. D refused to sign the form and was held in contempt. The court of appeals upheld the contempt order, and the Supreme Court granted certiorari.

Issue. Is an accused's act of executing a consent form giving the prosecution access to his bank accounts a testimonial communication?

Held. No. Judgment affirmed.

♦　　D claims that his signing the consent form has testimonial significance that will incriminate him, and thus is barred by the Fifth Amendment. D's approach would make every written and oral statement that is significant for its content a testimonial communication under the Fifth Amendment. The correct test, however, is whether the accused's communication itself, explicitly or implicitly, relates a factual assertion or discloses information.

♦　　D may not be forced to reveal, directly or indirectly, his knowledge of facts relating him to the offense or to share his thoughts and beliefs with the government. In most cases, a verbal statement, whether oral or written, does in fact convey information or assert facts, and would fall within the privilege.

♦　　The consent directive in this case, however, is not testimonial. It does not refer to a specific account, it does not acknowledge that D has an account in any institution, and it does not describe any documents or other information that may exist. While it does give the government access to a potential source of evidence, it does not direct the government toward any information; if the government finds any information, it will do so only by its independent efforts.

♦　　The form does not admit or assert D's consent; it merely states that it shall be construed as consent for purposes of the foreign laws. It explicitly states that it was signed pursuant to a court order, so that it does not reveal D's actual intent or state of mind. If the government does receive any records with the form, the only factual statement made by anyone is the bank's declaration that it believes the accounts are D's.

H. THE SCOPE OF THE EXCLUSIONARY RULES

1. **Standing to Object to the Admission of Evidence.** It is a basic principle of constitutional law that a person has no standing to complain of the violation of another's constitutional rights. The result in search and seizure cases, therefore, is that only the person who is "aggrieved" by an unlawful search can invoke the exclusionary rule.

   a. **Federal courts.** If the police violate the constitutional rights of A (*e.g.,* search her apartment without a valid warrant), may evidence that they find be used in the prosecution of others whose rights were not invaded (*e.g.,* drugs belonging to B that are found in the apartment)? The federal courts have held that other persons must have (i) "some interest in the property seized" or the premises searched, or (ii) some "reasonable expectation of freedom from government intrusion" in order to have standing to raise the constitutional issue on their own behalf. [*See* Rakas v. Illinois, *infra*]

   b. **State courts.** Some state courts have held that a person has standing if anyone's constitutional rights were invaded to obtain the evidence. [People v. Martin, 290 P.2d 855 (Cal. 1955)]

   c. **Fourth Amendment rights are "personal."** In *Alderman v. United States*, 394 U.S. 165 (1969), the Court dealt with the question of who has standing to object to the admission of evidence that was the product of an electronic surveillance in violation of the Fourth Amendment. The Court held that it was any person (i) whose conversations were so overheard, or (ii) on whose premises such conversations occurred, whether or not that person was present or participated in the conversations. "Fourth Amendment rights are personal rights which . . . may not be vicariously asserted."

      1) **No standing to assert Fourth Amendment by private party.** Under *Alderman*, the supervisory power of the court does not authorize a federal court to exclude evidence obtained by an illegal search that did not violate the defendant's Fourth Amendment rights, but that was obtained from a private party who was not the victim of the challenged practices. Defendants in these cases do not have standing to raise the Fourth Amendment violation. [United States v. Payner, (*supra*)]

   d. **"Automatic standing"—interest in the property seized.**

      1) **History of the rule.** A party has standing when he has and can show a legally protected interest in the property seized. But when the property seized is narcotics or some other contraband prop-

erty, possession of which is in itself a crime, the defendant is in an awkward position. To suppress such evidence, he would have to allege ownership or possession that is in itself unlawful, which could then be used as an admission against him. Thus a defendant could only assert what he believed to be a valid Fourth Amendment claim by waiving his Fifth Amendment privilege against self-incrimination. To alleviate this problem, the Supreme Court held that when a defendant is being prosecuted for possession of contraband, he is not required to admit any interest in the property in making his motion to suppress the contraband as having been illegally seized; *i.e.,* he is deemed to have "automatic standing." [*See* Jones v. United States, 362 U.S. 257 (1960)]

2) **"Automatic standing" rule reversed.** Twenty years later, *Jones* was overruled by the Court, which held that defendants charged with crimes of possession may only claim the benefits of the exclusionary rule if their own Fourth Amendment rights have in fact been violated. [*See* United States v. Salvucci, 448 U.S. 83 (1980)]

e. **Expectation of privacy.** In *Jones*, the Court also held that anyone "legitimately on the premises" has a reasonable expectation of privacy sufficient to confer standing. The question of when standing is conferred was further elucidated in *Mancusi v. DeForte*, 392 U.S. 364 (1968), in which the Supreme Court upheld the standing of a union official to seek suppression at a state trial of union documents seized from a union office that he shared with others. Justice Harlan stated that standing depended not on a "property right" in the invaded place but on whether the area was one in which there was "a reasonable expectation of freedom from governmental intrusion." Here the union official shared a large room with several other officials and spent a considerable amount of time in the office. Moreover, he had custody of the papers at the moment of their seizure.

f. **Current approach.**

1) **"Legitimately on the premises" test insufficient--**

Rakas v. Illinois, 439 U.S. 128 (1978).

Facts. Police stopped the car in which Rakas and others (Ds) were passengers. The car was suspected as the getaway car from a recent robbery. Police searched the car and found a rifle and shells under the front seat and in the glove compartment. Ds did not own the car (the owner was driving), nor did they claim a possessory interest in the rifle or shells. At trial, Ds moved to suppress the evidence, but the motion was denied because Ds lacked standing. Ds were convicted and appeal.

Issue. Do all persons "legitimately on the premises" have standing to challenge a search of those premises?

Held. No. Judgment affirmed.

♦   *Alderman, supra,* established the personal nature of Fourth Amendment rights. Ds argue for a "target" theory that would give any defendant at whom a search was "directed" standing to challenge the search and to move for suppression. But the Fourth Amendment provides no protection against incriminating evidence obtained by a search of a third person's premises or property.

♦   The *Jones* phrase "legitimately on premises," implies an overbroad measurement of Fourth Amendment rights. The true test is whether the defendant has a legitimate expectation of privacy in the premises he was using.

♦   Ds here had no property or possessory interest in the car or the property seized and did not show any legitimate expectation of privacy in the areas in which the evidence was found (glove compartment and under the front seat). Therefore, they do not have standing to challenge the search.

---

2)   Mere ownership insufficient--

Rawlings v. Kentucky, 448 U.S. 98 (1980).

Facts. Rawlings (D) and Cox, D's companion of a few days, were visiting in Marquess's house. D was carrying several illegal drugs, which he put in Cox's purse shortly before police arrived with a warrant for Marquess's arrest. The police did not find Marquess, but they went to get a search warrant for the house and would not let D or Cox leave without a consensual body search. When they obtained the second warrant, the police made Cox empty her purse. When she did so, D claimed his drugs. At the suppression hearing, D admitted that he did not think the purse would be free from governmental intrusion. The state courts held that D had no standing to challenge the search. D appeals.

Issue. Does ownership of items kept in someone else's purse necessarily entitle the owner to Fourth Amendment rights against search of the purse?

Held. No. Judgment affirmed.

♦   D could not claim any legitimate expectation of privacy in the purse. He had known Cox for only a few days and had no right to exclude others from her purse. He did not expect that the purse would be free from searching. Although his ownership of the drugs is a fact to consider, it is not sufficient, by itself, to constitute a legitimate expectation of privacy. Thus, the police did not violate any legitimate expectation of privacy held by D.

Concurrence (Blackmun, J.). The right to exclude may be determinative of a legitimate privacy interest, but D's possessory interest alone was insufficient.

---

3) **Passenger in car sufficient.** In *Brendlin v. California*, 551 U.S. 249 (2007), the Court held that a passenger, as well as the driver, is "detained" or "seized" when an officer stops the car. Therefore, the passenger may challenge the constitutionality of the stop. The reason is that a reasonable passenger would believe that no one in the car was free to depart without police permission. In that case, officers had stopped the car without any grounds and recognized a passenger as a parole violator. They arrested him and searched him, finding drugs. The Court held that the trial court should not have denied his suppression motion on the ground that he was seized only upon the arrest.

4) **Brief invited stay insufficient--**

Minnesota v. Carter, 525 U.S. 83 (1998).

Facts. An informant told a state police officer that he had seen people putting white powder into bags in a ground-floor apartment. The officer looked through the same window, through a gap in the closed blind, and observed the bagging activity of Carter and Johns (Ds), and Thompson, the apartment's lessee. The officer notified his headquarters to get a search warrant. When Ds left the building, they were arrested. A search of their vehicle uncovered cocaine. A search of Thompson's apartment pursuant to a warrant uncovered more cocaine. Ds, who were only temporary out-of-state visitors and had been in the apartment for only two-and-a-half hours, were convicted of state drug offenses. The trial court denied Ds' challenge to the legality of the officer's intrusion into Thompson's apartment. The state supreme court reversed, holding that Ds had standing because of their legitimate expectation of privacy in the apartment. The Supreme Court granted certiorari.

Issue. Does an invitee to a person's home have an expectation of privacy in the home if the invitee stays only a few hours in the home?

Held. No. Judgment reversed.

♦   The Fourth Amendment is a personal right that must be invoked by an individual. The extent of the protection depends on where the person is. The capacity to claim Fourth Amendment protection depends on whether the person claiming protection has a legitimate expectation of privacy in the invaded place.

♦ The text of the Fourth Amendment suggests that its protections extend only to people in "their" houses, but the cases have recognized a legitimate expectation of privacy in someone else's house in certain circumstances, such as when the invitee is an overnight guest. It is not enough, however, that the invitee was legitimately on the premises.

♦ In this case, Ds were in the apartment for only a few hours. Their visit was commercial in nature, not residential. Therefore, Ds did not have a Fourth Amendment protection against any search that may have occurred.

Concurrence (Scalia, Thomas, JJ.). The obvious meaning of the Fourth Amendment is that each person has the right to be secure against unreasonable searches and seizures in his own person, house, papers, and effects. This meaning extends to an overnight guest, on the basis that it is a temporary residence, but it cannot extend to the use of an apartment for packaging cocaine. If an invitee is to be protected against governmental searches of the room in which business is conducted, the state and federal legislatures must create that protection, because the Fourth Amendment does not.

Concurrence (Kennedy, J.). Almost all social guests have a legitimate expectation of privacy in their host's home. Ds could have no protection against a search of Thompson's apartment unless they can establish a meaningful connection to that apartment. But here all Ds can show is a fleeting and insubstantial connection with the apartment, so they had no legitimate expectation of privacy.

Dissent (Ginsburg, Stevens, Souter, JJ.). An invited guest should share the host's shelter against unreasonable searches and seizures. The home has a special status under the Fourth Amendment. A homeowner who chooses to share the privacy of the home with a short-term guest satisfies the twofold requirement that (i) both host and guest have exhibited an actual expectation of privacy, and (ii) that expectation is one our society is prepared to recognize as reasonable. This is still a less extensive protection than the "legitimately on the premises" approach that was rejected in *Rakas*.

———————

2. **"Fruit of the Poisonous Tree" Doctrine.** To prevent the acquisition of evidence by illegal means (such as by an unlawful search and seizure), the evidence *directly* acquired by such means shall not be used, nor shall that which is *indirectly* acquired (*i.e.,* evidence that the illegally seized evidence leads to) be used.

   a. **Consequences of illegal arrest or search followed by incriminating statements.**

1) **Introduction.** It was clear before *Wong Sun, infra,* that goods illegally seized were not admissible; the same is true for testimony about such goods. For example, evidence about matters observed during an unlawful invasion are excluded. *Silverman v. United States*, 365 U.S. 505 (1961), excluded matters overheard (verbal statements) during such an illegal invasion.

2) **Witnesses.** *Wong Sun v. United States*, 371 U.S. 471 (1963), carried the "fruit of the poisonous tree" doctrine a step further. Here the police unlawfully entered the defendant's bedroom and unlawfully arrested him. The defendant immediately confessed, and his confession led to other witnesses. The Court held that the confession and the other witnesses must be excluded. The confession did not result from an intervening "independent act of a free will." The government argued that the defendant's confession was "voluntary" and did not come as a result of any "psychological coercion."

b. **Confession as the fruit of an illegal arrest or search.**

1) **Circumstances considered.** In *Brown v. Illinois*, 422 U.S. 590 (1975), the Court held that whether an incriminating statement is the product of free will under *Wong Sun* depends on a number of factors—the time elapsing between the illegality and the statement, the presence of intervening circumstances, and particularly the flagrancy of the illegality.

a) The fact that the *Miranda* warnings are given before the statement is made does not alone make the statement a product of free will. All the circumstances must be considered.

b) *Brown* reversed a state conviction based on an admission made two hours after unlawful arrest, the *Miranda* warnings having been given at the time of arrival at the police station.

2) ***Miranda* warnings insufficient.** In *Dunaway v. New York*, 442 U.S. 200 (1979), the Court reaffirmed the *Brown* notion that *Miranda* warnings alone are insufficient to dissipate the taint of an improper arrest.

c. **In-court identification by victim--**

United States v. Crews, 445 U.S. 463 (1980).

Facts. Crews (D) was illegally arrested. While D was in custody, the police photographed him, then released him. A robbery victim identified D's photo, and later identified D at a lineup. D was then indicted and convicted. The trial court suppressed all pretrial identifications but not the in-court identification at trial. The court of appeals reversed, holding that the in-court identification should have been excluded as tainted by the illegal detention (which was an arrest without probable cause). The United States appeals.

Issue. May an in-court identification by a victim be suppressed because the defendant was first identified as a result of evidence obtained during an unlawful arrest?

Held. No. Judgment reversed.

♦ The victim's presence in the courtroom at D's trial is not tainted because her identity was known to the police before any Fourth Amendment violation.

♦ The illegal arrest of D did not taint the victim's ability, acquired at the time of the crime, to accurately identify D.

♦ D cannot claim immunity from prosecution on the basis that his appearance in court resulted from an illegal arrest. D's face is not a suppressible "fruit" of the illegal arrest.

---

d. **Confession after *Payton* violation.** In *New York v. Harris,* 495 U.S. 14 (1990), the police went to Harris's apartment to arrest him without a warrant in violation of *Payton v. New York, supra.* Harris waived his *Miranda* rights and admitted that he had committed the homicide. At the police station, he again admitted his guilt and signed a written inculpatory statement. At trial, the court suppressed the confession made in his apartment. The state courts also held that the later confession was inadmissible as the fruit of the *Payton* violation. The Supreme Court reversed, holding that *Payton* is designed to protect the physical integrity of the home, not to protect against subsequent lawful custody. The police had Harris in lawful custody when he made the written statement.

e. **"Independent source" upon which the warrant was secured.** In *Segura v. United States, supra,* agents entered an apartment without a warrant and without permission and observed drug paraphernalia in plain view. A search warrant was not issued until approximately 19 hours after the initial entry by agents. The Supreme Court held that the fruits of the judicially authorized search were untainted because the information upon which the search warrant was derived came from sources wholly unconnected with, and independent of, the entry and was known by the agents before the entry. The Court stated that evidence will not be excluded unless the illegality is at least the "but for" cause of the discovery of the evidence. This holding was followed in *Murray v. United States*, 487 U.S. 533 (1988), when the Court declined to require exclusion of evidence that was seized during a valid warrantless entry, even though the evidence had been observed during an earlier illegal entry.

f.   Tainted witness--

United States v. Ceccolini, 435 U.S. 268 (1978).

Facts. A police officer in Ceccolini's (D's) flower shop was conversing with an employee (Hennessey) and discovered an envelope with unlawful bets in it. Without disclosing that he knew its contents, the officer asked Hennessey to whom it belonged. Hennessey indicated that it belonged to D. Four months later, without disclosing that the officer had told them about the envelope, police interviewed Hennessey. A year later, D testified before a grand jury that he had never taken illegal bets at his shop. Hennessey testified to the contrary. D was indicted for perjury. Hennessey testified against D at trial. After finding D guilty, the district court granted D's motion to suppress Hennessey's testimony and set aside the guilty finding. The court of appeals affirmed.

Issue. Should the exclusionary rule be implemented without considering the degree of free will exercised by the witness and the period of time elapsed between the time of the illegal search and the initial contact with the witness?

Held. No. Judgment reversed.

♦   Since the cost of excluding live witness testimony often will be greater than excluding other evidence, a closer, more direct link between the illegality of the search and that kind of testimony is required than exists here.

♦   Witnesses often come forward and offer evidence on their own. The more willing a witness is to freely testify, the more likely it is that she will be discovered by legal means, and there is less incentive to conduct an illegal search to discover the witness. Furthermore, exclusion would prevent a witness from testifying about relevant and material facts, no matter how unrelated such testimony is to the purpose of the prior illegal search or the evidence discovered during the search.

Dissent (Marshall, Brennan, JJ.). No logical distinction can be drawn between verbal and physical evidence for purposes of the exclusionary rule. The independent-source rule (if knowledge of evidence is gained from a source independent of police illegality, it should be admitted) would cover the situation of a witness whose identity is discovered in an illegal search but who later comes to the police with the desired information for reasons unrelated to the official misconduct. But that is not the case here.

g. **"Inevitable discovery" doctrine--**

Nix v. Williams (Williams II), 467 U.S. 431 (1984).

Facts. In the trial of Williams (D) for murder, evidence was admitted of the condition of a child's body as it was found, articles and photographs of her clothing, and results of post mortem chemical tests. The trial court concluded that the State (P) had proved that if a search by volunteers for her body had not been suspended and D had not led police to her, her body would have been discovered within a short time and in essentially the same condition as it was found. The United States District Court denied habeas corpus relief and adopted the inevitable discovery exception to the exclusionary rule. The Eighth Circuit reversed, because an inevitable discovery exception requires proof that the police did not act in bad faith and the record could not support such proof.

Issue. Should the ultimate or inevitable discovery exception to the exclusionary rule be adopted and, if so, does it require a threshold showing of police good faith?

Held. Yes. Judgment reversed.

♦ The inevitable discovery exception to the rule should be adopted, but no showing of good faith by the police is required.

♦ Exclusion of physical evidence that would inevitably have been discovered adds nothing to either the integrity or fairness of a criminal trial. It would have taken an additional three to five hours to discover the body if the search had been continued; but had the search continued, the body would inevitably have been found. Fairness can be assured by placing P in the same position it would have been in had the impermissible conduct not taken place. If P can prove that the evidence would have been obtained inevitably, there is no rational basis to exclude the evidence.

♦ There is no requirement that the police prove an absence of bad faith. The social costs of the exclusionary rule in withholding from juries relevant evidence far outweigh any possible benefits of deterrence that a good faith requirement might produce.

Concurrence (Stevens, J.). P adduced evidence that demonstrated that a search was under way, which would have discovered the body. Because the burden of proof is on P, the inevitable discovery rule does not permit P to avoid the uncertainty it would have faced but for the constitutional violation.

---

3. **Use of Illegally Obtained Evidence for Impeachment Purposes.** As a general rule, illegally obtained evidence is inadmissible for any purpose. How-

ever, an exception has been made in certain narrow circumstances involving the impeachment of a defendant's testimony when he appears to be committing perjury (based on the illegally seized evidence).

a. Voluntary confession obtained in violation of *Miranda*--

Harris v. New York, 401 U.S. 222 (1971).

Facts. Harris (D) was being prosecuted for a drug charge. After arrest and prior to trial, in violation of D's constitutional rights (as set forth in the *Miranda* case concerning custodial interrogation), D made statements concerning the sale of drugs by him to an undercover agent. At trial D took the stand and testified that he never made the sale. Evidence was then offered by the prosecution concerning D's statements after arrest; the purpose of the statements was to contradict D's testimony that he never made the sale. The trial court instructed the jury that this testimony was to be considered only in deciding D's credibility.

Issue. May statements made by a defendant that are otherwise inadmissible be used to impeach a defendant's credibility?

Held. Yes.

◆   A statement obtained in violation of the *Miranda* rule, although inadmissible against D as part of the prosecution's case on guilt, may be used to impeach D's testimony if he takes the stand at trial, provided that the statement is otherwise voluntary and trustworthy under proper legal standards.

◆   The "shield provided by *Miranda* cannot be perverted into a license to use perjury by way of a defense, free from the risk of confrontation with prior inconsistent utterances" even though unlawfully obtained.

Dissent (Brennan, Douglas, Marshall, JJ.). The choice to testify in one's own defense must be "unfettered." Thus it cannot be burdened by the risk that an illegally obtained prior statement may be used for impeachment purposes.

---

b. Exceptions.

1)   In *Oregon v. Hass, supra,* the Court applied *Harris* to the situation where the suspect was advised of his rights and asserted them (he asked for a lawyer), but the police refused to honor his request and continued to question him.

2)   But in *United States v. Hale*, 422 U.S. 171 (1975), the Court held that, pursuant to its supervisory powers (without deciding whether

Miranda required it), it was reversible error to permit cross-examination of a defendant concerning his silence during police interrogation (after he had received the *Miranda* warnings).

c. Statements made during cross-examination--

United States v. Havens, 446 U.S. 620 (1980).

Facts. At the suggestion of Havens's (D's) traveling companion, who had been seized for attempting to smuggle drugs, a customs official searched D's suitcase and found a cut-up T-shirt that matched pieces used to sew secret pockets in D's companion's shirt to smuggle the drugs. The customs official had failed to get a search warrant, however. At trial, D denied on direct examination that he had ever been involved in smuggling drugs. On cross-examination, D denied knowledge of having a T-shirt with missing pieces in his luggage. The prosecution then introduced the seized T-shirt to rebut D's credibility. The court of appeals reversed D's conviction, holding that illegally obtained evidence could be used for impeachment only of a statement made in direct examination. The Supreme Court granted certiorari.

Issue. May illegally obtained evidence be used to impeach statements made by a defendant during a cross-examination that is reasonably suggested by the direct examination?

Held. Yes. Judgment reversed.

♦   Attempts by the prosecution to bring in illegally obtained evidence by bringing out testimony for the first time on cross-examination and then rebutting it with the suppressed evidence violate the defendant's rights and are prohibited. However, this does not mean that only statements on direct examination may be rebutted.

♦   The exclusionary rule is not a license to use perjury by way of defense. If the cross-examination is reasonably suggested by the direct examination, then statements by the defendant may be rebutted with illegally seized evidence.

Dissent (Brennan, Stewart, Marshall, Stevens, JJ.). This new rule allows a reasonably talented prosecutor to work in evidence on cross-examination that is suppressed because of illegal police conduct. This will compel D to forgo testifying on his own behalf.

---

d. No impeachment of defense witnesses--

James v. Illinois, 493 U.S. 307 (1990).

Facts. James (D) was taken into custody as a murder suspect. He had changed his hair from a straight, reddish-brown style to curly black. He told police that he had done so to change his appearance, but these statements were suppressed because the police lacked probable cause to arrest D. At trial, five witnesses testified that the murderer had long straight reddish hair and that they had seen D previously with that hair color and style. D called a witness who testified that on the day of the murder, D's hair was black. The prosecutor impeached this witness using D's otherwise suppressed statements. D was convicted. The Illinois Supreme Court affirmed. D appeals.

Issue. May the prosecution use a defendant's illegally obtained testimony to impeach the defendant's witnesses at trial?

Held. No. Judgment reversed.

◆　　　To expand the class of impeachable witnesses from the defendant alone to all defense witnesses would significantly undermine the deterrent effect of the general exclusionary rule without promoting the truth-seeking function as much as the exception for impeaching the defendant himself. While a defendant facing prison may be more likely to perjure himself, a defense witness facing criminal prosecution for perjury is already discouraged from committing perjury.

◆　　　Applying the exception to all defense witnesses may chill defendants' ability to present a defense through others. It would also enhance the value of illegally obtained evidence by making it usable in more situations.

Dissent (Kennedy, J., Rehnquist, C.J., O'Connor, Scalia, JJ.). The Court has given the defense broad immunity to introduce whatever false testimony it can obtain from friendly witnesses. The Court has given the truth-seeking function of a criminal trial insufficient weight in balancing the competing interests. Depriving jurors of the knowledge that the defendant himself had revealed the falsity of a defense witness's testimony is misleading. Forcing the prosecution to remain silent in effect bolsters the falsehood.

━━━━━━━━━━━━━━━

e.　　**Use of pre-arrest silence.** In *Jenkins v. Anderson*, 447 U.S. 231 (1980), Jenkins turned himself in to police two weeks after a killing. At his murder trial, Jenkins testified that he had acted in self-defense. On cross-examination, he was questioned as to why he waited two weeks if he had truly acted in self-defense. The Supreme Court affirmed Jenkins's conviction, holding that the Constitution does not prohibit the use of a defendant's pre-arrest silence for impeachment purposes.

f.　　**Use of post-*Miranda* warning silence to rebut insanity defense.** In *Wainwright v. Greenfield*, 474 U.S. 284 (1986), the Court held that a defendant's silence or request for counsel after receiving *Miranda* warnings cannot be used to rebut an insanity defense.

4. Allocation of the Burden of Proof.

    a. Burden of proof. Practices vary among the states on the issues of who has the burden of going forward with the proof of admissibility and which party bears the ultimate burden of proof. The approach of the federal courts is described here.

        1) Search pursuant to warrant. In the case of a search with a warrant, the accused has the burden of establishing that the warrant was issued without a sufficient showing of probable cause.

        2) Search without a warrant. However, for a search without a warrant, most courts hold that the government has the burden of showing the reasonableness of the search. If there has been an unlawful search, the government also has the burden of proving that challenged evidence is not the "fruit" of the search.

    b. Approach in New York--

People v. Berrios, 270 N.E.2d 709 (N.Y. 1971).

Facts. Police testified that the defendants dropped envelopes of heroin when approached. Then they were searched.

Issue. Does the accused bear the burden of proof when asserting the illegality of a warrantless search?

Held. Yes.

♦   Police bear the burden initially of going forward to show the legality of the police conduct in the first instance. But ultimately the defendant bears the burden of proof on a motion to suppress to show that evidence should not be admitted.

---

    c. Standard of proof on confessions. *Lego v. Twomey*, 404 U.S. 477 (1972), held that in a hearing before a trial judge to determine whether a confession is voluntary, the prosecution need only prove by a preponderance of the evidence that the confession is voluntary.

        1) As to evidence allegedly seized in violation of the Fourth Amendment, *i.e.,* search and seizure, or the Fifth Amendment, *i.e.,* confessions, the prosecution need not prove admissibility beyond a reasonable doubt.

2) A hearing as required by *Jackson v. Denno, infra,* is not designed to implement the presumption of innocence or insure the reliability of jury verdicts, but only to prevent the use of coerced confessions that violate due process—quite apart from the issue of truth or falsity.

3) Justices Brennan, Marshall, and Douglas dissented in *Lego v. Twomey*, stating that such a rule is a violation of due process and self-incrimination rights.

d. **Waiver.** Under *Colorado v. Connelly, supra*, a waiver of *Miranda* rights need be proven only by the preponderance of evidence.

e. **Other issues relating to the hearing.**

1) **Testimony by the defendant.** Generally, the defendant may testify in a hearing to determine the admissibility of evidence without waiving her right to decline to take the stand in her own defense at trial.

2) **Holding the hearing in the presence of the jury.** Many jurisdictions, including the federal courts, follow the procedure of holding hearings on the admissibility of allegedly illegal confessions or search and seizures outside the presence of the jury.

3) **Specific findings.** Normally, the judge need not make specific and formal findings of fact or write an opinion, but his conclusion must be clear from the record.

4) **The jury's presence.** *Jackson v. Denno*, 378 U.S. 368 (1964), held that it denies a defendant due process to allow the jury to hear an allegedly involuntary, but true, confession in order to decide upon its voluntariness. The State must provide the defendant with a separate and preliminary hearing on the issue of voluntariness; only if the confession is found to be voluntary can the jury then hear it as evidence. However, it is not improper for a trial court to conduct a hearing, in the jury's presence, on a constitutional challenge to the admissibility of evidence, such as an in-court identification that was allegedly tainted by an improper pretrial identification procedure. [Watkins v. Sowders, 449 U.S. 341 (1981)]

III. THE COMMENCEMENT OF FORMAL PROCEEDINGS

A. PRETRIAL RELEASE

1. Bail.

    a. Setting bail. Bail is typically set by the committing magistrate, before whom the defendant must be presented within a certain time after arrest. In the state system, the magistrate is usually a municipal court judge who sets (i) a time for a preliminary hearing and (ii) the amount of bail. In the federal system, the local United States commissioner warns the defendant of her rights and sets bail. The few statistics available on the bail system are not very accurate.

        1) One study showed that 50% of all cases were finally disposed of within 36 hours of arrest. This is a good record—until it is realized that drunk driving cases were included and made up 30 to 40% of all the arrests.

        2) The more serious cases often involve a long wait before final disposition, and this wait is sometimes spent in jail.

    b. Purposes of bail.

        1) **To insure appearance.** The United States (by statute) and all states (by statute or state constitution) give the right to bail before trial in noncapital cases, but most do not in capital cases (where death is a possible penalty). Since the only purpose of bail is to insure the defendant's presence at trial, it is improper to deny bail or set excessive bail in order to detain a defendant unless it can be shown that no other alternative exists that will insure her appearance at trial.

            a) **Excessive bail--**

Stack v. Boyle, 342 U.S. 1 (1951).

Facts. The district court set bail at $50,000 each for 12 men (Ds) charged with violating the Smith Act. Ds moved to reduce bail on the ground that it was excessive under the Eighth Amendment; in support they submitted statements on their financial resources, family relationships, health, prior criminal records, etc. The government showed only that in another, earlier situation, four persons alleged to have violated the Smith Act had skipped bail.

Issue. May the court consider the actions of past defendants in setting bail?

Held. No. Judgment reversed.

♦ Federal law has always provided for bail for noncapital offenses, based on the presumption of innocence. It allows preparation of a defense and avoids punishing before conviction.

♦ But release on bail is dependent on the accused giving adequate assurance that he will stand trial. Bail may not be set (under the Eighth Amendment) higher than is reasonably calculated to fulfill this purpose. Additionally, bail must be set individually and be based on the standards relevant to the purpose of assuring the presence of each defendant. It was not here.

♦ Bail is excessive here. Conviction could bring five years and up to $10,000 in fines; the bail set is higher than usual for like penalties. When it departs from the norm, the government must show good reasons for doing so. Ds should make a motion to the federal district court for reduction of bail.

---

2) **Crime control.** Although analytically having only one function, bail is often used to accomplish many other things. These aims can be analyzed under the heading of crime control.

a) **Rationale.** Just because we operate our system on the basis of individual rights and the presumption of innocence is no reason why we cannot give effect in some cases to the interest of society in being protected from more crime and violence on the part of people whose conduct has already shown the futility of more conventional crime control methods.

(1) The vast majority of those who are arrested and charged with a crime are guilty. There is sufficient evidence to try them.

(2) If they are let out before trial, they may not appear for trial.

(3) Already limited resources will have to be expended in tracking these people down.

(4) Defendants out on bail may commit further crimes, since they are unrestrained by the deterrence of the criminal law.

(5)   Many first and minor offenders are apt to have their cases dismissed or to be put on probation or fined and given suspended sentences—all dispositions having little effect on future conduct. A short stay in jail might be an effective deterrent device.

(6)   The stay in jail encourages guilty pleas. People who know they are guilty would rather get it over with than spend weeks or months in jail waiting for trial.

b)   **Added sentence.** The most objectionable part of the present bail system, even if the crime control model were accepted, is the fact that time spent in jail before trial is like an added sentence for a crime, since this time is often not credited to sentence time; furthermore, no bail is a terrible injustice to those who are really innocent.

c)   **Due process model.** A distinction may be made between the status of a defendant and one who has been convicted of a crime. In order to allow a defendant to prepare her case, to maintain the interests of her family, and to assert all the rights that are hers without intimidation, release on adequate assurance that she will return for trial must be allowed. Whatever devices will insure this can legitimately be used—bail is only one such method. In any event, bail must not be set at a figure that a defendant cannot meet (if a defendant is indigent and cannot meet bail, then alternative methods should be used to insure an appearance).

c.   **Problems with the bail system.**

1)   Most people who are defendants cannot make bail, even a very small one. A federal study showed that 63% cannot raise $100 for bail or even the fee for a very small bail bond. The system is very discriminatory—the rich get out while the poor stay in jail.

2)   The vast majority of defendants who are released on bail would come back if released without bail.

a)   Exercising a minimal amount of discretion in selection, based on family or community ties, etc., can insure almost a 99% return rate for defendants released on their own recognizance. Therefore, the bail system could be abolished without making any difference in criminal law enforcement.

b)   Letting defendants out saves money by not having to support them in jail and allows defendants to work and not lose their jobs, keeping their families off the welfare rolls.

c) Those who would skip are the ones who do it under the bail system anyway.

d. Possible solutions.

1) Release on own recognizance. In the federal system and several states, release on a nonmonetary basis is the presumptive form of release. Releasing defendants on their own recognizance (in most situations) has many advantages. Wealthy defendants are out anyway under the present system.

2) Speedy trial. For those who appear likely to skip, one possible solution is to let all good risks go and try the rest quickly. An experiment in Philadelphia has kept all defendants accused of violent crimes in jail but requires that they be tried within 30 days. However, this raises equal protection problems—can a fair line be drawn in letting some out and keeping others in?

3) Retention of portion of bail bond. In *Schlib v. Kuebel*, 404 U.S. 357 (1971), the Court upheld a state provision that gave the option of depositing 10% of the bond amount instead of the full bond amount, but the state would retain 10% of the deposit for "bail bond costs."

4) Bail Reform Act of 1984. The preferred form of release is upon the person's own recognizance, but the guiding principle is what will reasonably assure the person's appearance as required. Conditional release is often beneficial; it may allow the accused to continue working, for example. [*See* 18 U.S.C. §3142]

e. Bail for capital offenses. Most states limit the right to bail in capital cases. When the state's death penalty provisions are held unconstitutional, some states consider the bail limitations inapplicable because the possibility of losing his life was thought to be the accused's motivation to flee. Other states retain the restrictions because of the gravity of the offenses. In any state, however, the prosecution would have to justify imposition of the bail limitations by producing evidence showing the probability of conviction of a capital offense.

2. Preventive Detention.

a. Bail Reform Act of 1984. Like a number of state statutes, the federal Bail Reform Act of 1984 authorizes detention without bail under specific circumstances. If no conditions of release will reasonably assure that the accused will not flee or pose a danger to the community, bail may be denied. A rebuttable presumption arises that this situation is present where the accused has been convicted of other serious felonies committed while out on bail. [18 U.S.C. §3142]

b. **District of Columbia statute.** The District of Columbia bail statutes are essentially the same as the Bail Reform Act preventive detention provisions, including a provision making the safety of "any person or the community" a factor in imposing conditions on release, a provision establishing added penalties for crimes committed while on release, and provisions establishing sanctions for violation of release conditions. A judicial officer can order such pretrial detention in limited situations if there is a hearing and a showing of clear and convincing evidence that conditions are met, there are no conditions for release that will reasonably assure safety of other persons or the community, and there is substantial probability that the person committed the offense charged.

c. **Constitutionality of preventive detention--**

United States v. Salerno, 481 U.S. 739 (1987).

Facts. Salerno and Cafaro (Ds) were charged with numerous RICO, fraud, and other charges. After their arrest, the United States (P) moved to have Ds detained pursuant to section 3142 of the Bail Reform Act of 1984, which allows a federal court to detain an arrestee pending trial upon clear and convincing evidence that no release conditions will reasonably assure the safety of any other person and the community. At a hearing on the motion, P showed that Salerno was a crime family "boss" and that Cafaro was a "captain" in the same family and offered evidence that Salerno personally participated in two murder conspiracies. Ds dismissed the evidence, based primarily on wire-tapped conversations, as "tough talk." The district court granted P's motion, finding that Ds' activities would not cease upon arrest and would present a danger to the community. The court of appeals reversed, finding the statute unconstitutionally violated substantive due process because it was not limited to defendants who were likely to intimidate witnesses or otherwise jeopardize the trial process. The Supreme Court granted certiorari.

Issue. May Congress permit pretrial detention, without bail, upon clear and convincing evidence that no release conditions will reasonably assure the safety of any other person and the community?

Held. Yes. Judgment reversed.

♦ The Bail Reform Act was a response to several deficiencies of the prior federal bail process, and it was intended to authorize the courts to make release decisions that give appropriate recognition to the danger a person may pose to others if released. Section 3142 applies only to the most serious crimes. The judge must hold a hearing, at which the defendant has a right to counsel, to present witnesses, and to cross-examine other witnesses. The judge's findings must be written and supported by clear and convincing evidence. The statute enumerates the relevant factors to be considered. Finally, the decision may be reviewed on appeal.

- Ds claim the Act violates substantive due process because it permits pretrial punishment. However, the pretrial detention provided for is regulatory, not penal. A restriction, unless expressly intended to be punitive, is regulatory if it is not excessive in relation to the nonpenal purpose for the restriction. Congress's purpose of preventing danger to the community is a legitimate regulatory goal. The Due Process Clause does not prohibit pretrial detention; many cases hold that the government's regulatory interest in community safety through preventing crime may outweigh an individual's liberty interest.

- The procedures set forth in section 3142 satisfy the requirements of procedural due process, particularly in this case, which is a facial challenge to the Act.

- Ds claim the Act violates the Excessive Bail Clause of the Eighth Amendment. That amendment does provide that "Excessive bail shall not be required," but it does not specify that bail must be available. The clause does not create a right to bail in all cases.

Dissent (Marshall, Brennan, JJ.). The majority has now permitted Congress to jail a presumably innocent person for an indefinite period, so long as the government satisfies a judge that the accused is likely to commit crimes in the future, even if unrelated to the pending charges. The Court's punitive/regulatory distinction could be used to punish any groups that Congress determines to present a threat to the community. This is the kind of statute tyrants use.

Dissent (Stevens, J.). There may be circumstances that justify the brief detention of a person who has not committed any crime, but the evidence of imminent danger must be strong, and must not include the existence of pending charges.

B. THE DECISION WHETHER TO PROSECUTE

1. Prosecuting Attorney.

a. **Office and duties.** The county or district attorney, usually an elected official, prosecutes criminal cases and represents the local government in civil cases. On a citizen's complaint, or on the arrest of the suspect, the prosecutor determines whether there is probable cause to believe that the suspect has committed the offense. If she so finds, then the prosecutor drafts an information or indictment stating the charges against the suspect. The prosecutor then takes her case before a magistrate or the grand jury, which reviews her decision. If the magistrate or grand jury agrees with the prosecutor's determination, an arrest warrant will be issued.

b. **Prosecutor's discretion.** The courts have repeatedly held that the prosecutor has a wide latitude in deciding whether to file charges and that her decision is not subject to direct judicial review except when there is a glaring abuse of discretion.

c. **Factors in exercising discretion.** ABA Standards recommend considering the following mitigating factors:

1) Reasonable doubt of guilt.

2) Minimum harm of offense.

3) Excessive punishment relative to offense.

4) Improper motives of party complaining.

5) Reluctance of victim to testify.

6) Cooperation of accused in arresting others.

7) Likelihood of prosecution in another jurisdiction.

2. **Challenging the Prosecutor's Discretion.**

a. **The decision not to prosecute.** Generally, the court cannot force a criminal prosecution. In *Inmates of Attica Correctional Facility v. Rockefeller*, 477 F.2d 375 (2d Cir. 1973), the court dismissed a mandamus action brought by inmates of Attica to require federal and state officials to prosecute persons who allegedly violated certain federal and state criminal statutes in connection with treatment of inmates during a prison riot. Reluctance to force prosecution is based on separation of powers. The language of Congress in enacting the statute governing federal civil rights crimes does not require prosecution.

1) **Constitutional limitations.** In *Moses v. Kennedy*, 219 F. Supp. 762 (D.C. Cir. 1963), eight residents of Mississippi petitioned for a writ of mandamus to compel the United States Attorney General and the director of the FBI to investigate and prosecute a local official for alleged violation of petitioners' civil rights. 42 U.S.C. section 1987 states that federal officials are authorized and required to prosecute persons who have violated petitioners' civil rights. The court held that the courts cannot compel a prosecutor to take action. Article II, Section 3 of the Constitution (providing that the President shall take care that the laws be faithfully executed) vests the prerogative of enforcing the criminal law in the executive, not the judicial, branch of government. The decision to investigate, arrest, and prosecute depends on a number of factors—the likelihood of a guilty verdict (in turn resting on the weight of the evidence and the credibility of the witnesses), the gravity of the offense, present public policy, public opinion, and the need to test an un-

certain law with a strong case. The prosecution must be free to use its own judgment. While the Civil Rights Act appears to compel prosecution, nothing in the Act's legislative history shows an intent to grant the courts special control over the prosecutor.

2) **The district attorney and the grand jury.** A United States attorney refused to prepare and sign a grand jury indictment. In upholding a contempt conviction, the court held that the federal prosecutor must help prepare the indictment because he is working as part of the judicial branch of government. However, he need not sign the indictment, because to do so formally initiates a prosecution. After the grand jury returns an indictment, the prosecuting attorney can refuse to go forward on the case. [United States v. Cox, 342 F.2d 167 (5th Cir. 1965)]

3) **Checks on the prosecutor's refusal to prosecute.**

a) **The court.** Some jurisdictions place limits on the prosecutor's discretion after initial proceedings begin. For example, after an indictment or information is filed, some states permit the prosecutor to refuse to go forward, but other states leave that decision to the courts, or require court approval.

b) **The state attorney general.** At common law, and statutory law in many states, the state attorney general may intervene when the local prosecutor fails to act. The attorney general may initiate the prosecution or even supersede the reluctant prosecutor.

c) **Removal by the state legislature.** Most states permit the legislature to remove, by impeachment or other means, a reluctant district attorney.

d) **Grand jury.** In many states, indictment by grand jury overrides the prosecutor's discretion.

e) **Suit by private party.**

f) **Removal of prosecutor.**

b. **The decision to prosecute.**

1) **Selective enforcement.** The Equal Protection Clause of the Fourteenth Amendment does not preclude selective enforcement of the law, as long as the selectivity is not based on an unjustified standard, such as race, religion, or other arbitrary classification.

2) Selective prosecution--

United States v. Armstrong, 517 U.S. 456 (1996).

Facts. Armstrong and others (Ds) were indicted on charges of conspiring to possess with intent to distribute more than 50 grams of crack cocaine, following an investigation that used three confidential informants. These informants had purchased crack from Ds. The government (P) offered affidavits stating that the decision to prosecute Ds met the general criteria for prosecution, and that race played no role in the investigation. Ds submitted an affidavit alleging that an intake coordinator said there was "an equal number of Caucasian users and dealers to minority users and dealers." Ds also submitted an affidavit from a criminal defense attorney to the effect that nonblacks were prosecuted in state courts, while blacks were prosecuted in federal courts where sentences were more severe. Ds filed a motion for discovery or dismissal of the indictments on the ground that they were selected for prosecution because they were black. The district court granted the motion for discovery and ordered P to provide a list of cases involving cocaine and firearms showing the race of the defendants, and to explain its criteria for deciding to prosecute those defendants. P refused to comply with the discovery order, and the court dismissed the case. A three-judge panel of the court of appeals reversed, holding that to obtain discovery, Ds would have to provide a colorable basis for believing that others similarly situated have not been prosecuted. The court of appeals, en banc, affirmed the district court by holding that Ds were not required to show that P had failed to prosecute others who were similarly situated. The Supreme Court granted certiorari.

Issue. To establish a selective prosecution claim, must a defendant show that similarly situated defendants of other races could have been prosecuted but were not?

Held. Yes. Judgment reversed and case remanded.

♦ A claim of selective prosecution is not a defense on the merits but an independent assertion that P brought the criminal charge for reasons forbidden by the Constitution. The claim asks a court to exercise judicial power over a special province of the executive branch, in the face of the normal presumption that the executive branch properly discharges its official duties. Accordingly, the showing necessary to obtain discovery must be a significant barrier to the litigation of insubstantial claims in this area.

♦ Prosecutors normally have complete discretion to bring charges or not, so long as they have probable cause to support the charge. To dispel the presumption that a prosecutor has violated equal protection by directing prosecution at a particular class of persons, a defendant must present clear evidence.

♦ Applying ordinary equal protection standards to a selective prosecution claim, Ds must show that P's prosecutorial policy had a discriminatory effect and that it was motivated by a discriminatory purpose. A discriminatory effect in a race case means that similarly situated individuals of a different race were not prosecuted.

♦ The showing necessary to obtain discovery in support of a selective prosecution claim corresponds to the rigorous standard for the elements of the claim itself. To obtain discovery, Ds must produce some evidence that similarly situated defendants of other races could have been prosecuted but were not. The study Ds offered in this case failed this test, because it did not identify any individuals of other races who could have been prosecuted but were not.

Dissent (Stevens, J.). Ds' evidence was insufficient to support a right to discovery, but the district court could properly require some response from P. The extraordinary severity of the federal penalties for crack cocaine violations, combined with the fact that 88% of the federal offenders were black while 65% of the users were white, entitled the district court to require some explanation from P.

---

3) **Vindictive prosecution.** In *People v. Walker*, 200 N.E.2d 779 (N.Y. 1964), the court held that the defendant should be allowed wide latitude to prove her contention that the prosecution acted out of vengeance. Walker was prosecuted for building code violations. She argued that the prosecution was vengefully brought because she had recently exposed corrupt practices in the building department.

4) **Retaliatory prosecution--**

Dixon v. District of Columbia, 394 F.2d 966 (D.C. Cir. 1968).

Facts. Dixon (D) was stopped for traffic offenses by the police but was not given a ticket. Two days later, he turned in a written complaint about police conduct. A discussion was held where D agreed not to prosecute the complaint if the police did not prosecute the traffic violations. However, D went ahead anyway with the complaint. The prosecutor therefore began the action for the traffic violations.

Issue. Did the prosecutor abuse his discretion by prosecuting in retaliation for D's filing a complaint?

Held. Yes.

♦ There are limits to the discretion to prosecute. One such limitation is that the decision should not be based on any agreement with a possible defendant relative to a charge concerning police misconduct. Such bargains suppress complaints against the police that should be aired, they prevent prosecution of persons that possibly should be prosecuted, and they contribute to the police trumping up charges against persons with legitimate complaints in order to prevent hearings on police conduct.

---

5) Desuetude (nonuse)--

United States v. Elliott, 266 F. Supp. 318 (S.D.N.Y. 1967).

Facts. Elliott (D) was convicted under a 1917 law prohibiting conspiracies within the United States to commit crimes in foreign countries. His was the first prosecution in 50 years of the law.

Issue. Does prolonged nonuse of a statute render a new prosecution under the statute invalid?

Held. No.

♦ Nonuse alone does not abrogate the enforcement of the statute. While there had been no prosecutions under the law, it was not obsolete because it is still a politically desirable goal to prevent the use of the United States as a base for destruction of foreign property. The court finds no "fair notice" violations.

Comment. The court noted that there was no showing that D had been unjustly singled out for prosecution.

---

c. **Selection of the charge.** If two or more statutes cover the same offense, the prosecutor has the option of choosing among them.

1) **Overlapping provisions of a single federal statute--**

United States v. Batchelder, 442 U.S. 114 (1979).

Facts. Two provisions of the 1968 Omnibus Act prohibited convicted felons from receiving firearms, but each prescribed a different maximum penalty. Batchelder (D) was convicted under 18 U.S.C. section 922(h) and sentenced to five years' imprisonment as permitted through that provision. The court of appeals affirmed the conviction, but remanded for resentencing since 18 U.S.C.A. section 1202(a) was substantively identical but allowed a maximum sentence of only two years. The United States appeals.

Issue. If two statutory provisions overlap, may a defendant convicted of the offense under the provision carrying the greater penalty be sentenced only under the more lenient provision?

Held. No. Judgment reversed.

♦ The provisions are not void for vagueness. Although they overlap and might therefore cause uncertainty as to the actual penalty for violation, the adequate notice given by each provision is not thereby nullified.

♦ The settled rule permitting prosecutorial discretion in choosing between statutes with different elements also applies when a choice must be made between statutes with identical elements.

♦ The choice is still subject to constitutional constraints, and the prosecution is not thereby entitled to fix criminal penalties, for that duty remains with the sentencing judge.

---

2) **Overlapping federal and state statutes.** In *Hutcherson v. United States*, 345 F.2d 964 (D.C. Cir. 1965), the court found that the defendant could not challenge the prosecutor's choice to proceed under the federal penal statute when the applicable state statute provided for a less severe penalty. The court held that, in the absence of a prohibitory statute, the prosecutor may elect between two applicable statutes.

3) **Plea bargaining.** When the defendant's actions violate several statutes, or a single offense is covered by overlapping statutes as in *Hutcherson*, it is common practice for the prosecutor to charge the greatest number or the most severe charges in order to gain a plea-bargaining advantage. The overawed defendant often pleads guilty to a lesser offense to avoid prosecution for the more serious charge.

   a) A few states have invalidated statutes that allow the prosecutor to choose between misdemeanor and felony offenses for the same conduct.

   b) Often, the prosecutor's discretion works in favor of the defendant, as when the prosecutor charges a first offender with a lesser offense or with a misdemeanor instead of felony charge. Should this element of mercy be eliminated? Or does the real danger lie in the nonreviewability of the prosecutor's decision?

4)   Due process and substitution of a more serious charge--

Blackledge v. Perry, 417 U.S. 21 (1974).

Facts. Perry (D) had been tried and convicted of the misdemeanor of assault with a deadly weapon. When D exercised his right under state law to a trial de novo, the prosecutor brought an indictment for the same act but charging D with the additional elements of having an intent to kill or inflict serious bodily injury, a felony. D pleaded guilty but later filed an application for a writ of habeas corpus based on double jeopardy and due process. The district court granted the writ, and the court of appeals affirmed on the ground that the later prosecution violated D's rights under the Double Jeopardy Clause. The Government then petitioned the Supreme Court.

Issue. When the state has not shown that it was impossible to proceed on the more serious charge at the outset, is it constitutionally permissible for the state to respond to a defendant's invocation of his statutory right to appeal by bringing a more serious charge against him at the trial de novo?

Held. No. Grant of petition for habeas corpus affirmed.

♦   This is based on due process, and it is therefore unnecessary to reach the double jeopardy issue. Due process protects against possibilities of increased punishment when they pose a realistic likelihood of vindictiveness. Actual retaliatory motivation need not inevitably exist for such a situation to be found. Since the practical result of the Due Process Clause here is that the state could not permissibly require D to answer the felony charge, his plea of guilty did not foreclose him from attacking his conviction through a writ of habeas corpus.

Dissent (Rehnquist, J.). The prosecutor chose to proceed initially in the state district court, where felony charges could not be prosecuted. When D obtained a trial de novo in superior court, a court of general jurisdiction, the prosecutor was able to seek a felony conviction. This does not mean that the prosecutor was vindictive.

5)   Prosecutorial vindictiveness--

United States v. Goodwin, 457 U.S. 368 (1982).

Facts. Goodwin (D) was originally charged with misdemeanors, and his case was assigned to an attorney to try before a magistrate. D insisted on a jury trial, so the case was sent to a district court, which had authority to try felony cases. A new prosecutor obtained a felony indictment. D was convicted, but the court of appeals reversed. The Supreme Court granted certiorari.

Issue. Does a presumption of prosecutorial vindictiveness attach in a pretrial setting when a defendant receives a higher charge after he requests a jury trial?

Held. No. Judgment reversed.

♦　　In the pretrial stage of a criminal proceeding, numerous factors may operate to cause a change in the charging decision. A prosecutor's duty to determine the extent of the societal interest in prosecution should not be hindered by an unnecessary presumption of vindictiveness attached to a change from an initial charging decision.

♦　　The prosecutor in this case had no personal stake in having a bench trial as opposed to a jury trial and therefore had no reason to engage in self-vindication. The mere opportunity for vindictiveness here does not justify imposition of a prophylactic presumption rule.

♦　　Although no presumption applies, a defendant is not precluded from proving actual vindictive motivation.

Concurrence (Blackmun, J.). There is no reason to distinguish between pretrial and post-trial vindictiveness, but there was evidence here of a valid motive for changing the charges.

Dissent (Brennan, Marshall, JJ.). The increased charge posed a realistic likelihood of vindictiveness, and the fear of such vindictiveness may deter someone in D's position from exercising his right to a jury trial. A jury trial entails much more work for a prosecutor, and thus D's election would give the prosecutor reason to act out of vindictiveness.

C.　THE PRELIMINARY HEARING

1.　Introduction.

    a.　Requirement. In jurisdictions where prosecutions by information are permitted as alternatives to grand jury indictment, a preliminary examination is required before the prosecutor can file the information. In the federal court, where an indictment is required for all felonies, the accused is entitled to a preliminary examination if arrested before the grand jury indicts her. Preliminary examinations are not required in misdemeanor cases.

    b.　Procedure. In the states, the preliminary examination or hearing is held before a magistrate or an inferior court judge; in federal cases, it is before a special commissioner.

2. **Functions.**

   a. **Screening.** The primary purpose of the preliminary hearing is to examine the prosecution's case to determine if there is probable cause that an offense has been committed and that the person arrested is responsible for it. This helps to prevent groundless charges from coming to trial.

      1) In the federal courts, the issue is whether there is sufficient evidence for a defendant to be required to post bail. Determination of whether there will be a trial is normally left to the grand jury.

      2) In the state courts, practice differs. Some use the hearing to determine if a grand jury should be called; others use it to determine whether there should be a trial.

   b. **Discovery.** The hearing also serves to assist discovery. The defendant gets to see something of the prosecution's case and may cross-examine the prosecution's witnesses. Testimony taken at the hearing may be used to impeach witness testimony at trial.

   c. **Perpetuation of testimony.**

      1) If the prosecution and counsel for the accused agree, a transcript of the witness's testimony at the hearing may be used at trial in lieu of new testimony.

      2) *California v. Green*, 399 U.S. 149 (1970), held that the admission of preliminary hearing testimony is not unconstitutional if the defendant was represented at the hearing and counsel had an adequate opportunity to cross-examine the witness.

   d. **Other purposes.** The hearing serves other purposes, such as assisting in plea bargaining, determination of bail, and the terms of pretrial release.

3. **Waiver of the Preliminary Hearing.**

   a. The accused may waive the right to a preliminary hearing.

   b. A plea of guilty generally operates as such a waiver. The accused is directly bound over to the court for sentencing. In addition, some states permit the accused to plead guilty to a degree of the crime charged or to a lesser offense (thus, the hearing is a part of plea bargaining), and from the hearing the accused is bound over to the court for sentencing.

4. **Defendant's Right to a Preliminary Hearing.** When a grand jury has returned an indictment, no preliminary examination is required. [18 U.S.C.

§3060] The grand jury proceedings constitute a determination that there is probable cause against the accused. A preliminary examination would be superfluous.

    a.   **Federal courts.** Federal Rule of Criminal Procedure section 5(c) provides that a person taken into custody before indictment is entitled to a preliminary hearing. But a person arrested after a grand jury indictment does not have to be given a preliminary examination.

    b.   **State courts.** Most states follow the federal rule. When using prosecution by information, states divide over whether a preliminary hearing is required. Lower federal court opinions have held that direct filing of an information without a hearing violates the Fourth Amendment.

    c.   **Misdemeanors.** There is no preliminary examination in misdemeanor cases. Because of the lesser penalties involved, the accused goes directly to trial on a complaint without indictment or preliminary examination.

5.   **The Bindover Determination--**

State v. Clark, 20 P.3d 300 (Utah 2001).

Facts. Clark and Smith (Ds) were charged with forgery based on allegations that they each requested a bank to cash a check made out to him as payee, that the check was from a stolen book of blank checks, and that when the bank told him there was a problem with the account, he left the check and the bank. Ds claimed that this evidence was insufficient to show probable cause at a preliminary hearing. Ds moved to quash the bindover. The trial court agreed and dismissed the forgery charges against Ds on the ground that the state failed to show the requisite intent. The court applied a directed verdict standard. The state (P) appeals.

Issue. To bind a defendant over for trial, must the state produce evidence that would support a beyond a reasonable doubt standard?

Held. No. Judgment reversed.

    ♦   To bind a defendant over for trial, the prosecution must show probable cause at a preliminary hearing that the crime was committed and that the defendant committed it. The evidence required to show probable cause at this stage is relatively low, and the magistrate may not sift or weigh the evidence. He must view all evidence in the light most favorable to the prosecution.

    ♦   The standard of proof at a preliminary hearing is somewhere between the reasonable belief necessary to support a warrant and the preponderance of the evidence standard that applies in civil cases.

♦ In previous cases, the courts have equated the preliminary hearing probable cause standard with the standard for directing a verdict. This standard could improperly lead magistrates in preliminary hearings to improperly weigh the evidence. Instead, the proper standard requires the prosecution only to provide believable evidence of all the elements of the crime charged. The evidence at this stage need not support a finding of guilt beyond a reasonable doubt. This is essentially the same as the evidentiary requirement for an arrest warrant.

♦ The facts presented at the preliminary hearing satisfy the reasonable belief standard. The facts support two alternate inferences. Either Ds were unaware that the checks were stolen and assumed they had been defrauded so there was no reason to take the checks with them, or they knew the checks were stolen so they had no reason to take the checks back to the persons who gave the checks to them. In addition, Ds presented the checks only hours after the theft was reported, suggesting that they either stole the checks or knew they were stolen. This evidence, viewed in a light most favorable to P, constitutes probable cause.

Comment. Most appellate decisions are decided on an ad hoc basis without setting guidelines directing which kinds of inferences may be drawn by the magistrate.

---

6. **Preliminary Hearing Procedures.**

   a. **Rules of evidence.** There are no consistent rules in the federal courts establishing what types of evidence may be admitted at the hearing. The policy varies with the commissioner. The majority of states similarly lack consistency. However, California requires that hearing evidence must normally be admissible at the trial.

   b. **Scope of hearing.** In most jurisdictions, the prosecution must prove that there is competent evidence of each element of the offense on which the accused is held, and the accused must be given the opportunity to present any defense she wishes. In federal courts, the hearing is limited to the propriety of bail.

   c. **Right to counsel.** *Coleman v. Alabama*, 399 U.S. 1 (1970), held that the assistance of counsel must be provided at a preliminary hearing to determine the existence of probable cause against the accused.

D. GRAND JURY REVIEW

1. **Introduction.** In addition to its role as investigator, the grand jury serves the important function of helping protect the innocent from the prosecutor. Although all federal felony prosecutions must be based on a grand jury indict-

ment, many states permit use of informations as charging documents. The Supreme Court upheld this alternative for state prosecutions in *Hurtado v. California*, 110 U.S. 516 (1884). When a grand jury is convened, defendants may challenge grand jury composition, the evidence presented to the grand jury, and improper grand jury procedures.

2. **Challenges to Grand Jury Composition.**

   a. **Juror selection.** Grand jurors are usually drawn from the same pool from which petit jurors are drawn. Because grand juries sit for longer terms, hardship dismissals are more freely given. The presiding judge asks basic questions regarding qualification, and the prosecutor may also ask questions in many jurisdictions. It has not been settled exactly to what extent the petit jury equal protection requirements apply to grand juries. Generally, the courts require that no large and identifiable segment of the community be excluded from jury service.

   b. **Discrimination in foreman appointment.** Discrimination in the appointment of federal grand jury foremen does not constitute a violation of the Due Process Clause sufficient to warrant reversal of a conviction and dismissal of an indictment. Federal grand jury foremen perform essentially clerical tasks, so that discrimination in their appointment does not undermine the integrity of the indictment. So long as the grand jury as a whole does not have a large and identifiable segment of the community excluded from jury service, discrimination of one member of the grand jury does not conflict with due process interests. [Hobby v. United States, 468 U.S. 339 (1984)]

3. **Challenges to Evidence Before the Grand Jury--**

Costello v. United States, 350 U.S. 359 (1956).

Facts. Costello (D) was indicted for income tax evasion. The indictment was based entirely on hearsay.

Issue. May a grand jury issue an indictment based solely on hearsay evidence?

Held. Yes. Indictment affirmed.

♦   There are no constitutional limitations on the types of evidence that may be introduced in a grand jury investigation. Grand jurors should not be hampered by rigid rules of procedure or evidence, because they are primarily an investigatory body. In the trial on the merits, the defendant is entitled to strict observance of the rules of evidence. That is all that is necessary.

Concurrence (Burton, J.). I agree with the denial of the motion to quash the indictment, but not with the breadth of the declarations made by the Court. If the grand jury had before it no substantial or rationally persuasive evidence, that indictment should be quashed.

Comment. While *Costello* is followed by some of the states, it has been criticized as being too broad. Many states require evidence to be legally competent, which rules out an indictment based solely on illegally obtained evidence or hearsay. The New York courts, for example, direct the grand jury to consider only evidence that would be admissible at trial.

---

4. **Challenges to Grand Jury Procedures.** Most jurisdictions list the grounds for a motion to challenge an indictment (*e.g.*, less than the required number of jurors voting for indictment). Many states require that only these and constitutional grounds are sufficient; however, others leave the scope of the motion to case-by-case development.

   a. **Disclosure of exculpatory evidence not required--**

United States v. Williams, 504 U.S. 36 (1992).

Facts. Williams (D) was indicted by a federal grand jury for making false financial statements to obtain a bank loan. The financial statements included as current assets certain notes receivable that were not collectible in the short term. After arraignment, D moved for disclosure of all exculpatory portions of the grand jury transcripts. The district court granted the motion, and D discovered that the prosecution had failed to present "substantial exculpatory evidence" to the grand jury, including evidence that would show that he had consistently characterized the notes in the way he had on the bank loan application and thus had no intent to mislead the banks. The court dismissed the indictment without evidence on the ground that the withheld evidence was relevant to the essential element of intent and created a reasonable doubt about D's guilt. The court of appeals affirmed, pursuant to its decision in *United States v. Page*, 808 F.2d 723 (10th Cir. 1987), which required prosecutors to present substantial exculpatory evidence to a grand jury. The Supreme Court granted certiorari.

Issue. May a federal district court dismiss an otherwise valid indictment because the Government failed to disclose to the grand jury "substantial exculpatory evidence" in its possession?

Held. No. Judgment reversed.

♦ Prior decisions have held that federal courts may formulate procedural rules not specifically required by the Constitution or Congress. However, these decisions involved the courts' power to control their own procedures. The grand jury is an institution separate from the courts.

- The courts have power to dismiss indictments because of misconduct before a grand jury, but only if the misconduct violates a rule that has been drafted and approved by this Court and by Congress to insure the integrity of the grand jury's functions. No cases have extended the courts' supervisory power to allow the courts to prescribe the standards of prosecutorial conduct in dealing with grand juries.

- The grand jury is not mentioned in the body of the Constitution and belongs to no branch of the government. It acts as a buffer between the government and the people. Its relationship to the courts is at arm's length. A grand jury may appeal to the courts for assistance in compelling the production of evidence, for example, but it needs no authorization from the courts to initiate an investigation, and it operates without a presiding judicial authority. Grand juries are not bound by constitutional protections such as the Double Jeopardy Clause or many of the rules of evidence, such as the exclusionary and hearsay rules.

- The purpose of a grand jury is to decide whether there is adequate basis for bringing a criminal charge. Requiring a prosecutor to present exculpatory evidence would make the grand jury an adjudicatory body instead of an accusatory body. If as D claims the grand jury must make a balanced assessment of the situation, D should be allowed to provide a defense, which would undermine the whole function of the grand jury.

- Traditionally, an indictment may not be challenged for inadequacy of evidence presented to the grand jury. To allow a challenge based on the sufficiency of the prosecutor's presentation would undermine this historical understanding of a grand jury. If a change is to be made, it must be done by Congress, not by the courts.

Dissent (Stevens, Blackmun, O'Connor, Thomas, JJ.). The prosecutor's role is to see that justice is done, not to win a case. Prosecutors operate before grand juries without the check of a judge, a trained legal adversary, or public scrutiny. In this situation, the potential for abuse is so great that the judiciary has an obligation to protect against even the appearance of unfairness. While a grand jury is not assigned to a particular branch of government, it is convened by the court and remains subject to judicial control until it is discharged. A grand jury cannot adequately perform its important historic role if it is intentionally misled by the prosecutor, and the courts have power to establish and enforce rules to restrain prosecutorial misconduct. The courts should require a prosecutor to disclose to the grand jury substantial evidence that directly negates the guilt of a subject of the investigation.

---

b.   **Nonprejudicial misconduct by the prosecution--**

Bank of Nova Scotia v. United States, 487 U.S. 250 (1988).

Facts. The Bank of Nova Scotia and seven individual defendants (Ds) were indicted by a grand jury. Twenty-six of the original 27 counts were dismissed by the district court for pleading inadequacies. The United States appealed the dismissal. The court of appeals remanded the case to the district court to determine whether prosecutorial misconduct was an additional ground for dismissal. The district court then dismissed all 27 counts due to the following violations committed by the prosecution: (i) disclosure of grand jury material to IRS agents; (ii) failing to notify the court of such disclosure; (iii) disclosing the names of investigation targets to potential witnesses; (iv) allowing joint appearances by IRS agents to read transcripts to the jury; and (v) various abuses of witnesses. The court of appeals reversed, holding that the misconduct did not prevent the grand jury from exercising independent judgment. The Supreme Court granted certiorari.

Issue. May a district court dismiss an indictment for errors in grand jury proceedings when the errors did not prejudice the defendants?

Held. No. Judgment affirmed.

♦　　A federal court may establish procedural rules not required by the Constitution or the Congress, but this use of its supervisory power may not conflict with the Constitution or federal law. The Federal Rules of Criminal Procedure were adopted pursuant to express statutory authority and therefore are as binding as any federal statute.

♦　　The harmless error rule, Federal Rule of Criminal Procedure 52(a), provides that errors or defects that do not affect substantial rights must be disregarded. The courts do not have authority to disregard the balance between societal costs and the rights of the accused that Federal Rule of Criminal Procedure 52(a) set forth. The harmless error rule applies to this case, and the indictment could be dismissed only if the violation "substantially influenced the grand jury's decision to indict" or if there is "grave doubt" that the decision to indict was free from the substantial influence of such violations. This test differs from the court of appeal's analysis of independence, which does not focus on the grand jury's decision to indict.

♦　　The harmless error rule does not prohibit judicial action when fundamental errors are committed that compromise the structural protection of the grand jury such that the proceedings are fundamentally unfair. But this is not a fundamental error case.

♦　　Most of the misconduct found by the district court plainly did not affect the charging decision, and need not be considered further. The prosecution's abuse of an expert defense witness was cured by instructions by the prosecutors to the grand jury. The jurors were made aware that certain witnesses had received immunity, and that IRS witnesses were aligned with the prosecution. The joint appearances by IRS witnesses was technically a violation, but had no prejudicial effect because they did not give any of their own testimony.

- The violations took place during a 20-month investigation involving dozens of witnesses and thousands of documents. They did not have an effect on the grand jury's decision to indict, and the charges cannot be dismissed.

---

5. Improper Grand Jury Procedure Not Disclosed Until Trial--

United States v. Mechanik, 475 U.S. 66 (1986).

Facts. Mechanik (D) was indicted for drug-related offenses and conspiracy to commit such offenses. In a superseding indictment, the grand jury expanded the conspiracy charge. Unknown to D, two police agents testified in tandem at the second grand jury. Federal Rule 6(d) permits the presence at the grand jury of only one witness under examination at a time. At trial, after one of the agents testified, the prosecutor gave D a copy of the grand jury transcript, which revealed the joint testimony. D immediately filed a motion to dismiss, but the judge, who found that the joint testimony violated Federal Rule of Criminal Procedure 6(d), deferred ruling until after the verdict. D was convicted. The judge declined to set aside the conviction because D was not harmed by the error. The court of appeals reversed, and the Supreme Court granted certiorari.

Issue. Is a violation of grand jury procedure reversible error when the objection arises during the trial and the defendant is convicted?

Held. No. Judgment reversed.

- The grand jury rules protect against the danger that D might be required to defend against a charge for which there is no probable cause to believe D guilty. The error in this case could theoretically have affected the decision to indict D. But since D was convicted, there was not only probable cause, but there was no reasonable doubt of his guilt. Thus any error in the grand jury proceeding was harmless.

- Violation of grand jury procedures does not require automatic reversal of a subsequent conviction regardless of the lack of prejudice. The costs of retrial are acceptable when error deprives a person of a fair trial. But when the error has no effect on the outcome, society's interest in the prompt administration of justice, and the societal costs of reversal, must prevail.

Concurrence (O'Connor, Brennan, Blackmun, JJ.). The focus should be on the influence of the error on the charging decision, not the eventual result of the trial. Under the Court's rule, if the jury convicts, D's motion is denied; if it acquits, D's motion is moot. Focusing on the grand jury in this case, however, shows the error was harmless because of the abundance of other evidence.

Dissent (Marshall, J.). Motions such as D's almost always arise during trial. Under the Court's rule, a judge will always defer a ruling until after the verdict. Thus, Rule 6(d) is now unenforceable.

E. THE CHARGING INSTRUMENT

1. **Modern Pleading Requirements.**

    a. **"Bill of indictment."** A bill of indictment (written accusation of the crime) is the initial pleading submitted to the grand jury by the prosecuting attorney.

    b. **Pleading.** The indictment need only contain a simplified pleading of the elements of the crime. Basically, the same rules of pleading apply as in the case of an information (below).

        1) A few provisions, including the Federal Rules of Criminal Procedure, permit very abbreviated indictments (simply stating the offense charged)—recognizing the right of the accused to move for a bill of particulars if he wishes more information.

    c. **Information.** An information is the written accusation of crime prepared by the prosecuting attorney in the name of the state (an alternative to grand jury indictment in felony cases).

    d. **Contents of the information.** The prosecution is authorized to file an information as to any crime shown to have been committed by the evidence taken at the preliminary examination (not necessarily limited to that charged in the complaint), provided the crime is part of the same transaction. [Cal. Penal Code §739 (1970)]

        1) The information must "reasonably apprise the accused of the charges against him so that he may have an opportunity to prepare and present his defense." But this only requires that the essential nature of the offense be pleaded.

        2) Frequently, the information will also state the date, time, and place the offense was committed. However, these elements are not always essential, and errors here are usually deemed to be immaterial. [Cal. Penal Code §§955, 956 (1970)]

2. **Providing Notice Through the Pleadings.** The prosecution commences when the government files an indictment or information in whichever court

has jurisdiction of the offense charged. In misdemeanor cases, the accusatory pleading is simply the complaint (statement of the offense charged).

a. **Indictment.** An indictment is the product of a grand jury proceeding against the accused.

b. **Information.** An information is a written accusation of crime by the prosecuting attorney in the name of the state.

c. **Arraignment.** When any accusatory pleading (complaint, indictment, or information) is filed, the defendant must be called into the court having jurisdiction of the offense to inform him in a public hearing of the charges against him and to give him an opportunity to plead to it. This hearing is the arraignment.

   1) **Presence of the accused.** The accused's presence is required. If he has not yet been arrested, or if he is out on bail and does not appear, a bench warrant will be issued to compel his appearance. In many states, however, an accused charged only with a misdemeanor may appear through counsel at the arraignment.

   2) **Proceedings.** The accused is first informed of his constitutional rights, including the right to counsel. The indictment or information is then read to the accused, and usually a copy thereof is handed to him; and he is then called upon to plead thereto. [Fed. R. Crim. P. 10] In some states, the defendant has a reasonable time in which to answer. Frequently, the accused will also be asked at this point whether he wishes trial by jury or by the court without a jury. He then has a variety of possible motions or pleas that he may make at the arraignment.

d. **Specificity of the offense charged--**

Russell v. United States, 369 U.S. 749 (1962).

Facts. Russell and five others (Ds) refused to answer questions posed by a congressional committee and were convicted under a statute making such a refusal a criminal act. The indictment merely set forth the offense in the words of the statute, without specifying the elements of the offense. Ds appeal.

Issue. Is an indictment on a statutory crime sufficient if it simply sets forth the offense in the words of the statute?

Held. No. Judgment reversed.

♦   The indictment must set forth the elements of the offense charged. One reason is to apprise a defendant of what he must be prepared to respond to. These indictments failed to identify the subject under inquiry and were therefore defective.

♦ A cryptic form of indictment would require a defendant to go to trial with the chief issues undefined. It would enable his conviction to rest on one point and the affirmance to rest on another. It would give the prosecution a free hand on appeal to fill in the gaps of proof by surmise or conjecture. Therefore, the indictment must set out the specific offense, coming under the general description, so as to inform the court of the facts alleged so that it may decide whether they are sufficient in law to support a conviction, if one should be had.

Dissent (Harlan, Clark, JJ.). An indictment need not contain a statement of the actual subject under inquiry by the committee. If Ds wanted more specific information, they could have obtained it by requesting a bill of particulars.

Comment. Under modern criminal pleading, the information or indictment is frequently a short simple statement of the facts constituting the offense charged. The defense can, however, move for a bill of particulars, requiring the prosecution to plead the details of the alleged offense. [Fed. R. Crim. P. 7(f)]

♦ A bill of particulars is designed only to force the prosecution to plead the details of the alleged offense. It is not intended to advise the defendant of the prosecution's evidence, although it may have that effect. For example, it has been held that when the charge is the sale of narcotics, the defendant can request the name of the person to whom he was alleged to have sold narcotics. However, a bill of particulars cannot force disclosure of the names or addresses of the *witnesses* the government proposes to introduce at trial.

♦ The principal limitation of the bill of particulars as a "discovery" device is simply that the granting or withholding of the bill is discretionary with the court. A defendant has no absolute right to compel disclosure.

---

e. **Sufficiency of the term "attempt" in indictment--**

United States v. Resendiz-Ponce, 102 U.S. 549 (2007).

Facts. Resendiz-Ponce (D), after having been twice deported, approached a port of entry and tried to use his cousin's photo identification to enter the United States. Suspicious because D did not look like the photo of his cousin, agents questioned him. D was ultimately indicted. The indictment alleged that D "knowingly and intentionally attempted to enter the United States" on the specified date at the specified place, "after having been previously denied admission, excluded, deported, and removed from the United States." D moved to dismiss the indictment because it failed to allege an overt act, which is an essential element of the crime. The district court denied the motion, and D was convicted. The court of appeals reversed, holding that the indictment's omission of the overt act was a fatal flaw. The Supreme Court granted certiorari.

Issue. Is an indictment valid even if it alleges an "attempt" without specifying the overt act that, combined with intent, constituted the attempt?

Held. Yes.

- At common law, the attempt to commit a crime was itself a crime if the offender intended to commit the offense and performed an overt act that constitutes a substantial step toward completing the offense. When the indictment charged that D "attempted to enter the United States," it implicitly alleged that D engaged in the necessary overt act. The term "attempt" has long encompassed both the overt act and intent elements.

- In *Hamling v. United States,* 418 U.S. 87 (1974), the Court identified two constitutional requirements for an indictment: (i) it must contain the elements of the offense charged and fairly inform the defendant of the charge against which he must defend; and (ii) it must enable him to plead an acquittal or conviction in bar of future prosecutions for the same offense. In this case, the word "attempt," combined with a specific allegation of time and place, provided D with sufficient notice and protected against the risk of multiple prosecutions for the same crime.

- There are some crimes for which an indictment must be more specific and go beyond the words of the criminal statute, but this is not one of them. The law has moved away from the rules of technical and formalized pleading. Rule 7(c)(1) of the Federal Rules of Criminal Procedure requires only that an indictment be a plain, concise, and definite written statement of the essential facts constituting the offense charged. Therefore, the indictment in this case was sufficient.

Dissent (Scalia, J.).

- The word "attempt" contains two substantive elements that must be alleged in the indictment: (i) the intent to commit the crime, and (ii) the undertaking of some action toward commission of the crime. It is not enough to refer to the common understanding of the term "attempt," any more than an indictment could just charge "burglary."

- *Hamling* is distinguishable from the present case. *Hamling* involved the crime of publishing obscenity. Although "obscenity" is one of the elements of the crime of publishing obscenity, the various component parts of the constitutional definition of obscenity are no more elements of the crime of publishing obscenity than the various component parts of the definition of "building" are elements of the crime of burglary. Those definitions must be met for conviction but need not be set forth in the indictment.

♦   In this case, the government was required to state not only that D "knowingly and intentionally attempted to enter the United States," but also that he "took a substantial step" toward that end.

---

f.   **Omission of enhancement fact from indictment--**

United States v. Cotton, 535 U.S. 625 (2002).

Facts. Cotton (D) and others were indicted for conspiracy to distribute 50 grams or more of cocaine base. A superseding indictment returned five months later extended the alleged time period of the conspiracy and charged a conspiracy to distribute a "detectable amount" of cocaine. Section 841(b) of the United States Code provides threshold levels of drug quantity that lead to enhanced penalties. D was convicted. D was sentenced to life imprisonment, based on sentence enhancement provisions of section 841(b)(1)(A). D appealed on the ground that his sentence was invalid under *Apprendi v. New Jersey, infra*. The Fourth Circuit held that D's sentence was invalid under *Apprendi* and vacated the judgment because it did not have jurisdiction to impose a sentence of an offense not charged in the indictment. The Supreme Court granted certiorari.

Issue. Does the omission from a federal indictment of a fact that enhances the statutory maximum sentence justify vacating the enhanced sentence?

Held. No. Judgment reversed.

♦   Congress required a prison term of up to 20 years for drug offenses involving a detectable quantity of cocaine or cocaine base in section 841(b)(1)(C). The court in this case instead relied on the enhanced penalties of section 841(b)(1)(A), which requires a finding of drug offenses involving at least 50 grams of cocaine and provides a term of imprisonment up to a life sentence.

♦   The trial court found that D was responsible for at least 1.5 kilograms of cocaine base. D did not object to the fact that the sentence was based on an amount of drug quantity not alleged in the indictment.

♦   While D's case was pending in the Fourth Circuit, *Apprendi* was decided. *Apprendi* required that, other than the fact of a prior conviction, any fact that increases the penalty for a crime beyond the prescribed statutory maximum must be submitted to a jury and proved beyond a reasonable doubt. The Fourth Circuit noted that D had failed to raise an *Apprendi* argument before the district court, but vacated the sentence anyway because an indictment setting forth all the essential elements of an offense is both mandatory and jurisdictional.

♦ The conclusion that the omission from the indictment was a jurisdictional defect is based on *Ex parte Bain*, *infra*, but *Bain* relied on a different concept of jurisdiction than the courts apply today. Post-*Bain* cases confirm that defects in an indictment are not jurisdictional and do not deprive a court of its power to adjudicate a case.

♦ D is left with the plain-error test of his claim. The United States concedes that the indictment's omission of a fact rendered D's sentence erroneous under *Apprendi*. However, the error did not seriously affect the fairness, integrity, or public reputation of the proceedings because the evidence that the conspiracy involved at least 50 grams of cocaine base was essentially uncontroverted.

---

g. Unnecessary portions of an indictment may be disregarded--

United States v. Miller, 471 U.S. 130 (1985).

Facts. Miller (D) was indicted for several mail fraud violations, including a charge that he had arranged for a burglary at his place of business and then lied to his insurance company about the extent of the loss. At trial, the government did not offer any proof of the arranged burglary. D was convicted and appealed, claiming that the proof varied from the indictment. The court of appeals reversed, holding that the grand jury might not have returned an indictment based solely on D's exaggerated claim.

Issue. May unnecessary portions of an indictment be ignored to sustain a conviction as long as the offense was fully charged in other portions of the indictment?

Held. Yes. Judgment reversed.

♦ An indictment may not be amended by broadening the possible bases for conviction from that which appeared in the indictment. [Stirone v. United States, 361 U.S. 212 (1960)] However, unnecessary and independent portions of an indictment may be treated as a useless averment that may be ignored. As long as the proof upon which a conviction is based corresponds to an offense that was clearly set out in the indictment, the conviction may be sustained.

♦ The indictment fully and clearly set forth the offense of which D was convicted. D had notice that the offense was charged. Accordingly, D was not prejudicially surprised by the absence of proof about the alleged burglary scheme.

♦ D relies on *Ex parte Bain*, 121 U.S. 1 (1887), which held both that a conviction cannot stand if based on an offense that differs from that in the indictment, and that a narrowing of an indictment is no different from the adding of a new allegation not considered by the grand jury. The first proposition is good law, but the latter proposition is hereby explicitly rejected.

F. THE LOCATION OF THE PROSECUTION

1. Jurisdiction.

a. Jurisdiction over the person.

1) Extradition.

a) **Federal.** The Federal Extradition Act provides for the extradition of any fugitive upon the production by the requesting state of an indictment or an affidavit charging that the wanted party is a fugitive from the laws of the state and has committed treason, a felony, or other high crime.

b) **Uniform code.** The Uniform Criminal Extradition Act, subscribed to by a large majority of states, is more expansive than the federal act because it provides for the extradition of persons who are not technically "fugitives" from the requesting state.

c) **Governor.** Note that under both laws, the governor of the asylum state makes the initial determination to extradite the accused.

2) Self-help. In *Frisbie v. Collins*, 342 U.S. 519 (1952), the Court held that the forcible abduction of fugitives by the police or bail bondsmen back to the forum state does not invalidate a subsequent conviction, even though such an abduction may have violated the Federal Kidnapping Act, the rationale being that constitutional guarantees accorded at arraignment and trial will protect the defendant.

b. Subject matter jurisdiction.

1) Territorial principle. Generally, a crime must be committed in whole or in part within the forum state before that state can have jurisdiction.

2) Court limitations. Normally, courts have specific subject matter limitations, so prosecution of a crime must be brought before the correct court in the court system.

2. Venue.

a. Venue determined by definition of crime--

United States v. Rodriguez-Moreno, 526 U.S. 275 (1999).

Facts. A Texas drug distributor had 30 kilos of cocaine stolen from him. He hired Rodriguez-Moreno (D) to find the dealer and hold a middleman captive during the search. D and others drove from Texas to New Jersey, then to New York and Maryland. At the Maryland house, D handled a revolver. He told the distributor that they should abandon the search and kill the middleman. D put the gun to the middleman's neck but did not shoot. D and the others were tried in New Jersey with kidnapping and using a firearm in relation to the kidnapping. D moved to dismiss for lack of venue, on the ground that the firearm offense could only be tried in Maryland. D was convicted and sentenced to 87 months for kidnapping and a mandatory consecutive term of 60 months for the firearm offense. The court of appeals reversed, holding that the firearm statute is violated only in the district where the firearm is used. The Supreme Court granted certiorari.

Issue. May venue in a prosecution for using or carrying a firearm during a crime of violence be proper in any district where the crime of violence was committed, even though the firearm was used only in a single district?

Held. Yes. Judgment reversed.

♦　The locus delicti of a charged offense is determined from the nature of the crime and the location of the acts constituting it. The firearm enhancement statute, 18 U.S.C. section 924(c)(1), provides that whoever, during any crime of violence that may be prosecuted in federal court, uses or carries a firearm shall be sentenced to an additional five years in prison.

♦　The Third Circuit applied a "verb test" to determine the nature of the substantive offense, but this test, by itself, unduly limits the inquiry into the nature of the offense. Although the statute places the crime of violence element in a prepositional phrase instead of using verbs, D's violent acts are essential conduct elements. To prove a violation, the government must prove that the defendant used the gun during the kidnapping. The two elements are using and carrying a gun and committing the kidnapping.

♦　D claims that for venue purposes, the New Jersey kidnapping is irrelevant to the firearm crime because he did not use the gun during the New Jersey crime. But kidnapping is a unitary crime. Once begun, it does not end until the victim is free. Therefore, it does not matter that D used the gun only in Maryland because he did so during the kidnapping that started in Texas and continued through several states, including New Jersey.

♦ When a crime consists of distinct parts that have different localities, the whole may be tried where any part can be proved to have been done. Venue for the kidnapping here was appropriate wherever D took the victim. Where venue is appropriate for the underlying crime of violence, it was also appropriate for the firearm offense.

Dissent (Scalia, Stevens, JJ.). The firearm offense is separate from the kidnapping. D committed the firearm offense only in Maryland. Venue can lie only there. The Court has ignored the "during" requirement. The firearm offense is only committed where both acts are being committed simultaneously. D is being prosecuted for using a gun in a state and district where all agree he did not use it, contrary to the Constitution, Article III, Section 2, Clause 3.

---

b. **Constitutional limitations.** In *Travis v. United States*, 364 U.S. 631 (1961), the defendant executed false affidavits in Colorado and filed them in Washington, D.C. He was tried in Colorado and convicted. His conviction was reversed by the Supreme Court, which held that Article III, Section 2 of the Constitution provides for the trial to be held in the state where the crime is committed. The Court said it would not consider such chance events as the place of mailing or place of reception, but rather look to the nature of each crime to determine the proper venue. Since the law involved made it an offense to have false affidavits on file, then the venue should be the place of filing, not the place of execution. Note that in many federal offenses involving interstate commerce or conspiracy, the offense is viewed as continuing and triable in any state through which the commerce or conspiracy passed.

c. **Venue within the state.** Intrastate venue lies in the county where the crime is committed, with multiple venues possible when the crime begins in one county and ends in another.

d. **Change of venue.** Federal Rule of Criminal Procedure 21 provides for a change of venue from any district where prejudice against the defendant is so great that she cannot receive a fair trial in that district. This problem occurs most frequently when there is excessive pretrial publicity. If publicity has been nationwide, a transfer of venue may not be very effective. If publicity is of such an extensive and severe nature that the defendant may be deprived of a fair and impartial trial, the conviction must be reversed.

G. JOINDER AND SEVERANCE

1. **Joinder and Severance of Offenses.**

a. **Proper joinder.** Federal courts and a majority of the state courts permit the joinder of offenses in the following circumstances:

   1) The offenses are the same or similar in class or character.

   2) The offenses are different but related in time or space.

   3) The offenses spring from the same activity.

   4) The offenses are part of a long-term scheme.

b. **Improper joinder.** Generally, the courts will prohibit the joinder of offenses if there is a great danger that the jury will become confused by the joinder, or if the defendant is actually prejudiced by the joinder.

   1) **Forced testimony--**

Cross v. United States, 335 F.2d 987 (D.C. Cir. 1964).

Facts. Cross (D) was charged with two counts of robbery—first of a church and then of a tourist home a few months later. He took the stand to defend himself but wanted to testify only regarding the robbery of the tourist home. He was acquitted of the robbery of the tourist home but convicted of the other robbery.

Issue. May joinder be allowed if it significantly influences a defendant's fair choice of whether to testify?

Held. No. Judgment vacated and remanded for new trial on that count.

♦ A defendant may wish to testify on one count and not on another. His decision whether to testify on each will depend on several factors—the evidence against him, the availability of other defense evidence, the plausibility of his story, the possibility of impeachment, etc. However, once the defendant takes the stand on one count, he is open to impeachment on all counts. Furthermore, the jury may infer guilt from a defendant's silence on one count when he freely testifies to another. The danger of misleading the jury is too great to permit joinder of the offenses. Prejudice to D is shown by the fact that he was convicted on one count.

Dissent. The jury was not confused by the joinder, because it was able to convict selectively and convicted on the count with the weaker defense.

---

   2) **Cumulative guilt--**

Drew v. United States, 331 F.2d 85 (D.C. Cir. 1964).

Facts. Drew (D) was accused of the robbery of one of a chain of grocery stores and the later attempted robbery of another store in the chain. The issue at trial was identification of the robber. In each case, the robber followed a similar pattern and wore similar articles of clothing. D was convicted of both crimes after denial of his motion to sever. D appeals.

Issue. May a series of related crimes be joined in one trial?

Held. No. Judgment reversed and case remanded.

♦ A defendant may be prejudiced by joinder when (i) a defendant is embarrassed or confused when presenting several defenses at trial, (ii) the jury may use the evidence of one crime to imply a criminal disposition and guilt for the other crimes charged, or (iii) the jury may cumulate the evidence in all counts to find the defendant guilty, when it would not do so were each offense presented separately.

♦ Prior offenses may be admissible to show similarity, but each offense must be provable independently. This was not the case here. There was a strong likelihood that the jury was confused and used robbery number one to show a disposition to commit robbery number two.

---

3) **Factors showing lack of prejudice.** Courts frequently use the following arguments to show lack of prejudice:

   a) The jury is capable of following instructions regarding use of evidence.

   b) The jury, if it acquits on any charge, is capable of being selective.

   c) The defendant has no ground for complaint if she is convicted on several counts but received concurrent sentencing.

   d) Overwhelming evidence of guilt cures any prejudice by joinder.

c. **Proper severance of offenses.** There is no constitutional prohibition against multiple trials based on the defendant's criminal activity, as long as there is no more than one trial per offense.

d.   **Improper severance.** While the Constitution permits severance of offenses based on the same activity, the courts will not permit severance that is fundamentally unfair to the defendant.

2.   **Failure to Join Related Offenses—Collateral Estoppel.** A former conviction or acquittal that does not bar a later prosecution for a different crime arising from the same acts (the issue of double jeopardy) may still estop the prosecution from relitigating issues of fact necessarily determined in the defendant's favor in an earlier trial.

a.   *Blockburger* test--

United States v. Dixon, 509 U.S. 688 (1993).

Facts. Dixon (D) was released on bond after being arrested for second-degree murder. One of the conditions of his release was that D not commit "any criminal offense." A violation would subject D to prosecution for contempt of court. D was subsequently arrested and indicted for possession of cocaine with intent to distribute. At a contempt hearing, the court found that the government had established beyond a reasonable doubt that D had committed the cocaine offense and found D in contempt. D was sentenced to 180 days in jail. D moved to dismiss the cocaine indictment as a violation of double jeopardy. The trial court granted the motion. In a consolidated case, Foster's wife obtained a civil protection order ("CPO") that required Foster not to "molest, assault, or in any manner threaten or physically abuse" his wife. After Foster allegedly violated the CPO, the court held a hearing and found that Foster was guilty beyond a reasonable doubt of four counts of criminal contempt, based on his commission of assaults as defined by the criminal code. Foster was sentenced to 600 days' confinement. Foster was subsequently indicted for simple assault, three counts of threatening to injure another, and assault with intent to kill. The first and last counts were based on the events for which Foster had been held in contempt, while the remaining three counts were based on events for which Foster was acquitted of contempt. Foster moved to dismiss the indictment, but the district court denied the motion. The government in D's case and Foster both appealed to the District of Columbia Court of Appeals, which consolidated the cases and held that both subsequent prosecutions were barred by the Double Jeopardy Clause. The Supreme Court granted certiorari.

Issue. Does the Double Jeopardy Clause prohibit prosecution for an offense if the defendant has been previously found guilty of criminal contempt of court for committing the same offense?

Held. Yes. Judgment affirmed in part.

♦   The Double Jeopardy Clause protects against both successive punishments and successive prosecutions for the same criminal offense. In *Blockburger v. United States, supra,* the Court established a "same-elements" test whereby a person cannot be punished or tried for an offense that has the same elements as an offense for which he has been previously punished or tried. This test inquires whether each offense contains an element not contained in the other; if not, they are the "same offense" and double jeopardy bars additional punishment and successive prosecution.

♦ In *Grady v. Corbin*, 495 U.S. 508 (1990), the Court held that in addition to passing the *Blockburger* test, a subsequent prosecution must satisfy a "same-conduct" test to avoid being barred by double jeopardy. The *Grady* test provides that, "if, to establish an essential element of an offense charged in that prosecution, the government will prove conduct that constitutes an offense for which the defendant has already been prosecuted," double jeopardy bars the second prosecution.

♦ Under *Blockburger*, D's conviction for contempt required first that D be subject to a condition of release, and then that he violate the condition. The condition imposed by the judge incorporated the statutory cocaine offense. The "crime" of violating a condition of release cannot be abstracted from the "element" of the violated condition, so the underlying substantive criminal offense is a "species of lesser-included offense." D's drug offense did not include any element not contained in his previous contempt offense, so the cocaine indictment violates the Double Jeopardy Clause.

♦ The *Blockburger* test also invalidates the first charge against Foster, charging assault, because this charge does not include any element not contained in his previous contempt offense. However, the other four counts are not barred. The last charge required proof of specific intent to kill, which the contempt offense did not. The three remaining charges required proof of specific types of threat, which the contempt offense did not, while the contempt violation required willful violation of the CPO, which the three remaining charges do not require.

♦ Under the *Grady* test, the additional charges against Foster would have to be dismissed because they arise from conduct that constituted the contempt offense. However, the *Grady* test has proven unworkable and an exception has already been made for prosecution of conspiracy after a prosecution for the substantive offense. *Grady* was wrongly decided and is overruled.

Concurrence and dissent (Rehnquist, C.J., O'Connor, Thomas, JJ.). The Court's opinion is correct except for its application of the *Blockburger* test. Proper application of the test requires focus not on the terms of the particular court orders involved in a case, but on the elements of contempt of court. The traditional approach does not apply double jeopardy to bar a subsequent prosecution based on conduct for which a defendant has been held in criminal contempt. Two offenses are different for double jeopardy analysis if "each provision requires proof of a fact which the other does not." Contempt of court has two elements: (i) a court order made known to the defendant; and (ii) willful violation of the order. Proof that D committed a substantive offense does not satisfy the requirements of contempt, and D's guilt of contempt does not necessarily satisfy the requirements of the substantive offenses. Thus, these offenses are not analogous to greater- and lesser-included offenses, and they are separate and distinct for double jeopardy purposes.

Concurrence and dissent (White, Stevens, Souter, JJ.). The Court correctly holds that D's prosecution for the cocaine offense and Foster's prosecution for simple assault are barred. However, under the Double Jeopardy Clause, all the subsequent prosecutions in both cases should be impermissible. The prohibitions contained in the court orders duplicated those in the criminal statutes they incorporated. Thus, D and Foster were held in contempt for the same offense that they were subsequently charged with violating. In successive prosecutions, the risk is that a person will have to defend himself more than once against the same charges. The only way to protect against this risk is to set aside the CPO and compare the substantive offenses of which the defendants stood accused in both prosecutions. The *Blockburger* test by itself is not adequate protection, because a simple modification of statutory definitions can result in multiple prosecutions based on the same factual issues. The better approach is to bar successive prosecutions when the second prosecution requires the relitigation of factual issues already resolved by the first. For example, in Foster's case, he was acquitted of contempt for the arguably lesser-included offense of threatening "in any manner," and should not now have to defend a prosecution for specific types of threats based on the same conduct. The fact that the government had to prove the existence of the CPO in the contempt proceeding does not eliminate the prejudice to Foster of consecutive trials. Also, there is no basis for overruling *Grady*.

Concurrence and dissent (Blackmun, J.). *Grady* should not be overruled. Contempt proceedings serve unique interests in enforcing the courts' authority and protecting persons from harm. They should not be equated with criminal prosecutions.

Concurrence and dissent (Souter, Stevens, JJ.). All of the subsequent prosecutions should be barred. Analysis of claims of successive prosecution should be different from analysis of claims of multiple punishment. In the latter, double jeopardy assures that the court does not exceed its legislative authorization by imposing multiple punishments for the same offense. This is the focus of the *Blockburger* test, which emphasizes the elements of the two crimes. However, the legislature has power to authorize cumulative punishments under two statutes even if they both proscribe the same conduct. Successive prosecution, however, is prevented by the Double Jeopardy Clause to protect individuals from the expense and ordeal of such government action, as well as to avoid the higher risk of conviction of an innocent person. The *Blockburger* test is inadequate to fully protect against successive prosecution, and is not the only double jeopardy hurdle the government must clear.

Comment. The various opinions in this case resulted in the following votes: Six Justices voted that the prosecution of D's cocaine offense and Foster's simple assault charge were barred by double jeopardy. Three Justices voted that none of the subsequent prosecutions were barred. Four Justices voted that all of the subsequent prosecutions were barred. Five Justices voted to overrule *Grady*.

---

b. **Double jeopardy—continuing criminal enterprise.** In *Garrett v. United States,* 471 U.S. 773 (1985), the defendant contended that his conviction for engaging in a continuing criminal enterprise violated the test set forth in *Brown v. Ohio*, 432 U.S. 161 (1977). The government offered proof of the defendant's having pleaded guilty to the charge of importation of marijuana in order to satisfy its burden of showing three or more successive violations of a specified type needed to prove a continuing criminal enterprise. The defendant argued that the importation charge constituted a lesser-included offense of the continuing criminal enterprise offense and hence, under *Brown*, the Double Jeopardy Clause barred prosecution for the greater offense. A plurality of the Supreme Court held that *Brown* did not apply because the continuing criminal enterprise had not been completed at the time he was indicted for the continuing criminal enterprise charge.

c. **Defendant asks for separate trials--**

Jeffers v. United States, 432 U.S. 137 (1977).

Facts. Jeffers (D) was charged with conspiracy to distribute drugs and conducting a continuing criminal enterprise to violate the drug laws. D's objection to the government's motion to join the charges for trial was sustained. D later moved to dismiss the latter charge on double jeopardy grounds, but that motion was denied. D was separately convicted of both offenses and was given consecutive penalties for the two convictions.

Issue. If a defendant asks for separate trials without raising the issue that the trial on one offense would be for a lesser-included offense of the other, will the Double Jeopardy Clause bar the subsequent trial?

Held. No. Judgment affirmed.

♦   This is an exception to *Brown*. The result here might have been different if any action by the government contributed to the separate prosecutions on the lesser and greater charges. Since D had an alternative of being tried on both counts separately from the other defendants, he was not faced with the dilemma recognized in *Simmons v. United States, supra,* of asserting either of two constitutional rights but not both (here between a Sixth Amendment right to a fair trial and a Fifth Amendment protection against double jeopardy).

Dissent (Stevens, Brennan, Stewart, Marshall, JJ.). The grand jury's returning two indictments is evidence of government action contributing to the separate prosecutions on the lesser and greater charges.

---

d.   Collateral estoppel--

Ashe v. Swenson, 397 U.S. 436 (1970).

Facts. Ashe (D) was charged with the robbery of one of six poker players and found not guilty by a jury for "insufficient evidence." The prosecution clearly proved the robbery but could not prove the identification issue; *i.e.,* that D was one of the robbers. D was acquitted. D was subsequently brought to trial for the robbery of one of the other poker players. D moved to dismiss, but the motion was overruled. The witnesses who testified at the first trial testified again, but this time they identified D more clearly. D was convicted. The lower courts upheld the conviction. The Supreme Court granted certiorari.

Issue. Is the doctrine of collateral estoppel a part of the Fifth Amendment's guarantee against double jeopardy?

Held. Yes. Judgment reversed and case remanded.

♦   When an issue of ultimate fact is decided and final, that issue cannot be relitigated—here, identification of the robbers. Prosecution on a separate offense is not barred by double jeopardy, but collateral estoppel may bar retrial when a defendant is acquitted on a charge of a separate offense growing out of the same act or transaction.

♦   In this case, the sole issue in the first trial was whether D was one of the robbers. When the jury found that he was not, a second prosecution for the robbery was barred, even if the second trial involved a different victim of the same robbery.

Concurrence (Brennan, Douglas, Marshall, JJ.). Even if collateral estoppel did not apply in this case, the Double Jeopardy Clause would bar prosecution.

Dissent (Burger, C.J.). Collateral estoppel should not be applied here where the complainant in the second trial is not the same as the one in the first trial. The evidence in this case could support a verdict of guilty in the second trial even though D was acquitted in the first trial.

Comment. Once the jury determined that there was reasonable doubt as to whether D was one of the robbers, the state could not present the same identification issue in a second prosecution.

---

3.   **Joinder and Severance of Defendants.**

a.   **Confrontation and the Sixth Amendment.** The Sixth Amendment states that "[i]n all criminal prosecutions, the accused shall enjoy the right . . . to be confronted with the witnesses against him." This includes the right of a defendant to cross-examine witnesses called to testify against him.

    b.   **ABA standards.** Two or more defendants may be joined in the same trial:

        1)   When each defendant is charged with accountability for each offense included;

        2)   When each defendant is charged with conspiracy and some defendants are also charged with one or more offenses alleged to be in furtherance of the conspiracy; or

        3)   When the several offenses are part of a common scheme or plan or are so closely related in time, place, and occasion that it is difficult to separate the proof of one charge from proof of the others.

    c.   **Continuing joinder when joining charge fails--**

Schaffer v. United States, 362 U.S. 511 (1960).

Facts. Schaffer and two other parties (Ds) were each charged separately with interstate transportation of illegal goods. Each defendant had operated with a common middleman and they were therefore joined in a fourth count of conspiracy. All Ds were tried simultaneously in a single trial. Upon challenge, the trial court dismissed the conspiracy charge, but Ds were convicted of the separate substantive counts. Ds appeal, claiming that continued joinder after dismissal of the conspiracy count was improper.

Issue. When a conspiracy count, which originally justified joinder, fails, is continued joinder error as a matter of law?

Held. No. Judgment affirmed.

♦   Severance is required only if there is a showing of prejudice to the defendant as a result of joinder. Joinder here was properly granted initially, and failure of the conspiracy count does not retroactively invalidate the original joinder.

♦   The lower court judges were careful to see that there was no prejudice to Ds.

Dissent (Douglas, J., Warren, C.J., Black, Brennan, JJ.). The allegation of conspiracy, once proven false, should not be permitted to justify joinder when the defendants have not participated in the same series of transactions.

Comment. Federal Rule of Criminal Procedure 8(b) contemplates joinder of parties in two situations: (i) where the defendants participate jointly in a single act; and (ii) where the defendants participate in the same series of acts or transactions constituting an offense.

---

     d.   **Improper joinder of defendants.** As with improper joinder of offenses, joinder of defendants is reversible error when one of the defendants is prejudiced because the number of defendants or the complexity of evidence is so great that the jury might become confused; each defendant offers a contradictory defense; or it is otherwise impossible to use a co-defendant as a witness on behalf of the defendant.

         1)   **Inadequate redaction--**

Gray v. Maryland, 523 U.S. 185 (1998).

Facts. Bell confessed that he had participated in the fatal beating of Williams, along with Gray (D). Bell and D were indicted for murder and tried in a joint trial. The trial judge allowed the prosecution to use Bell's confession after it had been redacted to substitute D's name with a blank space or the word "deleted." When the officer finished reading Bell's redacted confession at the trial, the prosecutor asked whether D was arrested on the basis of information in the confession. Other witnesses testified that D and Bell participated in the beating. D testified and denied having participated. The jury was instructed not to use the confession against D. Both Bell and D were convicted. D appeals, claiming that the use of Bell's confession was unconstitutional.

Issue. Does the *Bruton* rule apply if the prosecution redacts a confession by a co-defendant to replace the defendant's name but keeps in the references to the unnamed defendant?

Held. Yes. Judgment reversed.

♦   In *Bruton v. United States*, 391 U.S. 123 (1968), the Court held that a confession by one co-defendant cannot be used against another co-defendant in a joint trial, even if a limiting instruction is given. The use of such a confession violates the co-defendant's right to confrontation. Limiting instructions are inadequate because of the inherent unreliability of such evidence, compounded by the inability to test through cross-examination.

♦   In *Richardson v. Marsh*, 481 U.S. 200 (1987), the Court limited *Bruton*, holding that the prosecution could use a redacted confession that eliminated all indications that anyone other than the confessing co-defendant and a third person was involved.

♦   The prosecution tried to comply with *Bruton* and come within *Richardson* by deleting D's name from the confession, but it left in the reference to another nonconfessing defendant. This type of redaction does not eliminate the special prejudice identified by *Bruton*. The jury will often realize that the confession refers specifically to the unnamed defendant in the trial. After all, if the confession referred to someone else, the jury would wonder why that person was not being tried instead of the defendant. The redaction encourages the jury to speculate about the reference.

♦ For these reasons, this case does not fall within *Richardson*, but instead falls within *Bruton*.

Dissent (Scalia, J., Rehnquist, C.J., Kennedy, Thomas, JJ.). The law assumes that jurors will follow their instructions. *Bruton* was a narrow exception to the rule and applies only when the facially incriminating confession of a nontestifying co-defendant is introduced at their joint trial. In *Richardson*, the Court declined to extend *Bruton* to confessions that incriminate only by inference from other evidence. A confession that redacts D's name is not facially incriminating. It is less likely to incriminate than a confession that contains D's name. In this case, Bell's confession named two others, but the evidence showed that five or six others participated. The level of incrimination in this case is not so powerful that the court must depart from the normal presumption that a jury follows its instructions. The extension of *Bruton* to name-redacted confessions seriously compromises society's compelling interest in law enforcement.

Comment. In *Cruz v. New York*, 481 U.S. 186 (1987), the Court held that *Bruton* applied to interlocking confessions (co-defendant confessions that interlock with the defendant's own confession). The interlocking nature of such confessions makes them even more devastating than a co-defendant confession standing alone.

———

2) **Other cases and comments.**

a) In *Tennessee v. Street,* 471 U.S. 409 (1985), the defendant testified at trial that his confession to murder and burglary had been coerced by the sheriff reading to him a confession made by a co-defendant. The co-defendant's confession was admitted in rebuttal to show the difference between the two confessions. The Supreme Court held that this use of the co-defendant's confession raised no Confrontation Clause concerns. Moreover, the trial court's limiting instruction that the confession was for the purpose of rebuttal only was, according to the Court, an appropriate way to limit the jury's use of the evidence in a manner consistent with the Confrontation Clause.

b) In *Nelson v. O'Neil*, 402 U.S. 622 (1971), the Court held that *Bruton* does not apply if the co-defendant takes the stand in his own defense and denies making an out-of-court confession implicating the defendant. The defendant has been denied no rights protected by the Sixth and Fourteenth Amendments.

    c)   In *California v. Green*, *supra*, the prosecution was allowed to introduce testimony from a former preliminary hearing of an unavailable witness. There the witness had been subject to full cross-examination by defense counsel at the preliminary hearing. The witness was not unavailable in the common law sense of death or insanity—or even out of state—but simply had a lapse of memory. The Court held that there was no denial of confrontation, as the defendant had a prior opportunity to cross-examine the witness. The defendant did not cross-examine the witness at the preliminary hearing for tactical reasons. The majority refused to distinguish cross-examination at trial from preliminary hearing. The dissent pointed out tactical differences and that a preliminary hearing is not a full-blown trial.

H. SPEEDY TRIAL AND OTHER SPEEDY DISPOSITION

    1.   **Constitutional and Statutory Provisions.**

        a.   **Sixth Amendment.** The Sixth Amendment provides that "[i]n all criminal prosecutions, the accused shall enjoy the right to a speedy . . . trial." The speedy trial provision of the federal Constitution is embodied in the Fourteenth Amendment Due Process Clause and hence is applicable to the states. [Klopfer v. North Carolina, 386 U.S. 213 (1967)]

        b.   **Purpose.** The purpose of the speedy trial provision is to relieve the defendant from anxiety, harassment, and lengthy imprisonment before trial and to protect her ability to refute the charges against her.

        c.   **Other protections.** In addition to constitutional provisions, statutes and court rules provide for dismissals of actions when there have been, without good cause, delays in filing an indictment or information or in bringing the defendant to trial. [Fed. R. Crim. P. 48]

        d.   **Speedy Trial Act of 1974.** The Speedy Trial Act provides that federal defendants are to be tried within 100 days of arrest. Several exceptions to the deadlines are allowed (*e.g.,* for hearings on pretrial motions).

        e.   **Balancing test--**

Barker v. Wingo, 407 U.S. 514 (1972).

Facts. Barker (D) was brought to trial on murder charges more than five years after his arrest. The delay was due to numerous continuances by the prosecution, which was trying to get D's co-defendant convicted first. D moved for dismissal, arguing that his Sixth Amendment right to a speedy trial had been violated. He had not objected to the first 11 continuances, however. D was convicted. The Supreme Court granted certiorari.

Issue. Is a delay of five years a violation of a defendant's Sixth Amendment right to a speedy trial per se?

Held. No. Judgment affirmed.

◆ The determination of whether a defendant's Sixth Amendment right to a speedy trial has been violated is done through a balancing test.

◆ The prejudice to D was minimal— he spent only 10 months of the five years in jail—and considering that the criminal charge was murder, the lower court was correct in dismissing D's petition.

Concurrence (White, Brennan, JJ.). Crowded dockets and limited public resources alone cannot justify an unreasonable delay in run-of-the-mill criminal cases.

---

2. **When Right to a Speedy Trial Attaches.** The right clearly attaches when the defendant is formally charged; and in most jurisdictions, the right is also deemed to attach after a complaint has been sworn out or the defendant has been arrested.

   a. **Pre-prosecution delay.** Very few delays in arresting or charging a person with a crime have been held to be within the right to a speedy trial, although such delays involve many of the same dangers as post-information delays.

      1) **Statute of limitations.** Usually the statute of limitations remains the sole control over this kind of delay.

   b. **Sentencing.** The right applies to delays in sentencing but not to delays in the appellate process.

   c. **Fifth Amendment rights.** Note that Fifth Amendment due process is involved in delays other than those involved in the right to a speedy trial.

3. **Waiver.** A defendant may waive her right to a speedy trial if she is the cause of the delay, if she enters a voluntary plea of guilty, or if she fails to present the claim prior to or at trial.

4. **Determining the Unreasonableness of the Delay.** Although statutes frequently impose specific time limits within which the accused must be brought to trial, violation of the constitutional right to a speedy trial is not established by delay alone. A delay violates the constitutional right to a speedy trial only if (i) its cause is improper, and (ii) the defendant suffers actual prejudice. Some courts, however, presume prejudice if there has been a denial of a speedy trial.

    a. **Defendant imprisoned in another state--**

Smith v. Hooey, 393 U.S. 374 (1969).

Facts. Smith (D) was serving a jail sentence in Kansas and was indicted for theft in Texas. D made a demand for a speedy trial in Texas but was told only that he would be granted a trial within two weeks of any date at which he could be present in Texas. D made repeated attempts over the next six years to get Texas to bring him to trial, but nothing was done. D made a motion to dismiss the charge for want of prosecution. The motion was denied. D appeals.

Issue. In order to keep a criminal charge against an out-of-state prisoner valid, must the state do anything more than indicate an intent to provide a speedy trial when the defendant is able to enter the state?

Held. Yes. Judgment reversed and case remanded.

♦   A delay in bringing an incarcerated defendant to trial on a different pending charge may result in as much oppression as that suffered by one who is in jail without bail on an untried charge. There is the possibility that the defendant already in prison might receive a sentence concurrent with the one he is serving, and this could be lost if trial of the pending charge is postponed. Also, serving a sentence with the possibility of being imprisoned in another state at the end of the first sentence can have a depressive effect on a prisoner that leaves him with little motivation to rehabilitate himself.

♦   Also, when the defendant is in prison in another jurisdiction, his ability to confer with potential defense witnesses is hindered, and, with the passage of time, witnesses disappear and memories fade. Thus, the possibilities that long delay will impair his ability to defend himself are significantly increased.

Comment. Some states have entered into a Uniform Agreement on Detainers to expedite such matters.

---

b. **Prejudice.** Actual prejudice is generally some impairment of the defendant's ability to defend (*e.g.,* destruction or disappearance of documentary or testimonial evidence). The burden of proving unreasonable delay and actual prejudice is generally on the defendant. However, this rule has been criticized as placing too difficult a burden on the defendant.

5. **Right to Other Speedy Disposition--**

United States v. Lovasco, 431 U.S. 783 (1977).

Facts. Lovasco (D) was indicted for possessing firearms stolen from the United States mail and for dealing in firearms without a license. D moved to dismiss the indictment on the basis that the offense occurred more than 18 months before the indictment was filed. The district court dismissed the indictment, while the court of appeals affirmed. The Supreme Court granted certiorari.

Issue. Does the prosecution of a defendant following investigative delay deprive him of due process, even if his defense might have been somewhat prejudiced by the lapse of time?

Held. No. Judgment reversed.

♦ To file charges without proper and complete investigation is undesirable from the perspective of defendants because it would increase the likelihood of unwarranted charges being filed, and would add to the time during which defendants stand accused but untried.

♦ To file charges without proper and complete investigation is undesirable from the perspective of law enforcement officials because it would cause fruitful sources of information to dry up before they are fully exploited.

---

6. **Remedy.** The only remedy for a violation of the defendant's right to a speedy trial is a dismissal of the prosecution entirely. This being so, the courts are noticeably reluctant to hold that there has been a denial of the right to a speedy trial. Such a dismissal, however, would not bar the refiling of the case unless: (i) the defendant was able to show prejudice resulting from the delay; (ii) the statute of limitations barred the prosecution; or (iii) the statute requiring dismissal because of the noncompliance with statutory speedy trial provisions also provides that the dismissal is a bar. [Strunk v. United States, 412 U.S. 434 (1973)]

IV. THE ADVERSARY SYSTEM AND THE DETERMINATION OF GUILT OR INNOCENCE

A. PRETRIAL DISCOVERY AND RELATED RIGHTS

1. Pretrial Discovery by the Defense.

a. Introduction. Other than being entitled to any exculpatory or mitigating evidence in the prosecution's possession, a defendant in a criminal case has no *constitutional* right to obtain discovery as to the prosecution's case against him (*i.e.,* to inspect physical evidence, to obtain names of persons who will testify as witnesses or copies of their statements, etc.).

1) One reason for this is a supposed balance between adversaries, since the defendant need not disclose his evidence or his defense. Also, there is the fear that a defendant, knowing the prosecution's case, will attempt to falsify evidence, make up false alibis, suborn perjury, or coerce or intimidate witnesses.

2) However, when the prosecution attempts to enforce an alibi rule against a defendant (requiring disclosure before trial of the details, witnesses, etc., of the defendant's alibi), due process requires that the defendant have a reciprocal right to discover the names and addresses of witnesses the state plans to use in refuting the defendant's alibi. [Wardius v. Oregon, 412 U.S. 470 (1973)]

3) The trend of thinking and court decisions is toward expanding the accused's right of discovery. For example, the ABA Standards recommend disclosure to the accused of prosecution's witnesses, all statements made by the accused or co-defendants, results of examinations, statements of experts, relevant grand jury testimony, etc.

b. Background. The following traditional methods of exploring the prosecution's case (in addition to discovery methods) usually supplied only a limited amount of information.

1) **Preliminary hearing.** The prosecution must put on enough evidence to establish a "probable cause" before the defendant can be held for trial. This allows the defense to see at least part of the prosecution's evidence.

2) Grand jury minutes. A few jurisdictions give the defendant a copy of the grand jury minutes, which contain the testimony of all prosecution witnesses. The majority of states and the federal courts ordinarily provide the defendant with a copy only of his own testimony before the grand jury; the balance is kept secret or for use only by the prosecution. In federal courts, however, a defendant may inspect the entire grand jury transcript upon a showing of "particularized need."

3) Bill of particulars. The bill of particulars can also be used to gain further information about the prosecutor's case.

4) Federal Rules of Criminal Procedure. [*See* Fed. R. Crim. P. 16, discussed *infra*]

c. State practice. Statutes, rules, and decisions on discovery in state courts vary enormously. For example, in *State v. Tune*, 98 A.2d 881 (N.J. 1953), the court refused to allow the defendant's attorney to obtain a copy of the defendant's pretrial confession. In *State v. Johnson*, 145 A.2d 313 (N.J. 1958), the court held that the defendant's counsel might be able to obtain the defendant's confession upon an adequate showing of need.

d. Federal practice. Rule 16 of the Federal Rules of Criminal Procedure provides a very broad right of discovery to an accused in a federal criminal proceeding:

1) Scope.

a) The accused is entitled to inspect his own pretrial statements, confessions, and grand jury testimony.

b) The results of medical and scientific tests and experiments are available (*e.g.,* autopsy reports, psychiatric reports, ballistics tests).

c) Inspection is allowed of any other books, records, or other physical evidence (*e.g.,* weapons) "material to the preparation of his defense" in the government's possession, except pretrial statements of third-party witnesses. The government does not have to disclose the identity of its witnesses (except in capital cases; *see* below) or the contents of statements made by them.

(1) However, once a government witness has testified at trial, the accused is then entitled to inspect any pretrial statements made by the witness (or reports by government agents of the witness's testimony) to aid in cross-ex-

amination. [Jencks v. United States, 353 U.S. 657 (1957); 19 U.S.C. §3500—The *Jencks* Act]

  (2) If the statement was oral, the government must furnish substantially a verbatim recital thereof. The court, on the government's request, will inspect a statement that is ordered to be produced to determine whether it relates to the subject matter of the witness's testimony and will excise portions of the statement that do not so relate. On the defendant's objection, the entire text can be preserved and made available to the appellate court reviewing the case.

  (3) The *Jencks* Rule does not extend to grand jury testimony that a witness gave unless "particularized need" is shown by the defendant.

  (4) In *In re United States*, 834 F.2d 283 (2d Cir. 1987), the court of appeals reversed the district court's ruling in *United States v. Gallo*, 654 F. Supp. 463 (E.D.N.Y. 1987), that the defendant was entitled to discovery of an undercover agent's written memorialization of the defendant's declaration made in the presence of the agent. The court of appeals applied a prior ruling that the written notes of an undercover agent who overhears oral statements of a defendant are not discoverable.

2) **Required showing.** Inspection of the accused's testimony and medical or scientific tests is apparently a matter of right; the accused need not establish "good cause" or any compelling necessity for the information sought. But the accused must show that any of the prosecution's other evidence is material to his defense and that the request is "reasonable."

  a) The government may in some instances be permitted to ask the judge to make an in camera determination of whether evidence in the possession of the government is material to the case. [*See e.g.,* Dennis v. United States, 384 U.S. 855 (1966)—disclosure of grand jury minutes subject to in camera delegation of extraneous material; Palermo v. United States, 360 U.S. 343 (1959)—in camera determination of whether the *Jencks* Act requires disclosure of documents to the defense]

  b) However, in some instances this determination is so complex and the margin of error so great that in camera hearings will be deemed inadequate to afford a defendant a fair trial. [Alderman v. United States, *supra*—refusing to permit in camera hearings on materiality of electronic surveillance records, even in a case involving national security]

3) **Capital cases.** Another rule in federal courts to implement discovery by the accused requires the prosecutor to give the defendant in a capital case the names and addresses of all persons whom the government intends to call as witnesses, at least three days before trial. [18 U.S.C. §3432]

4) **Habeas corpus proceedings.** More liberal discovery may be available in federal habeas corpus proceedings. Reflecting its historical background as a civil proceeding, the Court has held that a federal court, in aid of its habeas corpus jurisdiction, may issue discovery orders appropriate to criminal or civil proceedings (*e.g.,* interrogatories, depositions), or otherwise appropriate to the usages and principles of law. [Harris v. Nelson, 394 U.S. 286 (1969)]

2. **Discovery by the Prosecution.**

a. **Notice of alibi--**

Williams v. Florida, 399 U.S. 78 (1970).

Facts. Williams (D) sought an order excusing him from complying with Florida's notice of alibi rule, which required D to give the prosecution the names of his alibi witnesses, and which required the prosecution to give D the names of witnesses to rebut the alibi. The court denied D's request, and he was convicted when the prosecution successfully impeached D's alibi witness. D appeals.

Issue. Does a notice of alibi rule violate a defendant's Fifth Amendment right not to provide incriminating evidence?

Held. No. Judgment affirmed.

♦ The rule enhances the search for truth, is fair to both D and the prosecution, and complies with due process.

♦ The rule in effect merely accelerates the timing of the disclosure of D's alibi defense and does not force D to incriminate himself.

Concurrence (Burger, C.J.). The rule is useful from the point of judicial economy.

Dissent (Black, Douglas, JJ.). The rule violates the settled requirement that the state prove its own case without compelling D's assistance.

b. **Choosing when to testify.** The privilege against self-incrimination is broad; although it literally gives a defendant the right to refuse to testify, it also permits him to choose when to testify. In *Brooks v. Tennessee*, 406 U.S. 605 (1972), the Court invalidated a statute that required a defendant to be the first defense witness or lose his right to testify.

c. **Discovery during trial.** In addition to pretrial discovery rights under Federal Rule of Criminal Procedure 16, the trial court may grant the government discovery *during trial* pursuant to its inherent power to ensure that the fact-finding process at trial is enhanced. [*See* United States v. Nobles, 422 U.S. 225 (1975)—defense investigator can be prohibited from testifying as to impeaching statements obtained from prosecution witnesses, if defense refuses to give investigator's notes of conversations to the government; and such a sanction does not violate defendant's right to present evidence on his own behalf]

d. **In general.**

1) In most cases, the defendant will testify, thus subjecting himself to cross-examination by the prosecution.

2) Admissions by the defendant to the police are freely used at trial.

3) The body of the accused may freely be used to incriminate him—fingerprints, blood, urine, lineups, etc.

4) If he is not named as the defendant (by arrest, indictment, etc.), he may be called as a "witness" at grand jury hearings—thus forcing him to plead the privilege against self-incrimination to avoid testifying (ensuring his indictment).

5) Police can informally question the defendant's witnesses or the prosecution can question them more formally at the grand jury hearing.

e. **Sanctions for defense violations--**

Taylor v. Illinois, 484 U.S. 400 (1988).

Facts. Prior to the trial of Taylor (D) for attempted murder, the prosecutor filed a discovery motion for a list of defense witnesses. D's attorney provided a list of four persons, two of whom actually testified at trial. On the first day of trial, D's attorney added two additional witnesses in an amendment. After the two principal prosecution witnesses testified, D's attorney sought to make an additional amendment, claiming he had just been informed about them. Upon further questioning, D's attorney admitted he had known about the witnesses earlier, but did not have the address of one of them

(Wormley). The court then ordered that Wormley testify out of the presence of the jury. Wormley stated that he had not seen the incident, but had seen certain participants and heard their statements. However, Wormley did not meet D until two years after the incident (and four months before trial). Wormley also testified that D's attorney had met with him at his house the week before trial. Based on the contradictions with D's attorney's representations, the judge excluded Wormley's testimony as a sanction for the discovery violation. D was convicted. The state courts upheld the conviction and the Supreme Court granted certiorari.

Issue. May a trial court exclude defense evidence as a sanction for defense counsel's violation of a discovery rule?

Held. Yes. Judgment affirmed.

♦   The Compulsory Process Clause of the Sixth Amendment does not merely give an accused the power to subpoena witnesses. It also requires the government to assist in compelling the attendance of defense witnesses at trial and gives the accused the right to present relevant evidence to the jury. This right is not absolute, however.

♦   Unlike other Sixth Amendment rights, the compulsory process rights must be invoked by the accused. An accused's exercise of the right is subject to the necessary procedural rules that make orderly conduct of trials possible. Discovery rules are likewise intended to ensure full and fair presentation of the facts.

♦   While D admits the legitimacy of discovery rules as applied to defense witnesses, he claims that the sanction of excluding testimony is too drastic. Instead, D proposes use of a continuance or a mistrial, combined with sanctions against either D or his counsel. Such alternative sanctions may be appropriate in some cases, but they could be used to perpetuate the harm to the adversary trial process caused by violation of the discovery rules themselves. Therefore, the sanction of preclusion of evidence must be available as a sanction for defense violations of the discovery rules.

♦   In deciding what, if any, sanctions to apply, a judge must balance D's right to offer testimony against the integrity of the adversary process itself. In this case, the judge found that D's attorney's violation was willful and blatant; this justifies imposition of the most severe sanction.

Dissent (Brennan, Marshall, Blackmun, JJ.). The sanction of precluding a criminal defense witness from testifying is arbitrary and disproportionate to the purposes for discovery. D's witness should have been allowed to testify, and the prosecution could have explained to the jury the circumstances of the witness's testimony that cast a doubt on his credibility. At any rate, when D did not play any part in his attorney's violation, D's attorney, not D, should be punished for D's attorney's conduct.

3. **Access to Evidence by Defendant.**

   a. **Introduction.** The prosecution must provide the defense with evidence it has that is favorable to the accused and material to guilt or punishment. In addition, the Confrontation Clause protects a defendant's right to cross-examine witnesses. For example, in *Davis v. Alaska,* 415 U.S. 308 (1974), the Court held that a trial court could not prevent defense counsel from questioning a witness about the witness's juvenile criminal record, even though a state statute made this information confidential. The Confrontation Clause interest outweighed the interest in protecting the identity of juvenile offenders. The Compulsory Process Clause also gives defendants a right to the government's assistance in compelling attendance of witnesses at trial. An accused's right of access to evidence is not unlimited, however.

   b. **The *Brady* rule.** The prosecution's suppression of evidence favorable to an accused who requests the evidence violates due process if the evidence is material either to guilt or punishment. The rule was set forth in *Brady v. Maryland*, 373 U.S. 83 (1963). In that case, the prosecution failed to give the defense an admission by Brady's companion that he had done the actual killing. Brady was sentenced to death. The Court upheld a state court ruling permitting a new trial on the punishment issue, because the statement could have been used to support Brady's plea for leniency. The defense had, prior to trial, requested all of Brady's companion's statements. Such a discovery request is now frequently called a *Brady* request. The rule does not require prosecutors to deliver all their evidence to the defense.

   c. **Impeachment and exculpatory evidence.** For *Brady* purposes, it does not matter whether the evidence suppressed by the prosecution would be used for impeachment of government witnesses or just as exculpatory evidence. The reliability of the particular witness must relate to the determination of guilt to satisfy the materiality requirement of *Brady*, however.

   d. **Standards of materiality.** In *United States v. Agurs*, 427 U.S. 97 (1976), the Court described the varying standards of materiality that may apply in a *Brady* situation.

      1) **False prosecution evidence.** If the prosecution knowingly uses perjured or otherwise false evidence and does not disclose this to the defense, the evidence is automatically considered material unless the failure to disclose is harmless beyond a reasonable doubt.

      2) **Favorable defense evidence not requested.** If the defense does not make a *Brady* request, the defense must show some materiality greater than that required under the harmless error standard,

but not as great as that required for a motion for a new trial based on newly discovered evidence.

    3)   **Specifically requested evidence.** A somewhat lesser standard of materiality applies when the prosecution fails to disclose requested evidence, because such a failure is seldom excusable.

  e.   **Reasonable probability standard--**

United States v. Bagley, 473 U.S. 667 (1985).

Facts. Bagley (D) was indicted on federal narcotics and firearms charges. He requested information about any inducements that government witnesses received for their testimony. The prosecution did not reveal that two of the witnesses against D were paid for their assistance. Most of their testimony related to the firearms charges, of which D was acquitted. He was convicted of the narcotics charges and moved for vacation of his sentence after he learned about the payments. The district court denied D's motion, the court of appeals reversed, and the Supreme Court granted certiorari.

Issue. Is a defendant entitled to a new trial whenever the prosecution fails to respond to a *Brady* request and the defense does not discover the suppressed evidence until after the trial?

Held. No. Judgment reversed and case remanded.

♦   The purpose of the *Brady* rule is to ensure that a miscarriage of justice does not occur. Thus, suppression of evidence is a constitutional violation only if it deprives the defendant of a fair trial.

♦   The proper standard of materiality, whether a *Brady* request was made or not, is whether there is a reasonable probability that, had the evidence been disclosed to the defense, the result of the proceeding would have been different. When the defense makes a *Brady* request, nondisclosure is tantamount to a denial that the evidence exists. This in turn is likely to affect the defense's case preparation, and thus the eventual result, more than would a nondisclosure of unrequested evidence.

Concurrence (White, J., Burger, C.J., Rehnquist, J.). I agree that D cannot have his conviction overturned unless he can show that the evidence withheld was material. Evidence is material if there is a reasonable probability that, had the evidence been disclosed, the result of the proceeding would have been different. The court of appeals' failure to apply this standard necessitates reversal.

Dissent (Marshall, Brennan, JJ.). The Court now holds that there is no duty to disclose evidence unless nondisclosure would have a certain impact on the trial. The state's minimal interest in nondisclosure should instead yield to the great interest in searching for the truth.

Dissent (Stevens, J.). The Court has reduced the significance of deliberate prosecutorial suppression of specifically requested and potentially exculpatory evidence.

----

     f.   **Duty to assist in discovery of exculpatory evidence.** In *Evans v. Superior Court*, 522 P.2d 681 (Cal. 1974), the court held that in a proper case the prosecution had the duty to assist the defendant to discover possibly exculpatory evidence. There, several prosecution witnesses had indicated that they had seen the defendant commit the crime. The defendant petitioned the court, before trial, for a lineup to have the witnesses attempt to identify him before he became the defendant at the trial. It was held that the prosecution must assist the defendant to discover exculpatory evidence.

     g.   **Balancing state's interest in confidentiality with defendant's right of access to evidence--**

Pennsylvania v. Ritchie, 480 U.S. 39 (1987).

Facts. Ritchie (D) was charged with sexual offenses based on a report that D's 13-year-old daughter made to the Children and Youth Services ("CYS"). D served a pretrial discovery subpoena on CYS that covered all records relating to the charges, plus reports of prior allegations involving D's children. CYS claimed that the records were privileged under a state law that required its records to be kept confidential except under specific exceptions. D claimed that he should get the records because they might reveal favorable witnesses. The judge refused to order disclosure. The main witness at the trial was D's daughter. D's attorney cross-examined D's daughter extensively. D was convicted, but the appellate court vacated the conviction, holding that CYS's failure to disclose the records denied D the opportunity to cross-examine his daughter regarding her statements to CYS. The state supreme court affirmed, requiring the trial court to make the entire record available to D's attorney. The Supreme Court granted certiorari.

Issue. Is an accused entitled to review records of a public agency that by statute are to remain confidential, on the ground that the records might contain information useful for cross-examination of the prosecution's witnesses?

Held. No. Judgment affirmed in part and reversed in part, and case remanded.

♦   D claims the denial of access to CYS's records interfered with his right of cross-examination, because the records might have contained statements his daughter made to CYS that were inconsistent with her testimony at trial. The state supreme court relied on *Davis v. Alaska, supra*, in holding that the statutory privilege must fall before D's Confrontation Clause claims. This holding is too broad.

- The Confrontation Clause is not a constitutionally compelled rule of pretrial discovery. The right of confrontation is a trial right and prevents improper restrictions on the scope of cross-examination. The right to cross-examine does not include a pretrial right of access to all information that might be useful in cross-examining the witness. The Confrontation Clause only guarantees an opportunity for effective cross-examination. In this case, D was permitted to cross-examine his daughter, so the Confrontation Clause was not violated.

- The state supreme court also apparently held that the Compulsory Process Clause includes the right to have the government assist in uncovering arguably useful information. However, in this area compulsory process provides no protections greater than those provided by due process, so D's claims must be evaluated under due process principles.

- The government has a duty to provide an accused with evidence that it has that is favorable and material to guilt. Materiality depends on whether there is a reasonable probability that, had the evidence been disclosed, the result of the proceeding would have been different.

- In this case, the state law does not prohibit all disclosure of the CYS files; it sets forth exceptions, including a court order. Therefore, the trial court should review the file to determine whether it contains information that probably would have changed the outcome of D's trial. However, D's counsel is not entitled to review the files, any more than any defense counsel can freely search the government's files. The trial court has an ongoing duty to release information material to the fairness of the trial.

---

h. **Access to witnesses.** An accused's right of access to witnesses is limited. The government's duty to deport aliens, for example, outweighs an accused's right to access to such aliens who might be witnesses. [United States v. Valenzuela-Bernal, 458 U.S. 858 (1982)] However, the government may not refuse to disclose the identity of a key informer who was the sole participant, other than the accused, in the events giving rise to the criminal charges. When disclosure of the informer's identity is "essential to a fair trial," the government must make the disclosure. In *Roviaro v. United States*, 353 U.S. 53 (1957), the Court reversed a narcotics conviction because the government refused to disclose the identity of "John Doe," to whom FBI agents testified they had seen the defendant sell narcotics. The informer had helped set up commission of the crime, was present at its occurrence, and hence was a material witness on the issue of guilt. The factors combined to deprive the defendant of a fair trial when the government refused to disclose the identity of the informer. An accused does not have a right to have use immunity granted to his witnesses.

i. **Unavailable evidence.** The effect of the government's loss or destruction of evidence depends on the government's good or bad faith. While good or bad faith is irrelevant with regard to the state's failure to disclose material exculpatory evidence, the test is different when the issue is the government's failure to preserve evidence that could have been subjected to tests, the results of which might have exonerated the accused. The police do not have a constitutional duty to perform any particular tests, and unless an accused can show the police acted in bad faith, their failure to preserve potentially useful evidence is not a denial of due process. Thus, in *Arizona v. Youngblood*, 488 U.S. 51 (1988), the Court reversed a state court decision that threw out a sexual assault conviction because the state had not preserved semen samples on the victim's clothing. Although a test of the semen could have exonerated the defendant, the state did not act in bad faith, and the conviction was upheld.

j. **Compulsory process.** The Sixth Amendment right to subpoena witnesses is applicable to the states through the Fourteenth Amendment. In *Washington v. Texas*, 388 U.S. 14 (1967), the Court invalidated a state statute prohibiting the use of an accomplice as a defense witness. Although there was a possibility that "each accused would attempt to swear the other out of court," a defendant could not be deprived of this relevant and material testimony.

B. GUILTY PLEAS

1. **Background.** Eighty percent of all criminal prosecutions terminate in a guilty plea. Without this device our system of criminal enforcement would break down (too many cases to try).

   a. **Basis of plea.** The plea is essentially a waiver by the defendant of his right to trial and of his chance for an acquittal.

   b. **Sentencing.** Below are four views on whether to distinguish between pleas when sentencing.

      (i) The plea of guilty should have no effect in sentencing; if it did, defendants would be pressured into foregoing the right to trial.

      (ii) A guilty plea should have no independent significance in sentencing; but a defendant who goes to trial with a contrived defense should be treated more severely than one who admits his guilt, as he shows no interest in rehabilitation.

(iii) More lenient treatment should be given those pleading guilty. It is the first step toward rehabilitation (recognition and acceptance of guilt), and such pleas aid the administration of justice.

(iv) Guilty pleas should lead to lighter sentences in certain difficult-to-prove cases.

Most writers seem to agree that the guilty plea, all other things being equal, should not result in a lesser punishment. But the fact remains that courts do give lighter sentences to defendants who plead guilty. Plea bargaining is widely practiced and accepted, and an effort is now made to protect the rights of those who do so plead. A defendant may plead guilty or, with the consent of the court, nolo contendere. The court may refuse to accept a plea of guilty, and must not accept the plea without first determining that the plea is made voluntarily with understanding of the nature of the charge. [Fed. R. Crim. P. 11]

2. **Justifications for Guilty Pleas as a Factor in the Judge's Consideration of Final Disposition.**

   a. They are necessary to reduce the case load to a number that the courts can handle.

   b. The defendant has helped himself get prompt and certain application of correctional measures.

   c. The defendant has recognized and assumed responsibility for his guilt. However, (i) many people who stand trial did not commit the crime; (ii) in other cases (where guilt depends on negligence—*i.e.,* misdemeanor manslaughter—or the uncertain application of a law—*i.e.,* some forms of strict liability), the defendant needs the trial to find out if he is guilty; and (iii) the plea is not a recognition of responsibility; it is a deal, a reliance on the known policy of the courts to give defendants a break.

   d. Pleas obviate the need for a public trial. For example, in a sexual abuse case, it may be desirable to keep a young child off the stand.

   e. The defendant cooperates by giving information leading to the capture of other offenders.

   f. Note that the ABA Standards recognize all of these factors and indicate that it is proper to give lighter sentences for guilty pleas. But the National Advisory Commission Report (1973) recommends abolition of plea bargaining.

3. **The Plea in the Prosecutor's Office.** Most states (by statute) give a district attorney the power to grant a person complete immunity, usually in return

for full testimony that has some special value to the district attorney. This is required by the privilege against self-incrimination. The district attorney may give half immunity when the value of a defendant's testimony, weighed against the strength of the district attorney's case, indicates that some compromise is in order; the prosecutor lets the defendant plead to a lesser offense. Complete immunity does not involve the court in the dealing, while partial immunity does.

    a.   Alternatives. There are three ways for a district attorney to deal:

        1)   Recommend a lighter sentence. However, defendants who plead guilty on the prosecutor's promise to recommend a certain sentence run the risk that the judge will not accept the recommendation.

        2)   Plead the defendant to one count and dismiss several others in a multiple-count offense. This is an illusory deal since courts seldom impose consecutive sentences. Note that the court's approval is required to do this.

        3)   Allow a plea to a lesser included offense.

4.   Should a Court Accept a Plea?

    a.   They usually do. Courts never know all the facts in a case and so seldom have a real alternative to accepting the district attorney's recommendation.

    b.   Normally, in accepting a guilty plea, a court must at least secure an oral acknowledgment by the defendant of his guilt. The court asks, "Are you guilty?" The well-coached defendant says "Yes"; or the court asks if he expects to gain anything by his plea, and the response is "No." Both answers are of doubtful truth.

5.   Some Problems with Guilty Pleas. The easy cases are the ones where the judge makes an agreement to settle the case and then does not carry through with it after getting the defendant's guilty plea.

    a.   Coercion by the judge. There is greater likelihood of coercion of a guilty plea from the defendant when the judge participates in the bargaining process.

        1)   Example. The judge calls the parties before him and tells the defendant that the prosecutor's case is a good one and that he does not think the defendant can win; he then suggests that the defendant should consider taking the prosecutor's offer of a deal. If the defendant declines, he goes to trial before the same judge.

  a) Bargaining with the judge seems coercive, even when the judge has the defendant's interest at heart.

  b) But note that in most cases where the judge talks to the defendant, it is on the request of the defendant's attorney—an attempt to talk some sense into the defendant.

 2) **Knowingly made.** *Boykin v. Alabama*, 395 U.S. 238 (1969), noted that when a criminal defendant pleads guilty he waives his Fifth Amendment privilege against self-incrimination and Sixth Amendment rights to trial by jury and confrontation and cross-examination of witnesses—all made applicable to the states by the Fourteenth Amendment. The Court held that such waiver must be knowingly and intelligently made and that it is therefore a violation of due process for a judge to accept a guilty plea unless "on the face of the record" there is "an affirmative showing that it was intelligent and voluntary."

b. **Claims of innocence.** What happens when the defendant says "I didn't do it," but the case looks very bad against him and the jury is sure to convict?

 1) If the defendant pleads guilty, he does not have to tell anything more—*i.e.,* he does not have to describe the crime, give additional evidence, etc. The case is closed, and there is no further examination into whether the defendant actually committed the crime or not.

 2) But if when pleading guilty the defendant denies any guilt, the judge will usually vacate the plea.

 3) What if the bargain struck by the prosecutor and the defendant's attorney turns out to be a bad deal for the defendant? *McMann v. Richardson, infra,* held that "a deal is a deal" and that when a defendant pleads guilty, he is bound by the law and the judgment of his lawyer at the time of his plea, unless he can show such "serious dereliction on the part of counsel sufficient to show that his plea was not . . . a knowing and intelligent act." He cannot take advantage of new law after a plea is entered or a new lawyer's strategies even though he might have pleaded differently if later case law had been known or a different attorney had handled the strategy.

c. **Representation by counsel in the bargaining process.** The defendant should always be represented by counsel to protect his interests. The defendant's statements might be admissible evidence against him.

6. Rejected, Kept, and Broken Bargains; Unrealized Expectations.

a. Vindictiveness--

Bordenkircher v. Hayes, 434 U.S. 357 (1978).

Facts. Hayes (D) was indicted on a charge of uttering a forged instrument. During a plea-bargaining session, D refused to plead guilty even after the prosecutor informed him that he would seek a further indictment under the Kentucky Habitual Criminal Act if D refused to plead guilty. D was convicted under both charges. D petitioned a federal district court for a writ of habeas corpus. The writ was denied. The court of appeals reversed.

Issue. Is the Due Process Clause of the Fourteenth Amendment violated when a state prosecutor carries out a threat made during plea negotiations to reindict the accused on more serious charges if he does not plead guilty to the offense with which he was originally charged?

Held. No. Judgment reversed.

♦   There is no due process violation for vindictiveness so long as the accused is free to accept or reject the prosecution's offer.

♦   While threat of more severe punishment may have a discouraging effect on a defendant's assertion of his trial rights, such effect must be tolerated where plea bargaining is allowed.

Dissent (Blackmun, Brennan, Marshall, JJ.). The Due Process Clause protects against prosecutorial vindictiveness, and it makes no difference if the vindictiveness is used in attacking D's exercise of a legal right to refute his original conviction or in the give and take negotiation common in plea bargaining.

Dissent (Powell, J.). Implementation of a strategy calculated solely to deter the exercise of constitutional rights is not a constitutionally permissible exercise of discretion.

b. Fear of the death penalty--

Brady v. United States, 397 U.S. 742 (1970).

Facts. Brady (D) was charged with kidnapping and pleaded not guilty. On learning that his accomplice had pleaded guilty and would testify against him, he changed his plea to guilty. The federal statute allowed the jury to set the penalty and authorized a death penalty. D brings a habeas corpus action charging that his plea was involuntary in that fear of the death penalty coerced his plea. He was represented by counsel at the time of his plea. After the district court had found that the plea was voluntary, *United States v. Jackson,* 390 U.S. 570 (1968), held that the death penalty in the federal statute was unconstitutional because it penalized the assertion of Fifth (right not to plead guilty) and Sixth (jury trial) Amendment rights. At the original trial, D had been thoroughly questioned twice about his plea.

Issue. Does pleading guilty because of fear of the death penalty make that plea involuntary?

Held. No. Conviction sustained.

♦ D had competent counsel and a full opportunity to assess the advantages and disadvantages of pleading guilty.

♦ The decision was made in the light of all facts relevant at the time. There was no evidence that the plea was coerced or counsel incompetent. It makes no difference that subsequent events may make the plea subject to question in terms of whether D and counsel correctly assessed all of the facts.

Concurrence (Brennan, Douglas, Marshall, JJ.). The advice of counsel for D does not insulate the government from a finding in all situations that the plea was involuntary. For example, if D had shown that the cause of his guilty plea was solely the possible imposition of the death penalty, then *Jackson* would require that the conviction be reversed. But D did not make such a showing; other factors may have been the cause of the plea.

------

c. **Retraction of promise by judge.** In *United States ex rel. Elksnis v. Gilligan,* 256 F. Supp. 244 (S.D.N.Y. 1966), the court held that a defendant was denied due process when the judge promised him a sentence of no more than 10 years on his guilty plea, but retracted his promise after accepting the plea and gave the defendant a greater sentence.

d. **Requirement that promise be fully performed--**

Santobello v. New York, 404 U.S. 257 (1971).

Facts. After negotiations, Santobello (D) withdrew a not guilty plea and entered a guilty plea to a lesser included offense. The prosecutor agreed to make no recommendation as to sentencing. When time for sentencing arose, a district attorney newly appointed to the case asked for the maximum sentence imposed. The judge contended that the new district attorney's request for the maximum was not the reason the maximum was imposed and he was not influenced by it.

Issue. May a plea be withdrawn if the prosecution fails to fulfill all its promises, even if the result would have been the same had the prosecution kept its promise?

Held. Yes. Judgment vacated and case remanded.

♦ If the plea rests in any significant degree on a promise or agreement of the prosecution, even if implied to the defendant, such promise must be fulfilled or the defendant must be allowed to withdraw his guilty plea.

♦ If a promise or inducement is consideration for the plea, the plea is not voluntary unless the promise is carried out.

Concurrence (Douglas, J.). I favor a constitutional rule for this and future cases: When the plea bargain is not kept by the prosecutor, the sentence must be vacated and the court will decide in light of the circumstances of each case whether due process requires (i) specific performance of the plea bargain, or (ii) that the defendant be given the option to go to trial on the original charges.

Concurrence and dissent (Marshall, Brennan, Stewart, JJ.). When a prosecutor breaks the bargain, he undercuts the basis for the waiver of constitutional rights implicit in the pleas. This provides the defendant with ample justification for rescinding the plea.

Comment. In *United States v. Benchimol*, 471 U.S. 453 (1985), the Court held that a prosecutor need not explain his reasons for recommending a particular sentence pursuant to a plea bargain, so long as the sentencing court is aware of the recommendation and the plea bargain does not require the prosecution to do any more than make the recommendation.

---

e.   Violation of guilty plea agreements--

Ricketts v. Adamson, 483 U.S. 1 (1987).

Facts. Adamson (D) was charged with first degree murder. After his trial began, D negotiated a guilty plea agreement with the prosecutor that required D to plead guilty to second degree murder and to testify against other persons involved in the murder in return for a specific prison term and actual incarceration time. The original charges would be automatically reinstated if D violated the agreement. D testified as agreed and the other persons were convicted. When these convictions were reversed on appeal, however, D refused to testify at the retrial. By this time, D had already begun serving his specified sentence. The state charged D with first degree murder, and D moved to quash, claiming double jeopardy. The state supreme court held that the agreement provided for waiver of double jeopardy if violated, and that D's refusal to testify was a violation. D then offered to testify, but his offer was refused and he was himself convicted of first degree murder and sentenced to death. D sought a writ of habeas corpus in federal court, which the court of appeals granted. The Supreme Court granted certiorari.

Issue. If a person violates a plea bargain agreement after having pleaded guilty and having begun his sentence, may he be reprosecuted for the original charge?

Held. Yes. Judgment reversed.

♦   Assuming that second degree murder is a lesser-included offense of first degree murder, D would normally be protected against prosecution for first degree murder once he had been convicted of second degree murder for the same offense. The unusual circumstance in this case is that D breached the plea agreement, which provided for automatic reinstatement of the first degree murder charge.

♦   The agreement on its face clearly provides that if D breached the agreement, the parties would be "returned to the positions they were in before this agreement." This would leave D without a double jeopardy defense. Even if D did have a double jeopardy defense to waive, the agreement that the charges would be reinstated constitutes an agreement to waive a double jeopardy defense.

♦   D's purported uncertainty about whether he had to testify at a retrial is irrelevant because he knew that if he breached the agreement he would be retried, and he knew that a court would ultimately determine the extent of his obligation. D assumed the risk of his erroneous interpretation of the agreement when he chose not to testify at the retrial. Nor does it matter that D offered to testify when the court found that he had breached the agreement, for by then, the original charge had been reinstated.

Dissent (Brennan, Marshall, Blackmun, Stevens, JJ.). The critical issue is whether Adamson actually breached the agreement. Here, Adamson never took any act he knew or realized would constitute a breach of the agreement. Instead, he advanced an objectively reasonable interpretation of the contract, and advised the state that he was ready and willing to testify once the Arizona Supreme Court adopted the state's interpretation of the agreement.

---

7. **Professional Responsibility: The Role of the Prosecutor and Defense Counsel.**

    a. **Right to counsel.** In *Anderson v. North Carolina*, 221 F. Supp. 930 (W.D.N.C. 1963), Anderson was charged with rape. After investigating the case, Anderson's attorney had him plead innocent; later in the afternoon, Anderson pleaded guilty to a lesser charge. Meanwhile, the prosecutor and his staff had met with Anderson in his cell (without the presence of his attorney, but with the attorney's consent) and told Anderson that he would go on trial for his life, that the probability was the death sentence unless he agreed to a guilty plea to a lesser offense, and that if he so pleaded, he would get no more than 15 years, but the prosecutor would talk to the judge and Anderson would probably get no more than five. The court held that the constitutionality of the guilty plea was not questioned, but, that since it was a negotiated plea, the right to counsel meant that Anderson's attorney should be part of the negotiations, to assist him in making any decision.

b. **Discretion of the prosecutor--**

Newman v. United States, 382 F.2d 479 (D.C. Cir. 1967).

Facts. The United States attorney allowed D's co-defendant to plead guilty to a lesser offense while not permitting D to do so. D claims this denied him due process and equal protection, and appeals.

Issue. Must co-defendants be treated alike when plea bargaining?

Held. No. Judgment affirmed.

♦ The United States attorney is an executive officer, whose discretionary power in deciding when and whether to prosecute, what charges to make, etc., is subject to very limited, if any, judicial review.

♦ There may be differences between the co-defendants that the United States attorney considered.

c. **Prosecutor's refusal to disclose impeachment material prior to entering plea agreement--**

United States v. Ruiz, 536 U.S. 622 (2002).

Facts. Immigration agents found 30 kilograms of marijuana in Ruiz's (D) luggage. Federal prosecutors offered D a "fast track" plea bargain that would have reduced the otherwise applicable sentencing guidelines by six months (two levels down) in return for D waiving indictment, trial, and appeal. The plea agreement contained a provision that any known information establishing the factual innocence of D had been turned over to D. The agreement also required D to waive the right to receive information related to impeaching informants and other affirmative defenses. D refused to make the latter waivers, and the prosecutors withdrew the plea bargain offer. D was indicted and ultimately pleaded guilty anyway. The trial court declined to grant D the two-level downward departure. The Ninth Circuit vacated the sentence on the ground that the Constitution requires prosecutors to give impeachment information to D before trial, so D was entitled to receive the same information before entering the plea agreement. The Supreme Court granted certiorari.

Issue. Must federal prosecutors, before entering into a binding plea agreement with a criminal defendant, disclose impeachment information relating to any informants or other witnesses?

Held. No. Judgment reversed.

♦ A defendant who pleads guilty foregoes several constitutional guarantees, including the right to confrontation of one's accusers. A guilty plea must be voluntary, and any related waivers must be knowing and intentional.

♦ A guilty plea may be voluntary even without a pre-guilty plea disclosure of impeachment information. Impeachment material relates to the fairness of a trial, but does not relate to whether a plea is voluntary.

♦ A constitutional obligation to provide impeachment information during plea bargaining could seriously interfere with the desire of both the government and defendants generally to use the guilty plea option. It would risk premature disclosure of witness information and require the government to do more trial preparation prior to plea bargaining, depriving the process of its efficiency.

Concurrence (Thomas, J.). The "degree of help" of impeachment information is not relevant at the plea stage.

---

d. Prosecutor's discretion to charge and prosecute offenses--

In re **United States**, 345 F.3d 450 (7th Cir. 2003).

Facts. Bitsky (D), a police officer, assaulted an arrested person. D then tried to get another officer to write a false report justifying D's use of force and tried to prevent a third officer from informing on him. D was indicted for obstruction of justice and deprivation of civil rights under color of law. D agreed to plead guilty to one obstruction of justice count in return for the government dismissing the other counts. The trial court rejected the plea agreement because the 12-month maximum penalty for the obstruction of justice offense was less than half the 30-month maximum for the civil rights offense. D pleaded guilty anyway. The judge sentenced him to 16 months in prison (after denying him an acceptance of responsibility deduction). The government moved to dismiss the other counts, but the trial judge refused to dismiss the civil rights count and appointed a private lawyer to prosecute it. The government sought a writ of mandamus commanding the trial judge to dismiss the civil rights count and rescinding the appointment of the prosecutor.

Issue. May a federal judge refuse to dismiss a count of an indictment and appoint a private prosecutor when the federal prosecutor declines to prosecute the count?

Held. No. Mandamus granted.

♦   No statute authorizes the government to appeal from a trial court's refusal to dismiss a count, but mandamus is available as a remedy. Federal judges do not have the power to prosecute crimes, and mandamus functions to confine officials within the boundaries of their authorized powers.

♦   Section 48(a) of the Federal Rules of Criminal Procedure requires leave of court for the government to dismiss a count of an indictment, but the purpose of that rule is to protect a defendant against prosecutor harassment through repeated filing and dismissing of charges. A judge can require that a dismissal of a count be with prejudice.

♦   In this case, the government seeks a dismissal with prejudice. The district judge simply disagrees with the prosecutor's exercise of discretion. Under the Constitution, however, the executive branch has the power to prosecute, not the judicial branch. The prosecutor must balance resources and policy priorities with federal criminal statutes and sentencing guidelines and has enormous charging discretion, whether judges agree with it or not.

♦   The separation of powers assures that no one can be convicted of a crime without the concurrence of all three branches of government. A judge cannot exclude the executive branch by assuming the power to prosecute. Even if the judge could deny a motion to dismiss a criminal charge, he cannot appoint a prosecutor. Ultimately, the President has plenary power to pardon a federal offender, so a judge cannot win a confrontation with the executive branch over its refusal to prosecute.

---

8.   **Receiving the Defendant's Plea; Plea Withdrawal.**

    a.   **Entering the plea.** A guilty plea must be an unequivocal and knowledge-able admission of all elements of the offense charged. Anything less than that, or any qualified or ambiguous plea, will not be construed as a guilty plea.

    b.   **Voluntariness.** A plea of guilty is presumed to be voluntary, because no conviction based upon a guilty plea can stand unless the record of the proceedings establishes that the defendant voluntarily and intelligently waived his three basic constitutional rights, *i.e.,* trial by jury, confrontation of his accusers, and privilege against self-incrimination. [*See* Boykin v. Alabama, *supra*]

c.   **Understanding.** In most jurisdictions, the guilty plea is not deemed to have been made understandingly unless the accused comprehended (i) the meaning of the charge, (ii) what acts amount to being guilty, and (iii) the direct (as opposed to collateral) consequences of pleading guilty thereto—particularly the range of sentence that may be imposed. It is not clear whether there must be an affirmative showing that the defendant "understood" the nature of the charges, etc., but there must at least be some basis for inferring that the nature of the charge was explained sufficiently for the defendant to know what he was admitting. [*See* Henderson v. Morgan, 426 U.S. 637 (1976)]

d.   **Determining factual basis of guilty plea.** *Brady v. United States, supra,* held that a plea of guilty that represents an intelligent choice among the alternatives available to a defendant, especially one represented by competent counsel, was not involuntary because it was entered to avoid the possibility of the death penalty. In *North Carolina v. Alford,* 400 U.S. 25 (1970), the defendant pleaded guilty for this reason but continued to assert his innocence; the Court, nonetheless, held the plea voluntary, finding that the defendant had intelligently concluded that his interests required a guilty plea and that the record strongly evidenced guilt.

e.   **Plea withdrawal.** A guilty plea that was not voluntarily and understandably made may be withdrawn at any time. Failure to allow withdrawal of such a plea constitutes a denial of the federal constitutional requirement of due process of law; a person convicted by a state court can thus seek collateral relief by a writ of habeas corpus in the federal courts. A federal prisoner can seek collateral relief by a motion under 28 U.S.C. section 2255. [Machibroda v. United States, 368 U.S. 487 (1962)]

1)   **Timing.** Federal Rule of Criminal Procedure 32(d) provides generally that a motion to withdraw a plea of guilty or of nolo contendere be made only before sentence is imposed or imposition of sentence is suspended. After sentencing, the court can set aside the judgment of conviction only to "correct manifest injustice." State rules and statutes for the withdrawal of guilty pleas are similar.

a)   Before judgment (sentencing), most states authorize withdrawal of a guilty plea for "good cause shown," if the defendant was represented by counsel, and require the trial judge to set aside a guilty plea on a showing of "good cause," if the defendant was not represented by counsel.

> b) After entry of judgment, grounds for setting aside guilty pleas are more restrictive.

2) **Procedure.** The remedies to withdraw a guilty plea after judgment are a writ of coram nobis, or a motion to vacate judgment.

3) **Effect of withdrawn plea.** A withdrawn guilty plea is not admissible in most states in a criminal proceeding for the offense, either as an admission or for the purpose of discrediting the accused as a witness if he takes the stand.

4) **Federal Rules of Criminal Procedure.** [*See* Fed. R. Crim. P. 11(d)]

f. **Compliance with federal rules--**

McCarthy v. United States, 394 U.S. 459 (1969).

Facts. McCarthy (D) was indicted on three counts of income tax evasion; he pleaded not guilty. At trial he asked to plead guilty to the second count; the judge asked D if he knew that this waived his jury trial and subjected him to possible fine and imprisonment. D said yes. The prosecutor then indicated that the government would drop counts one and three for D paying all back taxes. The prosecutor asked the judge to inquire of D whether there had been any threats or promises. D said no. D appeals on the basis that Rule 11 was not complied with.

Issue. Did the judge violate Rule 11 of the Federal Rules of Criminal Procedure by not personally addressing D as to his understanding of the charge against him and the consequences of his plea?

Held. Yes. Judgment reversed.

♦ The judge must personally question the defendant to see that the plea was voluntary and that the defendant understands the charge and the consequences thereof.

♦ Also, the judge must determine whether there is a "factual basis" for the plea. This allows a determination of voluntariness and builds a record for review purposes.

♦ The remedy for a violation of Rule 11 is to allow the defendant to plead again.

---

g.   **Significance of compliance with requirements for receiving guilty plea--**

Blackledge v. Allison, 431 U.S. 63 (1977).

Facts. Allison (D) was charged with breaking and entering, attempted safe robbery, and possession of burglary tools. D pleaded guilty, allegedly thinking that his attorney had plea bargained with the prosecutor and judge for a 10-year sentence. D was sentenced to 17 to 21 years in prison. After exhausting his state remedies, D sought federal habeas corpus. The entire record from the trial court consisted of a 13-question checklist indicating that D realized the potential sentence and that no promises had been made to him to induce his guilty plea. In his petition D claimed that his attorney had instructed him to answer the questions as he did. The lower court dismissed the petition, but the court of appeals reversed.

Issue. Were D's allegations, when viewed against the record of the plea hearing, so palpably incredible or so patently frivolous or false as to warrant summary dismissal of the petition for habeas corpus?

Held. No. Judgment affirmed.

♦   In the light of the nature of the record and of the ambiguous status of the plea bargaining process in this state at that time, D's petition should not have been summarily dismissed.

h.   **Effect of a guilty plea on right to counsel--**

McMann v. Richardson, 397 U.S. 759 (1970).

Facts. Three defendants (Ds) petitioned for habeas corpus on the basis that their guilty pleas were not voluntarily given but were induced by prior coerced confessions. Ds were represented by counsel in determining their plea.

Issue. May a defendant challenge his plea when it was based on competent advice?

Held. No. Convictions sustained.

♦   Ds were represented by counsel. The issue was the strength of the government's case against them (and whether the confession would be thrown out). With reasonably competent advice, Ds made a decision on this issue.

♦   Thereafter Ds pleaded guilty. The guilty plea in this circumstance cannot be said to be involuntary or the product of the coerced confession.

◆ Waiving trial and pleading guilty (and accepting the benefits of this course of action) means that Ds must take the risk that their assessment and their lawyers' assessment of what the court would have done on the confession issue might be wrong.

---

i. **Constitutional violations before the guilty plea--**

Tollett v. Henderson, 411 U.S. 258 (1973).

Facts. Twenty-five years ago, Henderson (D) was indicted by a grand jury for murder. He pleaded guilty on advice of counsel. The grand jury had systematically excluded black people, and D was black. Counsel had not advised D that he may have had a defense to the indictment. D brings a habeas corpus action.

Issue. May a defendant, after pleading guilty, later succeed on a writ of habeas corpus because the indictment to which he pleaded was filed by an unconstitutionally selected grand jury?

Held. No.

◆ D was represented by counsel, which means that the issue is whether the plea was made with the competent assistance of counsel and was therefore voluntary. In this regard not every claim of unconstitutional conduct in the conviction of D will prove that D received the incompetent advice of counsel in making the plea.

◆ Proof that the grand jury was unconstitutionally selected does not render the attorney's advice incompetent.

C. TRIAL BY JURY

1. **Right to Jury Trial; Waiver.**

   a. **Right to trial by jury incorporated.** In *Duncan v. Louisiana*, 391 U.S. 145 (1968), the Court stated that the right to trial by jury in serious criminal cases is fundamental to the American scheme of justice and qualifies for protection under the Due Process Clause of the Fourteenth Amendment against violation by the states. After discussing the increase in the selective incorporation of other guarantees of the Bill of Rights into the Due Process Clause, the Court held the Sixth Amendment guarantee of a right to jury trial applicable through the Fourteenth Amendment to state criminal cases which, if tried in a federal court, would be covered.

b. **Length of sentence.** Any offense that carries a potential sentence of more than six months is a "serious" offense, so that a jury trial must be afforded on demand. This is true even in cases where the actual sentence imposed is less than six months. [Baldwin v. New York, 399 U.S. 66 (1970)] Conversely, where the maximum penalty authorized by statute is a fine or imprisonment for six months or less, trial by jury is not constitutionally required. [Dyke v. Taylor Implement Manufacturing Co., 391 U.S. 216 (1968)]

c. **Contempt cases.** Whether a defendant charged with contempt of court is entitled to a jury trial depends both upon whether the contempt is civil or criminal and upon the amount of punishment threatened. In civil contempt, no right to jury trial is recognized, but in criminal contempt cases, a limited right exists.

    1) **Civil or criminal contempt.** If the primary purpose of the contempt charge is to coerce the defendant to perform some act ordered by the court in connection with other litigation, the contempt charge is civil in nature (the defendant can purge himself of contempt by performing the act). If the primary purpose of the charge is to redress an affront to the dignity of the court itself, the contempt is criminal in nature. Thus, when the contempt is based on the defendant's refusal to testify after having been granted complete immunity from prosecution (hence no privilege against self-incrimination), and he is further given the unqualified right to be released from imprisonment by expressing his willingness to testify, the contempt is civil in nature (to coerce his testimony), and no right to jury trial exists. [Shillitani v. United States, 384 U.S. 364 (1966)]

    2) **Criminal contempt.** A right to a jury trial in criminal contempt does not exist if: (i) the punishment prescribed by the legislature makes the contempt a petty offense, as distinguished from a serious crime; (ii) no punishment is prescribed and the sentence imposed is six months or less [Cheff v. Schnackenberg, 384 U.S. 373 (1966)]; or (iii) probation is granted for up to five years and upon violation thereof there may be a sentence of six months or less [Frank v. United States, 395 U.S. 147 (1969)]. In *Muniz v. Hoffman*, 422 U.S. 454 (1975), the Court held that despite language to the contrary in the federal statute, situations where fines over $500 were imposed did not necessarily amount to a nonpetty offense requiring a jury trial (here a fine of $10,000 was imposed;

the Court looked to the fact that this amount was not "serious" for the large defendant labor union).

d. What constitutes "trial by jury"?

1) Number of jurors. The number of jurors in federal criminal trials is 12, but this is by statute [Fed. R. Crim. P. 23] and is not constitutionally required. State rules allowing use of less than 12 jurors (in noncapital cases) have been upheld. [Williams v. Florida, *supra*]

2) Unanimous verdict. Earlier federal decisions indicated that a defendant in a criminal case was entitled to a unanimous verdict under the Sixth Amendment. But in *Williams, supra,* the Court stated: "We intimate no view whether the requirement of unanimity is an indispensable element of the Sixth Amendment."

a) Unanimous verdict not required--

Apodaca v. Oregon, 406 U.S. 404 (1972).

Facts. A state statute provided that except for first degree murder cases, a defendant could be convicted on a verdict by 10 of 12 jurors. Apodaca (D) appeals his conviction for assault, burglary, and grand larceny.

Issue. Is unanimity of the jury required to convict a defendant?

Held. No.

♦   In a felony trial, conviction by less than a unanimous jury in a state trial (10 of 12) does not violate the Sixth Amendment or the Fourteenth Amendment.

Comment. In dicta, the majority did state that the Sixth Amendment requires a unanimous verdict in federal courts, but the distinction as to why is not clear. The majority also stated that such a verdict did not conflict with guilty beyond a reasonable doubt nor violate due process under the Fourteenth Amendment if the jury represented an adequate cross section of the community. Apparently under *Williams* and *Apodaca,* a less than unanimous verdict among six jurors might be held a conviction by a cross section of one's peers in the community (even if four to two or, in a seven-member jury, four to three). Justices Douglas, Marshall, Brennan, and Stewart entered strong dissents.

---

e. Waiver. In federal courts, the right to a trial by jury can be expressly and intelligently waived by the accused, even without the advice of counsel. [Adams v. United States, 317 U.S. 269 (1942)] Some states are more restrictive on waiver.

f.   Instructing the jury on disregarding the law--

United States v. Dougherty, 473 F.2d 1113 (D.C. Cir. 1972).

Facts. Dougherty (D) appealed his conviction on the basis that at trial, the trial judge refused to instruct the jury that it could acquit D without regard to the law and the evidence, and that the judge refused to give a similar jury instruction.

Issue. Does a defendant have an enforceable right to have the jury instructed of its power to nullify the law in a particular case?

Held. No. Conviction sustained.

♦   Juries undeniably have this right, but no specific instructions to this effect need be given. To do so would risk chaos in the legal system.

---

g.   Prosecution's right to jury trial--

Singer v. United States, 380 U.S. 24 (1965).

Facts. Singer (D) was charged with 30 violations of the mail fraud statute and sought waiver of a trial by jury. However, the prosecution refused to consent, and D was convicted by the jury. D appeals, claiming a constitutional right to waive jury trial.

Issue. Does a defendant have a unilateral constitutional right to waive trial by jury?

Held. No. Judgment affirmed.

♦   D's only constitutional right concerning the method of trial is to an impartial trial by jury. D may waive that right, but if either the prosecution or the trial judge refuses to consent to waiver, D is still subject to impartial trial by jury, which is all the Constitution guarantees him.

---

2.   Jury Selection.

a.   Constitutional requirements.

1) **Federal courts.** By virtue of the Sixth Amendment "impartial jury" requirements and its supervisory power over the administration of justice in the federal courts, the Supreme Court has held generally that jurors must be chosen from representative cross sections of the community, within the framework of minimum character and literacy requirements and state requirements for jurors.

   a) Thus, women, eligible under state law, cannot be excluded merely because of their sex. [Ballard v. United States, 329 U.S. 187 (1946)]

   b) Nor may federal employees be excluded from a panel trying a Communist because they are subject to a loyalty order. [Dennis v. United States, 339 U.S. 162 (1950)]

2) **State courts.** Although the Supreme Court has never held that state courts must use grand juries, it has held that in using both juries and grand juries they must comply with the Equal Protection Clause and Due Process Clause of the Fourteenth Amendment.

3) **Racial discrimination.**

   a) A statute that expressly excludes any racial group from jury participation is clearly unconstitutional. [Strauder v. West Virginia, 100 U.S. 303 (1880)]

   b) Most challenges have charged racial discrimination in the *application* of the laws governing selection of jurors, rather than in the laws themselves. [Whitus v. Georgia, 385 U.S. 545 (1967)—when the defendant shows a prima facie case of systematic discrimination on juries, the burden of proof shifts to the state to disprove actual discrimination]

   c) In *Avery v. Georgia*, 354 U.S. 559 (1953), the defendant's conviction was reversed because names of potential jurors were placed on different colored slips of paper according to race. In *Norris v. Alabama*, 294 U.S. 587 (1935), a conviction was reversed when it was shown that no blacks ever served, though many were qualified.

   d) In *Alexander v. Louisiana*, 405 U.S. 625 (1972), the defendant showed grand jury and trial jury discrimination where, in a rape case, there was an all-white grand jury from an area that was 21% black, and an all-white jury commission picked the jurors, knowing their race. This made out a prima facie case of discrimination and violated equal protection.

4) **Sex discrimination.**

    a) **Fair cross section requirement--**

Taylor v. Louisiana, 419 U.S. 522 (1975).

Facts. Women were given automatic exemption from jury duty with the result that almost all males were selected for jury duty. Taylor (D), a male, challenges this practice.

Issue. Do the Sixth and Fourteenth Amendments require that petit juries in both federal and state criminal trials be selected from a representative cross section of the community?

Held. Yes.

◆   Restricting jury service to only special groups or excluding identifiable segments playing major roles in the community is forbidden.

◆   Even though D is not a member of the group excluded, he has standing to challenge the group's exclusion on the ground that it denies him the right to an impartial jury drawn from a fair cross section of the community.

◆   However, the state may grant reasonable exemptions from jury duty to persons engaged in occupations requiring uninterrupted performance, as long as the jury panels are representative.

Dissent (Rehnquist, J.). D makes no claims of prejudice or bias. The Court does not provide any satisfactory explanation as to how this system undermines the role of the jury; instead it posits that a "flavor" is lost if either sex is excluded. This flavor is not of constitutional importance. This smacks more of mysticism than of law.

---

    b) **Overbroad exemption.** An automatic exemption from jury service for any women requesting not to serve, resulting in jury venires averaging less than 15% female, violates the Constitution's fair cross section requirement. A narrowly drawn exemption from jury service for women who have children to care for would be acceptable, but this exemption is overbroad. [Duren v. Missouri, 439 U.S. 357 (1979)]

    5) **Other discrimination.** The Fourteenth Amendment has generally not been applied by the Court to prohibit the exclusion or inclusion of persons on a jury for any reason other than color, sex, national origin, or descent. Thus, for example, convictions have been upheld in the following cases:

a) Jury selection was based on a poll tax that disqualified a higher proportion of blacks than whites. [Brown v. Allen, 344 U.S. 443 (1953)]

b) Although exclusion of daily wage earners as a class from juries in effect discriminates against blacks and is thus unconstitutional, mere disproportionate representation of such a class is not unconstitutional so long as their representation is substantial and not the result of mere tokenism or intentional exclusion. [Fay v. New York, 332 U.S. 261 (1947)]

b. Procedure for selecting trial jurors.

1) **Source of names.** A panel of jurors is assembled according to an established procedure (usually the same as that used for selecting juries for civil cases; *e.g.,* voters' registration lists, municipal directories). The panel can be challenged as a whole on grounds of "material departure" from the normal procedure or on constitutional grounds (*e.g.,* discrimination in selection on account of race).

2) **Examination of jurors (voir dire).** Questions may be directed to prospective jurors to determine whether there are grounds for challenge.

a) The trial judge, in her discretion, may allow counsel to question the jurors directly or have counsel submit such questions to her to be asked of the jurors.

b) The trial judge should not restrict questions that might properly be a ground for challenge for cause, but questions for the purpose of exercising peremptory challenges may be prohibited by the trial judge.

3) **Procedures not required--**

Hamer v. United States, 259 F.2d 274 (9th Cir. 1958).

Facts. Hamer (D) was charged with importing narcotic drugs and facilitating their sale. D requested a list of the names and addresses of prospective jurors in advance of trial. This request was denied. The court conducted voir dire directly, instead of allowing counsel to do so. The prosecutor used a jury book during voir dire to see how prospective jurors acted on previous juries. D's objections to these procedures were overruled. D was convicted. She appeals, claiming she had been deprived of the right to jury trial.

Issue. Is a defendant entitled to access to a prosecutor's jury book that sets out how prospective jurors acted or voted while on previous juries?

Held. No. Judgment affirmed.

♦ Congress requires that defense counsel be given advance notice, by service of jury lists, in certain classes of cases such as treason and capital offenses. Congress has decided such notice is not necessary for other types of cases, and D's remedy is a matter for Congress, not the courts.

♦ No constitutional right to a personal voir dire of the jury has been recognized by the courts. The court conducted the voir dire and asked D's counsel if he had any additional voir dire questions. D's counsel said he did not. The voir dire conducted by the court was sufficient.

♦ The prosecutor's jury book contained comments on about 300 jurors, describing briefly how each juror participated in previous juries, including references to how each voted. It is common for trial lawyers to share knowledge and experience, including information about jurors. If D's attorney had tried cases before some of the jurors on this panel, he would have used his experience to D's best advantage. D's argument would make it impossible for the government to prosecute in any situation where the defense attorney had less information about the jurors than the government did. This is impractical. Perfect equality in counsel can never be achieved.

Comment. Many states allow defendants access to jury lists in all criminal cases, while others allow it only in capital cases.

---

4) **Challenges.**

   a) **For cause.** Jurors will be dismissed for actual bias, implied bias, or for general cause. General cause is when the juror has been convicted of a felony or suffers from unsoundness of mind or defects in sensory faculties.

   b) **Peremptory.** Peremptory challenges are entirely within the party opponents' discretion. The number of such challenges varies from jurisdiction to jurisdiction. There is a split of authority on whether a defendant must exhaust his peremptory challenges to avoid waiving his right to object to the impartiality of a jury.

   c) **Challenges based on racial discrimination.** Equal protection does not require exact proportional representation of all the component ethnic groups of the community on every jury. However, if the prosecutors in a state systematically use their peremptory challenges to exclude members of a racial group from all juries in all cases, there is a violation of equal protection; but mere proof that members of a racial group were excluded from a particular jury by such means will not establish such a violation.

d) **Former approach to racial discrimination challenges.** In *Swain v. Alabama*, 380 U.S. 202 (1965), Swain, a black man, was convicted of rape. Twenty-six percent of the population of the county was black, but for several years only 10 to 15 percent of the jury panels were black, and no black persons had actually served on a jury for several years. In Swain's specific case, the black persons on the panel were struck by peremptory challenges. The Supreme Court sustained his conviction, holding that there need not be proportionate representation on panels or actual juries. The Court found that in Swain's case, the disproportion was not purposeful or invidious. Also, peremptory challenges are permissible, and striking black persons from the actual jury did not violate equal protection.

e) **Current approach--**

Batson v. Kentucky, 476 U.S. 79 (1986).

Facts. Batson (D), a black man, was indicted for burglary and receipt of stolen goods. At trial, the prosecutor used peremptory challenges to remove all the black persons on the panel. D moved to discharge the jury. The court denied the motion, stating that peremptory challenges may be used against anyone. D was convicted. The state courts affirmed and the Supreme Court granted certiorari.

Issue. Must a defendant prove an ongoing pattern of discrimination in order to attack the prosecutor's peremptory challenge of members of D's race from the jury?

Held. No. Judgment reversed and case remanded.

♦ A state may not deliberately prevent black persons from serving as jurors because of their race. The Equal Protection Clause forbids a prosecutor from challenging potential black jurors solely on account of their race.

♦ In *Swain v. Alabama, supra,* the Court permitted challenges to exclusion of blacks upon proof of repeated exclusions. That approach did not sufficiently protect the rights of a single accused to not be subject to invidious government discrimination.

♦ To establish a prima facie case, D: (i) must show that he is a member of a cognizable racial group and that the prosecutor has removed other such members through peremptory challenges; (ii) may rely on the fact that peremptory challenges can be used to discriminate; and (iii) must show that these facts raise an inference that the prosecutor purposefully discriminated.

♦ On remand, D must be given an opportunity to make his required showings.

Concurrence (Marshall, J.). Because neutral explanations are easily fabricated, the only real solution is to forbid peremptory challenges.

Dissent (Burger, C.J., Rehnquist, J.). If equal protection applies to peremptory challenges, defendants could object to challenges based on sex, age, religion, political affiliation, etc. This defeats the whole purpose of peremptory challenges, which reflect the challenging party's assumptions and intuitive judgments.

───────────────

5) **Limitation in capital cases.** When a capital offense is charged, prospective jurors are properly examined on their views toward capital punishment. Naturally, the prosecution will use its peremptory challenges to excuse jurors who indicate any scruples against the death penalty, and the defense will use its peremptory challenges on those who favor it. However, the question arises whether jurors can or should be excused *for cause* (bias) because they either favor or oppose the death penalty.

    a) **Jury composed only of jurors favoring the death penalty.** There is no assumption that a jury composed only of jurors favoring the death penalty will be more likely to find a defendant guilty than jurors opposed to the death penalty. However, to allow that same jury to decide the penalty (if it finds him guilty) violates due process and any death sentence imposed would be set aside. To put a person to death at the hands of a jury so selected ("a hanging jury") is to deny him due process. [Witherspoon v. Illinois, 391 U.S. 510 (1968)]

    b) **Standard applied: impairment of performance of duty.** Prospective jurors whose views on the death penalty (whether in favor or opposed) would prevent or substantially impair the performance of their duty with respect to the issues of guilt or sentence are properly excused. Such persons are not impartial jurors. [Wainwright v. Witt, 469 U.S. 412 (1985)]

    c) **Jurors opposed to the death penalty.** A prospective juror will not be excused for cause *merely* because he opposes the death penalty. However, the result would undoubtedly be different if the juror indicated on voir dire that he would automatically vote against the imposition of capital punishment (*i.e.,* without regard to any evidence that might be developed at the trial) or that his attitude toward the death penalty would prevent him from making an impartial decision as to the defendant's guilt.

D. MEDIA RIGHTS VS. FAIR TRIAL RIGHTS

1. **Introduction.** Two basic problems with trial publicity are determining what means of exercising control over what is published are permissible and defining the standards for determining a "fair" trial.

2. **Control over What Is Published.**

    a. **Restraint by newspapers.** Commissions that study the problems in this area often urge newspapers to adopt a code of ethics and practice more restraint in the things they publish—a useless suggestion. The ethic of the newspaper trade is aggressiveness, with the premium placed on getting "the story." Urging voluntary restraint is not sufficient.

    b. **English rule.** In England, the papers are forbidden, on punishment of contempt, to comment on a case before trial. Problems with this rule are:

        1) **Freedom of the press.** In the United States, such a policy would raise First Amendment problems.

        2) **Positive contributions by newspapers and news media.** There are some good reasons for wanting papers to oversee the process of justice in the United States.

            a) Our government system is never free of corruption. Papers have often been instrumental in exposing it.

            b) There have been numerous occasions when papers have helped draw public attention to the plight of innocent people, thereby gaining their release, or have been instrumental in helping catch fugitives who are at large.

        3) **The political process.** For the most part, judges in the United States are elected. This may suggest that they are involved in the political process already and that the papers have a right to tell them how to do their job.

3. **Pretrial Publicity and Jury Selection.**

   a. **Publication of inadmissible evidence.** It is extremely difficult for a juror to forget about a defendant's criminal record or about a confession (inadmissible at trial) that he read about out of court.

   b. **Confession and criminal record--**

Irvin v. Dowd, 366 U.S. 717 (1961).

Facts. Six murders were committed. Irvin (D) was arrested, and the prosecutor issued a press release stating that D had confessed, which was widely publicized. A change of venue to an adjoining county was given, but repeated requests for another change were denied. A barrage of headlines, pictures, etc., published during the seven months before D's trial, included information on D's criminal record. Over 90% of the 370 prospective jurors admitted having some opinion as to D's guilt; eight of those finally placed thought him guilty but on examination by the judge said they would put away their prejudices to decide the case.

Issue. May a defendant successfully challenge his conviction based on the jury's being prejudiced against him in violation of his constitutional right to a fair trial?

Held. Yes. Judgment reversed.

♦ Due process requires a fair trial before an impartial jury. This does not mean that a juror must be totally ignorant of the facts and issues involved, but he must be able to lay aside his impressions or opinions.

♦ There was a pattern of deep and bitter prejudice shown to exist throughout the community. Eight of 12 jurors admitted thinking D was guilty, and in light of the climate of opinion it is impossible to say that the jury was impartial enough to meet constitutional standards.

♦ This is a prosecution where D's life is at stake.

Comment. The decision in *Irvin* is further defined in a later case. Yount was convicted of murdering one of his high school students; the conviction was later reversed. At his retrial, Yount moved for a change of venue, arguing that the dissemination of prejudicial information by the press violated his right to a fair trial by an impartial jury. The Supreme Court held that the pretrial publicity did not reveal the kind of wave of public passion that would have made a fair trial unlikely. It noted that the second trial did not occur until four years later, at a time when public prejudice was greatly diminished. The relevant question, the Court ruled, is whether the jurors had such fixed opinions that they could not judge impartially the guilt of the defendant. [Patton v. Yount, 467 U.S. 1025 (1984)]

c. **Presumption of partiality.** Compare *Irvin* with *Murphy v. Florida,* 421 U.S. 794 (1975). The defendant in *Murphy* had a notorious criminal history, he was charged by state authorities with a robbery, and the case and his past had received extensive press coverage. The Court held that the defendant had not been denied a fair trial. The Court stated that *Irvin* does not stand for the proposition that juror exposure to information about a state defendant's prior convictions or to news accounts presumptively deprives the defendant of due process. Qualified jurors need not be totally ignorant of the facts and issues involved. At the same time, the juror's assurances that he is impartial are not dispositive. The defendant must demonstrate "the actual existence of such an opinion in the mind of the juror as will raise the presumption of partiality."

4. **Change of Venue--**

Rideau v. Louisiana, 373 U.S. 723 (1963).

Facts. The sheriff had a film made of Rideau (D), arrested for robbing a bank and killing a bank employee, as he was "interviewed" by the sheriff, during which D admitted the robbery and murder. This film was shown three times over the local television station; each time it was seen by between 20,000 and 50,000 people in a 150,000-person parish. Defense counsel moved for a change of venue, which was refused.

Issue. Must the defendant show actual prejudice when his confession was televised several times to the community from which the jurors were drawn?

Held. No. Judgment reversed.

♦ Three members of the jury had stated that they had seen the "interview"; two members of the jury were deputy sheriffs of the parish—challenges for cause by the defense were denied.

♦ When a defendant's trial is really conducted on television, no inquiry will be made into the voir dire examination of the jury members. Due process requires a trial before a jury drawn from a community of people who have not seen and heard D's televised interview.

♦ Although the jurors claimed neutrality, such claims in this circumstance are inherently implausible.

Dissent (Clark, Harlan, JJ.). Unless adverse publicity is shown to have fatally infected the trial, there is no basis for the Court's inference that the publicity "called up some informal and illicit analogy to res judicata, making petitioner's trial a meaningless formality." Furthermore, only three of the 12 jurors saw the interview and they testified that the interview would not influence their opinion. The judge determined that they would be impartial, a determination particularly within the province of the court.

Comment. A change of venue may be the only sufficient remedy to offset pretrial publicity. In *Groppi v. Wisconsin*, 400 U.S. 505 (1971), the Court invalidated a state law that did not permit venue changes in misdemeanor cases; no other available remedies were adequate.

---

5.   **Preventing Prejudicial Publicity.**

    a.   **Reporter and official conduct.** In *Sheppard v. Maxwell*, 384 U.S. 333 (1966), during Sheppard's murder trial, newspaper articles quoted prosecution officials and published unproven stories of his personal life, jurors were not sequestered and some read these accounts, the media was given substantial space in the courtroom and courthouse, newspapers printed the trial word for word, debates about the trial were conducted on the radio, and jurors were allowed to make telephone calls during their deliberations. The Court granted Sheppard's habeas corpus petition, finding that the adverse publicity and conduct of officials involved with the trial so prejudiced him as to amount to a denial of due process.

    b.   **Restricting public statements.** Rule 3.6 of the ABA Model Rules of Professional Conduct contains guidelines for trial publicity. Essentially, lawyers may not make extrajudicial statements if there is a reasonable likelihood that such comment will interfere with a fair trial or prejudice the administration of justice. In *Gentile v. State Bar of Nevada*, 501 U.S. 1030 (1991), Gentile, a defense attorney, held a press conference six months before the jury was to be empaneled to counteract negative publicity regarding his client. Among other things, Gentile claimed that his client was being used as a scapegoat and that a particular named detective was in the best position to have stolen the drugs and money. A Nevada rule prohibited lawyers, including defense lawyers, from making extra-judicial statements to the press that have a substantial likelihood of materially prejudicing an adjudicative proceeding. However, the rule's safe harbor provision allowed a lawyer to state without elaboration the general nature of the defense. Gentile had relied on this provision, but was disciplined for seeking to influence potential jurors. The Court ultimately upheld the rule, but also held that the "substantial likelihood of material prejudice" standard was void for vagueness because it did not furnish fair notice.

c.   Restricting the media--

Nebraska Press Association v. Stuart, 427 U.S. 539 (1976).

Facts. A local family of six was found murdered in their home. Simants was arrested and charged with the murders committed in the course of a sexual assault. The county court entered a restrictive order on publicity of the case. The Nebraska Supreme Court upheld the restraints as modified to include only (i) the existence and nature of confessions made to the police by Simants, (ii) confessions or admissions to third parties with the exception of the press, and (iii) other facts strongly implicative of Simants.

Issue. Is a court justified in imposing prior restraints on the publication of public court proceedings when it finds that a fair trial will be jeopardized?

Held. No. Judgment reversed.

♦   There is an extremely heavy burden required to justify the imposition of prior restraint by a court. A finding should be made that other methods, such as sequestering the jury or transferring or continuing the case, would be ineffective to ensure a fair trial before prior restraint can be justified. The courts below made no findings as to the effectiveness of the alternative methods.

♦   The restrictive order itself is defective because it prohibited the publication of evidence adduced at an open preliminary hearing and because it was too vague to meet the specificity required of orders restraining the press.

Concurrence (White, J.). This kind of restrictive order will likely never be found justifiable.

Concurrence (Powell, J.). One who undertakes to show the necessity for prior restraint on pretrial publicity bears a unique burden.

Concurrence (Brennan, Stewart, Marshall, JJ.). It is constitutionally impermissible to resort to prior restraints on the freedom of the press. Judges have a broad spectrum of valid options for insuring fundamental fairness.

Concurrence (Stevens, J.). I reserve judgment on whether the protection would apply to shabby, illegal, seriously intrusive, demonstrably false, or perversely motivated actions by the press.

---

d.   Closed proceedings. In *Gannett Co., Inc. v. DePasquale*, 433 U.S. 368 (1979), the Court held that neither the public nor the press had an en-

forceable Sixth Amendment right of access to a pretrial suppression hearing. However, in *Richmond Newspapers, Inc. v. Virginia,* below, the Court held that the public and the press have a First Amendment right to attend criminal trials, and this right was extended to preliminary hearings having some of the attributes of a trial. [Press-Enterprise Co. v. Superior Court, *infra*]

e.   **Public right to attend trials--**

Richmond Newspapers, Inc. v. Virginia, 448 U.S. 555 (1980).

Facts. Prior to his fourth retrial, the accused's motion to close the trial to the public was granted. Richmond Newspapers, Inc. (P) argued at a hearing that the judge had failed to consider less restrictive ways to ensure a fair trial. The judge refused to vacate the closure order, and the accused was acquitted. P appeals.

Issue. May a criminal trial be closed to the public upon the unopposed request of the defendant without proof that closure is necessary to ensure a fair trial?

Held. No.

♦   The First Amendment comprehends the right to receive information and ideas. It also assures the right of access to places traditionally open to the public, like criminal trials.

Concurrence (Brennan, Marshall, JJ.). The First Amendment plays a structural role in our system by ensuring informed public debate and confidence in the administration of justice.

Dissent (Rehnquist, J.). No constitutional provision prohibits the trial court's action in this case.

---

f.   **Closure standards--**

Globe Newspaper Co. v. Superior Court, 457 U.S. 596 (1982).

Facts. A state law required trial judges to exclude the general public from the courtroom during the testimony of minor victims of sex crimes. The trial judge closed the entire trial in a rape case, and Globe Newspaper Co. (P) sought injunctive relief. The state supreme court upheld the statute because of its narrow scope. The Supreme Court granted certiorari.

Issue. May a state require closure of criminal trials in narrowly defined cases?

Held. No. Judgment reversed.

♦ The state may deny access in order to inhibit disclosure of sensitive information if the denial is narrowly tailored to serve a compelling governmental interest. The state interests in protecting minor victims from further trauma and encouraging them to testify are compelling. But a mandatory closure rule is not narrowly tailored. Instead, the determination to close must be made on a case-by-case basis.

Dissent (Burger, C.J., Rehnquist, J.). States are permitted to protect minor defendants by closure, and they should be able to protect minor victims in the same way. The verbatim transcript is available after trial, so there is no denial of public access to information. Thus, the minimal impact on the First Amendment is justified here.

---

g. **First Amendment right of access to preliminary hearings--**

Press-Enterprise Co. v. Superior Court, 478 U.S. 1 (1986).

Facts. A person was charged with murdering 12 people with drug overdoses. He moved to have the preliminary hearing closed. State law permitted closure only if it is necessary to ensure a fair and impartial trial. Press-Enterprise Co. (P) sought release of the transcript. The court refused. P filed a writ of mandate. The state courts upheld the trial court's refusal to release the transcript. The Supreme Court granted certiorari.

Issue. Does the public have a right of access to a state preliminary hearing in the absence of a finding that only closure will ensure a fair trial?

Held. Yes.

♦ A preliminary hearing has the essential attributes of a criminal trial. Findings of probable cause usually lead to guilty pleas, but the hearing itself cannot result in a conviction.

♦ The public has a First Amendment right of access to proceedings having a tradition of accessibility and the functions of which are prompted by such access. Both considerations favor access here. To close the hearing, the court must make findings that there is a substantial probability that the defendant's right to a fair trial will be prejudiced by publicity that closure would prevent, and that reasonable alternatives to closure cannot adequately protect the fair trial rights. Such findings were not made here.

Dissent (Stevens, Rehnquist, JJ.). In California and other states, such hearings have been traditionally open but also subject to closure, so the tradition aspect is not satisfied in this case. The value of openness aspect would apply equally to grand jury proceedings. California preliminary hearings are functionally identical to the traditional grand jury.

---

6. **Televising Courtroom Proceedings.**

   a. **State proceedings.** A majority of states allow trial proceedings to be televised, although some allow a defendant to object and prevent televising.

   b. **Trial by television—inherently prejudicial--**

Estes v. Texas, 381 U.S. 532 (1965).

Facts. Estes (D), a well-known financier, was indicted for swindling. Portions of the trial were televised live, as was a pretrial hearing to determine if the trial should be televised. Other portions of the trial were filmed for later broadcasting. D was convicted; he appealed, claiming a denial of due process.

Issue. Did the televising of a criminal trial deny the defendant due process of law as guaranteed by the Fourteenth Amendment?

Held. Yes. Judgment reversed.

♦ Jurors and witnesses were made aware of the notoriety of the case, and four jurors saw or heard part of the telecasts. There are many possible prejudicial effects that such coverage might have on the jurors, witnesses, the defendant, the judge, and the attorneys in the case.

♦ No showing of actual prejudice is required of D. Instead, it will be presumed that, because of the state of television at that time and the nature of this particular trial, the broadcasting procedures used were inherently lacking in due process.

Concurrence (Harlan, J.). While the majority holding is too broad, in the case of a notorious trial such as this one, the factors against allowing televising so far outweigh the interest in televising as to require a holding that the televising infringed on the right to a fair trial.

Dissent (Stewart, Black, Brennan, White, JJ.). While televising trials might be extremely unwise, it does not rise to the level of a per se constitutional rule, and in this situation D's constitutional rights were not denied at all. I am concerned about the idea of imposing too many limits upon the public's right to know what goes on in the courts.

---

c. **Televised coverage allowed--**

Chandler v. Florida, 449 U.S. 560 (1981).

Facts. Some Miami Beach police officers (Ds) were charged with conspiracy to commit burglary, grand larceny, and possession of burglary tools, all counts stemming from breaking and entering a Miami Beach restaurant. Pursuant to an experimental program authorized by the Florida Supreme Court, portions of the trial (prosecutor's case and closing argument) were televised, despite Ds' objections. Ds were convicted by a jury of all counts and appealed, claiming that the procedures used had denied them a fair and impartial trial. The court of appeals affirmed the convictions, and the Florida Supreme Court denied review.

Issue. Do the procedures authorized by the Florida Supreme Court and used in the defendants' case violate the Due Process Clause of the Fourteenth Amendment?

Held. No. Judgment affirmed.

♦ *Estes v. Texas, supra,* did not establish a constitutional rule that all photographic, radio, and television coverage of criminal trials is inherently a denial of due process. *Estes* only held that television, as it existed at that time and as used in that case, resulted in a denial of due process. It does not stand as an absolute ban on state experimentation with an evolving technology.

♦ The Florida Supreme Court guidelines specify in detail the kind of electronic equipment that may be used in the courtroom and the manner of its use. The judge has the discretion to exclude coverage of certain witnesses and to forbid coverage when it may have a deleterious effect on the defendant's right to a fair trial.

♦ No one has presented empirical data sufficient to establish that the mere presence of the broadcast media in the courtroom inherently has an adverse effect on the judicial process. Furthermore, Ds have not shown that the media's coverage of their trial compromised the jury's ability to judge them fairly or that the broadcast coverage of their particular trial had an adverse impact on the trial participants sufficient to constitute a denial of due process.

Concurrence (Stewart, J.). Unlike the majority, I believe that *Estes* announced a per se rule that the Fourteenth Amendment prohibits television cameras from state courtrooms when a criminal trial is in progress. Rather than attempting to distinguish *Estes*, I would overrule it.

Concurrence (White, J.). *Estes* should be overruled.

E. THE CRIMINAL TRIAL

1. **Public Trial.** Most of the cases concern the requirement that a trial be "fair" in the sense that the defendant's right not be prejudiced by undue publicity, etc. However, there is also a requirement that a trial be "public" in the sense that the defendant not be tried in secret. This is to prevent the government from practicing unfair procedures on persons charged with crimes.

2. **Presence and Confrontation.**

    a. **Confrontation and the Sixth Amendment.** The Sixth Amendment states, "In all criminal prosecutions, the accused shall enjoy the right . . . to be confronted with the witnesses against him." This includes the right of a defendant to cross-examine witnesses called to testify against him. For example, in *Pointer v. Texas*, 380 U.S. 400 (1965), the prosecutor introduced at trial a witness's pretrial hearing testimony against the defendant even though the defense attorney had no opportunity to cross-examine the witness at the pretrial hearing. The Court held that this was a violation of the defendant's Sixth Amendment right of cross-examination.

    b. **Defendant's misconduct--**

Illinois v. Allen, 397 U.S. 337 (1970).

Facts. The trial judge warned Allen (D) to maintain order; D persisted in his disorderly conduct so that it was impossible to conduct the trial. The judge ordered D removed from the courtroom and continued the trial without him, over his objection.

Issue. Is a defendant's Sixth Amendment right to be present at his own trial absolute?

Held. No.

♦   Under the Sixth Amendment, a defendant has the right to be present at his trial. However, this right may be lost if the defendant is so disorderly that the trial cannot be continued with his presence.

♦   The judge has several alternatives in this situation: gagging D, removing him, or citing him for contempt. The judge has reasonable discretion in selecting the alternative to use.

♦   If the defendant is excluded, he may return on a promise to conduct himself properly.

---

c. **Waiver of right to confrontation.** In *Taylor v. United States*, 414 U.S. 17 (1973), the Court held that when a defendant voluntarily absented himself from the courtroom, this could be construed as a waiver of his right to confrontation, without a warning from the court.

d. **No right of access to witness competency hearing.** In *Kentucky v. Stincer*, 482 U.S. 730 (1987), the Court held that a defendant had no right to personally attend an out-of-court witness competency hearing, so long as his attorney participated and so long as he retained the opportunity for effective cross-examination.

e. **Holding the defendant in shackles at sentencing--**

Deck v. Missouri, 544 U.S. 622 (2005).

Facts. Deck (D) had his death sentence set aside. At his resentencing, he was shackled with leg irons, handcuffs, and a belly chain, which were visible to the jury. D was sentenced to death the second time, and the sentence was upheld by the Missouri Supreme Court. The Supreme Court granted certiorari.

Issue. May a defendant be held in shackles during the penalty phase of a capital case?

Held. No. Judgment reversed and case remanded.

♦ The common law has long required that a defendant must be brought to court without irons, shackles, or bonds, unless there is danger of escape. The purpose has been to prevent influencing the jury. This rule is a basic element of the due process of law. The Fifth and Fourteenth Amendments prohibit the use of physical restraints at trial unless the court determines that there is a potential security problem or risk of escape.

♦ Visible shackling undermines the presumption of innocence and suggests to the jury that the judicial system has already decided the defendant must be separated from society. Shackles also interfere with the right to counsel and the right to testify. They also undermine the dignity of the court.

♦ The concerns about shackles during the guilt phase continue through the penalty phase of criminal proceedings in capital cases. However, a judge can exercise discretion to impose restraint if necessary for security concerns, but only on a case-by-case basis. There were no findings in this case to justify shackling D.

Dissent (Thomas, Scalia, JJ.). A defendant's incentive to escape is greatest when he is in the courtroom for sentencing. This is the only time he is not jailed or restrained. Also, having been convicted, a defendant may be angry and may turn on his lawyer, a witness, or someone else in the courtroom. Furthermore, his appearance in shackles would not seem unusual to the jury and would not prevent him from communicating with his lawyer. And the restraints could be removed if he wanted to take the stand. The dignity of the court is not offended by having a convicted double murderer and robber appear before the court in visible physical restraints.

---

f.   Confrontation of out-of-court witness--

Crawford v. Washington, 541 U.S. 36 (2004).

Facts. Crawford (D) and his wife Sylvia went to the home of Lee, who allegedly had tried to rape Sylvia. D and Lee got into a fight, during which D stabbed Lee. D was arrested. He told the police that he had thought that Lee may have had a weapon. Sylvia, also a potential suspect, gave a statement while in police custody, in response to often leading questions, and after she had been told that whether she would be released depended on how the investigation continued. Her statement, at least arguably, undermined D's claim of self-defense. D was tried for assault and attempted murder. Sylvia did not testify because of the marital privilege, but the state invoked the hearsay exception for statements against penal interest and used her prior tape-recorded statements to show that D did not act in self-defense. D was convicted. D appealed, and the court of appeals reversed. The Washington Supreme Court reversed and upheld the conviction. The Supreme Court granted certiorari.

Issue. In a criminal trial, may a prior statement from a witness who is not present at the trial be admitted into evidence against the accused when the accused had no opportunity to cross-examine the witness when the prior statement was given?

Held. No. Judgment reversed and case remanded.

♦ D argues that admitting Sylvia's tape-recorded statements would violate his federal constitutional right to be confronted with the witnesses against him. In *Ohio v. Roberts*, 448 U.S. 56 (1980), we held that an unavailable witness's out-of-court statement may be admitted as long as it has "adequate indicia of reliability." The evidence must either fall within a "firmly rooted hearsay exception" or "bear particularized guarantees of trustworthiness."

♦ The early common law right to confront one's accusers required live testimony in court subject to adversarial testing. English law developed a right of confrontation to avoid injustice after the trial of Sir Walter Raleigh for treason. The primary evidence against him was an out-of-court statement made by his alleged accomplice. The court refused to require this witness to appear in court, and Raleigh was convicted and sentenced to death.

♦ The Confrontation Clause was directed at aspects of the civil law criminal procedure, especially the use of ex parte examinations as evidence against an accused. Accordingly, the right of confrontation is not limited to in-court testimony, but also applies to all testimonial statements of witnesses against the accused. Statements taken by police officers during interrogations, such as the one that produced Sylvia's statement in this case, fall within this class of statements.

♦ The ultimate goal of the Confrontation Clause is to ensure reliability of evidence, and reliability must be tested through cross-examination. The Clause involves, not only the desirability of reliable evidence, but also how reliability can best be determined. But the *Roberts* test allows a jury to hear evidence based merely on a judicial determination of reliability, thus replacing the constitutionally prescribed method of assessing reliability. Dispensing with confrontation because testimony is obviously reliable is like dispensing with a jury trial because the defendant is obviously guilty.

♦ The *Roberts* holding does not comply with the Confrontation Clause because it would admit testimonial statements that the Confrontation Clause is intended to exclude. This case demonstrates how *Roberts* is both unpredictable and inconsistent, since two appellate courts reached opposite conclusions about the reliability of Sylvia's out-of-court statement. Courts cannot substitute their own measures of reliability for the one mandated by the Confrontation Clause.

Comment. The Court noted that non-testimonial hearsay is governed by state hearsay law, while testimonial evidence is covered by the Confrontation Clause and cannot be admitted without a showing of unavailability and a prior opportunity for cross-examination. The scope of "testimonial" evidence is not clearly spelled out, but it does cover prior testimony at a preliminary hearing, before a grand jury, or at a former trial, as well as that obtained during police interrogations.

---

3.   **The Defendant's Right to Remain Silent--**

Griffin v. California, 380 U.S. 609 (1965).

Facts. Griffin (D) was accused of first degree murder and refused to testify on his own behalf. As permitted by the California Constitution, the prosecutor commented on D's refusal to testify, and the court gave jury instructions that included a reference to D's refusal to testify, although it stated that such a refusal does not create a presumption of guilt. D appeals.

Issue. Does comment by the prosecutor and in the jury instructions relating to a defendant's refusal to testify deny the defendant due process?

Held. Yes. Judgment reversed.

♦   Although earlier federal cases invalidating such comments were based on a federal statute, the spirit of the self-incrimination privilege would prohibit all such comments as a matter of basic due process.

Dissent (Stewart, White, JJ.). D has not been compelled to be a witness against himself. Also, the court's instructions would benefit D by not leaving the jury with their own, untutored instincts to guide them in making inferences from D's silence.

Comments.

♦   Upon a defendant's request, the court may instruct the jury that the defendant has a constitutional right not to testify in his own defense and that no inference of guilt can be drawn therefrom. The Court has also held that such minimal instructions, even if given over a defendant's objections, do not violate the defendant's privilege. [*See* Lakeside v. Oregon, 435 U.S. 333 (1978)]

♦   Recall that a defendant has a right to choose when to testify. [*See* Brooks v. Tennessee, *supra*]

---

4.   **Counsel's Arguments.**

     a.   **Introduction.** Argument of counsel can constitute reversible error. In criminal cases, the prosecution has the duty to see that justice is done, and accordingly improper prosecution argument can lead to reversal. Defense counsel's improper argument can lead to a mistrial. Certain conduct, such as an argument that refers to statements of witnesses that were not introduced into evidence, are clearly improper. The Model Rules of Professional Conduct and the ABA Standards, The Prosecution Function ("ABAS") set forth certain standards of prosecutorial conduct.

         1)   MRPC 3.4(e). "A lawyer shall not . . . state a personal opinion as to . . . the credibility [of] a witness . . . or the guilt or innocence of an accused."

         2)   ABAS 3-5.8(c). "The prosecutor should not use arguments calculated to inflame the passions or prejudices of the jury."

         3)   ABAS 3-5.8(d). "The prosecutor should refrain from argument which would divert the jury from its duty to decide the case on the evidence, by injecting issues broader than the guilt or innocence of the accused under the controlling law, or by making predictions of the consequences of the jury's verdict."

b.   Improper arguments must deny due process--

Darden v. Wainwright, 477 U.S. 168 (1986).

Facts. Darden (D) was charged with murder, robbery, and assault with intent to kill after he was identified by the deceased's wife and a neighbor who had arrived at the scene of the murder and was shot by the perpetrator. D had been arrested after his car was recovered a few miles from the murder scene, where D had crashed into a telephone pole. A gun was found near the crash site that matched the firing sequences that took place at the murder scene, as well as the bullet that killed the victim and wounded the neighbor. D was convicted and sentenced to death. During closing arguments, defense counsel and the prosecutor referred to the perpetrator of the crimes as an "animal." Defense counsel also opined as to the strength of the state's case. The prosecutor implied that the death penalty would be appropriate and exhibited emotional responses to the case, stating among other things that he wished someone had blown D away, or that D had been killed in the accident. The courts upheld the conviction and sentence. D sought federal habeas corpus relief, which the federal courts denied. The Supreme Court granted certiorari.

Issue. To obtain a reversal for improper prosecutor final arguments, must the defense show that the comments rendered the conviction a denial of due process?

Held. Yes. Judgment affirmed.

♦   In this habeas corpus proceeding, the proper standard of review is due process. The federal courts do not exercise their broad supervisory power in these cases.

♦   Even when a prosecutor's comments are undesirable or worthy of condemnation, reversal is appropriate only when the comments "so infected the trial with unfairness as to make the resulting conviction a denial of due process." The prosecutor did not manipulate or misstate the evidence. Some of the comments were invited by the defense counsel's opening argument. The trial court emphasized to the jurors that their decision must be based on the evidence, not arguments of counsel. And the weight of evidence against D was substantial. Therefore, D's trial was not fundamentally unfair.

Dissent (Blackmun, Brennan, Marshall, Stevens, JJ.). The prosecutor's argument violated several established standards of conduct. The evidence was not so overwhelming that it is clear the jury's verdict was not the product of the prosecutor's misconduct.

---

5.   Process of Proof, Argument, and Instruction of the Jury.

a. **Order of the proceedings.** Generally, criminal trials in most jurisdictions proceed according to the following order after the jury is impaneled and sworn:

1) The indictment or information is read to the jury by the clerk, and the plea of the defendant given.

2) The government attorney makes an opening statement, then the defendant or his counsel may make an opening statement (if authorized by the law of the jurisdiction).

3) The government attorney opens the case and offers evidence in support of the charge.

4) The defendant or his counsel may then open the defense (which may, depending upon the law of the jurisdiction, include the making of an opening statement) and offer his evidence in support thereof.

5) The parties may then respectively offer rebutting testimony only, unless the court, for good reason, in furtherance of justice, permits them to offer evidence upon their original case.

6) When the evidence is concluded, unless the case is submitted on either or both sides without argument, each side may argue the case to the jury, the government opening the argument and having the right to close.

7) The judge may then charge the jury and must do so on any points of law pertinent to the issue, if requested by either party, and she may state the evidence. The extent to which the judge will comment on the evidence varies greatly from one jurisdiction to another. In some jurisdictions, the judge may also give instructions to the jury on the law before the hearing of the evidence.

b. **Instructing the jury.**

1) **Instructing sua sponte.** The trial judge must—as a matter of process—instruct the jury on all general principles of law relevant to the issues raised by the evidence. This is true whether or not proper instructions have been requested by the prosecution or defense. It is the trial judge's duty to make certain that the jury is properly instructed.

2) **Requested instructions.** In most criminal trials, however, the parties—especially defense counsel—find it to their tactical advantage to *request* court instructions.

a) In a jury trial, requests for instructions must be made before argument, but requested instructions may be tendered after argument if the argument raised new issues.

b) What instructions should be requested depends, of course, upon the law applicable to the case and the evidence presented at trial. Most jurisdictions have a manual of approved jury instructions.

3) **Ruling on requested instructions.** The court, on request, must, before argument, decide whether to give, refuse, or modify the proposed instructions, decide which additional instructions it will give, and advise counsel of its decision. Often an informal conference will be held on instructions among the judge, prosecutor, and defense counsel.

4) **Hung jury charge.** If a jury announces its inability to reach a unanimous verdict, the trial judge may instruct the jury of its duty to decide and otherwise attempt to prevent a "hung jury" (minority jurors asked to consider the majority position, etc.). [Allen v. United States, 164 U.S. 492 (1896)] Such an instruction is invalid if it is "coercive," *e.g.,* threats to keep the jury locked up for an unreasonable time.

c. **Judge-jury relationship—motion for judgment of acquittal.** The trial judge may not direct a verdict of guilty. But she may take the case from the jury (on her own or the defendant's motion) for lack of sufficient evidence to support a conviction (motion for a directed verdict).

1) Normally, the standard applied is that "the defendant is entitled to acquittal if reasonable people could not conclude on the evidence taken in the light most favorable to the prosecution that guilt has been proved beyond a reasonable doubt."

6. **Deliberations and Verdict.**

a. **Deadlocked juries.**

1) While the type of charge given in *Allen v. United States, supra,* is not unconstitutional, some courts have discontinued its use as "coercive."

2) A judge may send a jury back for additional deliberations. At some point, however, such instructions become unreasonable.

3) Most states prohibit judges from commenting on the evidence and expressing opinions about the facts. The federal courts permit such comment within proscribed limits.

b. **Inconsistent verdicts.**

   1) Inconsistent verdicts between counts are upheld in jury trials, but not in judge-made verdicts.

   2) But normally verdicts by juries where they say "yes" and "no" to the same critical question are not upheld.

c. **Impeaching verdicts.** The time-honored rule was that jurors could not impeach their own verdicts (tell what went on in the jury room, etc.). Some states have changed this rule. *People v. De Lucia*, 229 N.E.2d 211 (N.Y. 1967), permitted juror testimony about outside influences on the jury (improper visit to the scene of the crime and some jurors acting out the crime).

7. **Jury's Role in Sentencing.** Most states permit the jury to determine the type and length of sentence, some in capital cases, some in other types, and some even when the jury has not determined guilt (as when a defendant pleads guilty). Since *Furman v. Georgia*, 408 U.S. 238 (1972), the jury cannot impose the death penalty without an authorizing statute that requires consideration of aggravating and mitigating factors, and the jury must be instructed on these factors.

F. DOUBLE JEOPARDY

1. **Introduction.** The Double Jeopardy Clause in the Fifth Amendment reads "No person . . . shall . . . be subject for the same [offense] to be twice put in jeopardy of life or limb."

   a. **Origins.** Double jeopardy originated from two common law defenses: already acquitted and already convicted. For a long time this common law maxim was used to deny appeals to convicted defendants.

   b. **History in the United States.** In the United States, it was also unclear whether the defendant could appeal (asking for a new trial), since allowing the new trial might violate double jeopardy.

      1) It was decided, in the federal system first, that a convicted defendant could appeal.

      2) Then it was decided that after a successful appeal the defendant could be retried. The defendant was said to "waive" his double jeopardy defense by asking for a new trial. The rationale was that there is no double jeopardy until the defendant has had one proper trial.

2. **Reprosecution After a Mistrial.**

a.   Mistrial based on unintentional procedural error--

Illinois v. Somerville, 410 U.S. 458 (1973).

Facts. The trial judge declared a mistrial of Somerville's (D's) first trial because the indictment against D was fatally defective. Two days later, the grand jury filed a second indictment.

Issue. Does a second trial following a mistrial constitute double jeopardy?

Held. No.

♦   Even though the defendant has a valued right to have his trial completed by an initial tribunal, that right may in some instances be subordinated to the public interest for justice.

Dissent (White, Douglas, Brennan, JJ.). The purpose of the Double Jeopardy Clause is to protect a defendant from continued exposure to embarrassment, anxiety, expense, and restrictions on his liberty, as well as to preserve his "right to have his trial completed by a particular tribune." I cannot find "manifest necessity" for a mistrial to compensate for prosecutorial mistake.

Comment. Even though jeopardy would normally have been held to have attached at the first trial, there are instances where a second trial is permitted after jeopardy has attached: after a successful appeal by a defendant, where misconduct causes a mistrial, and where a jury is unable to reach a verdict.

b.   Mistrial caused by defendant or counsel--

Arizona v. Washington, 434 U.S. 497 (1978).

Facts. In 1971, Washington (D) was found guilty of murder. In 1973, the Superior Court of Arizona ordered, and the Arizona Supreme Court affirmed, a new trial because the prosecutor had withheld exculpatory evidence. The second trial began in 1975. During voir dire and in his opening remarks, defense counsel forcefully mentioned the prior withholding of evidence and that the state supreme court granted a new trial as a result. The prosecutor, following both opening statements, moved for a mistrial. Without expressly finding "manifest necessity" or that he had considered alternative solutions, the trial judge granted the motion. The Arizona Supreme Court refused review. D's petition for habeas corpus to the federal district court was granted because of the judge's failure to *expressly* find "manifest necessity" or explicitly consider alternative solutions. The court of appeals affirmed.

Issue. Did the trial judge's failure to expressly demonstrate "manifest necessity" or consider alternative solutions invalidate the granted motion for a new trial?

Held. No. Judgment reversed.

♦ Unlike the situation where trial has ended in an acquittal or conviction, retrial is not automatically barred when granted in mid-proceeding. However, the prosecutor has a heavy burden of showing a high degree of "manifest necessity."

♦ At one extreme are cases where the prosecutor moves for mistrial in order to buttress weaknesses in his case. Double jeopardy prohibits this, and the requisite high degree of "manifest necessity" is never met. At the other extreme is the classic mistrial based upon the trial judge's belief that the jury is deadlocked. The judge's discretion in such a situation is given great deference.

♦ The present case fits into the latter end of this spectrum of appellate scrutiny, where the trial judge's determination is entitled to great respect. Adoption of a stringent standard of appellate review would just impede the trial judge. He is far more conversant with the relevant factors than any reviewing court. However, if the judge acts irresponsibly, his decision cannot stand.

♦ Defense counsel's remarks were improper and may very well have affected the impartiality of the jury. However, even though the trial judge is given great autonomy in determining the degree of bias, he must weigh that bias against the importance of defendant's right to conclude the trial confrontation once and for all.

♦ The record reveals that the judge acted responsibly and deliberately in this balancing process and, as a result, the mistrial is supported by the requisite high degree of "manifest necessity." Such a finding need not be expressly stated in the record as long as the record reveals such proper deliberations. Though explicit reasoning would be helpful to a reviewing court, it is not constitutionally required.

---

c.   **Standard for allowing reprosecution after a mistrial--**

Oregon v. Kennedy, 456 U.S. 667 (1982).

Facts. Kennedy (D) was tried for stealing an oriental rug. During redirect examination of an expert witness on the value of the rug, the expert stated that he had never done business with D. The prosecutor then asked, "Is that because he is a crook?" On the basis of the question, D was granted a mistrial. At retrial, D unsuccessfully asserted a double jeopardy objection. The appellate court reversed on the ground of prosecutorial overreaching. The Supreme Court granted certiorari.

Issue. Does double jeopardy attach when a mistrial is ordered at the defendant's request because of the prosecutor's conduct, but the prosecutor did not intend to provoke the mistrial request?

Held. No. Judgment reversed.

♦ In *United States v. Dinitz*, 424 U.S. 600 (1976), the Court held that double jeopardy does attach when the defendant is prejudiced by governmental actions intended to provoke mistrial requests. But that opinion also indicated that actions taken in bad faith by the prosecutor would also implicate the Double Jeopardy Clause. The latter standard is too broad, however.

♦ Retrial due to prosecutorial conduct that constitutes overreaching or harassment may be barred only if the prosecutor intends to subvert the double jeopardy protections. This rule provides relative certainty and adequately protects D's interests.

Concurrence (Powell, J.). A court must rely on objective facts and circumstances to determine prosecutorial intent.

Concurrence (Stevens, Brennan, Marshall, Blackmun, JJ.). The Court has improperly restricted the protection provided by the Double Jeopardy Clause. The protection should arise whenever a court is persuaded that egregious prosecutorial misconduct has rendered unmeaningful D's choice to continue or stop the proceeding.

---

3. **Reprosecution Following an Acquittal.**

    a. **Dismissal pursuant to defendant's motion--**

United States v. Scott, 437 U.S. 82 (1978).

Facts. Scott (D) was indicted on three counts and repeatedly sought dismissal of the first two on grounds that pre-indictment delay was prejudicial. Following presentation of the evidence, the trial court granted D's motion. The United States appealed the dismissal, but the court of appeals affirmed, holding that the Double Jeopardy Clause barred further prosecution under *United States v. Jenkins*, 420 U.S. 358 (1975). The United States appeals.

Issue. If a defendant successfully moves for dismissal before a trier of fact determines his guilt or innocence, may the government appeal the dismissal?

Held. Yes. Judgment reversed. *United States v. Jenkins* is overruled.

♦ To protect against undue harassment of defendants, a judgment of acquittal is not appealable by the prosecution if based on a jury verdict or on a ruling by the court that the evidence is insufficient to convict.

♦ If a defendant successfully seeks to avoid his trial prior to its conclusion, a second prosecution does not violate the Double Jeopardy Clause. In such a case, the defendant has elected to waive his right to have the first trier of fact determine his guilt or innocence.

♦ Here, D chose to avoid conviction not because the government failed to make its case but because of a legal claim of prejudice. D is not oppressed by permitting the government to appeal; the appeal is merely the result of D's voluntary choice.

Dissent (Brennan, White, Marshall, Stevens, JJ.). An appeal of a midtrial examination is improper if it requires further proceedings concerning factual issues.

Comment. In *Serfass v. United States*, 420 U.S. 377 (1975), the Court held that if the defendant was indicted but the indictment was dismissed on motion by the defendant before trial, the government could appeal the motion, and if the dismissal was reversed on appeal, the government could then try the defendant without jeopardy attaching. The jury had not been sworn in nor any evidence entered, so there had not been a trial.

---

b. **Post-trial ruling appealed--**

United States v. Wilson, 420 U.S. 332 (1975).

Facts. Wilson (D) was convicted by a jury of converting union funds to his own use. The court dismissed the indictment on a post-verdict motion. The government attempted to appeal the dismissal.

Issue. Does the Double Jeopardy Clause absolutely prevent the government from appealing?

Held. No.

♦ A government appeal of a post-trial court ruling does not constitute double jeopardy. There is no danger of subjecting D to a second trial for the same offense. If the government were to win on the appeal of the motion, then the jury's verdict of guilty would simply be reinstated.

---

4.   Reprosecution Following a Conviction.

a.   The *Ball* rule. As modified by *Burks v. United States,* 437 U.S. 1 (1978), the *Ball* rule permits reprosecution when a convicted defendant has successfully set aside his conviction on grounds other than insufficiency of the evidence. [Ball v. United States, 163 U.S. 662 (1896)] However, no reprosecution is permitted if the defendant is acquitted.

b.   Reprosecution following a conviction--

Lockhart v. Nelson, 488 U.S. 33 (1988).

Facts. Nelson (D) pleaded guilty to burglary and theft. Because he had prior convictions, D was sentenced under the Arkansas habitual criminal statute, which provided for an enhanced prison term of 20 to 40 years if the person being sentenced had previously been convicted of four or more felonies. The prior convictions must be proven beyond a reasonable doubt. At the sentencing hearing, the prosecution introduced certified copies of four prior felony convictions of D. D did not object, even though D stated he believed that one of the convictions had been pardoned. In fact it had been, but the prosecutor was unaware of this and suggested that D was confusing a pardon with a commutation to time served. D agreed with this, and received an enhanced sentence. D's sentence was upheld on appeal. Several years later, D sought a writ of habeas corpus. The district court held the enhanced sentence to be invalid based on evidence of the pardon. When the state announced it would resentence D using a separate felony conviction as a replacement, D asserted a double jeopardy claim. The courts agreed that the state could not resentence D. The Supreme Court granted certiorari.

Issue. May an accused be retried if the original conviction is reversed because evidence was erroneously admitted against him, when there would have been insufficient evidence to support a conviction without the inadmissible evidence?

Held. Yes. Judgment reversed.

♦   The Double Jeopardy Clause does not prevent a successive prosecution after a defendant successfully gets his first conviction set aside because of an error in the proceeding. An exception to this rule applies when the conviction is reversed for insufficient evidence. [Burks v. United States, *supra*] The reason is that a reversal for insufficient evidence is equivalent to an acquittal.

♦   A reversal for insufficient evidence is different from a reversal for a defective process, such as the incorrect receipt or rejection of evidence. D's case involved a trial error; the judge should not have admitted the pardoned conviction. But with that evidence admitted, the enhanced sentence was supported by sufficient evidence.

♦   A retrial in this circumstance gives D an opportunity for a fair readjudication of his case free from error. If D had offered evidence of the pardon at his hearing, the trial judge would have given the prosecution an opportunity to offer evidence of another prior conviction.

Dissent (Marshall, Brennan, Blackmun, JJ.). The majority has not explained whether in a double jeopardy case the reviewing court should look to all the admitted evidence, or just the properly admitted evidence. As a matter of law, the document the prosecution offered to prove the fourth conviction was devoid of probative value and should not have been considered.

---

c. Implied acquittals--

Green v. United States, 355 U.S. 184 (1957).

Facts. Green (D) was charged with arson and first degree murder of a woman killed in the fire. The judge instructed the jury that they could find D guilty of first or second degree murder (because the latter was included in the former). The verdict was guilty of second degree murder and arson; nothing was indicated about first degree murder. D appealed the second degree murder conviction, and the conviction was reversed with remand for a new trial. At this trial, D was convicted of first degree murder; he appealed on the basis of double jeopardy.

Issue. Can a defendant be retried for an offense on which he was tried at a previous trial but was not convicted?

Held. No. Judgment reversed.

♦   A verdict of acquittal is final; the first trial amounted to an acquittal on the first degree murder charge. The appeal was for the second degree murder charge; D may be retried for this offense.

---

5. Reprosecution by a Different Sovereign.

a. Reprosecution in a sister state--

Heath v. Alabama, 474 U.S. 82 (1985).

Facts. Heath (D) hired two men to kill D's wife. On the appointed day, D left his house in Alabama, met with the killers in Georgia, and then led them back to his house where D gave them the keys to his car and house. The men kidnapped D's wife, took her to

Georgia, and shot her in the head, leaving her in the car in Georgia. Both Georgia and Alabama investigated the crime. D was convicted of murder in Georgia and received life imprisonment. Later, a grand jury in Alabama indicted D for murder during a kidnapping. D challenged his trial on double jeopardy grounds, but the courts rejected his claims and D was convicted and sentenced to death. The Supreme Court granted certiorari.

Issue. Does the dual sovereignty doctrine permit successive prosecutions under the laws of different states, which would be barred by double jeopardy if the same sovereign brought both charges?

Held. Yes. Judgment affirmed.

♦   The Double Jeopardy Clause precludes successive prosecutions for the "same" offenses. The offenses in this case may be assumed to be the "same" because they are greater and lesser offenses.

♦   The dual sovereignty doctrine is based on the principle that a crime is an offense against the sovereignty of the government. Thus, a single act may violate the peace and dignity of two sovereigns, and may thereby constitute two offenses.

♦   The dual sovereignty doctrine has been applied with regard to the states vis-à-vis the federal government. States are no less sovereign with respect to each other than they are with respect to the federal government. Therefore, successive prosecutions by two states for the same conduct are not barred by the Double Jeopardy Clause.

Dissent (Marshall, Brennan, JJ.). The compelling need for the dual sovereignty doctrine in federal-state relationships is greatly diminished when different states are involved. A state's desire to further a particular policy should not be permitted to deprive D of his constitutionally protected right not to be tried more than once on essentially the same charges.

───────────

b.   **Reprosecution by a state after a federal trial--**

Bartkus v. Illinois, 359 U.S. 121 (1959).

Facts. Bartkus (D) was acquitted in federal district court for robbery (a federal offense) of a federally insured savings and loan association. Then he was indicted by an Illinois state grand jury, the facts recited being nearly identical to those contained in the prior federal charge, for violation of an Illinois robbery statute. D was convicted and sentenced to life. D appeals.

Issue. Does the Double Jeopardy Clause bar a state prosecution following a federal prosecution for the same act?

Held. No.

♦ Even though the federal government turned over all its evidence to the state, collected more after it tried D, and cooperated in making witnesses available to the state, there is insufficient evidence to warrant a finding that the second prosecution was really a federal one, that the state was merely a tool of the federal authorities providing a cover for a second federal prosecution.

Comment. The Court has also ruled that a prior state court prosecution does not bar federal prosecution. [Abbate v. United States, 359 U.S. 187 (1959)]

G. SENTENCING

1. **Introduction.** Sentencing is the driving element for decisions throughout the criminal justice process, starting with the prosecutor's decision about what crime to charge. Defendants and their counsel make decisions regarding plea bargains largely based on sentencing factors. Ultimately, the sentencing judge makes a decision based on the crime itself and additional factors involving the particular circumstances, including the defendant's personal background.

   a. **Purposes.** Four basic purposes of punishment affect the determination of the sentence. These are (i) rehabilitation, (ii) deterrence, (iii) incapacitation, and (iv) retribution. The modern trend makes rehabilitation a more significant factor than it had been in the past.

   b. **Sentencing guidelines.** Congress established the United States Sentencing Commission to review and rationalize the federal sentencing process. In so doing, Congress specified that honesty in sentencing was a priority, diminishing the discretion of the parole commission. Congress also sought increased uniformity in sentencing and proportionality so the sentences reflected the offenses.

2. **Control of Discretion.** Traditionally, sentencing judges had broad discretion to impose sentences within the ranges established by statute. This led to arbitrary results, with different judges imposing disparate sentences for similar offenses. In response, the federal government and nearly all of the states have established mandatory minimum penalties. Many of the states have adopted mandatory minimum sentences for repeat offenders. The federal government and many states have also adopted sentencing guidelines that must be followed by judges. Variations from a specified range must be justified by finding certain facts specified in the statutes.

3. **Constitutional Limitation on Sentencing Procedure.** Because of the importance of the sentencing procedure, constitutional protections have been recognized to assure due process. Statutory control of the sentencing process is also subject to constitutional limitations.

   a. **Information used by sentencing judge--**

Williams v. New York, 337 U.S. 241 (1949).

Facts. Williams (D) was convicted of first degree murder, committed during a burglary. The jury recommended a life sentence. The sentencing judge received a presentence investigation report. D was brought to court to be sentenced, and claimed innocence. His lawyers asked the court to accept the jury's recommendation. The court responded that a death sentence should be imposed because the presentence investigation revealed that D had been involved in 30 other burglaries and that D had a "morbid sexuality." The judge classified D as a "menace to society." D and his counsel did not challenge these conclusions or request an opportunity to refute them. The judge imposed a death sentence. D appeals, claiming the judge should not have used information not subject to confrontation.

Issue. May a judge in a sentencing proceeding consider evidence not presented at trial that is also not made subject to confrontation by the defendant?

Held. Yes. Judgment affirmed.

♦ Due process requires that no person shall be tried and convicted of an offense unless he is given reasonable notice of the charges against him and is afforded an opportunity to examine adverse witnesses. Historically, sentencing judges were not limited by the same constraints. Out-of-court affidavits are commonly used, including reports made by probation officers.

♦ A sentencing judge is not confined to the narrow issue of guilt. A defendant's other misconduct, while excluded from the guilt phase, is relevant to the selection of an appropriate sentence. Modern penology seeks to fit the punishment to the offender and not merely the crime. For example, there is a distinction between first and repeated offenders. Reformation and rehabilitation have become as important as retribution.

♦ The objectives of fair sentencing would be undermined if sentencing judges could not have access to information provided by probation officers and other similar sources. The Due Process Clause does not require that the evidential procedure of sentencing be governed by the same rules as the trial itself.

Dissent (Murphy, J.). A judge should be willing to increase a jury's recommended sentence only with the most scrupulous regard for the defendant's rights. Due process requires that the person accused of a crime be accorded a fair hearing through all the stages of the proceeding.

Comment. Williams was 18 years old at the time of the murder, with no prior convictions. However, his victim was a 15-year-old girl, and the judge concluded there was a strong possibility that he had attempted to molest her because he had been accused in a prior burglary of molesting a seven-year-old girl. He had also assaulted the victim's younger brother during the burglary, an offense not charged.

---

b.   Burden of proof--

McMillan v. Pennsylvania, 477 U.S. 79 (1986).

Facts. McMillan (D) was convicted of aggravated assault after he shot the victim. The Pennsylvania Mandatory Minimum Sentencing Act provided that anyone convicted of certain enumerated felonies is subject to a mandatory minimum sentence of five years in prison if the sentencing judge finds, by a preponderance of the evidence, that the person "visibly possessed a firearm" while committing the offense. The trial judge found this Act unconstitutional and sentenced D to a term less than five years. The Commonwealth of Pennsylvania (P) appealed. The Pennsylvania Supreme Court reversed and upheld the Act. The Supreme Court granted certiorari.

Issue. May a state impose a mandatory minimum sentence for an offense when aggravating factors are proven only by a preponderance of the evidence?

Held. Yes. Judgment affirmed.

♦   The Due Process Clause requires the government to prove beyond a reasonable doubt every fact necessary to constitute the crime charged. But in *Patterson v. New York*, 432 U.S. 197 (1977), the Court held that the state is not required to prove beyond a reasonable doubt those facts that are linked to the severity of punishment but are not elements of the offense.

♦   Under P's Act, visible possession of a firearm is not an element of the crimes set forth for mandatory minimum sentencing. It is merely a sentencing factor. Visible possession does not change the maximum penalty or create a separate offense; it merely raises the minimum sentence, thus limiting the sentencing court's discretion in selecting a penalty within the established range.

---

   c.   **Use of prior conviction.** In *Almendarez-Torres v. United States*, 523 U.S. 224 (1998), the Court upheld a sentence that was enhanced due to a prior conviction. The crime of unlawfully reentering the country after deportation normally has a maximum sentence of two years, but if the defendant has prior convictions, the maximum is increased to 20 years. The defendant received a sentence of 16 years. The Court held that it was not necessary for the prior conviction to be an element of the crime. The prior conviction aspect was merely a sentencing factor comparable to the traditional sentencing factor of recidivism. The Court also noted that the prior conviction enhanced the maximum permissive sentence but not the mandatory minimum.

d.   Aggravating facts other than prior convictions must go to the jury--

Apprendi v. New Jersey, 530 U.S. 466 (2000).

Facts. Apprendi (D) fired several bullets into the home of an African-American family. The arresting officer said that D stated he did not want the family in the neighborhood because of their race, but D later denied that and said he was not biased against African-Americans. D pleaded guilty to two counts of firearm possession, each punishable by five to 10 years. After accepting the plea, the judge held a hearing on the issue of D's purpose for shooting at the house. The judge found by a preponderance of the evidence that D acted to intimidate the family, and used the "hate crime" enhancement statute to sentence D to 12 years on the second count. D appeals.

Issue. Does due process require that a factual determination authorizing an increase in the maximum prison sentence for an offense be made by a jury on the basis of proof beyond a reasonable doubt?

Held. Yes. Judgment reversed.

♦   The term "sentencing factor" was coined in *McMillan v. Pennsylvania, supra,* where the Court upheld the use of facts not found by the jury that could affect the sentence imposed by the judge. However, the Court stated that there are constitutional limits to a state's authority to define away facts necessary to constitute a criminal offense and that a state scheme that keeps from the jury facts exposing defendants to greater punishment may raise serious constitutional concerns. Furthermore, the holding in that case is limited to cases that do not involve the imposition of a sentence more severe than the statutory maximum for the offense established by the jury's verdict.

♦   In *Almendarez-Torres, supra,* the Court allowed the use of prior convictions to enhance the sentence, but that case involved the sufficiency of the indictment, not the right to a jury trial. The defendant there did not challenge the accuracy of the fact of the prior conviction.

♦   The state's procedure in this case allowed D to be convicted of a second degree offense by the jury, but then allowed the judge to impose a sentence identical to that allowed for a first degree offense. This procedure violates the rule that any fact that increases the penalty for a crime beyond the prescribed statutory maximum must be submitted to a jury, and proved beyond a reasonable doubt. The only exception to this is the fact of a prior conviction.

Dissent (O'Connor, J., Rehnquist, C.J., Kennedy, Breyer, JJ.). The majority has imposed a new constitutional rule. Until now, the accepted rule was that not every fact that bears on D's punishment need be charged in an indictment and found by the jury beyond a reasonable doubt. The legislature had discretion to define the elements of an offense, subject only to constitutional limits. The Court has rejected this approach and created a clear limitation on the power of legislatures to define crimes. This new constitutional rule has never been applied before. The legislature could easily circumvent this rule by permitting larger sentences for offenses, with reductions in the absence of aggravating factors. All the state did in this case was take a factor traditionally considered during punishment, D's motive, and specified the weight that should be given to that factor.

Comment. *Apprendi* has created uncertainty in the courts about the application of mandatory minimum sentences, especially in drug cases where the sentence depends on the quantity of drugs involved.

---

e.   **Constitutionality of Federal Sentencing Guidelines--**

United States v. Booker, 543 U.S. 220 (2005).

Facts. Based on evidence that he had 92.5 grams of cocaine base, or crack, in his duffel bag, Booker (D) was convicted of violating 21 U.S.C. section 841(a)(1). That section required a sentence of 10 years to life. The Federal Sentencing Guidelines required a "base" sentence of 210 to 262 months in prison. The judge held a post-trial sentencing proceeding and concluded by a preponderance of the evidence that D had possessed an additional 566 grams of crack. These findings increased the range of the sentence to between 360 months and life. The judge gave D a 30-year sentence. The Seventh Circuit held that the sentence violated the Sixth Amendment. In a companion case, another defendant convicted of cocaine offenses had his sentence enhanced to 15 or 16 years instead of the five or six years authorized by the jury verdict alone. The Supreme Court granted certiorari.

Issue. Does *Apprendi* apply to the Federal Sentencing Guidelines?

Held. Yes. Judgment of the Seventh Circuit affirmed; the other sentence is vacated.

♦   (Stevens, Scalia, Souter, Thomas, Ginsburg, JJ.). Under the Constitution, a defendant can be convicted only upon proof beyond a reasonable doubt of every fact necessary to constitute the crime with which he is charged. A defendant also has a right to have a jury make the decision.

> In *Apprendi*, the Court held that, other than the fact of a prior conviction, any fact that increases the penalty for a crime beyond the prescribed statutory maximum must be submitted to a jury and proved beyond a reasonable doubt. In *Blakely v. Washington*, 542 U.S. 296 (2004), and *Ring v. Arizona*, 536 U.S. 584 (2002), the Court held that *Apprendi* applies to a finding of aggravating factors as well as to both discretionary and determinate sentence enhancement findings.

> The Federal Sentencing Guidelines are mandatory in nature, not advisory. As such, they have the effect of laws. Departures from the Guidelines are allowed only in a few specific circumstances. In this case, D's actual sentence was 10 years longer than the jury verdict alone would have allowed. This type of enhancement makes the jury's finding of the underlying crime less significant than the judge's determinations about enhancement and makes it essential for *Apprendi* to apply to these Guidelines.

♦ (Breyer, J., Rehnquist, C.J., O'Connor, Kennedy, Ginsburg, JJ.). The provision of the federal sentencing statute that makes the Guidelines mandatory is incompatible with the Court's constitutional holding that *Apprendi* applies to the Guidelines. This constitutional requirement would transform the sentencing scheme into something that Congress would not have created and would destroy the system by eliminating the judge's ability to customize a sentence to reflect actual circumstances. Accordingly, the Guidelines are now advisory.

Dissent in part (Stevens, Souter, Scalia, JJ.). None of the parties has suggested any need to invalidate the Guidelines to avoid violations of the Sixth Amendment in administering the Guidelines. Ninety-five percent of all federal criminal prosecutions are terminated by a plea bargain, and in almost half of the cases that go to trial there are not sentencing enhancements. The Court's remedy is overbroad, but more importantly, the Court has no authority to invalidate legislation without a showing that it is unconstitutional.

Dissent in part (Scalia, J.). The Court has decided that in order to rescue from nullification a statutory scheme designed to eliminate discretionary sentencing, it discards the provisions that eliminate discretionary sentencing.

Dissent in part (Breyer, J., Rehnquist, C.J., O'Connor, Kennedy, JJ.). *Apprendi* and *Blakely* were wrongly decided, as there is no history of a right to jury trial regarding sentencing facts. Judges have traditionally resolved disputes about sentencing facts. Requiring jury findings for sentencing would risk unwieldy trials and lead to changes in the role of the federal judges, depriving the legislatures of the power to specify sentences.

V. APPEALS, POST-CONVICTION REVIEW

A. POST-TRIAL MOTIONS AND APPEALS

1. **Motions.** A post-trial motion is a defendant's formal pleading requesting that the trial judge review alleged trial errors. The motions are usually filed, in writing, before the appeal and often as a prerequisite to appeal.

    a. **Motion for acquittal or directed verdict.** This motion attacks the sufficiency of the evidence against the defendant and may be made at the conclusion of the prosecutor's case in some jurisdictions, or after the jury has returned a verdict in others.

    b. **Motion to arrest judgment.** Under Federal Rule of Criminal Procedure 34, this motion is filed if (i) the court does not have jurisdiction over the offense or (ii) the indictment fails to charge an offense.

    c. **Motion to correct or reduce the sentence.** This motion may be made for a limited time after sentencing, or for an indefinite time if the defendant was illegally sentenced.

    d. **Motion for a new trial.** This motion may be based on:

        1) Alleged trial error, *e.g.,* improper evidence, improper joinder, verdict contrary to law.

        2) Newly discovered evidence. The motion may be made up to two years after conviction or longer if the court so decides. [Fed. R. Crim. P. 33] The court is restrictive in granting the motion, however. The defendant must demonstrate that (i) the newly discovered evidence was unknown at the time of trial, (ii) the evidence is material, (iii) the evidence will probably bring an acquittal, and (iv) the defendant made a diligent effort to uncover the evidence at the time of trial.

2. **The Right to Appeal.**

    a. **Appeals by the defense.**

        1) **No constitutional right.** While there is no constitutional right to an appeal, all states now provide some method of appeal from criminal convictions.

2) **Bail.** The Bail Reform Act provides for the release of the defendant pending appeal under the same conditions as for bail pending trial. Bail may be denied if:

a) The appeal is groundless;

b) The appeal is a delaying tactic;

c) There is no sufficient guarantee that the defendant will not jump bail; or

d) The defendant is a threat to the community.

3) **Due process and imposition of harsher punishment--**

North Carolina v. Pearce, 395 U.S. 711 (1969).

Facts. Two defendants, one convicted of rape, the other of burglary, appealed. Their convictions were set aside. On retrial, each was convicted again. This time each received a more severe penalty than after their first trials. They appeal.

Issue. May defendants be given a longer sentence upon reconviction than for the first conviction?

Held. Yes.

◆ The Constitution does not forbid the imposition of a longer sentence on reconviction of the same offense; however, such longer sentence must be for proper reasons and may not be for the purpose of punishing the defendant for having appealed and succeeding in getting his original conviction set aside.

◆ Thus, the reasons for a longer sentence on reconviction, and the factual data in support thereof, must affirmatively appear on the record and "must be based upon objective information concerning identifiable conduct . . . occurring after the time of the original sentencing proceeding."

Concurrence (White, J.). The Court should authorize an increased sentence on retrial based on any objective, identifiable factual data not known to the trial judge at the original sentencing.

Concurrence and dissent (Black, J.). I agree that it would violate the Constitution for any judge to impose a higher penalty solely because a defendant had taken a legally permissible appeal. However, the particular detailed procedure set forth by the Court for assuring the absence of such a motivation is not constitutionally required. This is pure legislation.

Comments.

- **Retrial in higher court.** A harsher sentence may be imposed even without new data in those states that have a two-tier system, whereby, after a conviction or plea of guilty in an inferior court, the defendant has the right to a trial de novo in a higher court. In such a case, there is no risk of vindictiveness by the same court that imposed the original sentence; hence, the due process considerations of *North Carolina v. Pearce* do not prevent imposition of a harsher sentence if the accused is found guilty after the second trial. [*See* Colten v. Kentucky, 407 U.S. 104 (1972)]

- **Jury determination of sentence.** The new data requirement applies only when the sentence is determined by the trial judge. If the sentence is determined by a jury, and the jury is not informed of the prior sentence, there can be no concern about "vindictiveness"—and the jury on retrial can therefore recommend or determine a harsher sentence with or without new data. [*See* Chaffin v. Stynchcombe, 412 U.S. 17 (1973)]

- **Interim criminal conviction.** The Due Process Clause does not forbid enhanced sentences or charges, but only enhancement motivated by actual vindictiveness toward the defendant for having exercised guaranteed rights. When there is a criminal conviction obtained in the interim between an original sentencing and a sentencing following retrial, consideration of this conviction during sentencing is manifestly legitimate and rebuts any presumption of vindictiveness, notwithstanding that the "conduct" upon which the conviction is based occurs prior to the time of the original sentencing proceeding. [Wasman v. United States, 468 U.S. 559 (1984)]

---

4)   Greater sentence upon retrial permitted--

Texas v. McCullough, 475 U.S. 134 (1986).

Facts. McCullough (D) was convicted of murder. He elected to be sentenced by the jury and received 20 years' confinement. D moved for a new trial based on prosecutorial misconduct. The prosecution did not contest the motion and the trial court granted it. The prosecution produced additional evidence of D's egregious conduct at the second trial and D was again convicted. D elected to have the judge impose the sentence. She sentenced D to 50 years in prison and explained why on the record: the new evidence added to the sentencing case; the fact that D had been released from prison only four months before the murder was brought out only at the second trial; and she believed that the first sentence was too lenient. The state court of appeals reversed under *North Carolina v. Pearce, supra*. The Supreme Court granted certiorari.

Issue. May a judge impose a greater sentence upon retrial than was imposed at the original trial if the reasons are explained and there is no suggestion of vindictiveness?

Held. Yes. Judgment reversed.

♦ The *Pearce* rule was intended to protect against judicial vindictiveness, not the possibility of enlarged sentences after a new trial. Existence of vindictiveness depends on the circumstances of a particular case.

♦ The facts in this case do not support a presumption of vindictiveness. The judge granted a new trial herself—she was not reversed on appeal. She agreed that D's claims had merit. The fact that D chose to be sentenced by the judge clearly shows that he believed she would be fair. She was a different sentencer as well; she had no reason to vindicate the original sentence.

♦ Even if the *Pearce* presumption applied here, the judge's findings overcome the presumption. Justifications for an increased sentence are not limited to events occurring after the first trial. Here, objective information justifies the increased sentence.

Concurrence (Brennan, J.). Under these circumstances, the possibility that the increased sentence upon retrial resulted from judicial vindictiveness is sufficiently remote that the *Pearce* presumption is inapplicable.

Dissent (Marshall, Blackmun, Stevens, JJ.). The mere grant of a motion for a new trial is not an indication that the judge had no resentment toward D. She may resent having to either publicly acknowledge the error or being reversed on appeal. This is especially true if she feels the errors do not cast doubt on D's guilt. The prosecution, by not contesting the motion, may have desired a retrial to get a stiffer sentence. Proving actual prejudice is so difficult that the presumption of vindictiveness is an essential protection. By emasculating the *Pearce* rule, the Court resurrects the chill felt by defendants who want to contest their convictions.

Comment. In *Alabama v. Smith*, 490 U.S. 794 (1989), the Court held that the presumption of vindictiveness does not apply to a higher sentence imposed after a subsequent conviction when the defendant's original guilty pleas were vacated.

---

    b.   **Appeals by the state.** While some states deny the prosecution the right to appeal, most states grant appeals limited to cases where the court has:

        1)   Quashed the indictment;

        2)   Granted a motion to arrest judgment;

3) Dismissed the prosecution before the defendant has been placed in jeopardy; or

4) Granted a new trial.

3. Scope of Appellate Review.

a. **Introduction.** Normally, appellate review is limited to questions of law. However, in criminal cases, where the standard for conviction is that guilt be established "beyond a reasonable doubt," the appellate courts will consider whether evidence has been presented that is sufficient, as a matter of law, to permit reasonable inferences establishing the required elements of the crime.

b. **The harmless error concept.** Appellate courts do not reverse for every error. It must appear that the error was likely to have resulted in prejudice to the accused; that, but for the error, a different result may have been reached.

1) **Contribution to verdict--**

Chapman v. California, 386 U.S. 18 (1967).

Facts. At the time of Chapman's (D's) murder trial, state law permitted the prosecution to comment on D's failure to testify. The prosecutor did so, the judge instructed the jury that it could draw adverse inferences from D's failure to testify, and D was convicted. After the trial, the Supreme Court held, in *Griffin v. California*, *supra*, that neither the prosecution nor the jury instructions could comment on an accused's failure to testify. The California Supreme Court held the constitutional error to be harmless. The Supreme Court granted certiorari.

Issue. May any federal constitutional errors be deemed harmless?

Held. Yes. Judgment reversed on these facts.

◆ The harmless error doctrine has been followed by all the states and by Congress, and there has not been a distinction between federal constitutional errors and other types of errors. Thus, there may be some constitutional errors that are so unimportant that they may be deemed harmless.

◆ An error under the federal Constitution must be evaluated under a federal, not state, standard.

◆ The basic consideration in federal harmless error cases is "whether there is a reasonable possibility that the evidence complained of might have contributed to the conviction." Some violations involve such basic constitutional rights that they result in automatic reversal. Others may affect substantial rights of an accused and so would not be harmless.

♦ To find a federal constitutional error to be harmless, the judge must find that the error was harmless beyond a reasonable doubt. In this case, it is impossible to say that the prosecutor's comments and the jury instructions did not contribute to D's conviction.

---

2) **Harmless error situations.** In *Harrington v. California,* 395 U.S. 250 (1969), the Court held that although a co-defendant's confession implicating the defendant was erroneously admitted in evidence, it was harmless error because the other evidence of the defendant's guilt was so overwhelming that there was "no reasonable doubt" that the jury would have convicted the defendant even without the inadmissible confession. In *United States v. Hasting, supra,* the Court held that the "harmless error" test should be applied when the prosecutor commented on the defendant's failure to rebut the victim's testimony, when there existed overwhelming evidence of the defendant's guilt, and when the defendant's evidence was scanty and inconsistent.

c. **Automatic reversal required.** A line has been drawn between those errors that can be subjected to the "harmless error" standard and those constitutional errors that require automatic reversal.

1) As a matter of law, the introduction of a coerced confession cannot be harmless. [Haynes v. Washington, 373 U.S. 503 (1963)]

2) The denial of a defendant's right to counsel is never harmless. The only general standard that the Supreme Court has suggested is that these errors are "so basic to a fair trial" that reversal is automatic. [Gideon v. Wainwright, *supra*]

d. **Harmless error and omission of element of offense--**

Neder v. United States, 527 U.S. 1 (1999).

Facts. Neder (D) was charged with filing false income tax returns by failing to report more than $5 million in income he obtained from allegedly fraudulent real estate loans. The indictment included language regarding the materiality of false statements, but the district court instructed the jury that it did not need to consider the materiality. D was convicted and sentenced to 147 months' imprisonment. The court of appeals affirmed, despite finding that the district court erred in failing to submit the materiality element of the tax offense to the jury, by concluding that the error was harmless because materiality was not in dispute. The Supreme Court granted certiorari.

Issue. Does the harmless error rule apply to a jury instruction that omits an element of an offense?

Held. Yes. Judgment affirmed in part.

◆ Under Federal Rule of Criminal Procedure 52(a), any error that does not affect substantial rights shall be disregarded. Most constitutional errors can be harmless.

◆ An error regarding the omission of an element of the offense in a jury instruction differs from constitutional violations that have been previously subjected to harmless error review. This type of error affects the framework within which the trial proceeds and infects the entire trial process. But it does not necessarily make the criminal trial fundamentally unfair.

◆ D notes that in *Sullivan v. Louisiana*, 508 U.S. 275 (1993), the Court held that a defective "reasonable doubt" instruction was not subject to harmless error analysis because it vitiated all the jury's findings. In this case, the error only prevented the jury from making a finding on the element of materiality.

◆ The Court has previously applied harmless error review in cases where the jury did not render a "complete verdict" on every element of the offense. It would be consistent with those cases to apply harmless error review to this case.

◆ On the other hand, if the Court adopted D's position, it would call into question the common problem of misdescription of an element of the crime, both in state and federal courts, which would require reviewing courts to ascertain the elements of each offense. In this case in particular, D underreported $5 million and did not contest the element of materiality at trial. D does not claim he would offer evidence at retrial bearing on materiality. The Sixth Amendment does not require modifying the law to reverse in these circumstances.

◆ Applying the harmless error rule in this case, the inquiry must be whether it is clear beyond a reasonable doubt that a rational jury would have found D guilty absent the error. When an omitted element is supported by uncontroverted evidence, as it was in this case, it is appropriate to ask whether the jury verdict would have been the same absent the error.

Concurrence and dissent (Scalia, Souter, Ginsburg, JJ.). Depriving a criminal defendant of the right to have the jury determine his guilt of the crime charged, including his commission of every element of the crime charged, can never be harmless. The Court acknowledges that D's right to trial by jury was denied in this case, but upholds the conviction because the judges can tell that he is unquestionably guilty. But the Constitution does not allow judges to make determinations of criminal guilt. The Court's opinion does not specify how many elements can be taken away from the jury with impunity, so long as appellate judges are persuaded that the defendant is surely guilty.

e.   **Issues not properly raised.** Appellate courts ordinarily will not consider issues that were either not raised at trial or were improperly raised (some questions must be raised before trial, some at trial, etc.). Due process requires, however, that a defendant have "reasonable opportunity" to raise objections. Also, an appellate court may consider an error not properly raised below if it is "plain error" affecting substantial rights.

B.   POST-CONVICTION REVIEW: FEDERAL HABEAS CORPUS

1.   **Translations.**

   a.   "Habeas corpus" means bring forth the body.

   b.   "Coram nobis" means before us ourselves (the court).

2.   **Constitutional Provisions.** Article I, Section 9 of the Constitution provides: "The Privilege of the Writ of Habeas Corpus shall not be suspended, unless when in Cases of Rebellion or Invasion the public Safety may require it."

3.   **Remedy.**

   a.   The traditional characterization of the writ of habeas corpus is that it is an original (except perhaps when it is issued by the Supreme Court) civil remedy for the enforcement of the right to personal liberty.

   b.   It lies to test any restraint contrary to "fundamental law" (*i.e.,* the Constitution).

   c.   Restraints by federal or state authority that are contrary to "fundamental law" may be challenged on federal habeas corpus. It may be invoked at any stage of a criminal proceeding.

4.   **Historical Development of Habeas Corpus.**

   a.   **At common law.** At the time the first Judiciary Act was written, conferring habeas corpus jurisdiction on the federal judiciary, there was authority for the proposition that it was available to remedy any kind of government restraint contrary to fundamental law. The Constitution probably allows a construction of the power of the federal courts generous enough to encompass the extent of the power at common law.

   b.   **Federal courts.** At first, habeas corpus in federal courts did not apply to prisoners in state custody, as the first Judiciary Act did not extend it this far. Congress removed this limitation in 1867.

      1)   With the passage of the Fourteenth Amendment and the application through due process of many of the Bill of Rights provisions to the states, habeas corpus became a very broad power.

2) With respect to the federal criminal system, the remedy has been held to extend to prisoners held in violation of federal law and not merely of the Constitution. The cases here, however, are not uniform—there are some that deny relief on allegations merely of error of law.

c. **Current statute.** Federal habeas corpus relief is governed by 28 U.S.C. sections 2241-2266. Congress established new restrictions in 1996 as part of the Antiterrorism and Effective Death Penalty Act ("AEDPA").

5. **Procedure.** An application or petition for the writ of habeas corpus must be in writing by the person for whose relief it is intended or by someone acting on his behalf. The petition must allege the facts concerning the petitioner's commitment or detention, and the cause of the alleged illegality of it.

a. **Issuance of the writ of order to show cause.** The judge entertaining the application for the writ must either award the writ or issue an order directing the person alleged to be detaining the petitioner to show cause why the writ should not be issued, unless it appears from the application that the petitioner is not entitled thereto. [28 U.S.C. §2242] Issuing the writ does not entitle the petitioner to release; it merely orders that the petitioner be produced before the court so that the legality of his detention can be determined. However, in federal court the petitioner need not even be produced in the court if the writ and the return present only issues of law. [28 U.S.C. §2243] The order to show cause can be used to determine whether the writ should be issued and a preliminary hearing held.

b. **Hearing.** The court summarily hears and determines the facts and disposes of the matter as "law and justice require." [28 U.S.C. §2243]

c. **Appeal.** In the federal courts, a final order on a habeas corpus proceeding may be appealed. [28 U.S.C. §2253] In some states, only the prosecution is granted the right to appeal; the defendant can obtain appellate review only by filing another original habeas corpus proceeding in the appellate court.

6. **Issues Cognizable.**

a. **Generally.** In *Fay v. Noia*, 372 U.S. 391 (1963), the Supreme Court noted that the fundamental principle behind habeas corpus is that the government must be accountable to the judiciary for a person's imprisonment. An individual whose imprisonment does not conform to fundamental requirements of law is entitled to immediate release. Accordingly, and pursuant to the Judiciary Act of 1867, federal courts have habeas corpus authority over state prisoners. This authority must be exercised in light of principles of comity so as not to unduly interfere with state judicial processes, but states cannot preclude federal courts from exercising federal habeas corpus authority.

1) The Court has held that the federal habeas corpus remedy extends to federal prisoners in as broad a range of cases as it applies to state prisoners. For example, the Court applied federal habeas corpus to a claim that a federal prisoner was convicted on evidence seized through unconstitutional means. [Kaufman v. United States, 394 U.S. 217 (1969)]

2) In *Schneckloth v. Bustamonte, supra*, Justice Powell's concurring opinion, joined by Chief Justice Burger and Justice Rehnquist, takes the view that federal collateral review of a state prisoner's Fourth Amendment claims should be confined solely to the question of whether the prisoner was provided a fair opportunity to raise the question in state courts. Federal courts should not redetermine constitutional claims bearing no relation to the question of the prisoner's innocence. The constitutional claim raised should cast doubt on the finding of guilt. If such a doubt is not raised, the federal court should only look to see whether there was a fair opportunity to raise such doubt at the state trial. Freeing a clearly guilty prisoner defeats the interest of society.

b. **Exclusionary rule--**

Stone v. Powell, 428 U.S. 465 (1976).

Facts. Two defendants were convicted of first and second degree murder in state court proceedings. They both raised the issue of illegal search and seizure, moved for exclusion of the evidence in the state court actions and on appeal, and had a full and fair opportunity to litigate the issue. After losing on appeal, they filed habeas corpus actions in the federal courts, seeking release on the ground of illegal search and seizure of evidence.

Issue. Is a habeas corpus proceeding available to a defendant who has had a full and fair opportunity to litigate the exclusion of evidence obtained in an illegal search and seizure in the state court system?

Held. No.

♦ The exclusionary rule is a deterrent on police conduct and does not rise to the level of a due process guarantee.

♦ Illegally obtained evidence is not excluded for all purposes; therefore the full and fair opportunity to litigate the issue in the state courts is not subject to collateral attack.

Dissent (Brennan, Marshall, JJ.). The Court effectively limited the operation of the exclusionary rule by imposing the limitation on federal habeas corpus review. The finality of state court actions should give way to the overriding concern for protecting federally guaranteed rights, including those of the Fourth Amendment. Congress conferred the habeas corpus jurisdiction on the courts and should be the forum for limiting that jurisdiction, rather than the Court.

----

      c.   *Miranda* **violations.** [*See* Withrow v. Williams, *supra*]

  7. **Waivers, Defaults, and Other Bars to Relief.**

      a.   **Contemporaneous objection rule--**

Wainwright v. Sykes, 433 U.S. 72 (1977).

Facts. Sykes (D) was convicted of third degree murder. D talked about his wrongdoing after being read his *Miranda* rights. D, neither at trial nor on appeal, objected to the admission of his earlier testimony on the ground that he had not understood his *Miranda* rights. On a motion to vacate the conviction, he then challenged the statement for the first time. The state courts would not vacate his conviction due to a state procedural rule that required that all such claims be raised by a pretrial motion to suppress. D then filed for federal habeas corpus on the same ground. The court of appeals granted the writ.

Issue. Does a state contemporaneous objection rule bar granting of federal habeas corpus review absent a showing of "cause" and "prejudice" attendant to such a state procedural waiver?

Held. Yes. Judgment reversed and case remanded.

♦   The former test for determining habeas corpus review in light of a state contemporaneous objection rule, that of deliberate bypass, was too broad and encouraged the defense attorney to avoid raising a constitutional issue at trial, as well as giving too little deference to the state court.

♦   The contemporaneous objection rule serves many interests that require deference unless a defendant can actually show cause for noncompliance and prejudice resulting from his inability to subsequently raise the constitutional issue.

Concurrence (Stevens, J.). I believe the Court has wisely refrained from attempting to give precise content to its "cause" and "prejudice" exception to the rule. Matters such as the competence of counsel, the procedural context in which the asserted waiver occurred, the character of the constitutional right at stake, and the overall fairness of the entire proceeding may be more significant than the language of the test. In this case, competent trial counsel could well have made a deliberate decision not to object to the admission of D's statement.

Dissent (Brennan, Marshall, JJ.). Almost every procedural default is the result of an error by counsel, and D should not suffer forfeiture of his constitutional rights because of his lawyer's mistake. The deliberate bypass test should be upheld since it enforces only intentional but not inadvertent procedural defaults by a defendant.

---

b. **Successive applications for a writ.** To avoid abuse, 28 U.S.C. sections 2254 and 2255 provide limitations on successive applications for writs of habeas corpus. All claims must be presented at one time. However, a second application is permissible if (i) the application presents a new ground or a ground not previously determined on the merits or (ii) the judge is satisfied that justice requires further inquiry into a ground previously determined adversely to the defendant. [*See* Sanders v. United States, 373 U.S. 1 (1963)]

8. **Retroactive Application of New Rules--**

Teague v. Lane, 489 U.S. 288 (1989).

Facts. Teague (D), who is black, was convicted by an all-white jury. The prosecutor had used all 10 of his peremptory challenges to exclude blacks from the jury, claiming he was trying to obtain a balance of men and women. The state courts upheld the conviction, so D filed a habeas corpus petition in federal court. The district court denied relief under *Swain v. Alabama, supra.* While D's case was on appeal, the Supreme Court overruled part of *Swain* in *Batson v. Kentucky, supra.* The court of appeals denied relief on the ground that *Batson* would not apply retroactively to cases on collateral review. The Supreme Court granted certiorari.

Issue. Do new rules for the conduct of criminal prosecution generally apply retroactively to cases on collateral review?

Held. No. Judgment affirmed.

♦   The Court has held that the *Batson* rule does not apply retroactively on collateral review of convictions that became final before *Batson* was announced. Therefore, D cannot take advantage of the *Batson* rule on that ground.

♦   Retroactivity of new constitutional rules of criminal procedure should be determined at the time of the decision. A rule may be considered "new" if it breaks new ground or imposes a new obligation on a state or the federal government. Another way to state the concept is that a new rule arises if the result was not dictated by precedent existing at the time the defendant's conviction became final. Under this approach, a rule applying the fair cross section requirement that applies to jury venire to petit juries would be a new rule.

- New rules apply retroactively to all cases pending on direct review and those not yet final (a case is final when the availability of appeal or certiorari is exhausted). As to collateral review, the approach of Justice Harlan is most correct.

- Justice Harlan believed that new rules generally should not apply retroactively to cases on collateral review, since collateral review is not a substitute for direct review. Habeas corpus is designed to insure that trial and appellate judges conduct judicial proceedings consistently with the Constitution; therefore, a habeas court must apply the constitutional standards that prevailed when the original proceedings took place. A more expansive rule would undermine the principle of finality that gives the criminal law a deterrent effect.

- There are two exceptions to Justice Harlan's general rule: (i) new rules that place certain kinds of individual conduct beyond the power of the criminal law-making authority to proscribe; and (ii) new rules that require observance of procedures that are "implicit in the concept of ordered liberty." The latter exception is limited to those procedures without which the likelihood of an accurate conviction is seriously diminished.

- Consequently, habeas corpus cannot be used as a vehicle to create new constitutional rules of criminal procedure unless the new rules would be applied retroactively to all defendants on collateral review through one of the two exceptions.

- Application of the fair cross section requirement to petit juries as D requests is not the kind of absolute prerequisite to fundamental fairness that comes within the second exception.

Concurrence (Stevens, Blackmun, JJ.). Generally, Justice Harlan's approach is correct. However, the plurality has unduly limited the scope of the second exception.

Dissent (Brennan, Marshall, JJ.). The habeas corpus proceedings were intended to permit federal courts to inquire into any constitutional defects in a state criminal trial, so long as the petitioner is in custody due to a conviction in that trial. The plurality has limited habeas to the narrow two exceptions it sets forth. This substantial contraction of habeas corpus lacks precedential authority and is unwise.

---

9. **Impact of AEDPA Provisions--**

(Terry) Williams v. Taylor, 529 U.S. 362 (2000).

Facts. Williams (D) received a death sentence after being convicted of robbery and capital murder. At the sentencing hearing, D's lawyer presented D's mother, two neighbors, and a taped statement by a psychiatrist, but he spent most of his closing argument explaining that it was difficult to find a reason why the jury should spare D's life. The state courts denied D collateral relief on the ground that although mitigating evidence about D's mistreatment as a child and the possibility that he was borderline mentally retarded had been omitted due to the ineffectiveness of his counsel, there was no reasonable possibility that the omitted evidence would have affected the jury's sentencing recommendation. D then sought a federal writ of habeas corpus. The federal court found that but for D's trial counsel's unprofessional errors, the proceeding would have been different. The court concluded that the Virginia Supreme Court's decision was contrary to federal law. The court of appeals reversed. The Supreme Court granted certiorari.

Issue. Under the rules specified in AEDPA, may a federal court grant a writ of habeas corpus where the state courts have applied a rule contrary to established federal law?

Held. Yes. Judgment reversed.

♦ Under AEDPA, a federal habeas court must first test the determination of the state court against clearly established federal law, as determined by the Supreme Court, and second, refuse to issue the writ unless the state court's decision is contrary to, or involved an unreasonable application of, that clearly established law.

♦ AEDPA codifies *Teague v. Lane, supra*, to the extent that *Teague* requires federal habeas courts to deny relief that is contingent upon a rule of law not clearly established at the time the state conviction became final. The merits of D's claim are squarely governed by *Strickland v. Washington, supra*, which is clearly established federal law as determined by the Supreme Court. Thus, the Virginia Supreme Court was required to apply *Strickland* in considering D's ineffective assistance claim.

♦ Under AEDPA, D is entitled to relief if the Virginia Supreme Court's rejection of his ineffective assistance claim was either "contrary to, or involved an unreasonable application of," the established law.

♦ This second part of the AEDPA requirement basically means that a habeas writ should not be issued unless the state court was wrong as a matter of law or unreasonable in its application of law in a given case. This requires independent review by the federal courts.

♦ State court decisions that do not "conflict" with federal law will rarely be "unreasonable," but the "unreasonable" language in AEDPA may still apply where the state judgment is infected by constitutional error.

◆ Although there have been exceptions to *Strickland*, such as *Lockhart v. Fretwell*, 506 U.S. 364 (1993), the Virginia court should have applied *Strickland* itself to this case because those exceptions did not apply here. Under *Strickland*, D's counsel's unprofessional service prejudiced D. By relying on the inapplicable *Lockhart* exception, the court's analysis was both contrary to established law and an unreasonable application of the law.

◆ The Virginia Supreme Court's prejudice determination was unreasonable because it failed to evaluate the totality of the available mitigation evidence. While this evidence might not have undermined the prosecution's death eligibility case, it might have altered the jury's selection of penalty.

Concurrence (O'Connor, J.).

◆ Justice Stevens's conclusion that AEDPA does not alter the prior rule of independent review is contrary to the intent of Congress to change the law regarding habeas corpus. His conclusion is based on his failure to give independent meaning to both the "contrary to" and "unreasonable application" clauses.

◆ The term "contrary to" means diametrically different and requires that the state court's decision be substantially different from the Supreme Court's relevant precedent. This phrase means the federal courts must not issue a writ unless the state court applies a rule that contradicts the governing law set forth in Supreme Court cases. It does not mean that federal courts who disagree with the application of a correct rule can issue a writ.

◆ The "unreasonable application" clause applies if the state court: identifies the correct governing legal rule but unreasonably applies it to the facts of a particular case; unreasonably extends a legal principle to a new context where it should not apply; or unreasonably refuses to extend it to a new context where it should apply.

◆ A federal habeas court applying this clause must decide whether a state court's application of clearly established federal law was objectively unreasonable. Even if the federal court concludes that the state court decision applied federal law erroneously or incorrectly, a writ should issue only if the application was also unreasonable.

◆ In this case, the Virginia Supreme Court's adjudication of D's claim was both contrary to and involved an unreasonable application of the Supreme Court's clearly established precedent.

Comment. Justice O'Connor's opinion with respect to the interpretation of section 2254(d)(1) was the opinion of the Court on that issue.

Abbate v. United States - 295
Adams v. United States - 263
Adams v. Williams - 95
Aguilar v. Texas, - 69, 70, 71
Agurs, United States v. - 242
Ake v. Oklahoma - 32
Alabama v. Smith - 304
Alabama v. White - 94
Alderman v. United States - 177,179, 238
Alexander v. Louisiana - 264
Allen v. United States - 286
Almeida-Sanchez v. United States - 96
Almendarez-Torres v. United States - 297, 298
Anders v. California - 32
Anderson v. North Carolina - 253
Andresen v. Maryland - **66**, 164
Apodaca v. Oregon - 9, **262**
Apprendi v. New Jersey - 217, 218, **298**, 299, 300
Argersinger v. Hamlin - **26**
Arizona v. Hicks - 83
Arizona v. Roberson - 137
Arizona v. Washington - **288**
Arizona v. Youngblood - 246
Arkansas v. Sanders - 87, 88
Armstrong, United States v. - **199**
Ash, United States v. - **157**
Ashe v. Swenson - **228**
Avery v. Georgia - 264

Bagley, United States v. - **243**
Bain, Ex parte - 218
Baldasar v. Illinois - 27
Baldwin v. New York - 261
Ball v. United States - 292
Ballard v. United States - 264
Bank of Nova Scotia v. United States - **210**
Barker v. Wingo - **232**
Bartkus v. Illinois - **294**
Batchelder, United States v. - **201**
Batson v. Kentucky - **268**, 312
Beckwith v. United States - **131**

Bellis v. United States - 172, 173, 174
Benanti v. United States - 116
Benchimol, United States v. - 252
Berger v. New York - 113
Berkemer v. McCarty - 131
Berrios, People v. - **189**
Betts v. Brady - **24**, 25, 26, 33
Bivens v. Six Unknown Named Agents - 60
Blackburn v. Alabama - 149
Blackledge v. Allison - **259**
Blackledge v. Perry - **203**
Blair v. United States - **163**,166
Blakely v. Washington - 300
Blockburger v. United States - 154, 224, 225, 226
Blue, United States v. - 128
Booker, United States v. - **299**
Bordenkircher v. Hayes - **250**
Boumediene v. Bush - **19**
Boyd v. United States - **164**
Boykin v. Alabama - 249, 257
Brady v. Maryland - 242, 243
Brady v. United States - **250**, 257
Branzburg v. Hayes - 166
Braswell v. United States - **173**
Breithaupt v. Abram - 10
Brendlin v. California - 180
Brewer v. Williams (Williams I) - **150**, 151
Brooks v. Tennessee - 240, 283
Brown v. Allen - 266
Brown v. Illinois - 182
Brown v. Mississippi - 123
Brown v. Ohio - 227
Bruton v. United States - 230, 231
Burks v. United States - 292
Bute v. Illinois - 25

Calandra, United States v. - 60, **166**
California v. Acevedo - **87**
California v. Carney - **85**
California v. Green - 205, 232
California v. Greenwood - **62**

California v. Hodari D. - 94
Camara v. Municipal Court - 95, 97
Caplin & Drysdale, Chartered v. United States - 51
Cardwell v. Lewis - 89
Carnley v. Cochran - 34
Carroll v. United States - 86, 87, 88
Ceccolini, United States v. - **184**
Chadwick, United States v. - 87, 88
Chaffin v. Stynchcombe - 303
Chambers v. Maroney - 86, 89
Chandler v. Florida - **278**
Chandler v. Fretag - 25
Chapman v. California - **305**
Chavez, United States v. - 117
Chavez v. Martinez - **143**
Cheff v. Schnackenberg - 261
Chewning v. Cunningham - 25
Chimel v. California - **82**, 83, 90
Cicenia v. La Gay - 124
Clark, State v. - **206**
Coleman v. Alabama - 207
Colorado v. Bertine - **91**
Colorado v. Connelly - **149**, 190
Colorado v. Spring - 130
Colten v. Kentucky - 303
Commonwealth v. Upton - 16
Connecticut v. Barrett - 136
Coolidge v. New Hampshire - 74, 89
Costello v. United States - **208**, 209
Cotton, United States v. - **217**
Cox, United States v. - 198
Crawford v. Washington - 14, **281**
Crews, United States v. - **182**
Cronic, United States v. - **45**
Crooker v. California - 123, 124, 126
Cross v. United States - **222**
Cruz v. New York - 231
Cupp v. Murphy - 82
Cuyler v. Sullivan - **46**, 47, 48

Danforth v. Minnesota - **14**
Darden v. Wainwright - **284**
Davis v. Alaska - 242, 244
Davis v. Mississippi - 95
Davis v. United States - 139

Deal v. Spears - **120**
Deck v. Missouri - **280**
De Lucia, People v. - 287
Dennis v. United States - 238, 264
Desist v. United States - 11, 12
Dickerson v. United States - 123, 128, **142**, 146
Dinitz, United States v. - 290
Dionisio, United States v. - **165**
Dixon, United States v. - **224**
Dixon v. District of Columbia - **200**
Doe, United States v. (Doe I) - **172**, 173
Doe, United States v. (Doe II) - **176**
Dorman v. United States - 85
Dougherty, United States v. - **263**
Douglas v. California - 29, 30, 31
Dow Chemical Co. v. United States - 65
Drew v. United States - **223**
Dunaway v. New York - 182
Duncan v. Louisiana - 8, 9, 260
Duren v. Missouri - 265
Dyke v. Taylor Implement Manufacturing Co. - 261

Edwards v. Arizona - 13, **137**, 138, 139
Edwards, United States v. - 81
Elksnis v. Gilligan, United States *ex rel.* - 251
Elliott, United States v. - **201**
Escobedo v. Illinois - 124, **125**
Estelle v. Smith - **141**
Estes v. Texas - **277**, 278
Evans v. Superior Court - 244
Evitts v. Lucey - 39

Faretta v. California - **34**, 37
Fay v. New York - 266
Fay v. Noia - 309
Fisher v. United States - **171**, 173
Florida v. Bostick - 93
Florida v. Meyers - 16
Florida v. Riley - 63
Florida v. Royer - 94
Forrester, United States v. - 115
Frank v. United States - 261
Franks v. Delaware - 72
Frisbie v. Collins - 219

Fuller v. Oregon - 23
Furman v. Georgia - 287

Gagnon v. Scarpelli - **33**, 34
Gallo, United States v. - 238
Gannett Co., Inc. v. DePasquale - 274
Garrett v. United States - 227
Gastelo, People v. - 76
Gault, *In re* - 34
Gelbard v. United States - 119
Gendron, United States v. - 106
Gentile v. State Bar of Nevada - 273
Gerstein v. Pugh - **79**
Gideon v. Wainwright - 11, **25**, 306
Gilbert v. California - 12, 156
Giordano, United States v. - 117, 119
Globe Newspaper Co. v. Superior Court - **275**
Godinez v. Moran - 35
Goldman v. United States - 116, 117
Gonzalez v. United States - 38
Gonzalez-Lopez, United States v. - **50**
Gooding v. United States - 75
Goodwin, United States v. - **203**
Gouled v. United States - 66
Gouveia, United States v. - 28
Grady v. Corbin - 225, 226
Grand Jury Proceedings, *In re* (Schofield) -
    165, 167
Grand Jury 87-3 Subpoena Duces Tecum, *In
    re* - 168
Grand Jury Subpoena Duces Tecum Dated
    November 13, 1984, *In re* - 174
Gray v. Maryland - **230**
Green v. United States - **293**
Griffin v. California - 12, **282**, 305
Griffin v. Illinois - 29, 30, 31
Groppi v. Wisconsin - 273
Gustafson v. Florida - 80

Halbert v. Michigan - 31
Hale, United States v. - 186
Hale v. Henkel - 164
Hamdi v. Rumsfeld - **17**
Hamer v. United States - **266**
Hamilton v. Alabama - 25
Hamling v. United States - 216

Harrington v. California - 306
Harris v. Nelson - 239
Harris v. New York - 129, **186**
Harris v. United States - 61
Hasting, United States v. - 15, 306
Havens, United States v. - **187**
Haynes v. Washington - 306
Heath v. Alabama - **293**
Heckenkamp, United States v. - **110**
Henderson v. Morgan - 257
Henry, United States v. - **152**, 153
Hensley, United States v. - 94
Hobby v. United States - 208
Hoffa v. United States - **102**
Holloway v. Arkansas - 47, 48
Horton v. California - 77
Hubbell, United States v. - **174**
Hudson v. Michigan - **58**
Hurtado v. California - 208
Hutcherson v. United States - 202

Illinois v. Allen - **279**
Illinois v. Andreas - 90
Illinois v. Gates - 16, 57, **70**, 71
Illinois v. Lafayette - 81, 91
Illinois v. Perkins - 134
Illinois v. Rodriguez - **100**
Illinois v. Somerville - **288**
Indiana v. Edwards - **37**
Inmates of Attica Correctional Facility v.
    Rockefeller - 197
INS v. Lopez-Mendoza - 60
Iowa v. Tovar - **36**
Irvin v. Dowd - **271**, 272

Jackson, *Ex parte* - 112
Jackson, United States v. - 251
Jackson v. Denno - 190
Jacobsen, United States v. - 60, 65
Jacobson v. United States - **108**
James v. Illinois - **187**
James v. Strange - 23
Janis, United States v. - 60
Jeffers v. United States - **227**
Jencks v. United States - 238
Jenkins v. Anderson - 188

Jenkins. United States v. - 290, 291
Johns, United States v. - 89
Johnson, State v. - 237
Johnson v. New Jersey - 12
Johnson, United States v. - 12, 13
Johnson v. Zerbst - 24
Jones v. Barnes - 38
Jones v. United States - 178, 179

Kaiser v. New York - 113
Karo, United States v. - 65
Kastigar v. United States - 170
Katz v. United States - **60**, 61, 62, 63, 64, 113,
    114, 117
Kaufman v. United States - 310
Kentucky v. Stincer - 280
Kimmelman v. Morrison - **41**
Kirby v. Illinois - **157**
Klopfer v. North Carolina - 232
Knights, United States v. - 98
Knotts, United States v. - 65
Kuhlmann v. Wilson - **153**
Kyllo v. United States - **63**

Lakeside v. Oregon - 283
Lassiter v. Department of Social Services - 34
Lee v. Florida - 116
Lego v. Twomey - 189, 190
Leon, United States v. - **56**, 57
Leyra v. Denno - 130
Linkletter v. Walker - 11
Lockhart v. Fretwell - 315
Lockhart v. Nelson - **292**
Lovasco, United States v. - **235**

Machibroda v. United States - 257
Maine v. Moulton - 151
Mallory v. United States - 122, 123, 145
Malloy v. Hogan - 126
Mancusi v. DeForte - 178
Mandujano, United States v. - **169**, 170
Manson v. Brathwaite - **159**
Mapp v. Ohio - 11, **55**, 59, 60, 83
Martin, People v. - 177
Martinez-Fuerte, United States v. - 96
Maryland v. Garrison - 75
Maryland v. Pringle - **73**

Massachusetts v. Sheppard - 57
Massachusetts v. Upton - 71
Massiah v. United States - **124**, 125, 150, 151,
    152
Matlock, United States v. - 100
Mayer v. Chicago - 30
McCarthy v. United States - **258**
McCoy v. Court of Appeals of Wisconsin - 32
McCray v. Illinois - **72**
McKaskle v. Wiggins - 35
McKnight, State v. - 130
McMann v. Richardson - 249, **259**
McMillan v. Pennsylvania - **297**, 298
McNabb v. United States - 15, 122, 123, 145
McNeil v. Wisconsin - 139, 154
Mechanik, United States v. - **212**
Michigan v. Chesternut - 94
Michigan v. Doran - 79
Michigan v. Long - 16, 95
Michigan v. Mosley - **136**, 137
Michigan v. Summers - **76**
Michigan v. Tucker - 129
Mickens v. Taylor - **47**
Middendorf v. Henry - 34
Miller, United States v. - **218**
Miller v. Fenton - 149
Mincey v. Arizona - 128
Minnesota v. Carter - **180**
Minnesota v. Olson - 85
Minnick v. Mississippi - **138**
Miranda v. Arizona - 12, 13, 58, 77, 123, **126**,
    127, 128, 129, 130, 131, 132, 133, 134,
    135,136, 137, 138, 139, 140, 141, 142, 143,
    144, 145, 146, 147, 148, 149, 150, 151, 154,
    169, 182, 183, 186, 187, 188, 190, 311
Missouri v. Seibert - **147**
Moore v. Illinois - 158
Moran v. Burbine - **139**
Morris v. Slappy - 49
Moses v. Kennedy - 197
Mulligan, Ex Parte - 17
Muniz v. Hoffman - 261
Murphy v. Florida - 272
Murray v. United States - 184

Nardone v. United States - 116

Nebraska Press Association v. Stuart - **274**
Neder v. United States - **306**
Neil v. Biggers - 160, 161
New Jersey v. T.L.O. - 97
Nelson v. O'Neil - 231
New York v. Belton - 90, 91
New York v. Harris - 183
New York v. Quarles - 129, **135**
Newman v. United States - **254**
Nix v. Whiteside - **42**
Nix v. Williams (Williams II) - **185**
Nixon, United States v. - 167, 168
Nobles, United States v. - 240
Norris v. Alabama - 264
North Carolina v. Alford - 257
North Carolina v. Butler - 136
North Carolina v. Pearce - **302**, 303, 304
North, United States v. - 170

Oates, People v. - 16
Ohio v. Roberts - 281, 282
Oliver v. United States - 63
Olmstead v. United States - 112
One 1958 Plymouth Sedan v. Pennsylvania -
    60
Oregon v. Bradshaw - 137, 139
Oregon v. Elstad - 130, **145**, 148
Oregon v. Hass - 129, 186
Oregon v. Kennedy - **289**
Ortiz, United States v. - 96

Padilla v. Rumsfeld - 19
Page, United States v. - 209
Palermo v. United States - 238
Palko v. Connecticut - 8
Patane, United States v. - **146**
Patterson v. Illinois - 151
Patterson v. New York - 297
Patton v. Yount - 271
Payner, United States v. - 15, 177
Payton v. New York - 12, 13, **84**, 183
Pennsylvania v. Muniz - 134
Pennsylvania v. Ritchie - **244**
Place, United States v. - 65, 95
Pointer v. Texas - 279
Powell v. Alabama - 39

Press-Enterprise Co. v. Superior Court -
    275, **276**

Quirin, Ex Parte - 17

R. Enterprises, Inc., United States v. - **167**
Rabinowitz, United States v. - 83
Rakas v. Illinois - 177, **178**, 181
Rasul v. Bush - 19, 20
Rawlings v. Kentucky - **179**
Resendiz-Ponce, United States v. - **215**
Rhode Island v. Innis - **133**
Richardson v. Marsh - 230, 231
Richmond Newspapers, Inc. v. Virginia - **275**
Ricketts v. Adamson - **252**
Rideau v. Louisiana - **272**
Ring v. Arizona - 300
Riverside, County of v. McLaughlin - 79
Robinson, United States v. - **79**, 80
Rochin v. California - **9**, 10, 103
Rodriguez-Moreno, United States v. - **220**
Rompilla v. Beard - **43**
Ross, United States v. - 87
Ross v. Moffitt - **30**, 31
Rothgery v. Gillespie County - **28**
Roviaro v. United States - 245
Ruiz, United States v. - **254**
Russell, United States v. - **107**
Russell v. United States - **214**

Salerno, United States v. - **195**
Salvucci, United States v. - 178
Samson v. California - **97**
Sanders v. United States - 88, 312
Santobello v. New York - **251**
Schaffer v. United States - **229**
Schlib v. Kuebel - 194
Schmerber v. California - 10, **81**, 155
Schneckloth v. Bustamonte - **99**, 310
Scott, United States v. - **290**
Scott v. Illinois - 27
Scott v. United States - 118
Segura v. United States - 84, 183
Serfass v. United States - 291
Shadwick v. City of Tampa - 75
Shea v. Louisiana - **13**

Sheppard v. Maxwell - 273
Sherman v. United States - **104**, 107
Shillitani v. United States - 261
Sibron v. New York - 94
Silverman v. United States - 117, 182
Simmons v. United States - 160, 227
Singer v. United States - **263**
Smith v. Hooey - **234**
Smith v. Maryland - **114**, 115
Smith v. Robbins - 32
Solem v. Stumes - 13
Sorrells v. United States - 104, 105
South Dakota v. Opperman - 86, 91, 92
Spano v. New York - 124
Spinelli v. United States - **69**, 70, 71
Stack v. Boyle - **191**
Stirone v. United States - 218
Stone v. Powell - 41, 141, 142, **310**
Stoner v. California - 100
Stovall v. Denno - **159**, 160
Strauder v. West Virginia - 264
Strickland v. Washington - **39**, 42, 44, 47, 314, 315
Strunk v. United States - 235
Sullivan v. Louisiana - 48, 307
Swain v. Alabama - 268, 312

Taylor v. Illinois - **240**
Taylor v. Louisiana - **265**
Taylor v. United States - 280
Teague v. Lane - 14, **312**, 314
Tehan v. United States *ex rel.* Shott - 12
Tennessee v. Garner - 78
Tennessee v. Street - 231
Terry v. Ohio - 76, **92**, 95
(Terry) Williams v. Taylor - **314**
Texas v. Cobb - **153**
Texas v. McCullough - **303**
Texas v. White - 89
Thornton v. United States - **90**
Tollett v. Henderson - **260**
Townsend v. Sain - 149
Travis v. United States - 221
Tune, State v. - 237
Turk, United States v. - **119**

United States, *In re* - 238, **255**

Vale v. Louisiana - 84
Valenzuela-Bernal, United States v. - 245
Villamonte-Marquez, United States v. - 96
Villarreal, United States v. - **111**
Virginia v. Moore - 80

Wade, United States v. - 12, **155**, 156, 157, 158
Wainwright v. Greenfield - 188
Wainwright v. Sykes - **311**
Wainwright v. Torna - 39
Wainwright v. Witt - 269
Walker, People v. - 200
Warden v. Hayden - 66
Wardius v. Oregon - 236
Washington, United States v. - 170
Washington v. Chrisman - 83
Washington v. Texas - 246
Wasman v. United States - 303
Watkins v. Sowders - 190
Watson, United States v. - **77**
Weeks v. United States - 54, 56
Weiss v. United States - 116
Welsh v. Wisconsin - 85
Wheat v. United States - **48**
White, United States v. - 103
Whitus v. Georgia - 264
Williams, United States v. - **209**
Williams v. Florida - 9, **239**, 262
Williams v. New York - **296**
Wilson, United States v. - **291**
Winston v. Lee - 82
Witherspoon v. Illinois - 269
Withrow v. Williams - 142, 311
Wolf v. Colorado - **55**, 56, 59
Wong Sun v. United States - 182
Wong, United States v. - 169

Yarborough v. Alvarado - **132**
Yarborough v. Gentry - 42
Ybarra v. Illinois - 73, 74, 76
Youngstown Sheet & Tube Co. v. Sawyer (the Steel Seizure Case) - 16

Zurcher v. Stanford Daily - **67**

NOTES

NOTES

NOTES

NOTES

NOTES

NOTES

NOTES

NOTES

NOTES

NOTES

NOTES

NOTES